St. Clair Augustin Mulholland

The Story of the 116th Regiment, Pennsylvania Infantry

War of Secession, 1862-1865

St. Clair Augustin Mulholland

The Story of the 116th Regiment, Pennsylvania Infantry
War of Secession, 1862-1865

ISBN/EAN: 9783337249304

Printed in Europe, USA, Canada, Australia, Japan

Cover: Foto ©ninafisch / pixelio.de

More available books at **www.hansebooks.com**

THE

STORY OF THE 116TH REGIMENT,

PENNSYLVANIA INFANTRY.

WAR OF SECESSION,
1862--1865.

By

BREVET MAJOR GENERAL
ST. CLAIR A. MULHOLLAND.

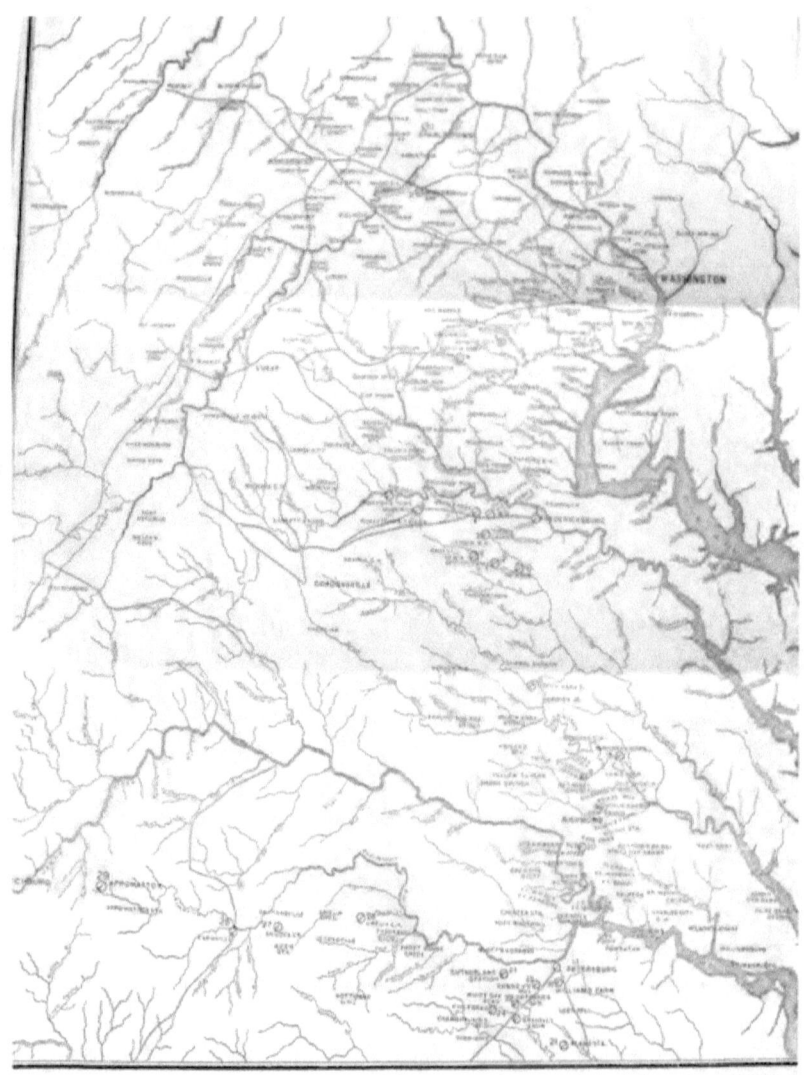

re of War in which the One Hundred and Sixteenth Pennsylvania Volunteers fought. Gettysburg, and Falling Waters, are not shown in this

MDCCCXCIX.

PRINTERS,
F. McMANUS, JR. & CO.
PHILADELPHIA.

BREVET MAJOR-GENERAL ST CLAIR A. MULHOLLAND.
Colonel 116th Pennsylvania Infantry.

DEDICATION.

TO the Members of my Regiment, living and dead, these pages are dedicated with very great affection.

To you, also, my beloved friends and comrades, who with me shared the honors, glorious triumphs and vicissitudes of the greatest war the world has ever seen; to you who have stood with me on many battlefields, rejoicing in the hour of victory, sorrowing in the hour of defeat, whom the bond of fire has rendered nearer and dearer than brothers, whose joys, tears and blood have been mingled with my own, to you I offer and dedicate this book, a story of brave deeds and brave men, a tribute to your heroism and excellence, a chaplet of fadeless laurel, well deserved and nobly won, which, with great reverence, I lay on the graves of those of my comrades who are gone, and gladly place on the brows of those who are still with us, happy in the thought that I have been permitted to record their splendid valor, in the hope that they may live long to read in these pages their own honored names, so that when they, too, shall be no more, their children may look on it exultantly, and make it their proudest boast that "Father was a soldier of the Union".

PREFACE.

WAR with its pomp and pageantry, glories, honors, horrors and bloodshed has, from the beginning of time, entered largely into the history of nations.

In every age, and in every clime, the story of the nation's brave has been the principal topic of the historians, the most sublime theme of the poet.

In every century, since the arts became a part of civilization, the sculptor and painter have plied the chisel and brush to perpetuate in marble and bronze, and depict on the less enduring canvas, the deeds of the heroes who, in the flame and tempest of battle, have stood, sword in hand, to defend the national honor or contend for a principle which they believed to be just.

The record of a warrior is too often but that of a fearless man or unscrupulous conqueror, and often, whilst we would fain admire the dauntless bravery that made the soldier distinguished among his fellows, we are forced to condemn the cause for which he fought. But in the case of the men who, during the War of Secession, formed the grand army that fought for, and preserved us a nation, we can both applaud the hero and endorse the motive.

The soldiers who gathered around our flag, in this great war, were not only heroes but patriots and saints as well. Theirs was the holiest, noblest, purest and best cause that ever summoned men to arms. Moses and Joshua fought to destroy and annihilate, that they might found a nation. Our army fought to preserve and secure—even to those whom they strived to conquer—the rights and liberties that they themselves hoped to enjoy.

Our soldiers fought to preserve that great legacy—more dear and valuable than all else gained by the sword on earth—the first real Republic that has ever existed; to demonstrate that human freedom was not a myth and a dream, but a splendid reality; to preserve intact, for all man who love liberty, that vast territory over which our flag floats, the glorious land that stretches from the storm-swept coasts of the Atlantic to the golden shores of the Pacific, that reaches from the frozen lands of Alaska to the orange groves of sunny Florida—the land that will, in the boundless future, shelter in its bosom so many happy homes and countless millions of freemen.

The Army of the Union fought to keep alive that sacred torch of human liberty which burns brighter and more brilliantly as the years roll on, and which is indeed destined to illumine the world and shine with so resplendent a glory as to teach all, even the most benighted of nations, that men can live in peace, purity and honor without being subjects that the laws for the well-being and happiness of society can be well and wisely administered by the servants of a people who will not tolerate masters. It is the history of a gallant regiment, composed of these men, that I propose to record.

But how many volumes it would take to tell the history of a regiment of more than a thousand noble men! The naming of the brave deeds of any one of them would, of itself, fill many glowing pages. Space, necessarily limited, will not suffice to allow justice being done to the individual, I can only write of the organization; of the marches, trials, triumphs, and sufferings of the members as a body; record the glories in which all were alike participants; live over again the days of victory, and hear again the inspiring cheers of the victors, as they rushed over the works of the foe or hurled them back in defeat; of other days, when disaster, rather than victory, was our lot, and when, maybe, our lines were forced back, leaving the ground strewn with dead and wounded—our well-loved companions; of the midnight march and bivouac; of marches in the deadly heat of summer, when men fell by the wayside, killed by sunstroke; of other marches during winter, when men died of the extreme cold; of the camp and picket line; of happy days in old Virginia, when sunshine and peace would prevail for a time, and cause the shadows of soldier life to pass away.

Then again, in writing this volume, I feel that I am but fulfilling a duty to comrades whom I have reason to, and do, sincerely love, so that the memory of their noble deeds shall not be forgotten, but will live, when they have gone to join those whose brave souls went out in the storm of battle.

And this is truly the history of a regiment on whose record there is no stain or blemish, a command that never turned its back upon the foe, or shrank from any duty, no matter how dangerous; that never failed to defend, in the most heroic manner, the position it was placed to hold, or charge, with the highest courage and most reckless daring, the line of works that it was commanded to take—a command, the bones of whose members bleach on thirty battlefields; a regiment whose colors, shattered, torn and bloodstained were, after three years of arduous service, returned to our State with honor.

I rejoice that I can testify to the excellence of that Regiment and to the heroism, devotion and gallantry of all its members; and can here declare that all who touched elbows and marched under the flag of the One Hundred and Sixteenth Regiment, Pennsylvania Volunteers, are worthy of having their names inscribed herein.

And this story of the organization is intended, not only as a memorial to the original members, but to all and every one who at any period of the three years, fought with the command; to those who, at a later date, came from Allegheny, Fayette and Schuylkill Counties to fill the depleted ranks, and who, by their magnificent conduct in the Wilderness and Petersburg campaigns, brought so much honor and glory to the command, as well as to those who were with us from the first, or who fell early, in the great struggle.

NOTE.—At a meeting of the Survivors of the organization it was Resolved, "that no portraits of any members of the Regiment should appear in the History except officers killed in battle or who had died while in the service, and the portrait of author.

CONTENTS.

	PAGE
MAP	1
DEDICATION	3
PREFACE	4
BATTLES AND SKIRMISHES	12
ROLL OF HONOR	13

CHAPTER I. 23

    Organization of the Regiment. Starts for the Seat of War. In Washington. First Night in Camp. Assigned to the Irish Brigade. Harper's Ferry. The First Fight. The March to Fredericksburg.

CHAPTER II. 43

    General McClellan takes leave of the Army and is succeeded by General Burnside. Arrival at Falmouth. The Battle of Fredericksburg. Death of Lieutenants Montgomery and Foltz.

CHAPTER III. 78

    After Fredericksburg. Funeral of Lieutenant Montgomery. Christmas Day in Camp. The Regiment is Consolidated into a Battalion of Four Companies. General Hooker succeeds General Burnside in Command of the Army. Corps marks are adopted. St. Patrick's Day in Camp. The President visits and reviews the Army. "Home Sweet Home".

CHAPTER IV. 104

    The Battle of Chancellorsville. The Regiment saves the guns of the Fifth Maine Battery.

CHAPTER V. 120

    Chancellorsville to Gettysburg. General Couch leaves the Second Corps, and is succeeded by General Hancock. Company B is detailed to Division Headquarters as Provost Guard. General Meagher resigns and takes leave of the Brigade. Itinerary of the March to Gettysburg.

CONTENTS.

CHAPTER VI. 131

Gettysburg—the Battle of the Century. Notes on the Battle. Gettysburg to the Rapidan. Death of Lieutenant Bibighaus. Orders received to organize six new Companies and raise the Battalion to a Regiment.

CHAPTER VII. 154

General G. K. Warren takes Command of the Second Corps. Battle of Bristoe Station. Fight at Auburn, or Coffee Hill. General Meagher, Colonel Peel and Marshal Prim visit the Brigade. Reorganization of the Regiment.

CHAPTER VIII. 172

The Wilderness Campaign. General Meade addresses the Army. The Regiment Camps on the Battlefield of Chancellorsville. The Battle of May 5th and 6th.

CHAPTER IX. 182

The Battle of Todd's Tavern or Corbin's Bridge. From prayer-meeting to battle. A Religious Army. The Battle of the Po.

CHAPTER X. 194

Spottsylvania, May 12th. Lieutenant-Colonel Dale holds a prayer-meeting in the darkness of early morning. Glorious charge of the Regiment—among the very first to cross the enemy's works. Capture of a Confederate Battery, several stands of colors, and many prisoners. Colonel Dale falls dead in the hour of victory. Death of Lieutenant Keil. Battle of Spottsylvania Court House, May 18th. Captain Lieb greatly distinguishes himself. Battle of North Anna River, May 24th. Fight at the Pamunkey River, May 28th. Battle of Totopotomy, May 30th and 31st. Lieutenant Yocum distinguishes himself on the Picket Line. Colonel Mulholland wounded.

CHAPTER XI. 222

Cold Harbor. Severe Losses in the Second Corps. Death of Colonel Byrne, commanding Brigade. Losses in the Regiment during the month of May.

CHAPTER XII. 231

The Command withdraws from the works at Cold Harbor. March over historic ground. Arrival before Petersburg. Battle of June 16th. Splendid charge of the Regiment. Death of Colonel Kelly, commanding Brigade. Battle of June 18th.

General Birney takes command of the Second Corps. Battle of William's Farm, June 22d. Severe Losses in the Regiment. Captain Cosslett, Lieutenant Cope, Sergeant-Major Burke and many of the men captured by the enemy. General Mahone tells of the fight. The Regiment leaves the Irish Brigade.

Chapter XIII. 250

First Deep Bottom, or Strawberry Plains, July 27th and 28th. Second Deep Bottom, August 14th and 15th. Terrible suffering from excessive heat.

Chapter XIV. 257

Battle of Reams Station. General Barlow leaves the Army and is succeeded in command of the Division by General Nelson A. Miles. Heavy Fighting. Severe loss in the Regiment. Death of Captains Nowlen and Taggart. Captain Crawford and Lieutenant Springer are captured by the enemy. Letter of the Confederate General Heth.

Chapter XV. 274

Siege of Petersburg. General Hancock's letter. On the Picket Reserve. Ghost stories. Colonel Mulholland returns and assumes command of the Brigade. "The Old Canteen."

Chapter XVI. 288

Turning movement against Lee's right, October 27th. Capture of a Confederate Fort. Death of Captain Henry D. Price. Major Teed returns from prison and resigns. A Sunday afternoon at Petersburg. Fight at Hatcher's Run, December 9th. The last Christmas in the Army. Fight at Hatcher's Run, February 5th. The Regiment is authorized to place the names of nineteen Battles on the colors.

Chapter XVII. 303

Spring time again. Battles of Gravelly Run and Five Forks. Death of Lieutenant Brady. Fight at Sutherland Station. Color Sergeant Kelly wounded. The Confederate Retreat. Amelia Court House. Sailor's Creek. Farmville. Death of General Smyth. Appomattox. Officers who were prisoners in the South return, and Major Cosslett tells of prison life. Return march to Washington. Assassination of the President. Lieutenant Tyrrell's story of the arrest of the assassins. The Regiment passes through Richmond. The last Review in Washington. The Last Muster on Gettysburg field. The Roster.

ILLUSTRATIONS.

	PAGE
MAP	1
PRESIDENT ABRAHAM LINCOLN	96
GOVERNOR ANDREW G. CURTIN	24
GENERAL U. S. GRANT	182
MAJOR-GENERAL PHILIP SHERIDAN	309
MAJOR-GENERAL GEORGE B. MCCLELLAN	44
MAJOR-GENERAL GEORGE G. MEADE	132
MAJOR-GENERAL AMBROSE BURNSIDE	56
MAJOR-GENERAL JOSEPH HOOKER	104
MAJOR-GENERAL EDWIN V. SUMNER	88
MAJOR-GENERAL WINFIELD S. HANCOCK	140
MAJOR-GENERAL DARIUS N. COUCH	122
MAJOR-GENERAL G. K. WARREN	158
MAJOR-GENERAL ANDREW A. HUMPHREYS	298
MAJOR-GENERAL NELSON A. MILES	258
MAJOR-GENERAL DAVID B. BIRNEY	238
MAJOR-GENERAL FRANCIS A. BARLOW	251
BRIGADIER-GENERAL THOMAS FRANCIS MEAGHER	32
BRIGADIER-GENERAL THOMAS A. SMYTH	176
LIEUTENANT-COLONEL RICHARD C. DALE	202
CAPTAIN AND BREVET MAJOR GARRETT NOWLEN	264
CAPTAIN AND BREVET MAJOR SAMUEL TAGGART	270
CAPTAIN AND BREVET MAJOR HENRY D. PRICE	290
CAPTAIN GEORGE HALPIN	278
CAPTAIN GEORGE F. LEPPINE	110
LIEUTENANT ROBERT B. MONTGOMERY	81
LIEUTENANT EUGENE BRADY	304
LIEUTENANT CHRISTIAN FOLTZ	65
LIEUTENANT ROBERT T. MCGUIRE	72
LIEUTENANT WILLIAM H. BIBIGHAUS	152
WILKES BOOTH, AND IRONS INTENDED FOR PRESIDENT LINCOLN	362
THE WILDERNESS	172
CHANCELLORSVILLE, AFTER THE BATTLE	119
SPOTTSYLVANIA, ONE YEAR AFTER THE BATTLE	210
THE REGIMENTAL MONUMENT AT GETTYSBURG	366
FATHER CORBY GIVING GENERAL ABSOLUTION ON THE BATTLE-FIELD AT GETTYSBURG	373
COL. AND BREVET MAJOR-GENERAL ST. CLAIR A. MULHOLLAND	3

116th Regiment, Pennsylvania Infantry.

BATTLES AND SKIRMISHES.

Charlestown, Va.	October 16, 1862
Snicker's Gap, Va.	November 12, 1862
Fredericksburg, Va.	December 12 and 13, 1862
Chancellorsville, Va.	May 1, 2, 3 and 4, 1863
Gettysburg, Pa.	July 2 and 3, 1863
Falling Waters, Md.	July 12, 1863
Auburn, Va.	October 14, 1863
Bristoe Station, Va.	October 14, 1863
Mine Run, Va.	November 28 and 30, 1863
Morton's Ford, Va.	February 6, 1864
Wilderness, Va.	May 5 and 6, 1864
Todd's Tavern, Va	May 8, 1864
Po River, Va.	May 10, 1864
Spottsylvania, Va.	May 12, 1864
Spottsylvania Court House, Va.	May 18 and 19, 1864
North Anna River, Va.	May 23, 1864
Pamunkey River, Va.	May 28, 1864
Totopotomy, Va.	May 30 and 31, 1864
Cold Harbor, Va.	June 3, 1864
Assaults on Petersburg, Va.	June 16, 17 and 18, 1864
William's Farm, Va.	June 22, 1864
Siege of Petersburg, Va.	June 19, 1864, until March 28, 1865
Deep Bottom, Va.	July 26, 1864
Strawberry Plains, Va.	August 14 to 18, 1864
Reams Station, Va.	August 25, 1864
Hatcher's Run, Va.	December 9, 1864
Dabney's Mill, Va.	February 5, 1865
Gravelly Run and Five Forks, Va.	March 29 to April 1, 1865
Sunderland Station, Va.	April 2, 1865
Amelia Court House, Va.	April 6, 1865
Sailor's Creek, Va.	April 6, 1865
Farmville, Va.	April 7, 1865
Appomattox, Va.	April 9, 1865

"Their bones are dust,
Their good swords rust,
Their souls are with the saints, we trust."

ROLL OF HONOR.

(The dead of the 116th Pennsylvania Volunteers.)

LIEUTENANT COLONEL RICHARD C. DALE, killed at Spottsylvania, May 12, 1864.

CAPTAIN AND BREVET MAJOR GARRETT NOWLEN, killed at Reams Station, August 25, 1864.

CAPTAIN AND BREVET MAJOR SAMUEL TAGGART, killed at Reams Station, August 25, 1864.

CAPTAIN AND BREVET MAJOR HENRY D. PRICE, killed at Petersburg, October 27, 1864.

CAPTAIN GEORGE HALPIN, died at close of war, of disease contracted in Confederate Prison.

LIEUTENANT ROBERT MONTGOMERY, killed at Fredericksburg, December 13, 1862.

LIEUTENANT CHRISTIAN FOLTZ, killed at Fredericksburg, December 13, 1862.

LIEUTENANT EUGENE BRADY, killed at Five Forks, March 31, 1865.

LIEUTENANT PATRICK CASEY, died of gun-shot wound, Sept., 1862.

LIEUTENANT WILLIAM H. BIRIGHAUS, died in Washington, June, 1863.

LIEUTENANT HENRY KEIL, killed at Spottsylvania, May 12, 1864.

LIEUTENANT ROBERT T. McGUIRE, died at close of war, of gun-shot wound received at Fredericksburg.

COMPANY "A".

PRIVATE JOHN S. ALTEMUS, died December, 1863, of wounds received at Gettysburg, July 2, 1863.

PRIVATE JOHN CORLOY, died in prison (Belle Island), date unknown, taken prisoner at Bristoe Station.

SERGEANT THOMAS DOUGHERTY, drowned in Acquia Creek, Virginia, May 1, 1864.

PRIVATE FREEMAN DYSON, died at Petersburg, October, 1864.

PRIVATE JOHN GOLDEY, killed at Petersburg, November 2, 1864, wounded at Gettysburg. Grave 1295, Poplar Grove Cemetery, Va.

PRIVATE GEORGE TURNER, killed at Gettysburg.

PRIVATE JOHN WOODWARD, died in prison (Belle Island), date unknown, taken prisoner at Bristoe Station.

COMPANY "B".

PRIVATE BENJAMIN CUMMINGS, died September 3, 1864. Buried at Cyp Hill Cemetery, L. I.

PRIVATE JAMES CARROLL, killed at Petersburg, June 16, 1864.

PRIVATE ——— CARTER, ———. Buried at Winchester, Va.

PRIVATE EDWARD FAGAN, killed at Spottsylvania C. H., May 18, 1864.

PRIVATE JOHN S. LEGUIN, killed at South Side R. R., April 2, 1865.

PRIVATE JAMES McHUGH, died July, 1863. Buried in National Cemetery, Philadelphia.

PRIVATE MANUEL MARTIN, died July 19, 1863. Buried in National Cemetery, Philadelphia.

PRIVATE JOHN RODGERS, killed at Fredericksburg, December 13, 1862.

PRIVATE CHARLES WALTING, died April 14, 1865.

COMPANY "C".

SERGEANT FRANCIS MALIN, killed at Gettysburg, July 2, 1863.

SERGEANT FRANKLIN B. MISSIMER, killed at Fredericksburg, December 13, 1862.

SERGEANT ELHANAN W. PRICE, killed at Fredericksburg, Dec. 13, 1862.

SERGEANT THOMAS M. ROWLAND, killed at Fredericksburg, December 13, 1862.

CORPORAL WILLIAM E. MARTIN, died December 13, 1862.

CORPORAL SAMUEL J. WILLAUER, killed at Fredericksburg, December 13, 1862.

PRIVATE GEORGE W. BIDDLE, killed at Fredericksburg, Dec. 13, 1862.

PRIVATE WILLIAM CAWLER, killed at Fredericksburg, Dec. 13, 1862.

ROLL OF HONOR.   15

PRIVATE ROBERT A. FULTON, died December 25, 1864, at Annapolis, Md.
PRIVATE WILLIAM GALLAGHER, died December 29, 1862, of wounds received at Fredericksburg.
PRIVATE ANTHONY HEFFNER, killed at Gettysburg, July 2, 1863.
PRIVATE A. S. HENDRICKS, died just after the battle of Fredericksburg.
PRIVATE GLENN HARRISON, killed at Fredericksburg, Dec. 13, 1862.
PRIVATE JOHN HOOP, killed at Deep Bottom, August 14, 1864.
PRIVATE ALLEN LANDIS, died October 2, 1864.
PRIVATE AARON J. LANDIS, killed at Fredericksburg, December 13, 1862.
PRIVATE A. LANDENBERGER, killed at Fredericksburg, Dec. 13, 1862.
PRIVATE DAVID E. MAJOR, died near Falmouth, November 17, 1862.
PRIVATE MICHAEL SPENCER, killed at Gettysburg, July 2, 1863.
PRIVATE DANIEL ULRICK, killed at Gettysburg, July 2, 1863.
PRIVATE DAVID WHITMEYER, died Sept. 27, 1864, at City Point, Va.

COMPANY "D".

SERGEANT ANDREW E. KER, killed at Fredericksburg, Dec. 13, 1862.
SERGEANT WILLIAM L. LOTT, killed at Reams Station, August 25, 1864.
CORPORAL JOHN H. CURRY (Color Guard), killed at the Wilderness, May 5, 1864.
CORPORAL JOHN HUGHES, died in prison, October 28, 1864. Captured at Reams Station.
PRIVATE JOHN T. BENSON, killed at battle of Wilderness, May 5, 1864.
PRIVATE ROBERT CONWAY, killed at battle of Wilderness, May 5, 1864.
PRIVATE MATTHEW GLASGOW, died March 27, 1865.
PRIVATE FREDERICK HILCAR, died on the eve of the battle of the Wilderness, May 4, 1864.
PRIVATE JAMES HANNA, died November 5, 1864. Captured by the enemy at Reams Station.
PRIVATE JOHN HUGHES, died October 9, 1864, of wounds received in front of Petersburg.
PRIVATE JOHN HUSS, died November 11, 1864, in Salisbury Prison.
PRIVATE JACOB MILLS, died on the way to Gettysburg.
PRIVATE JOHN MORRISSEY, killed at Petersburg, June 29, 1864.
PRIVATE JOHN MYERS, died in Andersonville Prison, July 22, 1863.
PRIVATE THOMAS O'BRIAN, died February 7, 1865.
PRIVATE JOHN B. QUIGLEY, died August 29, 1864, of wounds received at Petersburg, June 16.
PRIVATE GEORGE RUSHWORTH, killed at Chancellorsville.

PRIVATE CHARLES SERROSS, died in Andersonville Prison, September 30, 1864, of wounds received at William's Farm, June 22, 1864.
PRIVATE FRANCIS SHERIN, killed at Gettysburg.
PRIVATE JOHN A. SMITH, died July 26, 1864.
PRIVATE THEODORE A. WALKER, killed at Chancellorsville, May 3, 1863.

COMPANY "E".

SERGEANT HENRY KELLY, died September, 1862.
SERGEANT JOHN MURREY, died in Andersonville Prison, date unknown.
CORPORAL THOMAS SHARP, killed at Cold Harbor, June 3, 1864.
CORPORAL AARON TOMLINSON, died at Alexandria, Va., June 18, 1864, of wounds received at Cold Harbor, June 3. Grave 2181.
CORPORAL LOT TURNEY, killed at Cold Harbor, June 3, 1864.
CORPORAL HENRY MASTERS, died in Salisbury Prison, Nov. 13, 1864. Captured at Reams Station.
PRIVATE RICHARD BARKER, killed at Spottsylvania C. H., May 18, 1864.
PRIVATE GEORGE A. DODD, killed at Cold Harbor, June 3, 1864.
PRIVATE CHARLES ELFERT, killed at the Wilderness, May 6, 1864.
PRIVATE JACOB YARD, died November 25, 1864.
PRIVATE FREDERICK LEWDERS, killed at Deep Bottom, August 16, 1864.
PRIVATE HUGH LAYCOCK, died in Andersonville Prison, August 11, 1864.
PRIVATE JOHN LOGUE, died December 25, 1864.
PRIVATE THOMAS MURPHY, died September 22, 1864.
PRIVATE ALBERT NELSON, died in Andersonville Prison, 1864.
PRIVATE DAVID SHANNON, killed at Petersburg, June 16, 1864.
PRIVATE SILUS YOUNG, wounded and captured in Wilderness, died in Salisbury Prison.
PRIVATE WILSON TURPIN, killed at Cold Harbor, June 3, 1864.
PRIVATE JOHN M. WILEY, died in Andersonville Prison, October 10, 1864.
PRIVATE MALCHOIR ZANG, killed at Po River, May 10, 1864.
PRIVATE GEORGE ADAMS, killed at Wilderness, May 5, 1864.

COMPANY "F".

CORPORAL DANIEL B. BERKHEISER, killed at Reams Station.
CORPORAL CHRIS DIEFFENDERFER, died in Salisbury (N. C.) Prison.
CORPORAL WILLIAM MOSER, died June 14, 1864, of wounds received at Cold Harbor.
CORPORAL ADAM WAGNER, killed at Petersburg, June 14, 1864.
PRIVATE HENRY A. BERGER, killed at Po River, May 10, 1864.

ROLL OF HONOR.

PRIVATE JOHN A. BERGER, killed at Cold Harbor, June 3, 1864.
PRIVATE JOHN BAXTER, killed at Fredericksburg, December 13, 1862.
PRIVATE JAMES DAY, died in Salisbury Prison, December 20, 1864.
PRIVATE JOSHUA EVELY, killed at Tolopotomy River, May 31, 1864.
PRIVATE JOHN FREEZE, died June 29, 1864
PRIVATE CHARLES T. HOUCK, killed at Cold Harbor, June 3, 1864.
PRIVATE JOHN J. HUNKER, died April 20, 1864.
PRIVATE LEVI HERRING, died September 13, 1864.
PRIVATE LOUIS HEINBACK, killed at Petersburg, June 16, 1864.
PRIVATE PERAMUS HOFFMAN, died October 14, 1864.
PRIVATE JOSEPH M. JOHNSTON, killed at Po River, May 10, 1864.
PRIVATE THOMAS KRAMER, died March 13, 1865.
PRIVATE AMOS REPPERT, died October 27, 1864.
PRIVATE CHARLES K. REICHERT, died June 20, 1864, of wounds received at Cold Harbor, June 3.
PRIVATE JOSEPH B. REBER, died in Salisbury Prison, January 26, 1865.
PRIVATE NATHAN RAUSH, died July 22, 1864, of wounds received at Petersburg, June 16, 1864.
PRIVATE RICHARD SHOENER, killed at Cold Harbor, June 3, 1864.
PRIVATE JAMES WHITE, killed in Wilderness, May 5, 1864.
PRIVATE JOHN WAGNER, died January 7, 1865.
PRIVATE JOHN WEBBER, died in Andersonville Prison, September 7, 1864.
PRIVATE JOSEPH WAGNER, died July 17, 1864, of wounds received at Petersburg, June 22, 1864.
PRIVATE WILLIAM WANNER, died January 5, 1865.

COMPANY "G".

SERGEANT JOHN C. MARLEY, killed at Fredericksburg, Dec. 13, 1862.
CORPORAL ABRAHAM FOUST, died at Richmond, Va., of wounds received at Spottsylvania, May 12, 1864.
PRIVATE ADAM BUCHNER, died in Andersonville Prison, July 27, 1864.
PRIVATE JOHN BARR, died May 25, 1864.
PRIVATE JOHN G. COOK, died November 7, 1862.
PRIVATE THOMAS COOPER, killed at William's Farm, June 22, 1864.
PRIVATE HENRY DEITZLER, died March 28, 1865.
PRIVATE EDWARD L. GEBBERT, died October 16, 1864.
PRIVATE JACOB HUMMELL, died in Andersonville Prison, date unknown.
PRIVATE JOHN HEINBACH, died in Andersonville Prison, Oct. 12, 1864.

PRIVATE WILLIAM HEINBACH, died in Andersonville Prison, date unknown.
PRIVATE WILLIAM HARE, killed at Fredericksburg. December 13, 1862.
PRIVATE GEORGE KRAMER, killed at Fredericksburg, October 30, 1864.
PRIVATE JAMES KELLY, killed at Fredericksburg, December 13, 1862.
PRIVATE JOHN C. MARBERGER, died September 8, 1864, of wounds received at Ream's Station.
PRIVATE JONATHAN MOYER, died August 12, 1864, of wounds received at Cold Harbor.
PRIVATE FRANK PUFFENBERGER, killed at Spottsylvania C. H., May 18, 1864.
PRIVATE CYRUS RUCK, died in prison August 17, 1864. Grave 4952, Poplar Grove Cemetery, Va.
PRIVATE MARTIN V. RYAN, died July 24, 1864.
PRIVATE ADAM SHERMAN, killed at Cold Harbor, June 3, 1864.
PRIVATE JOHN SHERMAN, died June 30, 1864.
PRIVATE HENRY H. TRUMBO, killed at Spottsylvania, May 12, 1864.
PRIVATE WILLIAM TUCKER, died August 5, 1864.
PRIVATE SQUIRE H. VANNATTA, died December 25, 1864.
PRIVATE ANDREW WILSON, died in Salisbury Prison, February 10, 1865.
PRIVATE FRANKLIN WANNER, died December 25, 1864.
PRIVATE JOHN WALLS, died of wounds received at Fredericksburg.

COMPANY "H".

SERGEANT HENRY W. CASE, died August 13, 1864, of wounds received at Spottsylvania, May 12.
SERGEANT JOHN FARLEY, killed at Fredericksburg, December 13, 1862.
FIRST SERGEANT JOHN A. GRAHAM, killed at Cold Harbor, June 3, 1864.
SERGEANT FREDERICK SHAWN, died July 31, 1864, of wounds received at Petersburg, June 24.
CORPORAL HORACE GREENLEAF, killed at Fredericksburg.
CORPORAL GEORGE SHIP, died in prison at Salisbury, N. C., November 8, 1864. Captured at Ream's Station.
CORPORAL JAMES SLAVIN, killed at Fredericksburg, December 13, 1862.
CORPORAL WILLIAM WERTZ, killed at Spottsylvania C. H., May 18, 1864.
PRIVATE JOHN BRILHARTZ, died in Andersonville Prison, Oct. 14, 1864.
PRIVATE RUDOLPH BEITER, died June 23, 1864, of wounds received at Cold Harbor.
PRIVATE JOHN DOOR, died February 15, 1865.

PRIVATE JOHN S. FREIDLE, died in Salisbury Prison, December 25, 1864.
PRIVATE SAMUEL S. GILLESPIE, killed at Five Forks, May 31, 1865.
PRIVATE JOHN HAUGHY, died July 25, 1864, of wound received at Cold Harbor.
PRIVATE S. HEINBACH, died in Andersonville Prison, August 14, 1864.
PRIVATE CALVIN J. LEFEVER, died July 4, 1865.
PRIVATE FRANK LEONARD, died in prison September 10, 1864. Grave 4958, Poplar Grove Cemetery, Va.
PRIVATE CHARLES MCCARTY, died in Salisbury Prison, January 10, 1865.
PRIVATE DANIEL MCCARTY, killed at Fredericksburg.
PRIVATE C. STETZLER, died November 6, 1864.
PRIVATE ISAAC SHULTZ, killed near Petersburg, October 8, 1864.
PRIVATE JOHN SWISHER, died July 31, 1864, of wounds received at Cold Harbor. Buried in National Cemetery, Philadelphia.
PRIVATE MATTHIAS SEIFRITZ, died September 8, 1864, of wounds received at Cold Harbor.

COMPANY "I".

SERGEANT GEORGE COLE, killed at Fredericksburg, December 13, 1862.
CORPORAL ALEXANDER DOWNEY, died January 6, 1863, of wounds received at Fredericksburg.
PRIVATE JOHN ALLEN, died October 22, 1864, of wounds received at Cold Harbor.
PRIVATE J. CARTER, died March 15, 1864.
PRIVATE PATRICK FLEMING, killed at Wilderness, May 5, 1864.
PRIVATE WILLIAM GAW, killed at Fredericksburg, December 13, 1862.
PRIVATE HANNIBAL HATCH, killed at Wilderness, May 5, 1864.
PRIVATE WILLIAM C. HARVEY, died October 14, 1864.
PRIVATE BARTHOL W. JOHNSTON, killed at Fredericksburg, December 13, 1862.
PRIVATE JOHN LEECH, killed at William's Farm, June 22, 1864. Grave 1521, Poplar Grove Cemetery, Va.
PRIVATE SAMUEL MCCLUNE, killed at Fredericksburg.
PRIVATE SAMUEL PRICE, died July 11, 1864, of wounds received at Cold Harbor.
PRIVATE EDWARD SHEA, died June 3, 1864, of wounds received at Wilderness.
PRIVATE WILLIAM A. SEARIGHT, died July 25, 1864, of wounds received at Spottsylvania.

PRIVATE ALBERT J. VAN DIEN, killed at Fredericksburg, Dec. 13, 1862.
PRIVATE ANDREW WALLACE, died in Andersonville Prison, July 12, 1864.
PRIVATE JOHN WINCHESTER, killed at Fredericksburg, Dec. 13, 1862.

COMPANY "K".

SERGEANT DANIEL ROOT, killed at Fredericksburg, December 13, 1862.
SERGEANT EDWARD SPENCE, died June 24, 1864, of wounds received at Petersburg, June 16.
SERGEANT WARREN S. KILGORE, killed at Spottsylvania, May 12, 1864.
CORPORAL ROBERT J. BROWNFIELD, died June 12, 1864, of wounds received at Spottsylvania, May 12, 1864.
CORPORAL JOSEPH HUDSON, killed at Fredericksburg, December 13, 1862.
PRIVATE C. BURKHOLDER, killed at Cold Harbor, June 3, 1864.
PRIVATE JOHN BURNS, killed at Fredericksburg, December 13, 1862.
PRIVATE HENRY J. BELL, killed at Spottsylvania, May 12, 1864.
PRIVATE PARKS A. BOYD, killed at Wilderness, May 5, 1864.
PRIVATE DANIEL C. CRAWFORD, killed at Spottsylvania C. H., May 18, 1864.
PRIVATE MICHAEL CLEMMER, killed at Cold Harbor, June 3, 1864.
PRIVATE WILLIAM A. CONN, killed at Spottsylvania C. H., May 18, 1864.
PRIVATE STEPHEN H. DEAN, died in Salisbury Prison, Dec. 3, 1864.
PRIVATE PETER FINEGAN, killed at Fredericksburg, December 13, 1862.
PRIVATE LEVI GILMORE, died July 17, 1864, of wounds received at Cold Harbor.
PRIVATE ROBERT GLENDINNING, died July 17, 1864, of wounds received at Spottsylvania C. H.
PRIVATE ABRAHAM HULL, died June 23, 1864.
PRIVATE GEORGE W. HAVAN, killed in Wilderness, May 6, 1864.
PRIVATE JOHN HAUS, died in Andersonville Prison, August 1, 1864.
PRIVATE JOHN J. HULL, died, date unknown.
PRIVATE JOSEPH J. HAYNAN, died March 29, 1864.
PRIVATE SCOTT HUTCHINSON, died July, 1864.
PRIVATE WILLIAM HALL, died, date unknown.
PRIVATE JOHN H. INKS, died June 15, 1864, of wounds received at Tolopotomy River.
PRIVATE JOSHUA LUCKEY, died April 8, 1864.
PRIVATE JACOB MAUST, died March 8, 1864.
PRIVATE DAVD J. RIFLE, killed at William's Farm, June 22, 1864.
PRIVATE MILTON RATHBURN, killed at Spottsylvania, May 12, 1864.

ROLL OF HONOR. 21

Private Daniel Sickels, died in Andersonville Prison, July 9, 1864, of wounds received at Spottsylvania.
Private James Smith, killed at Spottsylvania, May 12, 1864.
Private John W. Smith, died June 14, 1864, of wounds received at Cold Harbor.
Private Joseph J. Smith, killed at Spottsylvania, May 12, 1864.
Private Benjamin Taylor, died May 5, 1864.
Private John Tiernan, killed in Battle of Wilderness, May 6, 1864.
Private Thomas Thorndell, killed at Five Forks, Va., March 31, 1865.
Private Newton Umble, died in Salisbury Prison, October 19, 1864.
Private John Williams, died February 9, 1863.
Private Thomas Wilson, killed at Fredericksburg.

CHAPTER I.

JUNE, 1862.

THE War of Secession had been in progress for over a year. Great armies had been reorganized, and great battles had been fought. The theatre of operations had extended until it embraced a territory more vast than ever occupied by any war in the world's history. Tens of thousands of armed men were marching and fighting on the long battle line that reached from Washington to the Mississippi. McClellan, with the army of the Potomac, had just fought and won the battle of Fair Oaks. Grant had captured Forts Henry and Donaldson, and advancing along the Tennessee, had fought and won at Pittsburg Landing, and at Shiloh.

It seemed as though the Civil War between the Northern and Southern States must soon end in triumph and final victory for the former, but peace was still far distant, and many thousands were yet to fall before the end came; and as the days passed it became evident that more stupendous efforts must be made by the general government if the union of states was to be preserved, so in the spring of this year (1862), a call was made for more troops. Pennsylvania, the Keystone State, always loyal and true, was prompt to respond, and the great War Governor, Andrew J. Curtin, whose administration extended over the six most eventful years of the Commonwealth's history, and whose memory will ever be cherished in every home in all the State wherever the name of a soldier is honored, quickly began the work of organizing new regiments.

The One Hundred and Sixteenth Pennsylvania Infantry was one of those then authorized. Dennis Heenan, a well-known and much respected citizen of Philadelphia, a soldier who had many years experience in the National Guard of the State, who had risen from the ranks through successive grades to that of Lieutenant-Colonel, and who had served in that capacity for three months with the Twenty-fourth Regiment in the Shenandoah Valley Campaign was chosen Colonel. The writer of this was commissioned Lieutenant Colonel, and George H. Bardwell, Major. Major Bardwell had served in the beginning of the war as Captain on the staff of General James S. Negley. He came of a long line of soldiers, his forefathers having been in every war in which the country was ever engaged, even back to the earliest times in the Indian wars, when the first of his name arrived in Boston in 1660.

On the 11th of June, headquarters were opened on Market Street, above Seventh, and recruiting actively begun. A camp was established in a beautiful spot at Jones' Woods, about three miles from the city on the Lancaster Pike. The first officer of the regiment mustered into the service of the United States was Edmund Randall, First Lieutenant of Company G, the required number of men being secured to entitle the company to an officer of that grade, and on the 8th day of July Lieutenant Randall was sworn in and took command of the new camp.

During the three summer months recruiting was slow, as many other regiments were organizing at the same time. In August the second battle of Bull Run, or Manassas, was fought in Virginia, and being a defeat to the Union troops, and a disaster to the Union arms that resulted in a menace and danger to the National Capitol, more men became an urgent necessity, and, without waiting for the completion of the organization, the regiment, on September 1st, was ordered to the front. On that date only about seven hundred men had been enrolled and the command started for Washington with many of the companies incomplete.

FORMING THE REGIMENT.

Camp was broken on the afternoon of September 2d, and the regiment, preceded by martial music, marched into the city and through the principal streets to the Cooper Shop Refreshment Saloon, and after enjoying an excellent meal and spending the last hour in Philadelphia in the most happy and agreeable manner, marched to the depot of the Philadelphia, Wilmington and Baltimore Railroad and embarked for Washington.

At the depot the crowd that accompanied the command through the streets slowly dispersed. Mothers, wives and sweethearts lingered on the platform until the very end, with the last warm kisses—alas! for many, the very last on earth—still burning on their lips, and saw through their fast-falling tears the train move slowly away with the loved ones, many of whom would never return.

The train arrived in Baltimore early next morning, and after being breakfasted by the citizens, proceeded to Washington, arriving there September 3d. The roster of the command was as follows:

Colonel—Dennis Heenan.
Lieutenant Colonel—St. Clair A. Mulholland.
Major—George H. Bardwell.
Adjutant—J. Robinson Miles.
Quarter Master—David S. Bunnell.
Surgeon—John P. Ashcom.
Assistant Surgeon—John W. Rawlins.
Assistant Surgeon—Philip A. Boyle.
Chaplain—Rev. Edward McKee.
Sergeant Major—George M. Book.
Quarter Master Sergeant—George McMahon.
Commissary Sergeant—Daniel Reen.
Hospital Steward—Frederick Wagner.

COMPANY "A".

Captain—vacant.
First Lieutenant—William M. Hobart.
Second Lieutenant—Henry D. Price.

COMPANY "B".

Captain—Thomas Murray.
First Lieutenant—Timothy J. Hurley.
Second Lieutenant—

COMPANY "C".

Captain—John Teed.
First Lieutenant—Seneca G. Willauer.
Second Lieutenant—John B. Parker.

COMPANY "D".

Captain—William A. Peet.
First Lieutenant—Jacob Ridgway Moore.
Second Lieutenant—George L. Reilly.

COMPANY "E".

Captain—John McNamara.
First Lieutenant—Joseph H. G. Miles.
Second Lieutenant—Robert J. McGuire.

COMPANY "F".

Captain—vacant.
First Lieutenant—Joseph B. Kite.
Second Lieutenant—Louis J. Sacriste.

COMPANY "G".

Captain—Lawrence Kelly.
First Lieutenant—Edmund Randall.
Second Lieutenant—Garrett Nowlen.

COMPANY "H".

Captain—John Smith.
First Lieutenant—Francis T. Quinlan.
Second Lieutenant—vacant.

COMPANY "I".

Captain—vacant.
First Lieutenant—John Stevens.
Second Lieutenant—Robert B. Montgomery.

COMPANY "K".

Captain—John O'Neill.
First Lieutenant—Patrick Casey.
Second Lieutenant—Bernard Loughery.

IN "WASHINGTON".

SEPTEMBER 30, 1862.

After a rest at the Baltimore and Ohio Depot, which was then at the foot of Capitol Hill, the ranks were formed. Officers put on their white gloves, tightened their belts, stepped briskly to their posts and drew their bright and untried swords. The men straightened up and tried to look their best, touched elbows to the side of the guide. "column forward, guide right, march!" and in column of company front the regiment swept up the broad avenue, but, much to their astonishment, no one seemed to mind the new soldiers a bit. The martial music and fine marching were all wasted and thrown away. Ambulances dashed past, mounted orderlies rushed here and there, officers galloped in all directions, but every one seemed too busy to pause and admire the new command. No crowds of interested citizens were gathered to see it pass. No bevies of pretty ladies waved "good bye". The good people of Washington had become accustomed to the music and marching.

Five hundred regiments had passed over the same pavement within a few months, and this one furnished no new spectacle; and so it moved along and wheeled into Seventh Street, en route for Long Bridge.

As the corner was turned, every man looked back at the Capitol—that splendid mass of Virginian marble towering to the skies—the majestic home of the Republic. The flag floated over the Senate and House where eight of the States had then no representatives. The dome was still in course of erection; the colossal statue of Liberty had not as yet been placed in position, and the men who were filing across the Potomac where going there to determine, by force of arms, whether the nation, like the Capitol, should still remain unfinished, or Liberty find a resting place in the calm heavens high above the halls of Congress —whether we should remain one country, a single people with but one destiny and one flag, or be torn into fragments with one portion of the land dedicated to human slavery!

Over the Long Bridge into Virginia! A hot, sultry day it was, and the dust settling on the new uniforms dimmed the bright blue, so that by the time a halt was called, a dull gray was the prevailing color.

And then the first taste of camp life, the excitement of getting up the tents, lighting the first camp fire, cooking the first camp coffee, eating the first "hard tack", mounting the first camp guard, and the hundred interesting incidents, so new, so fresh and so full of charm to the young patriots.

Then the dress parade: "arms stacked on the color front!" the sentries' monotonous tread; the "retreat", and, from the neighboring fort, the evening gun; the sad, sweet notes of "tattoo" sounding from the many camps and echoing from the woods and hills, all so charming to the men who, until now had only been playing soldiers, and who, but so short a time before, had been playing the more peaceful role of workman, busy in the marts of trade, wielding the implements of industry in the factory, or following the white wings of commerce over distant seas. Then a comrade's welcome greeting, for in the evening, the men from many other regiments swarmed into camp to meet the new comers. Ah! now indeed, it was real war. Now they were in the enemy's country, among real veterans who had been in real battles and showed real scars and told wonderful tales of hair-breadth escapes and fierce encounters.

One of the first visitors (Colonel McGrorty, Sixty-first Ohio), had been shot clean through the lungs, and the wound was still open, but he was on duty, and to-morrow he was going with an escort of cavalry to visit the battlefield of Bull Run to see about burying the dead. "Would any one like to go along?" Yes, the Major could go. He is the one officer of a regiment who seems to have no particular duty to perform and can run around and enjoy life—so he can go.

But just think! here at last, right in front of the enemy. Their pickets were just beyond the hill, and only an hour or two of a galop and one could look on a real battlefield where the dead were still unburied. One of the men picked up a real minie ball, and a real shell that had been fired by a Confederate gun. Ah, what an evening it was! And how eagerly the embryo heroes drank in the stories of camp and field with which the veteran visitors regaled them.

Night came at last. The newly made friends departed, the moon rose calm and serene, and the ranks lay down to sleep—to sleep and dream—to dream of home and friends, of mother's last blessing, of sister's last farewell, of wife and children who, in old Pennsylvania, were praying at that same hour for the loved ones absent, of the dear girl that gave him the last embrace, and whom he hopes some day, when this cruel war is over, to call his own.

Alas! how many of those homes will only be seen in dreams again. How many mothers, sisters and sweethearts will pray always for their soldier, but will look in vain for his return.

How many of the dreamers will never cross the Potomac again!

The first camp of the regiment on the soil of Virginia was established at Fort Craig, on Arlington Heights. Here the command remained for two days, the men greatly impressed with the new life and strange surroundings. Everywhere the evidence of active service and real war was visible. The earth was torn up in all directions, and strong forts topped every hill, a part of the immense line of earthworks raised to cover and protect the National Capitol, that was in plain view four or five miles away on the other side of the broad Potomac. September 6th, returned to Washington and drew ammunition and camp equipage. The arm furnished to the command was the "old pattern musket", that was loaded with a ball, calibre 69, and three buckshot. Sixty rounds was given to each man. On Sunday morning, September 7th, the regiment was ordered to march to Rockville, Md., and report to General D. N. Couch, commanding the Second Army Corps. Marched all day and reported as ordered, and immediately received orders to countermarch, return towards the Capitol and report to Colonel Morris, commanding the defences north of Washington. September 8th was spent in marching for the new field of duty, and on the evening of that day the regiment went into camp near Tennallytown. Here it remained until the 18th, and the time was well spent in drill and learning the many and various duties incidental to active warfare. Many of the men learned for the first time that the pick and spade were as much implements of war as the musket and bayonet. What astonishment was depicted in their faces, when a large detail for fatigue duty faced a wagonload of entrenching tools, and each one had to turn in for a long day's work. An officer of engineers of the regular army was in charge, and gave the men their first lesson in the very important branch of duty, "field fortifications". The work on which the regiment worked for two weeks was a square redoubt, with Abattis in front. The work, though of a very simple character, was most valuable to the command in teaching the important matter of getting under cover quickly, and of using the earth, rocks, trees, and everything that nature places within reach, as a means of gaining the end desired. The new soldiers were quick to learn, and after ten days of the work, it seemed almost wonderful to hear how each one could talk with facility on the subject. Lunettes, redans, and bastion forts, curtains, palisades, chevaux-de-frise, gabions, fascines, and many other military terms to which nearly all had been strangers a week before, became as familiar words, and were rattled off by glib tongues in the most astonishing manner. The work with the pick and shovel soiled the new clothes somewhat, and the line did not look quite so bright on "dress parade", but after becoming thoroughly acclimatized to Virginia dust and mud, a little dirt was not regarded with horror.

September 18th, marched to a point between Hall's Hill and Arlington Heights, near the Glebe House, and went into camp about six miles from Washington. Remained here until the 21st, when orders were received assigning the command to the Eleventh Army Corps, and to report to General Franz Seigel, commanding, at Fairfax Court House. September 23d, established camp within half a mile of that ancient town, and spent a week in vigorous work, the regiment being drilled and instructed by General Steinweir, a Prussian officer of distinction. October 6th, the regiment was ordered to proceed to Harper's Ferry and become a part of the famous Irish Brigade, commanded by General Thomas Francis Meagher. On the afternoon of that day broke camp, marched towards Washington, and formed camp near Bailey's Cross Roads. Entered Washington, en route, October 9th, and drew overcoats for the command. Left via Baltimore and Ohio R. R.

ARRIVAL AT HARPER'S FERRY.

The train carrying the regiment arrived at Sandy Hook near Harper's Ferry at daybreak, October 10th. The men woke up and tumbled out of the cars, sore, sleepy, and tired and formed line, and as the sun came over the hills, slowly moved through Harper's Ferry and climbed up the steep incline to Bolivar Heights. A halt for breakfast on the crest, and the men lit their little fires on ground that was literally covered with fragments of Confederates' shells, rested on the spot where Colonel Miles had made his stand and where he had surrendered to the enemy but a week or two before. Judging by the looks of the ground and evidence of the struggle one would think that he had reason to give up the fight when he did, the whole ground being strewn with pieces of shells, round shot, and debris of the battle.

While the boys were eating and looking around at the magnificent scenery, a very amusing though rather serious incident occurred. A regiment from Maine, a new regiment also, came up to join the Second Corps and halted to prepare breakfast, and finding plenty of thirty-pound parrot shells lying around used them to build fire-places—forming four or five of the oblong bolts in a ring with the points up, making an excellent resting place for the coffee pot. But when the fire in the centre began to roar and crackle and the coffee to boil, the shells began to explode, much to the amazement of the boys from the Pine Tree State. Half a dozen of the cooks were wounded, the coffee spilled, the whole corps had a good laugh, and the men of Maine had learned something.

Whilst eating breakfast, Colonel Moorehead, of the One Hundred and Sixth Pennsylvania Volunteers, rode up to shake hands and bid the men welcome. At noon the regiment fell in, marched over to the headquarters of the Irish Brigade and reported for duty. The Adjutant General, Major Tom O'Neill, assigned the command a spot on Bolivar Height, on a bluff overlooking the Shenandoah River, on which to pitch camp, and the streets were soon measured off and tents erected. Towards evening, when matters had gotten into something like order, the Brigade Commander, General Thomas Francis Meagher, came to make a visit of courtesy to his new command. He came in state, splendidly mounted, and surrounded by

BRIGADIER-GENERAL THOMAS FRANCIS MEAGHER.

a brilliant staff, the members of which seemed to wear a
deal more gold lace than the regulations called for.
Meagher was a handsome man, stately and courteous, with
a wonderful flow of language and poetic ideas. When the
canteen had been passed around the conversation became
animated—Meagher displayed a most gracious manner
that was captivating and charming to a remarkable degree,
forming a strange contrast to his mood at other times when
he tried to be stern, and his manner was not so affable.
A pleasant evening it was, and when the General and his
gorgeous staff rode away in the darkness, he left a pleasing
impression behind him. Whilst at Harper's Ferry the
state and national colors were presented to the regiment
with great ceremony, the presentation being made on
behalf of Pennsylvania, by Samuel P. Bates, deputy
secretary of the Commonwealth, and Sergeant William
H. Tyrrell, of Company K, was selected to carry the flag.
The camp at Harper's Ferry will always be remembered
by the members of the regiment with pleasure. The weeks
spent there were full of enjoyment. Plenty of drills and
work, to be sure, but still time enough for visiting through
the camps, and rambles through the old, historic town.
The ruins of the Engine House where old John Brown
made his last stand was a point of geat interest to all.
The magnificent scenery, the bright, sunshiny days, and
the visit to the army of many ladies all lent a charm to
the new life. That truly lovely woman, Mrs. General
Thomas Francis Meagher, spent a week or two in camp,
and many other wives of officers took advantage of the
peaceful days to visit the army. Then there was the
frequent target practice down by the river bank where the
boys fired away at imaginary Confederates and filled trees
full of buck and ball, with an implied understanding that
the trunks were Confederate Generals; the quiet picket
line, three miles out towards Halltown; the evening camp
fire, reviews, martial music, and all the pomp and display
of war rendered the days pleasing indeed.

The brigade to which the regiment had been assigned was a celebrated one, renowned for hard fighting and famous fun.

Instinctively one associates an Irishman with dash and courage, whether viewed as the presiding genius at Donnybrook Fair, or as the leader of armies. The very name of this brigade was redolent of dash and gallantry, of precision of evolution and promptness of action. It was commanded successively by General Thomas Francis Meagher, and was often referred to as Meagher's Brigade; Colonel Patrick Kelly, who was afterwards killed at Petersburg; General Thomas A. Smyth, who lost his life while in command of another brigade, and Colonel Richard Byrnes, who was killed in battle at Cold Harbor.

The First Division, Second Corps, of which the regiment had now become a part was known as Hancock's Division, and is celebrated as having done the hardest fighting and sustained the greatest loss of life. Within its ranks were the Irish Brigade, the Fifth New Hampshire, the One Hundred and Forty-eighth Pennsylvania, the Sixty-fourth New York, and other crack regiments. The losses aggregated 2,287 killed, 11,724 wounded, and 4,833 missing, making the appalling total of 18,844 men killed or wounded in this division during the war, yet it never at any one time numbered over 8,000 muskets. After the charge on Marye's Heights, which bloody assault it made under Hancock, it numbered only 2,800. Richardson, its First Commander, fell at Antietam. The Irish Brigade consisted of the Sixty-ninth, Eighty-eighth and Sixty-third New York and Twenty-ninth Massachusetts Regiments. The three former were Irish regiments, the latter like the One Hundred and Sixteenth was composed principally of Americans and had been placed in the brigade temporarily. The men quickly fraternized with the old regiments and were soon fast friends. There was very little sickness in the command and not one death during the time it was camped at Bolivar Heights, but in many other Pennsylvania regiments camped nearby there was a great deal of fever and many funerals. It seemed strange that the men of the regiment, chiefly from the city, from the factory and workshop, should stand the exposure of the camp better than the men who came from the country. The farmer boys fell quickly under the new conditions of life, and the citizen proved to have more stamina and better able to endure the vicissitudes of a campaign, and this rule seemed to hold good during the entire war.

At Harper's Ferry the command improved rapidly in every duty of the soldier. The picket line near Halltown ran through a delightful country. Firewood and food were plentiful, and picket duty was a pleasure rather than a pain. At one point the line ran between two farm-houses in which resided lovers—the boy within the Union line and his lady-love over the border. Neither were permitted to communicate, but they would come as close to the picket as allowable and look sweet at each other. Happy was the officer of the day who could eat breakfast with the lover and then cross the line and dine in the house of the beloved. He was sure to fare well in return for any brief message that he might carry.

While in camp at Bolivar Heights, General Edwin V. Sumner was succeeded in command of the second corps by General D. N. Couch; and here the regiment first met that prince of soldiers, General Winfield Scott Hancock, then commanding the division, and with whom the future was to be so closely linked—whom the command was to follow on so many bloody fields and whom all so soon learned to love and honor as one of the greatest of soldiers. On the evening of October 15th orders were received to march at daybreak next morning on a reconnoissance down the Shenandoah valley to Charlestown. What an evening of pleasurable excitement with a dash of anxiety it was! Men sat around the camp fires later than usual and talked of the morrow; or rolled up in their blankets, dozed and dreamed of the anticipated fight, for all knew that there would be a meeting of some kind, as a Confederate force was within a few miles. Candles flickered all over the camp where others were writing letters home, thinking maybe that that would be their last night on earth. Some packed their knapsacks and were all ready to march hours before the dawn. No doubt many never slept at all but sat by the smouldering embers of the camp fire in quiet thought, gazing at the dark mountains or listening to the wash of the Shenandoah's waters. One can hardly imagine a moment so full of subdued excitement, anticipative hope, fear, sadness, pleasure and all the emotions that human nature is subject to as the eve of a young soldier's first battle, and as the stars looked down on the calm, still night at Harper's Ferry they shone on many a beating though brave young heart; and on the morning of that eventful day when the new soldiers were to hear the whistle of the first hostile bullet, no reveille was necessary to call them to arms. Every man was ready long before the time to move.

The reconnoissance was made by the First Division, Second Corps, reinforced by Campbell's company of Horse Artillery and Tomkin's Rhode Island Battery and a squadron of cavalry. The column soon struck the enemy's picket which, after a few shots, retired towards the village of Charlestown. When within three miles or so of the town the advance suddenly encountered the enemy.

The two batteries galloped to the front and the cavalry passed to the rear. The infantry filed into the fields on each side of the road, quickly formed line and advanced. Meagher complimented the regiment by giving it the right of the brigade. Summer lingered late that year. Stacks of hay not yet gathered into the barns were still in the fields. The meadows were yellow with goldenrod, and the regimental line was formed in a field still green with rich clover. Ah, how beautiful that bright October morning when for the first time the command formed line to meet the enemy. Every face in the ranks beaming with

ARRIVAL AT HARPER'S FERRY.   37

patriotism, courage, enthusiasm and hope in that long line
of young men, the best of the land, men who had risked
their precious lives in defence of their country. The calm
bravery with which they swept over the flowered fields on
that Autumn morning was indicative of what was to be
expected on many other and bloodier fields that were to be
fought before the glorious morning of Appomattox was to
end the battles and the marches.

The batteries went into position near some large trees.
Shells began to fly and were seen bursting among the
guns. Then the order to advance; and when volunteers
were called for, to go ahead and tear down the fences,
every one was anxious to be first to rush into what would
seem to be a dangerous duty. How they made the fences
fly and clear the way! Then the advance in the clear,
bracing air. Oh, it was glorious war at last! Shells
screaming and bursting and the guns roaring and echoing.
But while men were killed and wounded in the batteries,
so far as the command was concerned the fight amounted
to but sound and smoke, for not a man of the regiment was
hit. The force of the enemy proved to be but one battery
of artillery supported by some cavalry and, after a vigorous
exchange of shots, retired before the advancing infantry.
Column was formed again and the march to Charlestown
resumed. When passing the spot where the batteries stood
the men had a chance to see a little of the horrors as well
as the glories of a fight. Men were already digging shallow graves in which to bury bleeding masses of human
flesh and bones that a few moments before had been men full
of life and vigor, standing by their guns and in turn hurling death and defiance—the wounded were being carried to
the rear on stretchers from which warm blood was dripping.
Mammoth trees had been pierced through by the shells;
and the earth was rent and torn in all directions. The
Confederates, considering their numbers, had made a most
gallant defence, and only yielded ground when the long line
of Union infantry advanced. The battery that had fought

the Union guns so nobly proved to be the Richmond Howizer Artillery, commanded by Captain B. H. Smith, Jr. The brave fellow with his leg shot off was lying by the road side rejoicing that his guns got away safely. The division occupied Charlestown without further opposition, and about one hundred Confederate soldiers were found in a church that had been turned into a hospital. They became prisoners. Lieutenant Edmund Randall, of Company G, was detailed to take charge of and parole them.

The regiment bivouaced in the field where old John Brown had been hanged, and great interest was manifested when the men learned of the fact. After dark the rain fell in torrents, soaking everyone. Lieutenant Frank T. Quinlan was sent out in command of the picket, and reported next morning that his line had been charged in the darkness by a flock of sheep with, it was thought, a serious loss of life on behalf of the latter. Remaining in the town until evening of the following day, the whole command started on the return to Harper's Ferry and camped in the fields near Halltown during the night. Quite a jolly evening it was. Everyone was in overflowing spirits. The camp fires crackled on all sides. Plenty of fence rails and even fresh bread seemed to come from somewhere, and fresh pork was plentiful. The regiment had not lost a man, to be sure, but had seen a genuine fight, heard the scream of the shells and seen a caisson blown up and men knocked over. Surely it was a taste of real war and now everyone could almost begin to feel like veterans.

While stationed at Harper's Ferry a call was made for volunteers to fill up the depleted ranks of some of the field batteries of the regular army. Twelve men of the One Hundred and Sixteenth volunteered, and were transferred to Battery A, Fourth Artillery, where they served until the close of the war. Of the number, Michael Hickey, William Miller, Joseph Meander, and John McCormack were wounded at Gettysburg, and Francis Tracey was wounded at Shiloh ; and Patrick Mullin greatly distinguished himself at Gettysburg, the gallant young Captain Cushing falling in his arms when killed.

October 26th tents were struck, and in the evening the army left Harper's Ferry, the second corps in the lead. The regiment, crossing the Shenandoah River on a pontoon bridge, passed around the base of Louden Heights into the valley, after marching three miles, and bivouaced —a cold uncomfortable night with a dash of snow, enough to whiten the ground, and a heavy frost, the first of the season and very early for that part of Virginia. Next day marched to Key's Pass where the command rested for a day, and was mustered for pay. The pay-rolls were sent off, and November 1st moved on again.

November 2d reached Snicker's Gap. Some cavalry were observed hovering on the left of the column, while the mountains of the Blue Ridge and Gap were on the right. It seemed improbable that the force could be a Confederate one, yet impossible that it could be Union troops; so Major Tom O'Neill, of the brigade staff, borrowing a guidon from one of the batteries, dashed over the fields to interview the strangers, Major George H. Bardwell galloping after him. O'Neill got there first and discovered, much to his annoyance, that he was a prisoner in the hands of a squadron of Confederate cavalry. Bardwell, discovering the mistake in time, wheeled around and made for his own column again and got away safely, although the boys in grey sent a shower of shots after him. Skirmishers were quickly thrown out, and line of battle formed, but after exchanging a few shots the cavalry withdrew out of sight and got away only to be captured by one of the Union cavalry regiments the same evening, Major Tom O'Neill being re-captured and restored to the brigade. On the afternoon of November 4th the Second Corps reached Upperville, the cavalry in front having an artillery duel with some of Stewart's Confederate Cavalry that were trying to escape through Ashby's Gap.

November 6th arrived at Rectortown, and on the 7th went into camp at Warrenton. The march down the Louden valley had been of the most delightful character. The weather, after the first night out, was charming. The air pure, clear and bracing; and as by slow marches the column moved along each day through a beautiful country, with the mountains of the Blue Ridge blazing with all the brilliancy of Indian summer, the fields aglow with the flowers of Autumn, the hearts of all were filled with joy. The evening camp fires during this period were the most enjoyable. The valley, as yet, had not been denuded of provisions; chickens, mutton and pork were plentiful, and fence rails made bright fires. Game was often added to the camp kettle, rabbits and partridges being in abundance; and one of the oddest incidents of the march was the swarms of rabbits that would go hopping over the fields in front of the line of battle as it swept across the country when the enemy would appear. At the same time coveys of partridge would rise from the stubble, and in bewilderment and fright fly into the men's faces. The negro servants caught quantities of the poor birds and killed thousands of rabbits. The odorous woods that skirted the base of the hills furnished lovely spots for the bivouac. The regiment enjoyed all the good things perhaps with a zest greater than that of the others around us, for it had not as yet lost a man, and the jest, story and song that passed the evening hours away were not yet saddened by the thought of the comrade who was missing and whose march was done.

At Warrenton General McClellan left the army and General Burnside assumed command. On the morning of November 15th the march was resumed in the direction of Fredericksburg. The march was steady but with all night rests; and on the evening of the 17th the regiment camped in a field within three miles of Fredericksburg. Shortly after dark on this evening, David E. Major, an enlisted man of Company C, became violently ill and died inside

of an hour, the first death in the regiment. His comrades
sat around him in silence, talked of his sudden departure,
of his boyhood, home, and friends. Many of his comrades
had been his schoolmates, and all felt his death deeply.
He was tenderly wrapped in his blanket and prepared for
burial next day, but at midnight orders came to march at
daybreak and so the boy had to be buried at once. The
men of Company C, were awakened and forming in line
formed a silent and sorrowful little procession. The body
was carried back for a mile to a little church yard that had
been passed on the road the evening before. The body
was laid on the ground while his companions stood sorrow-
fully around. Pine torches lit up the woods and gave
light to the men who with pick and shovel got ready the
lonely grave. The chaplain said a prayer, and so at midnight the first brave boy of the regiment was laid at rest,
his blanket marked U. S. his only shroud. The tears of
his comrades sanctified the soil where they laid him, and
though buried far from his home in old Pennsylvania,
hands as gentle and loving as brothers' gave him the last
sad rest.

> " No useless coffin enclosed his breast,
>   Nor in sheet nor in shroud we wound him,
>   But he lay like a warrior taking his rest
>   With his martial cloak around him.

Early the next morning, November 18th, the corps
marched on and the regiment went into camp in the woods
about a mile and a half from the old village of Falmouth.
A general feeling prevailed that the year's campaign was
ended and winter quarters were next in order. The pine-
covered hills and undulating slopes of meadow land,
broken up by the running brooks and rippling streams,
furnished the most inviting sites for pleasant camps, and
soon the dark woods were lit up by camp fires. Camp
fires fifty feet long, whole trees cut down, piled up and
forever kept cheerfully crackling and burning, around

which the whole company would gather and with their faces ruddy with the pleasant glow, spend the long evenings in uproarious fun, the day being filled up with marching, drilling, inspection, and reviews without limit. Thus passed three of the most agreeable weeks ever remembered in the regiment. This camp, which the command was destined to occupy for six months, was arranged strictly in accordance with regulations. The streets were laid out with a view of allowing the tall pine trees to stand, and these were the source of greatest pleasure, sheltering alike from sunshine and storm. The ground was on the rise of a hill, and generally healthful. A few, however, succumbed to the usual camp fever and sickness due to exposure. Corporal William E. Martin, of Company C, died a few days before the battle of Fredericksburg. He was an excellent soldier, and greatly beloved by his comrades. Several changes took place in the personnel of the officers; Lieutenant J. Ridgway Moore of Company D, was detailed as Aid-de-Camp on the staff of General David B. Birney, serving in that capacity until the end of the war, and greatly distinguishing himself. Lieutenant William H. Hobart of Company A, was detailed to the staff of General Winfield S. Hancock as Provost Marshal of the division, and he never re-joined the regiment, but remained until the end of the war at Division Headquarters. The Twenty-ninth Regiment, Massachusetts Infantry, Colonel Pierce, was detached from the Irish Brigade and replaced by the Twenty-eighth Regiment from the same State, commanded by Colonel Richard Byrnes, an officer of the regular army, and who was afterwards killed at Cold Harbor.

CHAPTER II.

FREDERICKSBURG.

IN the early days of November, 1862, the mountains of the Blue Ridge looked down upon one of those scenes of martial pageantry, a display of force and arms and men in battle array that happily our country but seldom witnesses.

For hours and days the great army of the Potomac, masses of gallant men, infantry, cavalry, and artillery, more than one hundred thousand in number, veterans of the Peninsula, victors of Antietam, swept by in serried ranks, with faultless step and perfection of discipline. Old hero Sumner was there, and Sedgwick, whom the men called "Father"; and Franklin, and the brilliant Sickles, and Averill, Reynolds, Smith, Couch, and Bayard, who was so soon to fall; Meade and the superb Hancock, and French, and Meagher, the orator-soldier from the Emerald Isle, and the impetuous Custer, whose golden locks were to fall in the Black Hills, and so in review they all passed by. Although the army had only a few short weeks before gained a glorious victory, as yet the greatest and most important of the war, a victory that had saved the National Capitol and checked the march of the Southern army towards the North, yet the occasion was one of the deepest sorrow, the saddest hour that the army of the Potomac ever knew. Every heart beat with a subdued throb, every eye was moist, and tears wet alike the cheek of the white-haired Sumner and the youngest drummer boy, for the great soldier who had organized and made this an army, the General who possessed the absolute confidence and love of every man there, was taking his farewell of those corps which he had formed and taught and led so well. It was the last review of the noble army by the only General who had, as yet, shown the ability to lead it, and who had just relinquished the command, and who had been relieved at the moment when he had made another victory almost a certainty, and the destruction of the army of Northern Virginia almost assured.

The order relieving General McClellan from command was received on the evening of November 7th, and a most ungracious moment was selected for his sudden removal, a moment pregnant with hope for the army and the cause. Never had his genius flashed forth with such lustre.

By the celerity of his movements and admirable handling of the army he had accomplished a most important strategic advantage.

Leaving Harper's Ferry on the 26th of the previous month he had, by forced marching and a series of the most brilliant cavalry battles and skirmishes, seized the passes of the Blue Ridge, and masked so well the movements of the main army as to completely deceive General Lee as to his whereabouts and purposes; and on the evening of November 7th when he had concentrated the army in the vicinity of Warrenton, he had succeeded in practically severing the two wings of the army of Northern Virginia —Longstreet, with his corps, was at Culpepper; and Jackson, with the remainder of the army, was at Millwood, west of the mountains, and two days' march away.

It was General McClellan's intention to strike Longstreet, and the early dawn of the following day would have found every corps in motion with that end in view, and with the forces of one hundred and twenty-seven thousand men, full of fight and hope and reliance on their leader, who could doubt the result? Longstreet would have been crushed before help could have reached him, and then he could have taken his own time to finish the work and Jackson.

MAJOR-GENERAL GEORGE B. McCLELLAN.

But, says some one, Longstreet would not have fought, but would have retired and formed a junction with the remainder of Lee's forces. Admit this, and still McClellan had the advantage. In order to connect with Jackson's corps, Longstreet would have to fall back upon Staunton, uncovering Richmond and leaving the road to that city open and clear. McClellan would then have moved promptly in, and the Union Flag would have floated over the Confederate Capitol.

"But then", says the Comte de Paris, "Jackson and Lee had certainly projected some bold movement upon McClellan's rear". This is not at all probable. It is known now, beyond a doubt, that General Lee had no such intention, and was not even aware of the position or whereabouts of the Union Army. Yet, admitting the surmises of the Comte de Paris as correct, General McClellan would have welcomed any such movement on the part of the enemy with delight. It would have more effectually separated their forces and rendered the final triumph more certain.

General McClellan had certainly succeeded in placing the Army of the Potomac between the two wings of the army of General Lee, and he could have failed only by the most lamentable blundering. He had placed the army in a position similar to that which Napoleon occupied in 1796, when he broke through the centre of the Austrian Army at Montenotte, and then defeated in succession, the two wings at Medesimmo Dego and Mondavi; and again in 1809, when opposed to the Archduke Charles, he pierced the centre of his too-extended line, and defeated successively the Austrian forces at Abensburg, Echmuhl and Ratisbon.

But, by his removal from the command of the army at this time the great advantages secured by General McClellan to the army and the nation were forever lost.

At noon, on November 11th, with the torn battle flags drooping to do him honor, and the most enthusiastic demonstration of affection by all the troops, General George B. McClellan, bidding adieu to the army, and saying: "We shall ever be comrades in supporting the Constitution of our country and the nationality of our people", left, and the soul of the army seemed for a time to go with him.

Not, indeed, that victories were not afterwards gained, or that the army ever failed to respond to every call. Under Burnside, the men without a murmur marched to death in a most hopeless contest. With Hooker they fought in a way that would have earned success had the head not failed.

With Meade they hurled back the enemy from Gettysburg and covered the battalions with new glory, and under Grant they stood up day after day, in battle after battle, with stubborn, unflinching courage, while brigades, divisions and corps were literally wiped from the face of the earth; but never again from that day until the end did the hearts of all the members of the army beat in sympathetic unison with that of the commander.

Then General Burnside, the gallant soldier and honorable gentleman, protesting against the responsibility forced upon him, with unsteady hand gathered up the reins and inaugurated the campaign that was to terminate in the impotent, useless, and sanguinary disasters of Fredericksburg.

The six corps were organized in three grand divisions, under Sumner, Franklin, and Hooker; and with Sumner and the Second Corps in the lead, marched for the Rappahannock.

On the evening of November 17th, the head of the column struck the river near the old Virginia town of Falmouth. On the opposite bank could be seen a battery of four guns, which promptly opened. General Sumner ordered Pettit's Battery to the front, and in just eight minutes from the time that Pettit fired his first shot the enemy had ceased firing and the four guns stood silenced and abandoned.

Sumner, whose seventy-two years, had not dampened the ardor of youth, carried away by the enthusiasm of the moment, called for troops to ford the river, seize the guns, and occupy the city.

The Irish Brigade had bivouacked in a field hard by and were cooking coffee and resting after a hard day's march, but in three minutes after receiving the order the brigade was going to the river on a run. Then Sumner, remembering that he had orders not to cross, and being too old a soldier to disobey, stopped the movement and sent back to General Burnside, asking permission to occupy the city, and the answer came, a peremptory "No!" So the army was compelled to look at the prize without grasping it.

How very odd the official report of this affair by General Lee when read along with the plain facts. He says: "The advance of General Sumner reached Falmouth on the afternoon of November 17th, and attempted to cross the Rappahannock, but was driven back by Colonel Ball, with the Fifteenth Virginia Cavalry, four companies of Mississippi Infantry, and Lewis' Light Battery".

Why the army did not cross the river and push on to Richmond has often been told, blundering by somebody and no pontoons ready. By and by, however, the pontoons arrived, but too late. Lee and Jackson and Longstreet had also put in an appearance, and from the bluffs one could see them busy, very busy indeed. Every day gave new evidence of their industry. Every hour saw new earthworks rising in front, redoubts, lunettes and bastioned forts, rifle-pits and epaulments for the protection of artillery arose in rapid succession until the terraced heights, which ran parallel to the city and two miles below and nearly a mile to the rear of it, were crowned with artillery, bristling with bayonets, and so formidable as to make an attempt to carry the place an act of insanity. The coming fight was to be an assault upon an intrenched position rather than an open battle.

Sometime about the first week in December a council of war was held at headquarters, at which General Burnside and the grand division and corps commanders were present. It is difficult at this day to tell just what was determined at this council. As one of those present afterwards remarked, they talked to General Burnside at arm's length. There would seem to have been a total absence of that harmony and unity of purpose so necessary to success between the commanding general and his lieutenants. A painful uncertainty, a vagueness of purpose hung over these meetings; but it was evident, however, that a flank movement by way of Skenker's Neck, twelve miles below the city, was discussed and determined upon, and the council adjourned, believing this to be the program. A few days after this, General Burnside sent for one of the corps commanders, General W. F. Smith, and invited him to ride with him along the high bluffs, Spofford Heights, that skirted the river in front of the city. He there told him that he (Burnside) had determined to change the order of battle and to cross and fight at the city, and gave as one of his reasons, that Colonel Hunt had called his attention to the excellent opportunity that Spofford Heights offered for the employment of all our artillery. The general officer in question, after being warned by General Burnside not to communicate the fact of the change to anyone, left him with a sinking heart and dark forbodings of the coming storm.

General Burnside, in a letter to General Halleck, dated December 19th, 1862, a few days after the battle, confirms the idea that the original intention, known to not only the grand division and corps commanders, but also to General Halleck and the President, was that of turning Lee's flank, and in this letter he magnanimously takes all the responsibility for the change and failure upon himself. He says:

"I have the honor to offer the following reasons for moving the Army of the Potomac across the Rappahannock sooner than was anticipated by the President, the Secretary of War, or yourself, and for crossing at a point different from the one indicated to you at our last meeting at the President's".

"This contemplated flank movement was discovered by the enemy, and General Lee, to be prepared for it, had sent General Hill's division to the vicinity of Skenker's Neck, and the balance of Jackson's corps was stationed so as to support him." This fact of Lee's army having been partially separated seems to have been the only reason for General Burnside altering, unknown to any of his subordinates, the plan of operations. He thought that by rapidly throwing the whole army across at Fredericksburg and striking a vigorous blow he could pierce the extended and weakened line and divide the forces of the enemy which were down the river from those on the crest in the rear of the town.

So the night of December 10th found the army in motion.

> "The midnight brought the signal sound of strife,
> The morn, the marshalling in arms—the day,
> Battle's magnificently stern array."

The roads leading to the front were filled with troops marching in silence to the fray. Camps deserted, the camp fires burning dim, the woods pouring out their thousands, everyone, everything moving towards the river; the infantry massing in rear of the bluffs by the stream, and the chief of artillery, Colonel Hunt, covering those heights with one hundred and forty-seven cannon. The pontoniers were hurrying the boats, planks and bridge material to the water's edge. Working rapidly, swiftly, but so noiselessly that those within one hundred yards of the enemy's pickets, who were lined on the opposite shore, were not heard, the pontoons were brought down and quietly let into the water. Great piles of planking arose, a multitude of spectral men were hurrying to and fro, cannon were gotten into position and more than one hundred thousand cavalry and infantry massed at hand. Yet there was no confusion, no clashing, so perfect the discipline, and the silence was profound—no audible sound save the lapping of the waves on the prow of the pontoons, and the moaning of the wind in the forest trees, and so the night wore on.

Two regiments of Engineers, the Seventeenth and Twentieth New York, stood prepared to build the bridges, and two regiments of Hancock's division, the Fifty-seventh New York, Colonel Chapman, and the Sixty-sixth New York, Colonel Bull, were on hand to cover and support them.

Towards dawn the work began. Swiftly fastening the boats to the bank, getting others into position, lashing them together, putting down the planking—so the work for a few moments went on. Then the sharp crack of a rifle broke the stillness of the night. A pontonier dropped his burden, fell forward into the dark, cold water, and went floating down with the tide, the first victim, the first corpse of the fight. More shots and balls went whistling through the fog. Then two loud reports of heavy ordnance pealed from Marye's Heights, echoed along the Valley of the Rappahannock and reverberated among the hills, the signal for the concentration of the Army of Northern Virginia, and the battle of Fredericksburg began. The firing becomes heavier, volleys of musketry, the rifle balls rattled on the planks and the boats were riddled. Many, very many of the pontoniers fell and went floating away.

It is so dark and the fog so dense that one could see but a few yards from the edge of the shore. Men went out on the bridge in the darkness and never returned. The fire was hot and deadly, but the men stuck to their work gallantly. Every moment the numbers of the artificers became less. Bull and Chapman returned the fire, but they were shooting at random and into the dark, while the enemy knew by the sound of the bridge building where to throw their iron. Colonel Bull was killed ; Chapman fell wounded, and the losses were so great that the engineers fell back and for a time gave up the attempt. Again they tried it and again they failed ; a third time they rushed at the work, but found it impossible to continue, and the brave little band fell back leaving the bridge half finished, slippery and saturated with blood.

Then daylight appeared. The work must be pushed. The bridge must be finished. The riflemen that checked the work must be driven out of their shelter, and for that purpose General Burnside decided upon treating the army to one of those rare and magnificently grand spectacles of war—the bombardment of a city ; so the order went forth to batter down the town, and about ten o'clock twenty-nine batteries, one hundred and forty-seven guns, opened. Then for an hour or two the firing was incessant, the sharp crack of the rifled guns, the heavy boom of the larger ordnance mingled with the echoes from the woods and hills, until separate sounds could no longer be distinguished and the roar became continuous. Clouds of sulphurous smoke rolled back from the masked artillery, the air became loaded, suffocating, with the odor of gunpowder. The fog still lay heavy in the river ; the water margins and the low lands and the city were almost hidden from view. One of the church spires shot up through the mist, glittering in the morning sun, and a few of the tallest chimneys and buildings struggled into sight. Tons of iron were hurled into the town. Shells, solid shot, shrapnel and canister raked and swept the streets. One could not see, but could hear the walls crumbling and timbers crashing ; then a pillar of smoke rose up above the fog, another and another, increasing in density and volume, rose skyward and canopied the doomed city like a pall. Flames leaped high out of the mist. The city was on fire. Again the engineers made an attempt to finish the bridge, but they found Barksdale with his Mississippians still at their posts and their fire as accurate as ever, and the effort was finally abandoned. Then Colonel Hunt suggested an idea, that a party be sent over in pontoon boats to drive the sharpshooters from the opposite shore. Strange that the simple device was not thought of before. Historic examples to suggest it were plenty. So late as 1799, this was successfully employed by Massena in the passage of the Limmat, where the bridges and boats were started simultaneously, and in three minutes from starting, six hundred French troops were landed, had captured the enemy's pickets and the bridge was then finished without further molestation. But better late than never. A dozen of the boats were lying by the river bank and plenty of volunteers were ready to man them. The Seventh Michigan and Nineteenth Massachusetts rushed down the steep bank, launched the boats and were off. The oarsmen pulled lustily, the Southern marksmen redoubled their fire, many in the boats were killed and wounded, but in a few minutes the further shore was reached. The men, leaping out, formed in line and dashing through the smoke and fire drove the sharpshooters from their shelter. Soon more boat-loads of men crossed over, the river front was soon in possession of the Union troops, and the work of building the bridges progressed to completion.

But the city was not yet captured. The first troops that crossed over the bridges thus constructed, had to fight for every foot of ground, and it was not until after dark, and after a sharp contest through streets, lanes and alleys, met at every step by the fire of Barksdale's men, from windows, roofs and every available point, that the Union line finally halted for the night on Carolina Street.

The dead were everywhere, in the street, on the cellar-doors, in yards of the houses, in the gardens by the river. Some few of the citizens had remained during the bombardment, taking refuge in the cellars, and two of them were killed, a man named Jacob Grotz and a negro woman.

FREDERICKSBURG.

On the left, half a mile below the city, where Franklin was to cross, but little difficulty had been met, and he had finished his bridges early in the morning.

It was then more than twelve hours since the signal-gun of General Lee summoned his divided army to concentrate, and as the sole hope of success on the part of General Burnside rested on being able to cross the river in force and take the enemy by surprise, it would look as though the Union cause had already sustained a heavy blow in this unfortunate delay. Moments were precious, yet the whole night of this day was suffered to pass without a move, and the Union troops did not begin crossing in force until the morning of the 12th, and by five o'clock of that day the grand division of Sumner had crossed into the city and that of Franklin had crossed on the lower bridges.

It was a cold, clear day, and when the One Hundred and Sixteenth Regiment filed over the bluffs and began descending the abrupt bank to cross the pontoons into the town, the crash of two hundred guns filled the valley of the Rappahannock with sound and smoke.

The color-bearers of the Irish Brigade shook to the breeze their torn and shattered standards·

> "That old green flag, that Irish flag,
> It is but now a tattered rag,
> But India's store of precious ore,
> Hath not a gem worth that old flag".

The Fourteenth Brooklyn ("Beecher's Pets") gave the brigade a cheer, and the band of Hawkin's Zouaves struck up "Garry Owen", as it passed. Not so pleasant was the reception of the professional embalmers who, alive to business thrust their cards into the hands of the men as they went along, said cards being suggestive of an early trip home, nicely boxed up and delivered to loving friends by express, sweet as a nut and in perfect preservation, etc., etc., The boys did not seem to be altogether pleased with the cold-blooded allusions to their latter end, and one of them from the Emerald Isle called out to a particularly zealous undertaker: "D'ye moind thim blankets. Well, only that we are in a bit of a hurry, we'd be after giving yez the natest koind av a jig in the air, and be damned to yez".

Then the One Hundred and Sixteenth passed over the river and was massed on an old wharf by the bank of the stream and rested during the afternoon and night of the 12th.

The streets were strewn with the dead. Some had been killed with the fire of the artillery and their bodies were shapeless masses of flesh, torn and mangled out of all resemblance to human beings.

Others killed by a rifle ball appeared as natural as life.

Numbers of Barksdale's men lay where they had fallen when disputing the passage of the stream. One group had an almost fascinating interest to the young men of the regiment, because every one of the party was boyish and handsome. They had fought in a garden by the riverside, where they had been somewhat sheltered from the fire, and had died just where they had been placed. There was not a sign of a struggle near the spot, and, singular to say, no indication of blood or wounds. They all had been shot through the body, and each had quietly dropped as he fired. The bodies were frozen hard, and all retained the appearance of life—eyes were open, faces placid and calm; and one bright looking youth seem to smile in his sleep. Gazing upon these brave Southern boys as they lay amid the frozen leaves and decaying flowers of the garden one's mind was apt to wander to the Southern homes where the sun was still shining and the roses still blooming, and the mournful Christmas there would be in many a far off Mississippi home whose soldier lad would never return again.

In the river by the wharf where the regiment bivouaced some barges ladened with tobacco had been sunk. The boys succeeded in fishing up great quantities of the weed

and lined their blouses with it. After the fight one heard
of many of the men whose lives had been saved by the
solid plugs of tobacco stopping the ball intended for their
heart, but there was no tangible evidence of the fact. The
fellow whose Bible stopped the deadly minie was around
in every camp, and he had his testament to show for it,
but the plug of tobacco that stood between the soldier and
death was chewed in to nothing, or the evidence went up in
smoke. The night of the 12th was exceedingly cold and
dismal, and, when morning came, the sun had a long
struggle with the chilling fog before full daylight filled the
valley. The men chewed on their hardtack and resumed
their pastime of fishing up tobacco, and listening to the
shells that passed over their heads in countless numbers.

The night of the 12th was to the men of the One
Hundred and Sixteenth one of the most dismal and miserable ever experienced. The cold was bitter and penetrating. The troops massed so close that there was not even
room enough for the men to lie down on the ground, and
it was a fortunate man who could secure a cracker box to
sit upon during the weary hours. Sleep was impossible,
it was so cold and chilly. Groups of officers occupied the
parlors of the fashionable residences, spending the night
in song and story; and Southern pianos played accompaniments to "Hail Columbia", and the "Star Spangled
banner". Fires still lit up portions of the town. The
firmament was aglow with a magnificent Aurora Borealis,
and the artillerists strove to rival the glories of nature and
illumined the sky with scores of shells whose trailing fuses
filled the air with streams of light.

When daylight came a few small fires were lit and some
of the men enjoyed a cup of coffee, but many chewed
their hardtack without a warm drink to comfort them.

The long hours of the night had slipped away and the
morning of December 13th broke chill and cold. It was
now thirty-six hours since the movement against Fredericksburg began, giving General Lee ample time to get his

corps together, destroying any virtue that might have existed in General Burnside's plan of attack and rendering it absolutely abortive. Owing to the delay in forcing the passage of the river the enterprise had been stripped of its only hope and the failure was complete. The only alternative was to withdraw the army or adopt an entirely new plan of battle.

To retire was not thought of, the fight must proceed. The evil genius of General Burnside seemed to irresistibly beckon him on to destruction. The silver lining of the cloud that was gathering was a suggestion that originated with General Franklin: "That the battle should be fought on the left : that a column of thirty or forty thousand men should be formed and at daylight, on the morning of the 13th, and make the main assault on the Confederate right with this body".

In preparation for this movement General Burnside visited the left at 5 P. M. of the 12th and discussed with Generals Franklin, Smith and Reynolds this order of battle, and at dark left them with the full understanding that it was adopted by him, promising to send the orders for carrying it into execution before midnight, thus giving time enough to General Franklin to get troops into position during the night.

Had this attack in Franklin's front been carried out it would most likely have been successful, and General Burnside would have gone down to posterity as a great General. But it was not to be, and instead of pushing the preparation for the only movement that contained a ray of hope, General Burnside went back to his headquarters and went to bed, leaving Franklin, Smith, and Reynold's anxiously awaiting orders that were to insure a victory. And how patiently they waited with their respective staffs, sitting up all night, thinking, wondering, trying to conceive what important event must have happened to prevent the arrival of the expected orders. At 7.30 o'clock, next morning, December 13th, General

MAJOR-GENERAL A. E. BURNSIDE.

Hardie handed to Franklin directions for a new plan of battle, not that which was discussed the night before, but the most remarkable, incogruous, disjointed plan of action, with the least possible hope of success that ever emanated from the brain of a commander: "That Franklin should keep his whole command in position for a rapid movement down the old Richmond road. That he should send out a division to seize the enemy's heights at Captain Hamilton's, on the extreme right of the enemy's line". He also ordered another column of a division or more from the command of General Sumner, to seize the heights in the rear of the town. Two isolated attacks by light columns, on distant positions, rendered almost impregnable and held by the flower of the Confederate Army!

Franklin selected the Pennsylvania Reserves for the almost superhuman task, for the reason that the division at the moment lay nearest the point of attack. General Meade, their commander, was one of the most discreet and able officers in the service, and the division was one of the most reliable. The selection was most admirable.

The line of march to reach the heights to be carried was across a level plain, over which hung a thick haze. The Reserves had been encamped here for some time the year before when attached to McDowell's forces and knew every inch of the ground to be marched over and fought for. So, having gotten his instructions, Meade started the division into the fog and into a fight that was to cover with glory himself and his command, though with the cost of nearly half their number, the objective point, the heights at Hamilton's, in a direct line, two miles away.

The division was formed with the First Brigade on the right, the Third on the left, and the Second in support.

Hardly had the march commenced when the enemy began firing. Although they could not see the Union lines they seemed to feel that something was going on, and solid shot and shells went flying over the fog-shrouded plain. Meade rode along the lines giving words of encouragement to each regiment. As he passed Colonel McCandless he said, alluding to a possible promotion, "A star this morning, William?" To which McCandless replied: "More likely a wooden overcoat". Then a shell passed through the horse ridden by McCandless, and he did the rest of his fighting for that day, on foot. And so for a half hour the march went on. Then young Confederate Major Pelham, of Stuart's Horse Artillery, from a point on the Port Royal road opened a telling fire on Meade's left flank, enfilading his whole line, and became so annoying as to cause him to halt. The line paused, and the four light batteries of the Reserves returned Pelham's fire so vigorously as to cause him to withdraw suddenly.

Stuart, with his cavalry, made threatening demonstrations, and General Doubleday deployed on Meade's left to check him.

Franklin instructed Gibbons to support Meade's right, and again the column moved forward. To meet the attack General Lee had arranged Jackson's Corps in the woods at Hamilton's with A. P. Hill's division in front, Early's and Taliaferro's divisions composing his second line, and D. N. Hill's division in reserve. The division of A. P. Hill forming the advanced line was composed of the brigades of Archer, Lane, and Pender, with the brigades of Gregg and Thomas directly in their rear.

As Meade neared the enemy's line the fog suddenly lifted, giving the Confederate artillerists a clear view of the advancing lines. Three batteries, those of Wooder, Braxton, and Carpenter, that had been pushed out on the skirmish line in front of Lane's Brigade, and the five batteries of Lieutenant-Colonel Walker's command, opened, using shell and canister, damaging the Union alignment considerably. The four light batteries of the Reserves replied energetically, and Meade pushed on. General Smith (Baldy), seeing the trouble from afar directed the fire of his Sixth Corps guns upon the three batteries first named and compelled their withdrawal. The crowd of skirmishers that covered the advance struck and drove in those of the Confederates.

The battle waxed hot, but Meade, oblivious to the roar, impetuously rushed on. With a great crash his infantry struck that of the enemy. The fighting, for a few moments, was extremely earnest. The men vied with each other in acts of noble daring. Many prisoners were taken, and one regiment, the Nineteenth Georgia, was captured entire, young Charles C. Upjohn, Company K, of the Second Reserves, tearing from the hands of the color-bearer, the flag of that regiment. The Union men drove Lane's Brigade back across the railroad into the woods, and crushing through the interval between the brigades of Archer and Pender flanked both their lines and compelled them to fall back. Then up the wooded crest with a rush so sudden, that General Maxey Gregg, the Confederate commander of the second line, could not believe that the advancing troops was the Union line, and fell dead while trying to prevent his South Carolinians from firing, but his men discovering the error poured a withering fire into Meade's line.

At this moment the divisions of Generals Early and Taliaferro swept forward at a double-quick, striking Meade with irresistible force and overpowering numbers, enveloping his flanks and endangering his whole command.

The situation became most critical, the surroundings awfully grand. The woods echoed and re-echoed every shot until the roar was appalling. Great shells went screaming through the forest, cutting down giant trees, and the crash of the falling timber added to the deafening sound.

In the midst of the tumult the reserves fell back and were soon out again on the open plain. In one short hour they had known the thrilling ecstacies of victory and disasterous defeat.

Meade halted after re-crossing the railroad, and reformed the division, but he was not allowed much time to rest. Early pushed after him, and the brigade of Atkinson and Hoke struck with vigor at the shattered ranks, forcing him to fall back rapidly and with some confusion. Franklin, forseeing the difficulty, had ordered Birney's division to the front, and he arrived just in time to check the advancing enemy and save what was left of the reserves. While Meade was moving on Hamilton's the troops in the city were prepared to strike.

About 9 o'clock whilst listening to the roar of battle on the left, the order to "Fall in" was given, and then until noon the command stood in line on one of the streets near the river and parallel with the stream. It was a trying ordeal for all. Shells were screaming overhead and frequently striking among the houses of the city, scattering the bricks and stones and wounding many. Although the noise of the artillery, flying shells and crumbling buildings was appalling, the silence in the ranks and the perfect order maintained was most admirable.

The wounded went past in great numbers, and the appearance of the dripping blood was not calculated to enthuse the men or cheer them for the first important battle. A German soldier sitting in a barrow, with his legs dangling over the side, was wheeled past. His foot had been shot off and the blood was flowing from the stump. The man was quietly smoking, and when the barrow would tip to one side he would remove the pipe from his lips and call out to the comrade who was pushing: "Ach, make right"! It seemed ludicrous and some of the men smiled, but the sight was too much for one boy in the regiment, William Dehaven, who sank in the street in a dead faint. The incident occurred just as the regiment moved off to go int the fight and the poor boy was left lying in the street. He recovered his senses to find his regiment gone, and the brave fellow picked up his musket and ran out alone onto the field and joined his company. And so the regiment stood. Under arms, listening to the sounds of the fight on the left and waiting patiently for their turn to share in the strife, while General Thomas Francis Meagher, mounted and surrounded by his staff, addressed each regiment of his (the Irish) brigade in burning, eloquent words besought the men to uphold in the coming struggle the military prestige and glory of their native land.

Green box-wood was culled in a garden near-by and Meagher placed a sprig in his Irish cap. Every officer and man followed his example, and soon great bunches of the fragrant shrub adorned the caps of every one. Wreaths were made and hung upon the tattered flags, and the national color of the Emerald Isle blended in fair harmony with the red, white and blue of the Republic.

At noon, Meade not having yet reached Hamilton's, General Couch ordered French and Hancock to the assault. French moved first, closely followed by "The Superb". As the troops wheeled into the streets leading towards the enemy they were in full view of the frowning heights and the march of death began. Nearly a mile away arose the position that the troops were expected to carry, and though not yet clear of the city they felt the pressure of the foe, the fire of whose batteries concentrated to crush the heads of the column as it debouched upon the plain. Solid shot, fired with light charges, ricochetted on the frozen ground, caromed on the pavement, and went tearing through the ranks, traversing the entire length of the streets and bounding over the river to be buried in the opposite bluff.

To charge an enemy or enter a battle when one knows that there is no hope of success, requires courage of a higher order than when the soldier is sustained by the enthusiasm born of hope.

It is recorded that a commander once gave to his subordinate the order to "Go there and die"! The reply was: "Yes, my General". When the Union troops, debouching from the town, deployed upon the plain in front of Marye's Heights, every man in the ranks knew that it was not to fight. It was to die.

As they moved out Hanover Street, the city seemed so deserted, and in a manner quiet, the men spoke in low whispers and earnest tones. A lone, solitary pussy cat sat on a gate-post mewing dolefully. Shells began dropping with destructive effect. One striking in the Eighty-eighth New York placed eighteen men hors du combat. The men of the regiment will ever remember the first one that burst in the One Hundred and Sixteenth, severely wounding the gallant Colonel, and cutting off the head of Sergeant Marley and killing three others. The men were struck by the instantaneousness of the deaths. The column had halted for a moment.

A sharp report, a puff of smoke, and four men lay stark dead their faces calm, their eyes mild and life-like, lips unmoved, no sign of suffering or indication of pain.

Sergeant Marley had not fallen but dropped upon his knees, his musket clasped in both hands and resting upon the ground.

Out in the open fields in the rear of the town, the regiment still marching in column of fours—soon reaching the canal to find that the bridge on which it was to cross had been shot away, only the stringers remaining. Some of the men plunged into the ice-cold water, others stepped quickly over the few remaining planks of the broken bridge. The shells still fell and now the whistle of the minie was heard mingling with their scream. Lieutenant Robert Montgomery, of Company I, as he stepped on the broken timbers of the bridge, fell over into the stream mortally wounded.

After crossing the stream a sharp rise in the ground hid the regiment from the enemy and gave the men a chance to take breath and to dress the ranks and prepare the column of attack, which was led by brigade front, General Kimball's brigade in the lead, followed by those of Colonel J. W. Andrews and Colonel Palmer. Hancock's division came next, with the brigades of Zook, Meagher and Caldwell in the order named. Here the thought occurred

"How different is the real battle from that which one's imagination had pictured." After the readings of boyhood, with heads filled with Napoleon and his marshals, and harrowing tales of gory fields of yore. With what realistic feeling one can see the wild confusion of the storm-swept field, charging cavalry, hurrying artillery, the riderless steeds madly rushing to and fro, their shrill neighing mingling with the groans, shrieks and screams of the wounded.

Here there was no disorder. The men were calm, silent, cheerful. The commands of the officers, given in a quiet, subdued voice, were distinctly heard and calmly obeyed, and the regiments manoeuvered without a flaw.

In this trying moment the guides were ordered out and the alignment made as perfect as on dress parade. The destruction of human beings is done with order and system. Yet is was terrible enough; the very absence of confusion and excitement but added to the dreadful intensity of the horror. As for the screams and shrieks, no one ever heard anything of that kind, either on the field or in the hospitals. It may be that soldiers of other nations indulge in cries and yells. The men of the War of 1861, took their punishment without a complaint or murmur.

Just before moving from this spot one of the young officers of the regiment, a brave boy from Chester County, Pennsylvania, Lieutenant Seneca G. Willauer, was badly torn by a shell which stripped the flesh from his thigh and left the bone, for four or five inches, white and bare. He approached the regimental commander and holding up the bleeding limb for inspection, said, with the most gentle manner and placid voice, "Colonel, do you think that I should go on with my company or go to the hospital?" No doubt had he been told to go on with his company he would have done so.

Then the advance was sounded. The order of the regimental commanders rang out clear on the cold

December air, "Right shoulder, shift arms, battalion forward, guide centre, march".

The long lines of bayonets glittered in the bright sunlight. No friendly fog hid the Union line from the foe, and as it advanced up the slope it came in full view of the Army of Northern Virginia.

The noonday sun glittered and shone bright on the frozen ground and all their batteries opened upon the advancing lines. The line of the enemy could be traced by the fringe of blue smoke, that quickly appeared along the base of the hills. The men marched into an arc of fire. And what a reception awaited them. Fire in front, from the right and left. Shells came direct and oblique, and dropped down from above. Shells enfiladed the lines, burst in front, in rear, above and behind; shells everywhere. A torrent of shells; a blizzard of shot, shell and fire.

The lines passed on steadily. The gaps made were quickly closed. The colors often kissed the ground, but were quickly snatched from dead hands and held aloft again by others, who soon in their turn bit the dust. The regimental commanders marched out far in advance of their commands and they too fell rapidly, but others ran to take their places.

Officers and men fell in rapid succession. Lieutenant Garrett Nowlen, who had just taken Willauer's place in command of Company C, fell with a ball through the thigh. Major Bardwell fell badly wounded; and a ball whistled through Lieutenant Bob McGuire's lungs.

Lieutenant Christian Foltz felt dead, with a ball through his brain. The orderly sergeant of Company H wheeled around, gazed upon Lieutenant Quinlan, and a great stream of blood poured from a hole in his forehead, splashing over the young officer, and the sergeant fell dead at his feet.

Captain John O'Neill, Company K, was shot in the lungs, the ball passing completely through his body.

LIEUTENANT CHRISTIAN FOLTZ.
Killed at Fredericksburg, December 13th, 1862.

But on, still onward, the line pressed steadily. The men dropping in twos, in threes, in groups. No cheers or wild hurrahs as they moved towards the foe. They were not there to fight, only to die.

Onward, still forward, the line withering, diminishing, melting away, every man knowing the desperation of the undertaking, but no one faltering or turning back. Still in good order the One Hundred and Sixteenth pushed forward until five hundred yards of the long half mile that lay between it and Marye's Heights were passed with the sharp whiz of the minie joining the loud scream of the oblong bolts. Soon the men forgot the presence of the shells in the shower of smaller missiles that assailed them. The hills rained fire and the men advanced with heads bowed as when walking against a hailstorm. Still through the deadly shower the ever-thinning lines pressed on. The plain over which they had passed was thickly spotted with the men of the Second Corps, dead, in twos and threes and in groups. Regiments and companies had their third or fourth commander, and the colors were borne to the front by the third or fourth gallant soul who had raised them. The gaps in the lines had become so large and so numerous that continued efforts had to be made to close them, and the command, "guide centre", was frequently heard. French neared the entrenchments of the Confederates' first line, and the enemy redoubling their efforts, the storm rose to greater fury. The struggle was hopeless. The attacking line waved like corn in a hurricane, recoiled, then broke, and the shattered mass fell back amid the shouts and cheers of Cobb's and Kershaw's Confederate Brigades that lined the trenches in their front. Now Hancock, with the division that never lost a gun or a color, swept forward, and being joined by many of the gallant men of French's command, made the most heroic effort of the day. Passing the furthest point reached by the preceding troops, he impetuously rushed on, past the brick house so conspicuous on the field. On, on, until his flags waved within twenty-five paces of the fatal stone wall. Then with a murderous fire everywhere around he realized the full absurdity of the attempt to accomplish an utter impossibility. His men had not yet fired a shot, and had only reached the spot where the work was to begin. Forty per cent. of the force had already fallen. No support within three-quarters of a mile. In front, line after line of works followed each other up the terraced heights to the very crest which was covered with artillery. To carry the assault further would be extreme madness. Even should the force take and occupy the first line it would simply be to meet the fire of the second and third. To fight the host in front was not possible. The men were here only to be shot down without being able to return the blow. The Irish Brigade had reached a point within thirty yards of the stone wall and began firing. All the field and staff officers of the regiment were wounded. The color sergeant, William H. Tyrrell, was down on one knee, (his other leg being shattered), but still waving the flag on the crest. Five balls struck him in succession; a dozen pierced the colors; another broke the flag-staff, and the colors and the color sergeant fell together. The orders to retire passed down the line and the command began falling back. All the color guard was down, and the flag in the grasp of young Tyrrell was still on the fire-swept crest. It was soon missed, and that fearless soldier, Lieutenant Francis T. Quinlan, ran back to save it. A hundred fired at him, but quickly seizing the broken flag-staff he threw himself on the ground and, with the flag tightly clasped to his breast, rolled back to where the command had halted, a noble deed, well done.

But Hancock would not be driven from the field, and halting where the formation of the ground afforded some shelter to his hard-tried command, he remained until relieved at nightfall and then withdrew to the town. It was a long, dreadful afternoon that awaited the thousands wounded, who lay scattered over the sad and ghastly plain.

The only place of cover was the brick house out near the stone wall. To this, hundreds of the wounded dragged themselves and a great mass of sufferers huddled together and struggled to get nearer the house that they might escape the fire. All around the great heaps of dead bore testimony to the fierceness of the combat. Near by, a color Sergeant lay, stark and cold, with the flag of his regiment covering him. Just in front of the stone wall lay a line of men of the Irish Brigade, with the green box-wood in their caps, and the two bodies nearest the enemy were those of Major William Horgan, and Adjutant John R. Young, both of the Eighty-eighth New York. It was not yet one o'clock when the assaulting column retired, and the wounded had nearly five hours to wait for darkness.

The sharpshooters of the enemy soon got a position from which they could infilade the brick house, and when any one moved among the mass of bleeding men it was the signal for the rifle balls to whistle around. Few expected to live until night, and but few did. Keeping very quiet, hugging the ground closely, the stricken men talked together in low tones. The bullets kept whistling and dropping, and every few moments some one would cease talking never to speak again. Quietly they passed away from the crimson field to eternity, their last gaze on their waving flag, the last sound to reach their ears the volleys of musketry and their comrades' cheers.

What a cosmopolitan crowd these dead and wounded were—Americans from the Atlantic Coast and the Pacific States, from the praries, from the great valleys of the Mississippi and the Ohio ; Irishmen from the banks of the Shannon and Germans from the Rhine and the blue Danube; Frenchmen from the Seine and Italians from the classic Tiber mingled their blood and went down in death together that the cause and that the Union might live. Every little while other columns emerged from the city, deployed upon the plain, marched forward, but never got so far as the brick house. The appearance of these troops would draw the fire of the batteries on the hills and hundreds of deadly projectiles would go screaming over, and could be seen bursting in the midst of the advancing lines. Evening came at last; the sun went down behind the terrible heights and the wounded anxiously watched the shadows lengthen and steal across the field of blood, creeping slowly over the plain, throw the houses of the city in the shade, then up the church tower until the only object that reflected the rays was the cross of burnished gold which sparkled a moment against the purple sky, and then the twilight deepened until it was difficult to discern objects. It was thought that the battle was ended, when, through the gathering darkness, loomed up the divisions of Hooker. Nobly they went to the work, with empty muskets and orders to carry the position with the bayonet. The dark mass passed the brick house and almost to the point that Hancock had reached. They had come in the gloaming unseen, and surged against the base of Marye's Heights.

Again the hills flashed fire, shook, rocked, roared and belched forth more tons of iron on the red plain, more minutes of useless carnage. The sombre wave rolled back, the last and most absurd attempt of the disastrous day had come to naught and seventeen hundred more had been added to the ponderous list of casualties. Clouds over-shadowed the skies, and, guided by the lurid fires still smouldering through the ebony darkness, the immense crowd of wounded began crawling, struggling, dragging themselves towards the city, those who were slightly hurt assisting the others who were more seriously injured; those with shattered limbs using muskets for crutches, many fainting and falling by the way. And when in the town, how hard to find a spot to rest, or a surgeon to bind up the wounds. More wounded than the city had inhabitants, every public hall and house filled to over-flow, the porches of the residences covered with bleeding men, the surgeons busy everywhere. In the lecture-room of the

Episcopal church eight operating tables were in full blast, the floor was densely packed with men whose limbs were crushed, fractured and torn. Lying there in deep pools of blood, they waited very patiently, almost cheerfully, their turn to be treated; there was no grumbling, no screaming, hardly a moan; many of the badly hurt were smiling and chatting, and one—who had both legs shot off—was cracking jokes with an officer who could not laugh at the humorous sallies, for his lower jaw was shot away. The cases here were nearly all capital, and amputation was almost always resorted to. Hands and feet, arms and legs were thrown under each table, and the sickening piles grew larger as the night progressed. The delicate limbs of the drummer boy fell along with the rough hand of the veteran in years, but all, every one, was brave and cheerful. Towards morning the conversation flagged, many dropped off to sleep before they could be attended to, and many of them never woke again. Finally the only sound heard was the crunching of the surgeons' saws and now and then the melancholy music of a random shell dismally wailing over-head. Few the prayers that were said, but the soft voice of a boyish soldier as he was lifted on the table, his limbs a mass of quivering, lacerated flesh, was heard as he quietly said "O my God, I offer all my sufferings in atonement for the sins by which I have crucified Thee".

Outside, the members of the Christian Commission were hard at work relieving all within reach, and the stretcher carriers were hurrying the wounded from the field. A few chaplains were quietly moving among the suffering thousands, giving them comfort, and soothing their dying hour. Out on the railroad at Hamilton's lay the body of the fearless commander of the Third Brigade of the Pennsylvania Reserves, General C. Fager Jackson, and at the Bernard House, where he had been carried, died at midnight the youngest general officer, and one of the most beloved of all that fell, General George

D. Bayard, of the cavalry. While conversing with some other officers early in the day a shell struck the group, passing through the overcoat of Captain H. G. Gibson, destroying his sabre. It crushed General Bayard's thighs and carried away a portion of his abdomen. He lived fourteen hours after being hit, and passed the time in quietly giving directions and in dictating letters to his friends. In one to Colonel Collum he said, "Give my love to General McClellan and say my only regret is that I did not die under his command." He was to have been married on the following Wednesday, and the bride awaited her cavalier who never came. *Bayard, sans peur et sans reproche!* The losses in some of the commands were unusually severe. The Eleventh Pennsylvania Reserves lost six color bearers inside of a few moments, and Company C, Twelfth Reserves, lost forty of the forty-nine present.

But the most appalling loss was in the division of General Hancock. Of the five officers composing his personal staff three were wounded and four horses were killed under them. The general himself was struck by a rifle-ball but not seriously hurt. Of the sixteen officers of the Sixty-ninth New York, every one was killed or wounded, and the regiment lost seventy-five per cent. of the enlisted men, and left the field with its fourth commander, three having been disabled. The Fifth New Hampshire lost seventeen out of twenty-three officers, and had five commanding officers during the fight. The One Hundred and Sixteenth Regiment, Pennsylvania Volunteers had all the field and staff and many of the line officers killed or wounded, and was taken off the field by the fourth officer in command during the fight. The Eighty-first Pennsylvania lost twelve out of sixteen officers and seventy-five per cent. of the enlisted men. The fourth commanding officer brought the regiment off the field. The Fifty-seventh New York lost nine out of the eleven officers present. The Sixty-sixth New York had four commanders during the battle, the three first having been killed or wounded. Many other regiments of the division suffered almost as severely, yet, on the morning of the following day, notwithstanding the great loss, when ordered to support the Ninth Corps, the command fell in, ready and willing, to join in the contemplated assault with the Ninth Corps, led by General Burnside in person—from which he was happily dissuaded by Generals Sumner and Hooker at the moment that all was ready to make the attack. During the fourteenth, the regiment rested in the streets of the city. Sergeant Abraham Detwiler, of Company C, begged to be allowed to carry the colors and he was accorded the honor. Well did he fill the position, and bore the flag during the Chancellorsville and Gettysburg campaigns until he was promoted lieutenant of his company. Lieutenant Edmund Randall was conspicuous in his efforts to rescue the wounded and get them over the river to a place of safety. He did noble work, and bursting shell and falling walls had no terrors for him where a man of the regiment could be saved. During the battle the regiment held the left flank of the Irish Brigade. The regiment and the Irish Brigade reached a point within thirty yards of the stone wall, and the bodies that lay nearest the enemy's line were those of the regiment and Brigade and, by actual measurement, within twenty-five paces of the Washington Artillery (Confederate). Lieutenant William E. Owens, of that famous corps, in his history of the Washington Artillery tells us, "That a soldier of the Irish Brigade was the nearest body to the stone wall and, by actual measurement, it lay within twenty-five feet of the wall." A British line officer, writing on the campaign of Fredericksburg (published by Keegan & Co., London), writes in laudation of the foreign-born soldier in America during the great Civil war. We quote his account of the attack of the Irish Brigade on December 13th, 1862: "Fifteen minutes passed and another division, Hancock's five thousand strong, rushed forward from the town. Zook's brigade led the way, but quickly recoiled, beaten back by that terrible artillery. Not so its successor. Under cover of the further bank of the ravine, the Irish Brigade composed of the Twenty-eighth Massachusetts, the Sixty-third, Sixty-ninth and Eighty-eighth New York, and the One Hundred and Sixteenth Pennsylvania, under General Meagher, threw off their haversacks and blankets and deployed into line. Resolutely they breasted the slope and faced the death-dealing storm; swiftly they passed the limit marked by three solitary colors, and shoulder to shoulder, their own green flag and the blue and scarlet of the Union standard waving above them, swept forward against the low wall which skirts the base of Marye's Hill.

So determined was their advance that Colonel Miller, commanding the Confederate Brigade confronting them—for General Cobb had already fallen—ordered his men to hold their fire for a space. And now occurred a strange and pathetic incident. Though high was the courage of that thin line which charged so boldly across the shot-swept plain, opposed to it were men as fearless and staunch; behind that rude stone breast-work were "bone of their bone, and flesh of their flesh"—the soldiers of Cobb's Brigade were Irish like themselves. On the morning of the battle General Meagher had bade his men to deck their caps with sprigs of evergreen, "to remind them," he said, "of the land of their birth." The symbol was recognized by their countrymen, and "Oh, God, what a pity! Here comes Meagher's fellows"! was the cry in the Confederate ranks. One hundred and fifty paces from the hill the brigade halted and fired a volley, while the round shot tore fiercely through the well ordered line. Still no sign from the wall, looming grim and silent through the battle-smoke; and again the battalions moved swiftly forward. They were but a hundred yards from their goal, unbroken and unfaltering still, they had reached a point where Walton's gunners, unable to depress

LIEUTENANT ROBERT T. McGUIRE.
Died at close of War, of wounds received at Battle of Fredericksburg.

their pieces further, could no longer harass them. Victory seemed within their grasp, and a shout went up from the shattered ranks. Suddenly a sheet of flame leaped from the parapet, and 1,200 rifles, plied by cool and unshaken men, concentrated a murderous fire upon the advancing line. To their glory, be it told, though scores were swept away, falling in their tracks like corn before the sickle, the ever-thinning ranks dashed on.

> " The charging blood in their up-turned faces
> And the living fill the dead men's places ".

But before that threatening onset the Confederate veterans never quailed; volley on volley sped with deadly precision, and at so short a range every bullet found its mark. For a while the stormers struggled on, desperate and defiant; but no mortal man could long face that terrible fire, scathing and irresistible as the lightning, and at length the broken files gave ground. Slowly and sullenly they fell back ; fell back to fight no more that day, for beneath the smoke-cloud that rolled about Marye's Hill the Irish Brigade had ceased to exist. Forty yards from the wall where the charge was stayed, the dead and dying lay piled in heaps, and one body, supposed to be that of an officer, was found within fifteen yards of the parapet. The Adjutant-General of Hancock's division, who witnessed the attack from the town, said that at the time he could not understand what had happened ; the men fell in such regular lines that he thought they were lying down to allow the storm of shot to pass over them. General Ransom, commanding one of the divisions which held Marye's Hill, reported that this assault was made " with the utmost determination ", and the eloquent words of the London Times special correspondent, who was present with the Confederates, record the admiration of those who beheld that splendid charge. ' Never wrote he, at Fontenoy, Albuera or Waterloo, was more undaunted courage displayed by the sons of Erin ; The bodies which lie in dense masses within fifty yards of the muzzles of Colonel Walton's guns are the best evidence what manner of men they were who pressed on to death with the dauntlessness of a race which has gained glory on a thousand battle fields, and never more richly deserved it than at the foot of Marye's Hill, on December 13th, 1862 ' ". During Sunday, the day after the battle, no assistance could be given to the wounded who lay in great numbers out on the plain, but after dark on Sunday evening, many of the men made heroic efforts to bring them in, although the enemy were vigilant and fired at every object seen moving against the sky. Sergeant Sheridan, of Company G, Eighty-eighth New York, lay far out on the field with a fractured leg, and four of his comrades determined to go to his relief. Working themselves out on their stomachs, they succeeded in reaching him, but found him very low. As he had a compound fracture of the leg, it seemed impossible to move him, his agony was so great. The men dared not stand up, and were at their wits' ends to know what to do, when Sergeant Slattery came to the rescue. Said he, " Begob, boys did yez ever see rats trying to get away with a goose egg ? One rat lies down, the others roll the egg on top av him, he holds it in place wid his four paws, and then they pull him off by the tail. Now I will lie down on my back, you lift Sheridan on top av me and I will do my best to kape his leg even ". The suggestion was adopted. The men would push themselves on a couple of feet, then pull Slattery, with his precious load, up to them, and so on until, before daylight, they all reached the city and had Sheridan attended to, and his leg amputated ; too late, however, to save the poor fellow's life. He died from exhaustion. The clothes were literally ground off Sergeant Slattery's back, and his cuticle so sore that he was unable to do duty for a week afterwards.

A gallant soldier of Company B, John Dempsey had almost as rough an experience as Sheridan. His leg was fearfully shattered and he fell far out on the field by the stone wall. Feeling that he would die if he remained on the field he threw the crushed leg over the good one and then dragged himself on his stomach for nearly a mile until he reached the town. Some stretcher bearers found him in the evening and carried him over the river, but the surgeons were busy and he did not have the limb amputated until after four days, but he lived and got well.

On every battlefield there are amusing incidents, and Fredericksburg furnished its share. As the One Hundred and Sixteenth regiment was advancing on Marye's Heights under a heavy fire, two Irishmen in Company H, began to quarrel. One had pushed the other a little and, whilst they still kept their places in line, belabored each other with their tongues. "Wait till Oi get up on top av the hill", said Dempsey, "and Oi'll knock you down wid me potstick"! (meaning his musket). "Bad luck to ye, Oi'll poke me bayonet down yer troat"! And so they kept on until they reached the crest, where both were killed. Some one asked Captain O'Neill where he was hit. "I'm wounded all over", replied the gallant Captain; and when one thinks for a moment of a ball smashing a fellow's ribs, passing through his lungs and whistling out somewhere in the vicinity of his backbone, it seems but natural that he should feel "wounded all over".

The day of the 14th passed without a renewal of the contest, but was made remarkable by an episode very unusual on such occasions. The flags of the regiments of the Irish Brigade had been torn to ribbons during the many contests in which it had participated, and the citizens of New York had procured others to present in their place. The standards arrived during the battle, and with them came a committee, who brought a very generous supply of the good things of earth wherewith to celebrate the presentation, and a banquet was determined upon. A concert hall in one of the upper streets was selected for the feast. Here the tables were spread and decorations improvised. Invitations were sent out, and at noon two or three hundred officers assembled to do honor to the event and toast the new banners. For two or three hours the hall teemed with wine and rang with wit and eloquence, and the flags were baptized amid speeches by Generals Couch, Hancock, Sturgis, Meagher, and many other distinguished and gallant officers. The enjoyment and festivities ran high, the enthusiasm was great, but the loud cheers drew the fire of the Southern batteries, and the enemy, envying perhaps the good time our friends were having, sent their compliments in the shape of shells, one of which, passing through the ceiling of the room, knocked the plaster down among the viands, and was suggestive of an early adjournment; so the company separated with rather unceremonious leave-taking—not on account of the shell, certainly not! but as some of the gentlemen remarked: "it being Sunday, they thought it well to close the feast a little early that they might attend Divine service". During the night of this day and on Monday, the 15th, the troops lay on their arms waiting the next event. After dark a rumor spread that the army was to move to the left and strike the enemy again the following morning, but soon the columns began marching over the river and through the storm and gloom back to their camps. Shortly after daylight, on the 16th, the last regiment, the Sixty-ninth Pennsylvania Volunteers, filed across the pontoons. With sturdy blows the pontoniers severed on the city side the lashings of the bridge which swung around with the current of the stream, landing on the other shore, leaving to the mercy of God and the enemy, the killed and many of the wounded of the gallant army. The battle was over; the result, a graveyard.

Save one regimental flag, no trophies of the fight remained. Yet the field was redolent with acts of noble daring. The troops that marched on Marye's Heights more than equalled, in the grandeur of their bravery, the gallant six hundred immortalized by the poet laureate, while by their sacrifice, though they did not gain a victory, they raised a monument more enduring than marble or brass to the valor and heroism of our times and our people; and in other ages, when the memories of the contest will have been mellowed by the lapse of centuries, in the bloodshed, will be seen a holocaust at the altar of freedom in the smoke of the battle, sweet incense at the shrine of human liberty. The Union troops failed—so did Leonidas of Sparta, yet what son of Hellas but shares even to this day in the glory of old Thermopylae, and what American even to the most remote period of the future but will share in the glories that cluster around the plain of Fredericksburg? Those fields, resplendent with the great deeds of our people, where the verdure and every blooming flower is nurtured and enriched by martyr blood, will ever be hallowed places in the land, around which will crystallize the warm, full gratitude of a nation saved.

CHAPTER III.

AFTER FREDERICKSBURG.

WHEN the battle was over and the troops once more on the North side of the Rappahannock, each command quietly marched back to the camp-ground that had been vacated a few days before. Fortunately, nearly all the wounded of the One Hundred and Sixteenth were brought over the river before the evacuation of the town, but their sufferings were intolerable. A cold dismal rain fell on the men as they lay on the wet ground, but as quickly as possible they were moved off to temporary hospitals and cared for. Orders to build winter quarters were issued, and soon the men were slashing trees and erecting huts in which to pass the winter. Four or five logs cut the proper length, were piled one on the other, the intersections filled with mud, and over all a shelter tent spread for a roof. A fire place was made at one end, and a chimney constructed of sticks and mud—a chimney, by the way, which frequently caught fire and threatened to burn up the household. In these dwellings, arranged in streets and forming regimental camps, the great army spent the winter. Immense camp fires blazed. Wood, for the time, was plenty, and when the building of the huts was finished, many an evening was spent by the men sitting in long lines, enjoying the heat and light, and chatting of the fight, recalling scenes in the city of Fredericksburg and the field beyond. There were plenty of incidents to fill the long evenings with interesting talk. Every comrade who had fallen was remembered, and each one's lovable characteristics recalled, nor were the wounded forgotten.

Not only were the dead and wounded comrades in arms, but, in many instances, they were near relatives. Allen Landis of Company C, mourned for his brother, Aaron J. Landis, of the same company, who fell by the stone wall; and Lieutenant Willauer, also of Company C, was sent home terribly wounded to carry to his aged parents the sad news of his younger brother's death, Corporal Samuel Willauer. First Sergeant Richard Ker, of Company D, left his brother, Sergeant Andrew E. Ker, dead on the field, shot through the head before he was seventeen years of age. And these were not the only members of this family who served their country as soldiers. Another brother, William W. Ker, was a gallant Captain in the Seventy-third Pennsylvania Infantry; and, still another, George J. Ker, served until the end of the war in the Fifth Pennsylvania Cavalry, coming out as a full Captain and Brevet-Major, only to die of his wounds. Then there were Alexander and Daniel Chisholm, brothers, in Company K, the only pair of brothers who got through without a scratch; and Colonel Mulholland and his brother, Captain Charles Cosslett, of Company E. Sergeants Jacob and Jefferson Carl, of Company C, were brothers, and two other brothers of the Carl boys, Henry and William, were enlisted in other regiments. Captain Henry D. Price, Company C, who was killed in front of Petersburgh, had a brother, Abraham D. Price a Major in the Sixth Cavalry, and another brother, Joseph D. Price, was a Lieutenant in the same regiment, while Sergeant Elhannan W. Price, who was killed at Fredericksburg, was a full cousin to Captain Henry D. Price. James Collins, of Company K, had a brother an Adjutant of the One Hundred and Forty-second Pennsylvania Volunteers who was killed on the second day at the Wilderness. Jim learned of George's death next morning, but never asked an hour off duty in consequence. He marched along in silence for some days, but fought nobly to avenge his brother's fall.

The brother of Captain Lawrence Kelly of Company G, was killed by his side; and Lieutenant Kite, of Company F, had his son a private in his company. Henry and George Wilt, of Company C, were brothers; and also, Thomas and Robert Scarlett, of Company A. Also, Daniel and William Price, of Company B.

In Company G, there was a young boy named H. M. Seitzinger who, at Cold Harbor, when Color Sergeant T. A. Sloan was shot, rushed forward, seized the flag, and waving it over his head led the charge, calling to his father, James M. Seitzinger: "Go in Pop, I'm coming".

There were numbers of others in the regiment, but it was not exceptional. Whole families went to the war; some returned and others fell, in many instances all were killed. In a quiet spot in Massachusetts there are five brothers sleeping side by side, the youngest seventeen, the eldest, twenty-eight, and all fell within a few months of each other.

In Lycoming County, in our State, there are five noble boys named Rankin, side by side, all killed in battle.

Lieutenant Willauer's brother died a very heroic death. He was first shot through the hand, then through the body, the ball passing near the heart, then both feet were cut off by a shell; he was still living, when, after dark, the stretcher-carriers took him from the field to the hospital where he died during the night. He was aged just twenty years and one month.

Lieutenant Robert B. Montgomery, who was killed in battle, was a very noble gentleman, of an amiable and gentle disposition, a man whom every one loved, and who was ever ready to sacrifice himself for the good of the service. He lived for some days after being wounded, the ball still lodged in his body, and died resigned, saintly and heroic. His body was sent home to Philadelphia, and buried in Machpelah Cemetery, corner Tenth and Washington Avenue. The funeral was on Sunday afternoon,

LIEUTENANT ROBERT B. MONTGOMERY.
Killed at Fredericksburg, December 13th, 1862.

December 28th and tens of thousands of citizens lined the streets as the cortege passed. He was buried with full military honors.

The following is from the *Philadelphia Inquirer* of Monday, December 29th, 1862 :

THE FUNERAL OF LIEUTENANT ROBERT B. MONTGOMERY.

"The body of Lieutenant Robert B. Montgomery, formerly of Colonel Heenan's One Hundred and Sixteenth Regiment, Pennsylvania Volunteers, was interred yesterday afternoon, about four o'clock, at Machpelah Cemetery, Tenth Street and Washington Avenue.

The Lieutenant died on the 14th inst., at the Patent Office Hospital, Washington, D. C., of wounds received at the battle of Fredericksburg. He was in the thirty-fourth year of his age. His remains were brought from Washington at the expense of his former fellow workmen in the Navy Yard. A large military escort was in attendance, including a portion of the Thirtieth Massachusetts and Arsenal Guards and Captain Rockafellow, together with the members of the Hope Hose and Steam Fire Engine Company, a number of the workmen of the Navy Yard, and a detachment of the police force of the Third Division.

The funeral took place from the residence of Mr. John Paul, No. 228 Saratoga Street. Dr. Brainerd, of whose church he was formerly a member, officiated. His remarks over the grave of the deceased soldier were very impressive. 'Of the evils of war in general,' the doctor said, 'they are legion, and only to be tolerated now in order to avoid the worse evils of universal anarchy and international strife and bloodshed likely to follow the breaking up of a great nation. We suffer war as a choice of great evils. War cannot last always. Over the graves of our country's martyrs we can say that the cause ennobles the victim. A life sold, not lost.' Of the battle of Fredericksburg, Doctor Brainerd said : 'It was a fearful time and disastrous to thousands. Other generations will shudder at its details. It unfolds to us the strength of that treason which we have to combat. It develops a love of country seldom surpassed. It has disciplined a great army to appalling dangers and linked thousands of bleeding hearts more closely to the cause of freedom. It has created in all Christian lands, among true men, a deeper loathing of the treason which has shed this blood, and a deeper abhorrence of the Northern semi-traitors who aided the rebellion. It will tend to lift from the high places the mean, the mercenary and the craven-hearted, and give prominence in the cabinet and field to men willing to suffer and die for their country.'

Of Lieutenant Montgomery the doctor said: 'He was a young man of excellent character and noble impulse. A native of Virginia, with his property and all his relatives there, he was like Abdiah, "faithful among the faithless found." He preferred his whole country to the State of his birth. On the battlefield he fought bravely, and fell. He was a true man, a citizen and a patriot.'

After the closing of the remarks by the reverend doctor, the usual honor was paid to his memory by the military, and the multitude in the vicinity slowly and quietly dispersed.

Thirty-two years after a little group gathered once more around the grave of the beloved Lieutenant and the remains being raised and fully identified, were with tender care taken to the National Cemetery at Germantown. The same paper of February 3d, 1895, finishes the story began more than a quarter of a century before.

VETERANS' TRIBUTE TO A DEAD HERO.

THE REMAINS OF LIEUTENANT MONTGOMERY WILL BE TAKEN OUT TO GERMANTOWN—A ROMANCE OF THE WAR—GENERAL MULHOLLAND, DEPARTMENT COMMANDER EMSLEY AND COLONEL EDMUND RANDALL SEE THAT A COMRADE WHO DIED IN BATTLE IS GIVEN FITTING RESTING PLACE—FOUR HUNDRED MORE BODIES WILL FOLLOW.

Three honored veterans stood around in the snow storm in Machpelah Cemetery yesterday morning and

AFTER FREDERICKSBURG.

watched while the remains of a one-time comrade, who had died under their eyes in battle, were lifted up and made ready for shipment to the Soldiers' Cemetery at Germantown.

Around the event is a most interesting story. The dead man was Lieutenant Robert B. Montgomery, of Company I, One Hundred and Sixteenth Pennsylvania Volunteers, of which General Mulholland, now Pension Agent, was then lieutenant-colonel. In marching out of the city the Colonel was wounded and Mulholland took active command. When the regiment went gallantly into the battle of Fredericksburg on December 13th, 1862, Lieutenant Montgomery received his death wound.

The ball, which entered his groin, and crushed his bones in a terrible manner, struck him as he was leading a charge across a frail bridge over the canal. As he was hit he toppled over into the water. His comrades pulled him out and he was sent to a hospital, where he died a few days later.

BURIED WITH HONORS.

General Mulholland was wounded soon after and was at his home in this city when the body of Lieutenant Montgomery was sent on here for burial. The funeral was held on Sunday, December 28th, 1862. On the occasion the crowds on the streets were immense. The young Lieutenant was interred with full military honors, Captain Rockafellow's command firing the salute.

Lieutenant Montgomery had few friends here, as he was a Virginian by birth, and at one time a slave-holder. On the outbreak of the war, however, he had abandoned everything and joined the Union army. He had several brothers in the Confederate army.

When the removal of the bodies from Machpelah Cemetery was begun General Mulholland thought of these events of thirty years ago, and determined to see that the body of the brave soldier was fittingly cared for. He hunted up the records of the cemetery, but in them he could not find any trace of the Lieutenant's interment. But the General protested that the body was there, and went on to point out the grave. The owner of the lot was hunted up and the General's memory was found to be correct.

THE REMAINS IDENTIFIED.

Yesterday, in company with Department Commander Emsley, who was also in the One Hundred and Sixteenth, and Colonel Edmund Randall, General Mulholland, went down to see the coffin opened, and the remains made ready for shipment. The coffin was found in good condition, and the skull and clothing were well enough preserved to make identification positive. The army buttons were taken from the coat and preserved by Colonel Randall. The remains will be buried with honors in the National Cemetery.

The bodies of four hundred other soldiers rest in Machpelah Cemetery. Many of their graves are marked with government tombstones. Through the agency of General Mulholland these will all be taken to the National Cemetery at Germantown for interment".

Lieutenant Christian Foltz was killed instantly, being shot through the head; his body was left on the field, and buried, after the fight, in front of the stone wall. He came from near Elizabethtown, Pennsylvania, was of German descent, a brave, unassuming, Christian soldier, and though a man advanced in years, he was as full of patriotic feeling, and ever as ready to share in the hardships and dangers as the youngest.

Many of the officers wounded in the battle never returned. Colonel Dennis Heenan suffered severely for months and finally lost the use of his right hand. Major George H. Bardwell also lost the use of his right hand, the ball having broken every bone. He was afterwards breveted lieutenant-colonel for his gallantry on the occasion.

Captain O'Neill was shot through the right lung, the ball making a terrible wound from which he never fully recovered, and finally caused his death. He was a veteran, having served some eight years in the regular army before joining the regiment; the wound received at Fredericksburg was his third. Lieutenant Robert T. McGuire was also shot through the lungs, and in the thigh, and died of the wounds shortly after the close of the war. He was a brave and most lovable officer. He was born in Philadelphia of Irish parents, and educated in the public schools of that city.

A few days after the battle, the thanks of the President was read to the regiments on "dress parade," and received by all with evident pleasure:

EXECUTIVE MANSION,
WASHINGTON, December 22d, 1862.

To the Army of the Potomac:

I have just read your Commanding General's report of the battle of Fredericksburg.

Although you were not successful, the attempt was not an error, nor the failure other than an accident. The courage with which you in an open field maintained the contest against an entrenched foe, and the consummate skill and success with which you crossed and re-crossed the river in the face of the enemy, show that you possess all the qualities of a great army, which will yet give victory to the cause of the country and of the popular government.

Condoling with the mourners of the dead, and sympathizing with the severely wounded, I congratulate you that the number of both is comparatively so small. I tender you, officers and soldiers, the thanks of the nation. ABRAHAM LINCOLN.

The winter of 1862 and 1863 seemed long to the men in camp on the Rappahannock. The cold was not intense, but the atmosphere damp and penetrating. The ground became frozen and sodden by turns, and when a few warm days would come and draw the frost out of the earth, the mud would become so deep that moving around was impossible. There was little chance for drill, and the days and nights in camp seemed very long. Ofttimes the doctor's call in the morning would be the only sound to disturb the camp. The guard would be changed without music, and the picket detail formed and marched off in the rain or snow in grim silence. During the winter the picket duty was extremely severe, and the detail large. The men of the regiment had to march three miles to the picket line which ran along the north bank of the Rappahannock, near the old town of Falmouth. Most of the march was through slush and mud, and by the time the detail reached the ground every one was wet and chilled, and in that condition began the turn of duty. No fires were allowed on the line, and frequently none on the reserve. After standing the two hours on the river bank, shivering in the wintry blast, or with the back to a blinding snow-storm, the men found scanty comfort when on the reserve. How cheerful and cosy the little hut seemed when, after the turn of duty on picket, they returned to camp! But the picket line, although so cold and trying, was not without its attractions. The river was narrow enough to permit the men of each army to see the other and often converse. Little or no firing was indulged in, and the men of both sides stood in full view of each other. Of course, during the darkness of night every one was vigilant and watchful, but during the day there was nothing to do but stand and let the hours go by. Contraband trading was carried on to a very great extent after dark, the men wading the river where fordable, and the Confederates visiting in return. Union coffee for Confederate tobacco constituted the principal commercial transactions. No harm resulted from the trade, and the officers, when patroling the line, would manage to look some other way, and fail to observe any visitors from the other side of the river who might happen to be among the Union men. Had they recognized the Confederate they would have been compelled to arrest him, but it was difficult to distinguish colors after nightfall, it being so very dark and the blue and the gray were so much alike. It was just the same on the other side. The officers and men acted honorably, and not one of the boys who crossed the river with his little bag of coffee was ever detained.

The regimental chaplain, Reverend Edward McKee, resigned December 24th. He had proven himself a brave and fearless officer, but his health gave way under the hardships of campaigning and he was compelled to return to private life.

Christmas Day, 1862, was celebrated in the camp; many boxes of good things from home were received, and shared by the recipients with comrades less fortunate. Some of the boys were a little homesick, to be sure, but enough were sufficiently light of heart to drive dull care away. A large Christmas tree was erected in the centre of the camp, and peals of laughter and much merriment greeted the unique decorations, tin cups, hard tack, pieces of pork and other odd articles being hung on the branches. At night the camp fire roared and blazed, the stars shone above the tall pines, the canteen was passed around, and care banished for the hour. It must have been a sad Christmas, however, to those at home whose friends had fallen by Marye's Heights and Hamilton's Woods. New Year's Day came and passed, and on January 16th an order was received to prepare for another march, the celebrated movement known in history as the "Mud Campaign." It was the last effort of General Burnside to justify himself and give battle to the enemy, but nature and the elements protested. On the twentieth the army broke camp and moved, or rather tried to move, but the downpour of rain upon the soaked earth was so copious and incessant, and the mud so deep that no movement was possible. No sooner had they left their different camps than men, trains and artillery became stalled in the mire, and it became a question of getting them extricated and back to their quarters, rather than one of striking the enemy. The members of the One Hundred and Sixteenth never left the camp ground during this period, as it was intended that the Second Corps should be the last to move. And the men found great consolation in the fact, especially when they saw the condition of the bedraggled infantry and mud-covered artillery, that was sunk hub-deep in the sea of liquid clay that was once a road. January 26th, that splendid old soldier, General Edwin V. Sumner, retired from command of the Right Grand Division, bade the army farewell, and shortly afterwards died. It is told of Sumner that, at Antietam, he was sending his son on an errand of great danger, and after giving him the order, the young man was about to gallop off when the general called him back and kissed him; then said, "Go on, my boy." January 26th, 1863, the regiment was consolidated with a battalion of four companies, and the following officers retained in command:

    Major commanding—St. Clair A. Mulholland.
    Adjutant—Lieutenant Garrett Nowlen.
    Quartermaster—Lieutenant Richard Wade.
    Surgeon—William B. Hartman.
    Sergeant Major—George Roeder.
    Quartermaster Sergeant—George McMahon.
    Company A—Captain, Seneca G. Willauer; first lieutenant, William M. Hobart; second lieutenant, George Halpin.
    Company B—Captain, Francis T. Quinlan; first lieutenant, Francis E. Crawford; second lieutenant, Thomas A. Dorwart.
    Company C—Captain, John Teed; first lieutenant, Henry D. Price; second lieutenant, William H. Tyrrell;
    Company D—Captain, William A. Peet; first lieutenant, Jacob R. Moore; second lieutenant, Louis J. Sacriste.

The consolidation of the regiment became necessary because of the fact that the command had not been recruited to the maximum strength at the beginning, and had lost heavily by death, sickness and detail. It was understood, however, that six new companies should be

MAJOR-GENERAL EDWIN V. SUMNER.
Commanded Second Corps, March 13th to October 6th, 1862

added to the command as soon as practicable. This was not effected until a year after the consolidation, and the command fought as a "battalion" at Chancellorsville, Gettysburg, Mine Run and Bristow Station. The supernumerary officers were honorably discharged, some entering the service again in other commands. Lieutenant-Colonel Mulholland was compelled to lose the rank of lieutenant-colonel and accept that of major, knowing that it would be but for a short time, or until the new companies were organized. Lieutenant Edmund Randall was one of the officers retained, but he tendered his resignation, and in April, Captain Francis T. Quinlan did likewise. These two young, brave and talented officers left the regiment, and their going was much regretted by the commanding officer and all their comrades. They were promising officers and had a brilliant future before them.

Shortly after the failure of the ludicrous fiasco, the "Mud Campaign", General Joseph Hooker succeeded General Burnside in command of the army of the Potomac, and the change for the time had a most happy effect. New life seemed to be given to every organization, and fresh vitality to every department. Many changes took place in the organization and personnel of the army. The grand division idea was definitely abandoned, and the corps-mark, or badge, was adopted. This feature consisted of a distinct emblem by which the division and corps to which every man belonged could be recognized. The emblem was worn on the cap, and the corps was designated by the emblem itself, and the division by the color. Red, white, and blue indicated the first, second and third divisions. The badge of the Second Corps was the trefoil or cloverleaf, and as the One Hundred and Sixteenth belonged to the First Division the badge of the regiment was red. The "corps badges", worn on the cap, became very dear to the troops, a source of pride and an incentive to emulation. They proved to be of great convenience to all, enabling every one to identify corps and divisions on the march or on line of battle without inquiry. The men of the Irish Brigade added to the red clover leaf an emblem of the same form, though of a different color—a small, green shamrock, this denoting the brigade organization as well as the division and corps.

February 28th Captain Peet resigned and Lieutenant Nowlen was soon after promoted to Captain of Company D, and Lieutenant Sacriste became Adjutant.

During February, March and April of this year, 1863, camp fever was prevalent, and many deaths occurred in the army, but the regiment was remarkably fortunate in the small number of cases of sickness and the very few fatalities. Every moment of fair weather was taken advantage of to drill and discipline the command, and at no time before or afterwards did the regiment attain such such perfection in all that pertains to the movements as a body under arms, or develop such a degree of excellent discipline of the individual soldier. Not only did the battalion gain unstinted praise on brigade, division and corps drills and reviews, but every man seemed to vie with each other in trying to outdo his comrade in personal appearance and soldierly accomplishments. The "reviews", "dress parades" and "guard mounts", and other occasions of ceremony were all admirable, and the rigid inspections told well for the *personnel* of every one. Every man was clean and neat, beyond anything that could be expected under the circumstances. Private Jacob Lutz, Company B", was awarded the credit of having the cleanest musket. Lutz, in fact, was a crank on the subject of cleanliness. His musket, however, was his especial pride and constant care. The boys used to say that he would sleep without cover on a wet night in order that he might wrap the piece in his blanket, and thus shelter it from the dampness.

On the morning after the battle, Sergeant Abraham L. Detweiler Company C, was promoted to be Color Sergeant, vice Tyrrell who had been severely wounded and who was shortly after commissioned. Sergeant Detweiler had behaved with great bravery in the fight and was the first to jump out of the ranks and volunteer to carry the flag when a new color sergeant was called for. He was not only a fearless man but intelligent and filled the position with ability. He carried the colors at Chancellorsville, Gettysburg, Auburn, Bristow Station and Mine Run and was promoted to a Lieutenancy in November 1863.

ST. PATRICK'S DAY, 1863.

St. Patrick's day in camp was celebrated with the usual gayety and rejoicing by the men composing the Irish Brigade. This time-honored national anniversary was observed with all the exhaustless spirit and enthusiasm of Irish nature. For days previous vast preparations had been made, a race-course marked out, and on every side, written in large, bold characters, was the following announcement:

GRAND IRISH STEEPLE-CHASE,

"To come off the 17th of March, rain or shine, by horses, the property of, and to be ridden by, commissioned officers of that brigade. The prizes are a purse of $500; second horse to save his stakes; two and a half mile heat, best two in three, over four hurdles four and a half feet high, and five ditch fences, including two artificial rivers fifteen feet wide and six deep; hurdles to be made of forest pine and braced with hoops".

The quartermaster was sent to Washington for liquors and meats, and brought for the banquet that was to follow the race the following moderate supply, which constituted the fare: Thirty-five hams, and a side of an ox roasted; an entire pig, stuffed with boiled turkeys; an unlimited number of chickens, ducks and small game. The drinking materials comprised eight baskets of champagne, ten gallons of rum, and twenty-two of whiskey. A splendid bower was erected, capable of containing some hundreds of persons, for a general invitation was issued to all the officers of the Army of the Potomac.

The evening previous to the races a committee was held on punch, as to who was the best qualified to mix that important compound. It was unanimously agreed that the General and staff were the best judges, and therefore the most proper to undertake it. It was ruled that the matter be left entirely in their hands. Captains Gosson and Hogan were voted masters of ceremonies, in which they labored so diligently that before the mixture was complete both felt overpowered by their labors and had to be relieved from duty.

The morning commenced with religious ceremonies, after which the different riders proceeded to dress themselves. The dresses were showy, but some rather incongruous. One officer appeared mounted in scarlet, the top of his head crowned with a green velvet smoking cap, the present of his lady-love. The reason he assigned for his peculiar taste was, he was from Galway, and his family had hunted with the Galway Blazers' Club, and dressed similarly.

At eleven o'clock the grand stand was crowded with distinguished generals, officers, and about a dozen ladies.

A large concourse of at least thirty thousand officers and soldiers had assembled to participate in the fun. Previous to starting, the course was the object of attraction for spectators. Large crowds of soldiers were congregated in the vicinity of the interesting points, which seemed to be, in their estimation, where the leaps were highest and the ditches deepest. The nature of the ground was favorable—a gently rolling stretch of land, over which the course ran for a mile and three-quarters in length—and at points about equal distances from each other, eight leaps had been erected or excavated. From the ground whereon the stand was, and where the flags marking the tracks waved, the hills, here and there crested with a growth of oak or cedar, sloped away towards the Rappahannock. The bluest of blue skies looked down on the gayly-dressed and eager crowds, on the dashing horsemen, whose steeds pranced by the side of others on which were riding gay and brilliant women, on the quiet hills the peaceful river, the two hostile armies, and seemed to shower its blessings and its beauties on the festive throng assembled for enjoyment and sport commemorative of the national holiday of old Ireland.

The start was named for eleven o'clock; ten minutes before that hour the Commander-in-chief of the Army of the Potomac, Major-General Hooker, attended by all the members of his staff not detained at headquarters or elsewhere on duty, and accompanied by Lieutenant-Colonel Bentley, and Captain John C. Lynch, of the Sixty-third, both of whom had waited on General Hooker earlier in the day, arrived on the ground. On the appearance of the Commander-in-chief he was greeted by warm cheers, which he gracefully acknowledged as he took his place on the grand stand. Before attempting to describe the sports of the day, it may be as well to notice some of the more prominent and distinguished of the invited guests. And let us first speak of the ladies, who added much, by their vivacity and their picturesque costume, by their brilliancy and witchery, to the entertainments and amusements of the day. Fortunate citizens, dwelling in their quiet homes, and having before their eyes, every hour of the day, graceful and lovely women, can have no idea of the chivalrous emotions which swell the hearts of even the roughest soldier, seeing on rude camp-covered hills the figures, the fair faces, which it may be, have not been looked on in these regions and by these men for many, many months. If the reader has any conception of these things, he can easily imagine with what deep yet subdued gladness, the ladies were greeted by all.

When a fitting opportunity offered, in recognition of the hospitable greeting that was accorded him, General Hooker proposed three cheers for "General Meagher and his Irish Brigade, God bless them".

The following horses only, out of a larger number entered for the first race, open to the officers of the Irish Brigade, started:

General Meagher's gray horse, "Jack Hinton"; rider, Captain John Gosson; dress, crimson jacket, sleeves, breeches and white cap.

Captain Hogan's bay horse, "Napper Tandy"; rider, Lieutenant Ryder; dress, blue jacket, white breeches, green cap.

Captain Martin's bay mare, "Kathleen Mavourneen"; rider, Captain Martin; Solferino jacket, white breeches, maroon cap.

Captain Langdon's black horse, "Nigger Bill"; rider, Lieutenant Byron; plaid jacket, white breeches, pink cap.

Quartermaster McCormick's bay horse, "Sharpsburg"; rider, Lieutenant O'Connor; red jacket, white breeches, blue cap.

Colonel Mulholland's chestnut horse, "Major"; rider, Quartermaster Wade; blue jacket, white breeches, red cap.

Judges: Colonel Von Schaick, Seventh New York Volunteers; Colonel Frank, Fifty-seventh New York Volunteers.

Umpire: Brigadier-General Caldwell.

Clerk of the Course: General Meagher.

A few minutes before eleven o'clock the bugle sounded to the post, the horses were uncovered, and the eager riders mounted. Precisely as the hand denoted the hour, the clerk of the course waved his whip, another sweet, inspiring note from the bugler, and they were off. Six horses, six gallant riders, the course, the leaps, innumerable throngs of spectators, met the eyes of those standing on the platform. The first leap was a hurdle almost five feet high. They came to it; and cleared it beautifully; two saddles were emptied; the bay mare bolted but was spiritedly and scientifically brought to it, and flew over magnificently. With varying fortune the other leaps and spaces were taken and passed over, the rider of the gray drawing towards him the attention of the throng, by the masterly manner in which he handled his horse. The home-stretch was reached, the gray, hard pressed by the bay, gained the winning post, and the umpire declared him the winner of the first heat. A wild, enthusiastic cheer went up from the jubilant throng. The start on the second heat was according to the formula of the first. All the horses cleared hurdle number one in fine style; the run home was headed by the gray again, this time the little black closing tightly on him, and the gray was declared the winner, amid thunders of applause for his dashing rider.

To this race succeeded a sweepstakes, open to all, and, as usual, all the incidents of an old-fashioned course happened. Eight horses contested for the prize, which was won by a fine chestnut, ridden by, it is said, a descendant of the Blucher of Waterloo fame.

It was one o'clock when General Meagher announced that all further operations would be postponed for half an hour, and invited the ladies, the generals present, and staffs, to a collation, prepared and awaiting destruction at his quarters, and thither the goodly company proceeded. In front of the quarters two Sibley tents had been pitched, separated by a space of ten yards, which space was enclosed by an awning. In and under these the guests thronged. Mountains of sandwiches disappeared, no doubt filling up those voids which nature is said to abhor. With the precision and promptitude of file-firing, pop, pop, went explosions that preceded copious draughts of rich wines. In and out, in fact everywhere, went the attentive officers of the brigade, attending to their visitors. What attracted most attention, however, and gratified every appreciative palate were potations of spiced whiskey-punch, ladled by Captain Hogan, the Ganymede of the occasion, from an enormous bowl, holding not much less than thirty gallons.

The following amusements followed :

First. A foot-race, one-half mile distance, best of heats; open to all non-commissioned officers and privates, the winner to receive $7, and the second $3.

Second. Casting weights, the weights to weigh from ten to fourteen pounds; the winner to receive $3.

Third. Running after the soaped pig—to be the prize of the man who holds it.

Fourth. A hurdle-race, one-half mile distance, open to all non-commissioned officers and privates; the winner to receive $7, the second $3.

Fifth. The wheelbarrow race—the contestants to be blindfolded, and limited to six soldiers of the Irish Brigade; the winner to receive $5; distance to be decided on the ground.

Sixth. Jumping in sacks to the distance of five hundred yards; the winner to receive $5.

Seventh. A contest on the light fantastic toe, consisting of Irish reels, jigs, and hornpipes; the best dancer to receive $5, the second best $3, to be decided by a judge appointed by the chairman.

The amusements of the day were followed by a grand entertainment at night, theatricals and recitations. Many a health was drank, many a friend was toasted, flowing bumpers, loving glances at the fair ones, songs and toasts went freely round. Captain Hogan presided at the nectarean mixture, which floated like a spiced island in a huge barrel. Captain Jack Gosson, in his most *recherche* uniform, bespangled with lace, aided and assisted. Around them were a lot of drummer-boys and soldiers. These Captain Jack dispersed in the most dignified manner, while they looked most longingly at Captain Hogan, as he ladled out the punch.

A poetical address was read by Dr. Lawrence Reynolds, of his own composition, giving a history of the career of the brigade. Dr. Lawrence, of the Sixty-third Regiment, was the poet laureate of the brigade.

"THE PRESIDENT VISITS THE ARMY".

In the latter part of April the President visited and reviewed the army. The One Hundred and Sixteenth

ABRAHAM LINCOLN

Battalion never looked better than on this occasion. The great review took place on the plains back of Spofford Heights, and occupied two whole days. Corps after corps filed past, one hundred and twenty thousand men ; infantry, cavalry and artillery, composing as General Hooker, in " grandiose " style, named it, " the finest army on the planet ". Every organization and every individual looked their best. But, although a joyous occasion, Mr. Lincoln wore that air of thoughtful sadness that every one recalls so well. While at Army Headquarters, in the morning surrounded by Generals and brilliant company, he seemed cheerful and full of life and gayety, but, as hour after hour he rode along the line of troops, he appeared like a man overshadowed by some deep sorrow. No doubt he thought of the coming campaign, of the great battle in the near future, and of the many who would fall. On the second day of the review he seemed more overcome than usual, and his strong, rugged face bore visible traces of his inmost thoughts. During the afternoon he became unusually silent, and rode for an hour without exchanging a word with the brilliant staff that galloped behind him. At one time his gait became very slow, and finally he reigned up his horse in front of a Pennsylvania regiment, and looking into the faces of the young soldiers who stood silently in line at a " present arm ", he let fall the lines on the horse's neck, and reaching out his arms towards the ranks, exclaimed, " My God, men, if I could save this country by giving up my own life and saving yours, how gladly I would do it ". As he spoke, the tears stole down his furrowed cheeks, and his great heart seemed bursting. Then he slowly passed on—but who can forget the scene? It was an episode called forth by the circumstances, the occasion and the man.

Abraham Lincoln had a heart overflowing with kindness and love for all mankind. No human being was too lowly to be an object of his tender thought and solicitude. On one occasion a sorrowful woman waited all day in the ante-room at the White house, anxious to secure an interview with him. The crowd of visitors was so great that it was almost evening before her turn came, and when she was finally admitted into the reception room it was to find many still ahead of her. Shrinking and overcome with grief, she sat alone in a corner quietly sobbing. Mr. Lincoln standing at his desk received one after another, attending to the business of each and dismissing them in succession, but every once in a while he would glance at the veiled figure sitting motionless in the corner. When the last visitor had departed he walked over to the poor soul and holding out both his large hands said: "Now, my poor little woman, what can I do for you"? The "poor little woman" had a son who was to be shot in the morning, for desertion. He had not meant to desert, but he was only a child and had gone home to see his mother. Well —he was not shot, but lived to prove himself a good soldier. The tears of the "poor little woman", friendless and alone, were as potent, and had as much influence on the great heart of Lincoln as an appeal from the grandest potentate on earth. One can scarcely conceive how, after a long day full of business and anxiety, interviewed by a host of eminent men on all sorts of important and pressing business, the President could have a moment left to give to a poor widow, yet, she received as much, and even more, consideration, as the greatest man in his audience, giving his hand and heart to the sorrowing mother with all the gentle tenderness of a great and noble nature. It was the crowning act of a well spent day, and how few days of Lincoln's life were not rendered sweet and sacred by such deeds. No doubt these incidents softened the habitual sadness that seemed to overshadow the life of the President. While ever full of sympathy and kindness for every one else, he never seemed to enjoy happiness himself except in the exercise of some good action.

On one occasion a committee of ladies called to plead with him to send the thousands of wounded from the hospitals around Washington to their own States, so that they might be near their homes. "Do this, Mr. Lincoln", said one of the ladies, "and the good deed will make you happy". He issued the order but said quietly to himself: "I will never be happy again".

The sadness that seemed to overshadow Mr. Lincoln during the afternoon of the review, continued to a great extent during the evening, and the brilliant company of officers and ladies gathered at General Sickles's headquarters was influenced in a great measure by the President's apparent sadness. A shadow seemed to rest on everyone, and while Mr. Lincoln made an effort to be cheerful his smile was full of pathos and his gayety evidently forced. As the evening progressed the situation became embarrassing. The gallant commander of the Third Corps seeing that something must be done to relieve the situation and banish the gloom thought of a plan that had an immediate and happy effect, but threatened, for a time, most unpleasant consequences. Among the ladies present was the Princess Salm Salm, a dark eyed, attractive little woman, the wife of the commander of the Eighth New York, a soldier of many wars, who was afterwards killed in the Franco-Prussian War of 1870.

General Daniel E. Sickles, taking her aside, suggested that in order to put life in the company and chase away dull care she should get the ladies to form a surprise party and each one kiss the President. There were ten or twelve ladies present, wives of the corps and division commanders, and visitors who had come to see the review. The Princess at first shrank from the suggestion, but finally, in a spirit of mischief and humor, consented. After quietly pursuading the others to enter into the scheme, she approached Mr. Lincoln who was standing by the fire, his tall form towering above everyone in the room, but how to reach up and kiss the lips so far above her was a momentous question. Not for long, however,

"Mr. Lincoln, let me whisper something," she said, and the tall form leaned over unsuspectingly to hear the secret, when a hearty kiss was delivered instead. The effect was electrical. The clouds passed away, and while the other ladies, amid much laughter and merriment, pushed forward to follow the example of the princess, the whole company joined in the spirit of the thing.

A most enjoyable evening followed, but there was one good lady who evidently did not appreciate the good-natured joke of General Sickles and the Princess. Mrs. Lincoln was extremely angry, and made no effort to conceal her feelings in the matter, and, as far as General Sickles was concerned, the situation became very strained when, on the following day, he received orders to escort President and Mrs. Lincoln back to Washington. Mrs. Lincoln was fully aware that the author of the mischievous proceedings of the preceding evening was the gallant General, and she took pains to manifest her displeasure. Mr. Lincoln tried by every means in his power to smooth the thing over, but without success.

At dinner he was specially gracious and full of wit and jest, but nothing could remove for an instant the grim expression on Mrs. Lincoln's face. She never once recognized or spoke to the brilliant commander of the Third Corps. Finally the President turned to him and exclaimed: "Sickles, they tell me that you have become very religious of late." This statement took the General by surprise, and not knowing whether the President was serious or still joking, replied: "Well, I cannot say that I am more so than usual. I am naturally of a religious nature." "Why," retorted Mr. Lincoln, "I hear that you not only have Psalms at your headquarters, but also, Salm Salms!" This sally disarmed Mrs. Lincoln. She burst out laughing, the kissing episode was forgiven, and Mrs. Lincoln and General Sickles were friends until she died.

As the spring approached, and the weather became better, picket duty on the river bank was not so trying, and in the balmy days of April and May became most desirable. It was picturesque and beautiful along the daisy and buttercup pied banks of the Rappahannock, and the fishing after dark was excellent. Then it was interesting to look over the river and speculate on what the enemy was doing; for the men were in full view and their drills and reviews could be seen.

Fredericksburg was always a point of deep interest. There was not a lady in our whole army, but many could be seen promenading the city streets and groups of children could be seen at play, recalling scenes at home. The music of the Confederate camps came softly floating over the still water, and crowds of citizens would gather on the opposite bank and on the city wharves, listening to the playing of the Union bands. On one sweet Spring evening a band on the Union side of the river played "Hail Columbia," and was promptly answered from the Confederates with "Bonnie Blue Flag." Then for an hour the songs of the Union and the Confederacy followed each other in answering harmony. Finally the Union musicians began playing "Home, Sweet Home". No derisive answer came to that tender chord, but the camps were quickly hushed, and on the calm of evening the air that touched every heart, both North and South, came echoing back from the Southern hills. It was a delightful episode, calling forth prayers and tears, and thoughts of dear and loved ones far away. One evening, during the siege of Sebastipole, the band of an English regiment played the sad and tender air of "Annie Laurie." The sound was taken up by others, the men of the whole army joined, and the chorus rose and swelled as forty thousand sons of the British Isles, in the trenches, united their voices in the song,

> " And for bonnie Annie Laurie,
> I would lay me down and die."

The effect must have been touching indeed, but only "Home, Sweet Home" could ever have joined the North and the South together in heart, song and sentiment just at this time.

The Rappahannock's stately tide, aglow with sunset light,
Came sweeping down between the hills that hemmed its
    gathering might,
From one side rose the Spofford slopes, and on the other shore
The Spottsylvania meadows lay with oak groves scattered o'er.
Hushed were the sounds of busy day; the brooding air was hushed,
Save for the rapid-flowing stream that chanted as it rushed.
O'er mead and gently sloping hills, on either side the stream,
The white tents of the soldiers caught the sun's departing beam—
On Spofford's Hills the Blue, on Spottsylvania's slopes the Gray:
Between them, like an unsheathed sword, the glittering river lay.
Hark! Suddenly a Union band far down the stream sends forth
The strains of "Hail Columbia", the pæan of the North.
The tents are parted; silent throngs of soldiers worn and grim,
Stand forth upon the dusky slopes to hear the martial hymn.

So clear and quiet was the night that to the farthest bound
Of either camp was borne the swell of sweet, triumphant sound.
And when the last note died away, from distant post to post
A shout, like thunder of the tide, rolled through the Federal host.
Then straightway from the other shore there rose an answering
    strain.
"Bonnie Blue Flag" came floating down the slope and o'er
    the plain.
And then the Boys in Gray sent back our cheer across the tide—
A mighty shout that rent the air and echoed far and wide.
"Star-spangled Banner", we replied; they answered, "Boys in
    Gray",
While cheer on cheer rolled through the dusk, and faintly
    died away.

Deeply the gloom had gathered round, and all the stars had come,
When the Union band began to play the notes of "Home, Sweet
    Home".
Slowly and softly breathed the chords, and utter silence fell
Over the valley and the hills—on Blue and Gray as well.
Now swelling and now sinking low, now tremulous, now strong,
The leader's cornet played the air of the beautiful old song;
And, rich and mellow, horn and bass joined in the flowing chords,
So voice-like that they scarcely lacked the charm of spoken words.
Then what a cheer from both the hosts, with faces to the stars!

And tears were shed and prayers were said upon the field of Mars.
The Southern band caught up the strain; and we who could
    sing, sang.
Oh, what a glorious hymn of home across the river rang!

We thought of loved ones far away, of scenes we'd left behind—
The low-roofed farm-house 'neath the elm that murmured in
    the wind;
The children standing by the gate, the dear wife at the door;
The dusty sunlight all aslant upon the old barn floor.
Oh! loud and long the cheer we raised, when silence fell again.
And died away among the hills the dear familiar strain.
Then to our cots of straw we stole, and dreamed the livelong night
Of far-off hamlets in the hills, peace-walled, and still, and white.

CHAPTER IV.

CHANCELLORSVILLE.

THE movement that culminated in the battle of Chancellorsville, began on April 27th.

On that day the Fifth, Eleventh and Twelfth Corps left the camps at Falmouth and began their march to Kelly's Ford, twenty-seven miles above Fredericksburg. The Irish Brigade broke camp also, on that same morning, and led the advance of Second Corps. Colonel Kelly with the Sixty-third and Eighty-eighth New York, halting at Bank's Ford, General Meagher with the One Hundred and Sixteenth Regiment, Sixty-ninth New York and Twenty-eighth Massachusetts, pushing on to United States Ford.

There is a charm and a dreamy balminess in the spring atmosphere of Virginia, and on one of the sweetest of mornings imaginable, the regiment left the old camp ground and moved for the ford, to cross the Rappahannock and strike the enemy once again.

The path of the column lay through virgin forests, blossoming and beautiful, and the perfumed air of the woods seemed laden with hope and promise. Many of the wounded of Fredericksburg had returned to the ranks. The men had, in a measure, forgotten that mournful field. The change of commanders had a most salutary effect upon all, and the morale of the army was excellent. A new life had taken possession of that army which, though often defeated, was never dismayed, destroyed or conquered.

MAJOR-GENERAL JOSEPH HOOKER.

The day was a beautiful one and the march, for some reason, exceedingly slow, with many halts and frequent rests. The road was lonely. Not a strange face was seen during the day, but the men were glad to leave the camp where they had spent the long dreary winter, and enjoyed the sunshine and fresh sweet odor of the deep woods through which they leisurely strolled.

Towards evening the regiment arrived at United States Ford. Looking over the river one could see the Confederate pickets on the further side, and the usual compliments, " Hello, Yank," " How are you, Reb?" were exchanged, but no firing took place. The boys across the stream seemed puzzled to know what the Union men were doing or why they had come, and as the picket line was in full sight of theirs, they talked together and wondered still more.

The woods along the river abounded in game. Rabbits hopped around in hundreds. Coveys of partridge and quail rose and with a loud whirr, flew further into the brush. A deer or two crashed through the timber and went flying past. The temptation to shoot was great but the orders "not to fire" were imperative and not a shot was fired. Many of the men secured a good supper, however, by knocking down a stray rabbit with a stick.

Darkness fell leaving the men to wonder why they had been sent to this lonely spot. Morning came and found them no wiser, and the day of the twenty-eighth passed, and another night and morning, and still the mystery remained; but towards dusk, on the twenty-ninth, Hancock and the balance of the division came up, and it was learned that three of the corps had crossed the river twenty miles above and that they were then coming down the opposite bank of the stream.

On the morning of the thirtieth, the pontoons were brought to the river's edge, the engineers began building the bridge, the enemy's pickets quickly withdrew without offering any resistance, and at 3.30 p. m., two divisions of the Second Corps began crossing. It was almost dark when the turn of the regiment came, and it crossed the river in the dusk. The enemy in retiring had left evidence of their hasty flight, the road for some distance being strewn with picks, spades and abandoned entrenching tools.

After marching a short distance, the Irish Brigade turned sharply to the left, and was put into position to cover a road leading to Bank's Ford. The regimental line ran through a swamp that skirted the edge of a dark wood. The darkness became dense. The ankle-deep ooze made lying down impossible and standing up most inconvenient, so fallen trees as roosting places were in great demand, some sitting and trying to balance themselves on a ragged tree stump with feet drawn up to avoid the wet. Water-snakes crawled around in great numbers, frogs croaked, and hundreds of whip-poor-wills filled the trees and made the long night more dismal by their melancholy calling. The long hours passed without alarm, and when daylight came the snakes went back to their holes, the frogs ceased croaking and the whip-poor-wills became silent. Looking around the men saw, not ten yards away, a beautiful dry ridge where they could have spent the night in comfort, had they but known it.

During Friday, May 1st, the regiment, together with three others of the brigade, maintained the same position, facing Bank's Ford, and in line, with the right reaching towards the plank road that runs from Fredericksburg to Chancellorsville, and the left reaching out towards the river. It was a peaceful day for the regiment. Not an enemy was seen, but one could hear the crash of musketry from time to time on the right and front, as the Union troops were pushing towards Fredericksburg. A long day it seemed, with every ear listening anxiously for news that was so difficult to obtain.

When evening came it was learned that the army was falling back to take up a new line and fight a defensive battle. Next morning, Saturday, May 2d, the brigade was moved to the extreme right of that line, to a point called Scott's Mills, and placed there to occupy and try to fill the gap that reached from the right flank of the army to the river.

The day was spent in listening to the roar of the musketry—which echoed and re-echoed through the dense woods, making sounds deafening and appalling—and in slashing timber to form revetments and abattis. The old buildings were loop-holed and turned into block-houses, and towards the end of the day the line was well prepared to give a cordial greeting to an enemy should he appear.

From time to time, during the afternoon, rumors of a column of the enemy moving across the front of the Union line to strike the right were heard and all felt anxious and nervous. General Meagher came down to the right of the brigade, where the regiment was stationed, addressed the men and begged them to make a good fight.

The line of works had just been completed and, with a strong abattis in front, all felt confident of being able to hold it.

But the flank of the One Hundred and Sixteenth, was in the air, nothing between it and the river, and the situation was grave enough. A line of pickets were out in front and extending well to the right, but not enough men could be spared to carry it to the river. Just as Meagher was speaking Sergeant Halpin ran in from the picket to report that the enemy's skirmishers were advancing. A deer came crashing through the abattis, leaped the works and went bounding to the rear, before the men had time to recover from their astonishment at the unusual incident, a tremendous storm of musketry broke out on the left. Stonewall Jackson's twenty-six thousand men had struck the right flank of the Union Army. More minutes of suspense—terrific peals of musketry—the roar rising, swelling, filling the woods with sound and fury—Every man in the ranks standing at "ready". A soldier was halted as he tried to run to the rear. Another soon arrived, then five, ten, fifty. Hundreds of them came running back, frightened demoralized. They were stopped in crowds by the men of the regiment (a part of the Eleventh Corps had given away). They got tangled up in the abattis, every one of them panic stricken, frantic, almost insane, their only desire to get to the rear.

The regiment, with the others of the brigade, stood calm and firm, stopping the fugitives in crowds. Meagher quickly changed direction of the left regiment of the brigade, so as to cover the main road, the better to check the disorderly flight.

The darkness was gathering, the volleys of musketry coming nearer. The scene was one of awful confusion and dismay, and withal, no man in the line of the regiment or brigade seemed to be even excited. As the sound of the firing came nearer, the fugitives were quickly gathered into squads, forced to the rear, and the front of the line was cleared for action. But the hour was growing late—darkness filled the forest. Another and final burst of musketry, a stream of whistling balls passed over, a random shell burst in the tree tops, the leaves and branches came showering down, "silence", "and the day was done". The picket line was rectified. Arms were stacked. The men lit little fires, cooked their coffee, and settled down to sleep as quietly as though at home in old Pennsylvania. Not a shot had been fired by the regiment, but a day full of anxiety had been passed.

At daybreak, on Sunday morning, May 3d, the battle was on again, and by five o'clock the continuous roar of artillery and volleys of musketry told that the fighting was fierce and deadly. The men cooked coffee, fried pork and enjoyed breakfast, calmly awaiting the next event. The presence of the Irish Brigade at Scott's Mills was no longer necessary, as the Frst Corps had extended the line of battle to the right and covered, in a manner, the vacant ground between the right flank of the army and the river.

By ten o'clock it was learned that the Union Army was falling back to a new line of battle which the engineers had prepared during the night, and shortly afterwards an order came for the Irish Brigade to move out to the Chancellorsville House and join the balance of the division which was at that time beating back the Confederate divisions of McLaws and Anderson, (then under the personal direction of General Lee). The brigade started for the front, passing along the road that ran from the United States Ford to the Chancellorsville House, with the regiment on the left. As it passed along the evidence of the struggle soon became manifest. Streams of wounded men flowed to the rear. Men with torn faces, split heads, smashed arms, wounded men assisting their more badly hurt comrades, stretchers bearing to the rear men whose limbs were crushed and mangled, and others who had no limbs at all. Four soldiers carried on two muskets, which they held in form of a litter, the body of their Lieutenant-Colonel who had just been killed. The body hung over the muskets, the head and feet limp and dangling, the blood dripping from a ghastly wound, a terrible sight indeed. Wounded men lay all through the woods; and here and there a dead man rested against a tree, where, in getting back, he had paused to rest and breathed his last. Shells screamed through the trees and, as the regiment approached the front, the whirr of the canister and shrapnel was heard and musket balls whistled past, but the men in the ranks passed on quietly and cheerfully, many of them exchanging repartee. During a moment's halt, with the shells falling and exploding around him, Sergeant Bernard McCahey looking back, waved his hand to the earth and air and in the most ludicrous manner exclaimed, "Good boi wurreld". Another son of Erin said to his companion. "What are we going in here for, Jimmy"? "To be after making history, Barney, to be sure".

The field officers were ordered to dismount, and move up the road on foot. As the writer walked at the head of the command, Major John C. Lynch, of the Sixty-third New York, walked by his side, and he chatted cheerfully and was full of gayety and life. Approaching the Chancellorsville House the brigade went "on the right by file, into line", along the edge of the road with the left (the One Hundred and Sixteenth Pennsylvania Volunteers) resting on the plateau in the middle of which the Chancellorsville House stands. As the writer passed to the left, he bade his friend, Major Lynch, "Good morning". A moment afterwards Lynch fell dead, a shell drove his sword through his body, killing him instantly, and the handsome, noble fellow who had walked up the road so full of life and happiness, lay by the wayside, an unrecognizable mass of quivering flesh and bones.

By the time the brigade had formed on the road all the army, except Hancock's division of the Second, and Geary's division of the Twelfth Corps, had gone to the rear to form on the new line. The men lay down along the edge of the wood and hugged the ground closely, to avoid the shells.

In order to gain time and hold the enemy in check until the new line was secure, General Couch sent the Fifth Maine Battery to take position to right of the Chancellorsville House and to the left of the regiment. The brave young commander of that battery, Captain Leppine, came dashing up the road followed by his five guns. Quickly placing them in line among the blossoming apple trees of the orchard, he opened fire on the masses of the Confederates, then plainly visible in the woods, on the other side of the plateau. To place a battery in such a position was a desperate thing to do. The plateau and orchard were racked by the fire of thirty guns, and hardly had Leppine fired his first shot, when they were all turned upon him. A scene of wild grandeur followed. The shells from the Confederate batteries seemed to fill the air, tearing up the ground, rending the men and horses limb from limb, blowing up the caisson, exploding and bursting

CAPTAIN GEORGE FREDERICK LEPPINE.
Commanding Fifth Maine Battery.   Killed at Chancellorsville May 3d, 1863.

everywhere. Young Leppine was soon carried to the rear dying, with his thigh crushed and torn. Lieutenant Kirby was sent, by General Couch, to take his place, and he fell mortally wounded, among the guns, before he was with them a minute. Men were blown up with the caissons, and their torn and bleeding limbs fell with the apple-blossoms. The orchard was a very hell of fire.

An orderly rode past and his head was taken off by a shell, but the momentum carried the headless trunk fifty feet before he fell and the riderless horse galloped into the enemy's lines.

Another passing orderly fell from his horse with his bowels protruding. Many of the regiment were wounded. Duffy, of Company A, was lying with a great piece of his skull crushed in. Another man lay beside him with his foot torn in a terrible manner. Dan Rodgers, a boy, had his shoulder-blade smashed; but still the men kept wonderfully calm. Captain Nowlen sat in the road, humming a tune, filled his pipe, lit it with the burning fuse of a Confederate shell, and began smoking. Corporal Emsley, of the color-guard, was passing jokes with Abe Detwiler, the color sergeant; and one would suppose that the boys were listening to the church bells, on that sweet Sunday morning, instead of the rush and scream of the shells. Twenty minutes had passed since the battery went into action. Nearly all the guns had been silenced. Five of the six caissons had been blown up. The men who remained were lying among the pieces torn and bleeding. Smoke was seen issuing from the Chancellorsville House and soon the building was in flames. It was filled with wounded, and the family were still in the house. Captain William P. Wilson, of Hancock's staff, and a few men of the Second Delaware, rushed in and began dragging the wounded out and laying them under the trees, and succeeded in saving a large number. The large mansion was wrapped in flames and the ladies of the family rushed out onto the porch. Colonel James Dickenson, of Sickles's staff, gallantly ran forward and offered to escort them into the lines. They all accepted the proffered service, and, with a courteous bow, he gave each an arm and brought them to a place of safety. One old colored woman ran towards the Confederate position and succeeded in reaching the line, but was wounded as she ran.

The scene was one of terror, dismay, and desolation.

Geary's division had gone and Hancock was withdrawing. Soon nothing was left near the Chancellorsville House except the Irish Brigade and the almost silenced battery. *One gun was still firing, however, and a gallant corporal and one man still clung to the piece and fired it when all others had gone. It was time for the last troops to fall back, and the order came to the One Hundred and Sixteenth Pennsylvania Volunteers to save the abandoned guns. One hundred of the men were quickly detailed to rush forward and surround the pieces and drag them to the rear, which was done in splendid style. When the guns were started down the road a few men of the One Hundred and Fortieth Pennsylvania Volunteers gallantly came forward to assist and help to take one of the guns to a place of safety. After seeing the wounded out of the burning house and safe Captain Wilson gallantly rushed to the rescue of the battery and never left until the last gun was saved. As a squad was tugging away at one of the guns, trying to get it started, a shell burst in their midst, killing Theodore Walker and George Rushworth of Company D, wounding half a dozen others and knocking everyone over on their backs. The men jumped to their feet and rushed at it again, laughing at the mishap, and pulled it off. Then the whole command started down the road. Young Sergeant George Halpin, seeing one of the caissons still standing, wished to take it off also, but the men were gone, and as he could not haul it off alone, he

---

* The writer had the pleasure of afterwards securing a Congress medal of honor for Corporal Lebroke and the private of the battery who so nobly stood to their guns, on this morning.

concluded to destroy it; so striking a match he lit a newspaper, threw it in, jumped back and the chest blew up. By some miracle, the brave boy remained uninjured himself. As the regiment passed down the road with the guns, the Confederates advanced and took possession of Chancellorsville, the One Hundred and Sixteenth Pennsylvania Volunteers being the last to leave that storm-swept ground.

Passing out of the woods into the open space near the Bullock House the regiment was met by General Sickles, who, rising in his stirrups, called for three cheers " for the regiment that saved the guns", and the boys felt proud and happy.

The five guns were turned over to the chief of artillery, and the command rejoined the brigade and went into position on the new line to the left of the road and facing Chancellorsville.

The line of works held by the Union army, during the fourth and afternoon of the third, were remarkably strong and solid—log revetments sufficiently strong to resist shell, with thick abattis in front. When the Union army retired to that line the battle of Chancellorsville was practically ended. The only fighting for the next two days was a severe skirmish in front of the Twelfth Corps, in which Major General Whipple was killed.

But while there was no general engagement, there was plenty of firing. The Confederate sharpshooters occupied every coign of advantage and were extremely vigilant. To show the head over the works was to court death, and there were many narrow escapes during the two days, as well as numerous casualties.

The night of the third was one to be long remembered, the enemy making continual demonstrations, the Union soldiers vigilant, awake and watchful. A lovely, cloudless night it was, with the planets quietly glittering in the azure above. General Meagher, in full uniform, walked up and down the brigade line. The men of the regiment lay, musket in hand; Sergeant Detwiler dozing, now and and then, with the colors tightly grasped. The men were tired, sleepy and dazed for want of rest, which they could not get on account of the frequent alarms.

Every time the boys slumbered, the sharp crack of a parrot gun or a crash of musketry would awaken them with a start, so the majority of them lay awake quietly chatting, some of the morrow, others of home. One group, lying on their backs looking up to the heavens, began talking about the stars. "Wonder if the people up there (in the stars) go to war." "Wonder if they have parrot guns." "Wonder if they allow foraging." "Wonder if the commissary gets up in time when the rations is out." "Wonder if they have sutlers and if their government allows them to charge three dollars a bottle for bad whiskey." And so the long night passed and another day came. A long beautiful spring day, with the sharpshooters vigilant. The afternoon brought with it a breeze, and as the wind was blowing towards the Union line, the enemy fired the woods with a view of annoying. The flames drifting towards the Union line were unpleasant enough, as they threatened the abattis. A flock of wild pigeons circled around through the smoke. Towards evening, the men on the picket line succeeded in extinguishing the fire before it had done much injury to the works.

So well had the builders done their work that when, thirty years afterwards, the writer passed over the ground, he found the work still standing and in good enough condition to occupy and fight behind. Bits of knapsacks, leather straps, broken shells and the usual debris of the battle were still visible along the line, but the scene was changed, and profound peace reigned in the lonely woods.

Where the men stood to deliver their fire from behind the works, the grass was growing fresh and green. Squirrels ran over the revetments and found quiet homes in the holes made by the shells. Wild honeysuckle knit together the withered branches of the abattis. Wild roses bloomed. The birds sang, and built their nests in the trees where sharpshooters had sat in the foliage watching for a shot, and when evening came, the whip-poor-will uttered, as of old, his complaining cry.

CHANCELLORSVILLE. 115

The picket line in front ran through a lovely bit of forest. The enemy's sharpshooters were exceedingly active, but Berdan's sharpshooters held the Union line and returned all compliments in the most vigorous manner. Many of them fell during the day and the ground at every post was stained with blood. Banks of violets bloomed and dead men lay in pleasant places where spring flowers perfumed the woodlands. Squirrels leaped affrighted, from bough to bough, wondering at the strange intrusion on their solitude, and birds flew screaming through the timber or circled around their nests in wild alarm. A shell would now and then go tearing through the trees, burst in the tops and send the branches and leaves showering down. Frequently a tree would be cut down entire, causing the sharpshooters who were esconsced in the upper foliage to calculate the chances of having their line of communication cut and getting an abrupt fall as well.

Evening came again, the sun went down, and another night was at hand. The rain began falling and by midnight was coming down in torrents, and, when darkness gathered on the sad field, the noble army that had been beaten by the incompetency of its commander, commenced evacuating the works and falling back to cross the river. All night long as the men stole away to the rear in the gloom, the wind tossed the tree-tops, and sobbed through the dripping pines. The silence and darkness were intense. Ever and anon the stillness would be broken by the sound of musketry coming from the picket line, as the men fired random volleys to deceive the enemy and make them believe the Union troops were still there. All night long the tramp of the infantry and rumble of artillery sounded on the pontoons.

No time to carry away the wounded or bury the dead, and they lay on the gory field with their white faces turned to the weeping sky. By day-break nearly all were gone, and the regiment was among the very last to cross the swollen river. The pickets hastily fell back and double-quicked for the bridge. The enemy rushed to intercept and cut them off, but they got there first and crossed, and the pontoons were cut away. A Confederate battery arrived on the bank and fired a few shots, as the last of the Union army disappeared over the bluff, and the Chancellorsville campaign was ended.

(*See page 328, Vol. XXV., Official Records of the War*).

REPORT OF MAJOR ST. CLAIR A. MULHOLLAND,
116TH REGIMENT PENNSYLVANIA VOLUNTEERS.

CHANCELLORSVILLE, May 4th, 1863.

SIR : In accordance with orders just received, I have the honor to submit the following report in regard to certain guns that were taken off the field of action by the men of my command, on the morning of Sunday, May 3d, 1863.

The Irish Brigade was engaged in supporting the Fifth Maine Battery, commanded by Captain Leppine, when the battery had been engaged with the enemy about one hour. All the officers and men belonging to it had either been killed or wounded, or had abandoned their pieces, with the exception of one man (Corporal James H. Letroke), and all the guns were silenced except one. About this time Major Scott of General Hancock's staff rode up to me, and requested me to take a sufficient number of men to haul the abandoned guns off the field, as they were in great danger of being captured by the enemy. My regiment being at the time on the left of the brigade, and nearest the battery, I at once led my men towards the abandoned battery and ordered them to haul the guns up the road. They obeyed with alacrity and removed three of the guns off the field and to the rear. After taking off the last piece I followed my men up the road and found another gun in possession of one of my lieutenants (L. J. Sacriste). This piece he had taken off without my knowledge, making in all, four guns saved by my command. The fifth piece taken to the rear was taken off the field by some men of the One Hundred and Fortieth Pennsylvania Volunteers, and was by them taken up the road about one hundred yards, where they were forced to halt, not having enough men to move the piece further. I at once sent some of my men to assist them and the guns were brought off successfully. I found it necessary, in removing the guns, to order the men to leave their muskets, as they could not work with them in their hands. Seventy-three of them did so. When the last gun was brought off I went back to the left to ascertain whether any more remained. I found eight or ten of my men coming up the road and ordered them back to gather up as many muskets as they could carry. I do not think that they succeeded in saving any. I was greatly aided in bringing off the guns by Lieutenant Wilson, of General Hancock's staff, who acted with great bravery, and personally assisted in bringing off the pieces.

ST. CLAIR A. MULHOLLAND,
Major Commanding 116th Penna. Volunteers.

To M. W. WALL,
    A. A. A. General.

(*See page 327, Vol. XXV., Official Records of the War*).

REPORT OF LIEUTENANT EDWARD WHITEFORD,
Aid-de-Camp.

CHANCELLORSVILLE, VA., May 3d, 1863.

CAPTAIN: In accordance with orders from General Meagher, I have the honor to report as follows:

During the heat of the action, personal orders were received from General Couch to advance the Brigade (then supporting the Fifth Maine Battery) through the woods in their front, but were immediately countermanded by him, and skirmishers ordered to be thrown out.

On returning, I found that the fire which the enemy had concentrated on the above battery compelled the men to desert the guns, the horses at the time being all killed or wounded. On reporting the fact to General Meagher, I was ordered by him to tell Major Mulholland, of the One Hundred and Sixteenth Regiment, Pennsylvania Volunteers, to save the guns with his men at any risk, and too much praise cannot be bestowed upon him for his cool bravery and that of the men under his command, having to take them (the guns) out of stiff yellow clay, where the guns were stuck, and under a galling fire of the enemy, by which many of his men were killed or wounded; but he succeeded, most fortunately, in obeying orders, and drawing the guns, five in number to within one mile of the pontoon bridge, where limbers were sent up, from the chief of artillery, to draw them to the rear.

I have the honor to be captain,

Most respectfully,
E. WHITEFORD,
Aid-de-Camp.

To CAPTAIN M. W. WALL,
    A. A. Adjutant General.

LETTER FROM CORPORAL J. H. LEBROKE, FIFTH MAINE BATTERY.

CAMP NEAR WHITE OAK CHURCH, VA., May 27th, 1863.

To the Editor of the Press:

Who brought off the guns of the Fifth Maine Battery?

As this question has caused much discussion, I thought I would let the friends of the battery know through the columns of your paper to whom the honor is due. It has been stated that Lieutenant Whittier deserves great credit for bringing off the guns after the horses were killed. Lieutenant Whittier did not bring off the guns, neither was he there at the time. After the battery had ceased firing, one of the gunners went to General Hancock for a detail to haul off the guns. He sent a detail from the Irish Brigade under the command of Lieutenant-Colonel Mulholland and Lieutenant Wilson, of Hancock's staff. The guns were hauled three miles by hand and the same brave men who exposed themselves to a severe fire of shot and shell from the rebel batteries to save our guns, lost their own muskets, for the enemy held the ground immediately after.

Truly yours,

J. H. LEBROKE,
Corporal, Fifth Maine Battery.

HEADQUARTERS FIRST DIVISION, SECOND CORPS.

NEAR FALMOUTH, VA., May 10th, 1863.

MAJOR: The Major-General commanding the division directs me to express to you his gratification at the manner in which you performed your duties as "Field Officer of the Day" for the division from May 3d to 6th.

The General was especially pleased with your action in reference to extinguishing the fire in front of the picket line. He had ordered the fire to be put out several times, but the order was not carried into effect until you were placed in command of the pickets. I am, sir,

Very respectfully your obedient servant,

W. G. MITCHELL,
A. D. C. and A. A. A. G.

To MAJOR ST. CLAIR A. MULHOLLAND,
116th Regiment, Penna. Volunteers.

CHANCELLORSVILLE
"When the Battery was saved."

HEADQUARTERS IRISH BRIGADE.

NEAR FALMOUTH, VA., May 10th, 1863.

MAJOR: The Brigadier-General (Meagher) commanding, directs me to add his own expressions of gratification to that of General Hancock, in his letter of commendation to you for your conduct at the Battle of Chancellorsville. I have the honor to remain,

Your obedient servant,

M. W. WALL,
A. A. A. G.

To MAJOR ST. CLAIR A. MULHOLLAND,
116th Regiment, Penna. Volunteers.

CHAPTER V.

CHANCELLORSVILLE TO GETTYSBURG.

A TIRED, hungry, sleepy and altogether weary set of men it was who, after passing over the pontoons, climbed up the steep, wet and slippery clay bank of the Rappahannock and took their way back to the old camp near Falmouth. Thirty-one of those who had crossed with the regiment but a few days before had been left on the other side, dead or wounded, but those who were slowly dragging their aching limbs along were too much depressed to talk of the missing ones.

Theo. Walker, of Company D, was among the dead. He was a man of remarkable attainments, educated and intelligent, with a wonderful flow of language. In any other army he would have been (as a private soldier) a phenomenon, but in any army that numbered thousands of college graduates in the ranks, he was only one of the many. He was a man who would be missed, however, around the camp fires of the future. Half way back to camp loads of hard tack was piled on the wayside to supply the returning troops. It was a welcome sight for the boys were badly in need of rations and the crackers, though soaked with rain, were eaten with relish. Then in the afternoon, in the old winter camp that the men never expected to see again—too tired to put up the tents—and it rained so hard! Everything was damp and wet. Nothing to do but to cut logs and start the camp fires and rest in the mud. To-morrow they would clean up once more, get the shelter tents stretched over the log huts and begin housekeeping all over.

When falling back from the field the men were excited to sympathy at the sight of a large and beautiful setter dog crouching beside a dead officer. No inducement they could offer would cause the noble brute to leave his friend, and he was left to become a prisoner of war when the enemy advanced. The dog was one of a number that shared the fate of the troops.

Captain Byron, Eighty-eighth New York had a little slut named Fan who went into every battle with her master. She realized the danger and would run behind the works the moment the firing began, and when a lull would follow she would run through the regiment as though trying to find out whether any of her friends were killed or wounded. She seemed to be endowed with an unusual amount of reason and never failed to seek shelter on the side of the log, tree, or field works furthest away from the enemy, and she never made a mistake as to which was the right side. During a breathing spell at Chancellorsville she was outside of the line hunting for rabbits among the abattis. At the whistle of the very first rifle ball indicating an attack she leaped the breast-high works and hugged close to the revetment. The instant the fight was over Fan was out again running among the men, seeming overjoyed to find some of them alive and well, but when she found one man, to whom she was much attached, mortally wounded, she threw herself on him, whining and crying, while the dying man feebly reached his hand and patted her head.

Shortly after the battle General D. N. Couch left the Second Corps. He was an officer beloved by all. He asked to be relieved and transferred to other scenes of usefulness because he had lost all confidence in the commander of the Army of the Potomac. He was a man of loyalty, courage and honor, and it was a pity that he did not remain a few weeks longer when a man after his own heart would be in command.

On the retirement of General Couch, General Winfield S. Hancock was assigned to the Second Corps as permanent commander, and General John C. Caldwell assumed command of the First Division.

Captain George Frederick Leppine, who was killed while in command of the battery that was saved by the regiment, was a brilliant young artillery officer. He was educated at a military school in Germany. He was born in Philadelphia, his father being German Consul in that city for some years. Captain Leppine failing to get a command from his native State, took the Fifth Maine Battery to the front.

A very high compliment was paid to the regiment by General Caldwell, the Division Commander, by the detail of Company B, entire, to division headquarters to act as Provost Guard, with Lieutenant William M. Hobart as Provost Marshall, and Lieutenants Henry D. Price and William H. Tyrrell as officers of the Guard. As it was customary to select only the most reliable and choice troops for this important service, nothing could so strongly testify to the efficiency and splendid condition of the regiment at this time than this detail.

The weeks of May passed swiftly. Drills, reviews and inspections without number. The battalion at this time became disciplined and drilled to perfection. The bayonet exercise and skirmishing were much indulged in, and many of the men became wonderfully proficient in the former. From reveille to taps there was not an idle moment in camp, and the picket line along the quiet and beautiful river was the place now most desired. Picket duty was very different during the sunny days of balmy May from the bleak days of the winter when the men were compelled to stand in the cold for hours and days at a time without being allowed to build fires. How the bleak winds whistled over the frozen stream those wintry days!

MAJOR-GENERAL D. N. COUCH.
Commanded Second Corps, from October 9th, 1862 to June 10th, 1863.

How chilled, cold and famished the men on picket then, and how comfortable the huts in camp. But in May, by the flowing river whose banks were pied with daisies and yellow buttercups, the picket line was the place most desired. The two hours of calm watching by the moving stream, and the alternate four hours of absolute rest in the reserve was far more agreeable duty than was to be found in the active camp where drill, guard mount, review and inspection followed each other so incessantly.

May 19th, General Meagher having resigned from the army, took leave of the brigade. The brigade being formed Meagher spoke for ten or fifteen minutes with more than usual fervor and eloquence. Then passing down the whole line in dead silence, he shook the officers and many of the men by the hand. The scene was most affecting and many were weeping. The members of the regiment, not having known him so long as the others were, of course, less moved than those of the other regiments of his command, but nevertheless they had learned to admire him, and they had followed him in two hard battles. As he stood there in the twilight with bared head and the tears streaming down his handsome face and said the last farewell.

Officers and soldiers, said he:

"My Countrymen and Comrades in Arms:

A positive conviction of what I owed to your reputation, to the honor of our race, and to my own conscience, compelled me a few days ago to tender to the President of the United States my resignation of this command. I shall not recapitulate the reasons which induced and justified me to do so. It would be superfluous. There is not a man in this command who is not fully aware of the reasons which compelled me to resign, and there is not a man who does not thoroughly appreciate and approve it. Suffice it to say that, the Irish Brigade no longer existing, I felt that it would be perpetuating a great deception were I to retain the authority and rank of a brigadier-general nominally commanding the same, which was no more; I therefore conscientiously, though most reluctantly, resigned my commission. That resignation has been accepted, and as your late general I now bid you an affectionate farewell. I cannot do so, however, without leaving on record the assurance of the happiness, the gratitude and pride with which I revert to the first days of the Irish Brigade, when it struggled in its infancy and was sustained alone by its native strength and instincts; and retrace from the field, where it first displayed its brilliant gallantry, all the efforts, all the hardships, all the privations, all the sacrifices which have made its history—brief though it be—sacred and inestimable. Sharing with the humblest soldier freely and heartily all the hardships and dangers of the battle-field—never having ordered an advance that I did not take the lead myself—I thank God that I have been spared to do justice to those whose heroism deserves from me a grateful commemoration; and that I have been preserved to bring comfort to those who have lost fathers, husbands and brothers in the soldiers who have fallen for a noble government under the green flag. My life has been a varied one, and I have passed through many distracting scenes. But never has the river that flowed beside my cradle, never have the mountains that overlooked the paths of my childhood, never have the old walls that claimed the curiosity and research of maturer days, been effaced from my memory. As at first—as in nature—the beautiful and glorious picture is indelible. Not less vivid, not less uneffaceable, will be the recollection of my companionship with the Irish Brigade in the service of the United States. The graves of many hundreds of brave and devoted soldiers, who went down to death with all the radiance and enthusiasm of the noblest chivalry, are so many guarantees and pledges that, as long as there remains one officer or soldier of the Irish Brigade, so long shall there be found for him, for his family and little ones, if any there be, a devoted friend in Thomas Francis Meagher"

The men felt sad enough, and sat around the fires that night quiet and subdued.

The officers of the One Hundred and Sixteenth Regiment assembled and all signed the following address which was presented to General Meagher before he left next morning:

HEADQUARTERS 116TH PENNSYLVANIA VOLUNTEERS,
IRISH BRIGADE, HANCOCK'S DIVISION,
SECOND ARMY CORPS, May 19th, 1863.

At a meeting of the commissioned officers of the One Hundred and Sixteenth Pennsylvania Volunteers, Major St. Clair A. Mulholland was called to the chair, and First Lieutenant Louis J. Sacriste was appointed secretary. The following preamble and resolutions were proposed and unanimously adopted:

"WHEREAS, By the acceptance of the resignation of our beloved general, Thomas Francis Meagher, we have been deprived of one who was always solicitous for our comfort and welfare; therefore, be it

RESOLVED, That by the resignation of Brigadier General Meagher this brigade, and especially this regiment, experiences an irreparable loss—one which is felt alike by officers and men, we have been deprived of a leader whom we all would have followed to death, if necessary; a leader whose name was sufficient to strike terror into the hearts of his foes, and excite admiration in the hearts of his co-patriots in arms.

RESOLVED, That in the discharge of his official duties he exhibited alike those qualities which only a true soldier can possess—when on duty a strict disciplinarian, and when off duty an affable, agreeable, and kind companion.

RESOLVED, That as a soldier he was foremost in the battle, offering his life as a sacrifice for the cause of liberty and the Constitution of his adopted country—which country has lost by his resignation one of its most patriotic generals, one of its most daring soldiers, and the army one of its brightest ornaments.

RESOLVED, That in his retirement to civil life he carries with him our most sincere wishes for his future welfare, and we earnestly hope that his future life may be as successful as his past career has been brilliant and honorable".

Henceforth, the Irish Brigade was be led by a new commander, the amiable, noble Patrick Kelly, Colonel of the Eighty-eighth New York Volunteers, who was destined, like Elias of old, to ascend to heaven in a chariot of fire. The brilliant Meagher was gone but his mantle had fallen on one who was most worthy to wear it. June 10th General Couch left the corps and Hancock, who had called the Irish Brigade his "right arm" assumed command, and on June 14th the second corps moved back from the river and began the long march that preceded the battle of Gettysburg.

ITINERARY OF THE MARCH TO GETTYSBURG.

The march of the first day was via Stafford Court House which was in flames as the column passed. On to Acquia Creek where the halt for the night was made. On the 16th marched through Dumfries to Wolf Run Shoals on the Occoquan River—and camped. The march, like that of the preceding day, was one of the greatest fatigue, the heat most oppressive. The dust rising in clouds stifled the men. Water was not to be had. Hundreds of men fell by the way to be picked up by the ambulances, which were soon filled with very sick, and in many cases, dying men. The regiment again proved the superiority of the city men over those who had come from the farm. Very few of the men of the regiment were missing at roll-call when the two dreadful days were ended, and no sooner was coffee cooked than almost every man in the command was swimming about in the stream. The pleasure of the bath was much lessened by the enormous quantities of water snakes that infested the vicinity. After dark a group of officers were enjoying the welcome swim, their clothes piled on the shore, when some one cried out that he felt something moving around his feet. A match was lit and a sight met the bathers' eyes that horrified and amazed them. The whole strand was a mass of writhing, squirming serpents! Snakes of all sizes, short and long, thick and lean, in groups and tied in knots. Snakes single and by the dozen. Snakes by the hundred, countless and innumerable. What a scramble for clothes before the match went out! What an embarassing predicament when it did! Dark as pitch, and a fellow's garments all tangled up with knots and rolls of serpents. How every one got back to camp with enough clothes to cover their nakedness is a mystery. No doubt, some of the One Hundred and Sixteenth literally shook snakes out of their boots, and by the light of the fire-flies looked for others in their blankets.

On the 17th, went into camp near Fairfax Station on the Orange and Alexander R. R., and from here all surplus baggage was sent to Alexander. Happy was the man who after that day had a piece of soap and a fine tooth comb—especially the latter.

June 19th, marched to Centerville, and bivouaced inside the fortifications of Washington. Rained heavily.

On June 20th left Centerville, marching through the village with flying colors. Moved via the Bull Run Pike, crossing Broad Run by wading. Passed over the left portion of Bull Run battlefield. Here the troops rested an hour, with the rain falling steadily. The bodies, or rather the skeletons of the dead of the battle were exposed and the men were evidently affected and depressed at the sight. Then, on again to Gainsville. Next to Haymarket. Still no halt or rest. Through slush, mud and rain, pushing on in the dark to Thoroughfare Gap, reaching the latter place at midnight, with the regiment resting in a swamp until daylight next morning. About six o'clock of this day's march, Captain Teed thinking that he would soon come to a halt, picked up a couple of nice sticks on which he intended to erect his shelter tent. An hour passed and no halt was called. Another hour and still another, and the tramp, tramp, tramp continued. Mile after mile was passed and still no camping for the night. The sticks became heavy but Teed was not going to be fooled by casting them away. He just knew that the column would halt right over that hill or when we would reach the valley then in view. But the hill was passed and the valley left behind and still onward went the column—the sticks were becoming so very, very heavy. Ten o'clock, eleven o'clock, and no rest. Half past eleven!—"Well, no use talking, gentlemen, we are going to march all night!" and away went the sticks after being carried for some fifteen miles. Half an hour afterwards the halt was called, but Teed's sticks were a mile away and he slept like the others—in the mud and without his shelter tent.

Rested two happy, sunshiny days at Thoroughfare Gap and enjoyed the pure air and magnificent scenery. Withdrew from the position on the morning of June 23d, and leaving the mountains suffused with the golden light of sunrise, moved to Haymarket where Stewart's Confederate Cavalry were encountered. Stewart put a battery in position and shelled the corps for a short time, killing and wounding half a dozen, but quickly disappeared when he saw the lines forming for a fight. Then on to Gum Springs, where bivouac was formed in a drenching rain. June 24th, marched at 6 A. M. and moved to Edward's Ferry and crossed the Potomac near the scene of the Ball's Bluff disaster. Moved four miles into Maryland and bivouaced. June 25th resumed the march, via Poolsville to Barnesville. One mile beyond that town halted for the night. June 26th marched at 10 A. M. Reached Sugar Loaf Mountain at noon. At Sugar Loaf Mountain the three armies of the service met. Cavalry, artillery and infantry, coming seemingly from three different directions. The whole army began singing and shouting the "Battle Cry of Freedom," which resounded and filled the valley with music and was echoed from every mountain side—a grand tableau of War never to be forgotten. Shortly after noon, reached the village of Urbana and found the people loyal and the Union flag flying from the houses, a cordial welcome and cheers for the Union Army. At night camped on the south bank of the Monocacy two miles from Frederick City. Two days of delightful rest with fresh bread and many city luxuries from the stores of Frederick. Candy was in great demand, and a bronzed veteran with a stick of candy in one hand and a doughnut in the other was not an unusual sight. The farmers flocked into camp with produce, and a grateful sense of gratified hunger prevailed in the ranks. In the evening songs were heard from all the camps, and fires blazed all over the country. Everyone's spirits rose and one of the happiest nights of the march passed away. While in camp here General Hooker was relieved from command of the army, and General George G. Meade replaced him. The news came on Sunday morning when listening to the very unusual sound of the church bells coming over the fields from Frederick town.

June 29th, left camp and crossed to the north bank of the Monocacy. Marched around the south-east side of Frederick City, by way of Mount Pleasant, passed through Liberty, Johnstown, Union Bridge and several other little villages. Forded innumerable streams during the day, and at 10 o'clock at night halted at Uniontown after making the longest march that the regiment was ever called upon to perform.

The road was thirty-three miles long, but counting several halts for rest, when the troops filed into the fields and were massed, etc., each man could not have marched less than thirty-four miles. The roads were better than those of Virginia, but the day was warm, and, of course, the fatigue extreme. The march was made in exactly twelve hours, an average of nearly three miles an hour. The fact of getting into Pennsylvania during the day seemed to have a wonderful effect upon the spirits of all the men of the regiment, and frequent inquiries were made during the day for the State line from the farmers who lined the fences by the way and gazed in wonder at the passing column. "Where does this road run to?" asked one of the men. "Oh," replied the intelligent citizen, "it runs right straight on!"

June 30th, Hancock thanked the troops of the corps for the long march of the day before, and the regiment was mustered for pay.

July 1st, marched at 8 A. M., via Tarrytown, and bivouaced within three miles of Gettysburg.

CHAPTER VI.

GETTYSBURG—THE BATTLE OF THE CENTURY.

IN a valley full of peace, calm, comfort and content, overlooked by ranges of high hills—blue, purple and exceedingly lovely—lies the old town of Gettysburg and the twenty-five square miles of territory over which the armies of the North and South struggled and fought during those three terrible days of July, 1863. No more beautiful country than this can be found in the State of Pennsylvania. No matter what part of the field one visits scenes of loveliness open in vistas on every side. The tongue of wood of McPherson's farm, where Reynolds fell, is a fine bit of American forest; and Willoughby Run, which meanders close by, and whose placid waters were crimsoned by the blood of brave men, is a sweet and charming stream where the lilies grow in shady places, and the birds come in springtime to build their nests along its banks. Then from Cemetery Hill, where the Union men made such a gallant stand against the "Louisiana Tigers", there is a splendid view as one looks over the town and across the fields to the Lutheran Seminary. Culp's Hill, too, is full of sweet spots; and through the dark forest, where the six hours' fighting took place on the morning of the third day, one can find much to admire, and many a grand old tree riddled by bullets and torn with shot and shell—forcible reminders of the awful morning of July 3d.

And what more picturesque than the wild and rugged scenery of the "Devil's Den?" Or where can one go to look for a grander or more sublime scene than that from the summit of "Little Round Top" where Vincent's men made their gallant fight. Gettysburg is certainly a magnificent spot, full of natural beauties; and of the many battlefields of the war none more suitable could have been selected upon which to erect the monuments that are intended to commemorate the heroism and valor of our troops. The field is fast becoming the National Mecca, and year after year the number of visitors to the ground increases, until tens of thousands of Americans annually make a pilgrimage to the holy ground and worship at the shrine where so many noble men laid down their lives in defence of the State and cause. England, has her Westminster, France her St. Denis, Italy her Pantheon and Germany her Walle-Halle. Every nation of the old Continent has some place dedicated to their noble and illustrious dead.

This country has not, as yet, reached that mature age when one can visit some hallowed spot set apart for the last resting place for the good and eminent men. In the State of Pennsylvania, the ground of Gettysburg is, however, of much greater interest, and much dearer to the American people than any of the celebrated sanctuaries of Europe.

Glorious Gettysburg! where five thousand of the bravest and best of the soldier-citizens sleep in honored graves on the field their valor won, is the National Sanctuary, the Pantheon, the Westminster of the Republic.

No kings, princes or potentates lie there, but five thousand gallant men, greater than kings, more splendid in their deeds and in their death than any of the princes or great ones who slumber within the fretted walls of Europe's grand Cathedrals—fathers, brothers and kinsmen, the men who came from eighteen states to shed their blood on Pennsylvania's soil in defence of the Union and human

MAJOR-GENERAL GEORGE G. MEADE.

liberty. No wonder, then, that year by year thousands of Americans visit the field, linger on the long line of battle, dwell on the memories of the fight, and meditate upon the heroism displayed in the battle.

From McPherson's woods and Willoughby Run to Cemetery Hill, Round Top, Culp's Hill and Rummel's Farm, the immense caravan of pilgrims yearly wander over the bloody field drawing inspirations from the green graves of those true heroes whose great souls went out in the flame of battle in the days when the National existence was hanging in the balance.

Gettysburg! What visions of those three summer days of July 1863 the magic word recalls. More than a quarter of a century has rolled away since the last shot was fired on the field yet to the veteran it seems but yesterday. To him the smoke of the guns still lingers in the valleys, the sound of the conflict, the roar of the artillery still echoes and reverberates among the verdure-clad hills. Gettysburg! the national battlefield of the war where gallant men from twenty-eight of the thirty-two States that then composed the Federal Union met in deadly conflict to decide by force of arms the future of the Republic, the only great battle of the war fought on the free soil of a Northern State. Fortunate indeed was the son of Pennsylvania who was present in that stupendous fight; and by a special Providence it would seem as though the battle fought on the soil should be, in a very great measure, by sons of the Keystone State. The eminent soldier who commanded the army, General George Gordon Meade, was a son of the State, General John Fulton Reynolds, the first great soldier to crimson the ground with his blood and give up his life in its defence, was a Pennsylvanian, and General Winfield Scott Hancock, "Hancock the Superb," he who galloped to the front at the first sound of strife, and who, from that hour until, in the moment of victory, he fell, crushed and bleeding, on the line of the Second Corps, did so much to win the fight, was a native of the grand old Commonwealth. The first regiment to fire a shot was the Fifty-sixth Pennsylvania Infantry. The First Brigade to especially distinguish itself was Roy Stone's, all Pennsylvanians.

When the second day's fight opened at the Peach Orchard almost the first troops to meet the advancing host of Longstreet were the men of Graham's Brigade, nearly all Pennsylvanians. Later, on that same afternoon, when Hood's Texans climbed the slopes of Little Round Top, they were met by the Eighty-third Pennsylvanians, and the splendid soldier who fell there, General Strong Vincent, fell on his native heath. Still later on that day, when the terrific fighting was progressing over the Wheat Field and Valley of Death, McCandless, with the Pennsylvania Reserves, swept over the bloody ground and made one of the most successful charges of the afternoon. And when the day was far spent and darkness settled over the field, one of the most brilliant feats of the whole battle was the splendid fight of the heroic Ricketts and his Pennsylvania Battery, when, with iron hand, he held the crest of Cemetery Hill against the rush of the Louisiana Tigers. The morning of the third day was ushered in by the charge of the White Star Division commanded by by another son of the State, General John W. Geary; and in the cavalry fight at Rummell's Farm, the greatest cavalry fight of the century, the Union forces was commanded by another, General D. McM. Gregg. In the last scene of all, when Picket crashed on the left centre with his eighteen thousand men, Pennsylvania was everywhere on the line to meet him; and the Philadelphia Brigade stood at the most important point on the field and gathered in the greenest laurels of the day. And the men of the One Hundred and Sixteenth Regiment have good reason to rejoice that their regiment had the happiness of participating in this, the most important battle of the century, and performing an honorable and distinguished part therein. The One Hundred and Sixteenth Regiment arrived near the field late on the evening of July 1st, and early on the morning of the 2d moved on to the line of Cemetery Ridge, to the left of the Umbrella Trees. The division was massed in brigade columns and the men enjoyed a grateful rest. Arms were stacked and the colors lay folded on the upturned bayonets. Every movement of the enemy was watched with interest, and the hours seemed long on that bright summer day. The pickets were more or less engaged all the morning—sometimes stray shots, then again volleys, now a rattling fire all along the front, and smoke would be seen here and there in the distant foliage. The men quietly looked on and when the Third Corps advanced on the Peach Orchard and became engaged, they were deeply interested and full of admiration at the splendid spectacle; and when they saw, in the distance, the Union troops recoil, and received the order to go to their assistance, it was a pleasure to do so. Quickly moving off, by the left flank, towards Little Round Top, the division, commanded by General John C. Caldwell, marched as it had stood, in brigade columns of regiments, closed en masse; and as it marched the enemy's batteries, out by Peach Orchard, opened fire upon the column, but without doing much damage. The solid shot falling on the soft soil of a newly ploughed field threw the earth in showers over the men. While passing the Trossell House, a woman on horseback and in uniform galloped back from the line of battle, asked for some information, and quickly returned to the front again. She was a nurse of the Third Corps, Anna Etheridge, and was directing the removal of the wounded. She was cool and self-possessed and did not seem to mind the fire.

As the column moved towards the left, Zook's Brigade was in the rear, and as that command was passing the Rose Farm, Colonel H. E. Tremaine, of General Sickles's staff, rode up to the general and requested him to halt and advance against the enemy who were breaking through the Union lines at that point. Zook at first refused to do so, as he had no authority from the division commander, General Caldwell, who was then far in advance at the head of the column, but Colonel Tremaine insisted and gave Zook a peremptory order in the name of General Sickles. The gallant Zook hesitated no longer but leaving the division column he quickly formed line, dashed into the woods, met the enemy and began fighting, while the other three brigades of the division continued marching towards Little Round Top, unaware of the fact that Zook's men had left the command and were fighting all alone. When the three brigades arrived at the foot of the hill, (Little Round Top), there was a short delay; then Cross deployed and went forward. Brook went in to his left, and the Irish Brigade counter-marched to the right, passing in rear of Cross, and after clearing his line, deployed and formed on the right of the division. As that brigade advanced it moved over exactly the same ground on which Zook's men had fought, passed over the line that they had reached, and struck the foe. Zook had been carried to the rear dying, and all the regiments of his brigade, after making a most gallant fight, had fallen back, and as the brigades of Brook, Cross and Kelly advanced and fought, the One Hundred and Sixteenth held the extreme right flank of the division line.

The men of the regiment went in at a "Right shoulder shift", and, although the ground was covered with huge boulders interspersed with forest trees, hilly and rough, the alignment was well preserved, and as it neared the crest, met the enemy and received a volley. But the shots were too high and did but little damage and the men rushed on. Soon the lines were but a few feet apart, and the men returned the fire with deadly effect. Captain Nowlen drew his revolver and opened fire; nearly all the other officers followed his example. Little Jeff Carl killed a man within six feet of his bayonet. That hero, Sergeant Francis Malin, was conspicuous by his dash and bravery, as his tall form towered above all around him—a noble soul. He soon fell dead with a bullet through his brain. For a few moments it was hand to hand, but the Confederates seemed to have no stomach for the fight; they were tired, weary and glad to call "enough," surrendered and were sent to the rear as prisoners of war. The regiment had met and fought the men of Kershaw's Brigade, the same who, at Fredericksburg, had poured their deadly fire into the regiment from the stone wall at the base of Marye's Heights. Then the brigade was halted and aligned where the monuments now stand. The meeting of the lines was unexpected to both the Confederates and Union men. As the latter were moving up one side of the hill the Confederates were ascending the other. They gained the crest first and seeing the Union men so close, they became excited and fired too quickly, resulting in the volley passing overhead, and but few of the men of the regiment were injured. On the contrary, the fire of the One Hundred and Sixteenth was delivered with precision and calmness, and every shot told. The Confederates were on a crest while the regimental line was below them, their feet about on a level with the heads of the men. When the One Hundred and Sixteenth charged and gained the ground on which the enemy stood, it was found covered with their dead, nearly every one of them being hit in the head or upper part of the body. Behind one large rock five men lay dead in a heap. They had evidently fallen at the first volley and all at the same time. One of them, in his dying agony, had torn his blouse and shirt open, exposing his breast and showing a great hole from which his heart's blood was flowing.

The large ball (calibre 69) and three buck shot with which the pieces were loaded, although a wretched ammunition for distant firing, was just right for close hand to hand work, and so, on this occasion the fire of the regiment was terrible in its effects, while the small rifle balls of the South Carolina men went whistling over the heads of the men of the One Hundred and Sixteenth. In front, and a little to the right, stood the Rose Farm House and barn. Over the little valley in the immediate front one could see the enemy massed and preparing for another attack. The dead of the One Hundred and Tenth Pennsylvania Volunteers lay directly in front, on the ground which that command had vacated but a half hour before, and one young boy lay outstretched on a large rock with his musket still grasped in his hand, his pale, calm face upturned to the sunny sky, the warm blood still flowing from a hole in his forehead and running in a red stream over the gray stone. The young hero had just given his life for his country. A sweet, childish face it was, lips parted in a smile—those still lips on which the mother's kisses had so lately fallen, warm and tender. The writer never looked on a soldier slain without feeling that he gazed upon the relics of a saint; but the little boy lying there with his blood coloring the soil of his own State, and his young heart stilled forever, seemed more like an angel form than any of the others.

> "Somebody's watching and waiting for him,
> Yearning to hold him again to her heart;
> And there he lies with his blue eyes dim,
> And the smiling child-like lips apart."

As the regiment stood in line waiting for the foe in front to advance, a column of the enemy, supposed to be Semm's and Wofford's Brigades, passed through the Peach Orchard, formed a line in rear and began to advance just as the line in front began moving forward. Orders were given for the division to retire, and under the circumstances it was done in fairly good order.

Passing to the left and going on a run towards Little Round Top, through the wheat field and emerging in the open ground, the command gained the Tawneytown Road and re-formed. Captain John Teed of Company C, Sergeant George Halpin and a few of the men were captured by the enemy. Captain Teed missed the way and walked into the enemy's lines. Halpin being shot was unable to get away. The fire, as the men passed through the wheat, was severe and destructive, and so close were the lines of the enemy between which the men ran, that they finally had to stop firing as they were hitting each other. Seven or eight of the men who were missing after the fight were probably killed in the wheat, only one of them being ever heard of afterwards. Young Martin Gallagher, whom the boys used to call "Jersey", fell at this point with a broken leg. It was afterwards learned that he was hit six or eight times after the first ball broke his leg, but he managed to recover from all his wounds.

The regiment re-formed on the Tawneytown Road and remained near the base of Little Round Top until the fighting on the left was over for the day. Then when the sun went down, moved back with the division and formed on the left of the Second Corps on Cemetery Ridge, on the ground it had occupied in the fore part of the day. The lines were dressed in the twilight, and darkness settled down over the field.

> "The bugle sang truce
> For the night cloud had lowered,
> And the sentinel stars set their watch in the sky,
> And thousands lay down on the ground overpowered,
> The weary to sleep,
> The wounded to die."

Daybreak, on the morning of July 3d, found Hancock on the line getting ready for the day that had dawned so brightly. He personally rectified the alignment of the brigade and placed the One Hundred and Sixteenth regiment to support the guns of Sterling's Second Connecticut Battery.

All morning the men sat around calmly chewing hard tack and waiting for the result of the fight at Culp's Hill, looking over towards that high land, seeing great volumes of smoke arise from the timber, listening to the crash of the musketry, watching the streams of wounded that poured out of the dark woods, seeing the re-enforcements hurrying to the assaulted point, and joining in the glad cheer that at eleven o'clock announced the victory of the Twelfth Corps and told the army that Culp's Hill was once more in possession of the Union Troops and the line was again intact. Then observing with deep interest the enemy, as artillery and infantry were massed in the Union front for the tremendous attack on the left centre. During the two hours of the artillery duel that preceded Pickett's charge, the men hugged the ground closely and, as they lay in front of Sterling's guns, his fire as well as that of the enemy, passed over them. The position, however, was most favorable. The Confederate gunners evidently misunderstood the location of the Union line, and threw their shells into the edge of the woods a hundred yards in rear, where they burst in great numbers. The men of Company B, who formed the Provost Guard of the division, were deployed in rear of the battle line, and during the fire, they suffered more than the men in front. When the fire of the two hundred and twenty-seven guns ceased and the smoke cleared away, one could see the long lines of Pickett's Division and Hill's Corps advancing to the attack. All the Union batteries opened and played upon them as they advanced over the fields. They were seen to fall by hundreds and thousands. Sterling's men made superb firing, their shells bursting in the faces of the advancing hosts. One of the Lieutenants of the battery, a very tall long legged fellow, could not restrain his delight at seeing the excellent work that his battery was doing, and when he would see a good shot and his shells bursting right in the ranks of the Confederates, the arms and legs flying, he would leap up, crack his heels together, and give a great scream of joy. Never was there such a moment of joy and happiness in the ranks of the command. Thousands of Confederates were seen advancing to sure destruction. It was Fredericksburg reversed. The right flank of the

MAJOR-GENERAL WINFIELD SCOTT HANCOCK.
Commander of Second Corps.

GETTYSBURG—THE BATTLE OF THE CENTURY.   141

assaulting line overlapped the division, and to the right, their left extended as far as the eye could reach. One could see the whole grand sight and when Pickett struck the Union line and the hand to hand struggle commenced at the Umbrella Trees, the excitement became intense.

The Confederate Brigade of Wilcox and Perry were directly in front of the Irish Brigade and it seemed impossible to restrain the men from firing.

Never were the men of the regiment so eager to rush into the fight. Finally as the enemy's line got within a hundred and fifty yards the order "Ready!" was given. The men grasped their muskets prepared to fire. The foe had disappeared for a moment in a sharp decline of the ground. The men waited to see the Confederate flags come over the hill, but instead of the red flag of the Confederacy a man crawled over the crest waving a white handkerchief, and ten minutes afterwards the larger part of the men of Wilcox's Brigade quietly walked into the Union line, as prisoners. Three men braver than their fellows, were seen running back over the fields with a stand of colors, and the men in admiration of their heroism, refrained from molesting them.

The firing suddenly ceased and Gettysburg became the victory that marked the beginning of the end of the war, for at the moment when the Army of the Potomac was hurling back, crushed and defeated from Cemetery Ridge, the Army of Northern Virginia, the cannon of the Army of the Tennessee was hammering down the defences of Vicksburg, the roar of Rosencran's Artillery was reverberating among the Cumberland Mountains and the Union lines were advancing along the Tennessee River. Vicksburg fell before the dead of Gettysburg were interred; and the cheers that announced the victory of the Union left wing in Pennsylvania found a loud echo among Grant's heroes of the right wing as they streamed into the captured city.

During the night of this day General Lee sent his wounded towards the south by the Fairfield Road, and during the night of the fourth retired by the same route with his whole army. During the forenoon of the fourth the regiment remained in the same position. It was rumored that the enemy was falling back, but the Confederate sharpshooters were active enough in their efforts to make one believe that all their army was still present. The rain fell in torrents. Rain! Rain! Why does it always rain after a battle? Rain after Antietam, after Fredericksburg, Chancellorsville and Gettysburg, as though the compassionate skies would weep for the fallen brave, send cooling showers to lave the angry wounds, or in sweet mercy hasten to wash away from the soiled earth the crimson stains.

In the evening it was known that the enemy had gone, and the regiment left the line of battle and marched to Two Taverns, a most grateful change. To get away from the tempest-torn ground, from the foul stench and noisome air, from the fray and excitement and blood-red streams, and once more enjoy the bright green of the meadows freshened by the showers, to breathe pure air, and drink clear sparkling water, was happiness indeed. How the men's spirits rose! And a delightful evening marked the calm after the storm. The men circulated through the massed regiments to learn the fate of friends; shook hands or wept with joy at meeting, or shed a silent tear at hearing of the noble end of some beloved one dead. While the survivors had much to regret they had also much to rejoice for. The Second Corps, whilst meeting with an appalling loss had borne a most honorable part in the battle. Laurels rested on every flag, and now, like a winged eagle, the corps had paused to take note of its wounds and to send forth a glad scream of victory. Hancock was gone, to be sure, and Zook, Cross, Shirrell, Kane, Tschudy, Willard, Rorty, and a host of the noblest and best lay with up-turned faces along Cemetery Ridge where their heroic souls had gone out in the hour of triumph. But the men of the Second Corps rejoiced, and who could object? Would not those of their comrades who filled the shallow graves on the line they had just left rejoice and be glad also if they were still alive, and looked upon the trophies of the fight?

Thirty-three battle flags, six thousand prisoners and thirteen thousand stands of small arms was truly a bountiful harvest to be gathered by the men who wore the trefoil.

> One dusk, long summers gone, the white-cheeked moon
>   Beheld this valley reel with war. But now,
> Where yon still hamlet's windows redly glow,
>   At eve, the housewives gossip, or else croon
> Soft lullabies. Through the long afternoon
>   The children gambol in the vale below,
>   The lustrous lilies at their moorings blow,
> The mowers move with scythes in merry tune;
>   Chime faintly far from out the white church spire,
> Those evening bells; slow moves the croaking wains,
>   Down purple glens ablaze with sunset fire,
> And low-necked kine trudge home through thick-leaved lanes,
>   Sweet vale, the only sword now there that's seen
> Is the moon's cimeter in skies serene.

Report of Major St Clair A. Mulholland.
Battle of Gettysburg.

In Camp at Sandy Hook, Md., July 17, 1863.

Sir: I have the honor to submit the following report of the part taken by command in the action at Gettysburg, July 2d and 3d.

After a long and fatiguing march we arrived, on the evening of July 1st, within three miles of Gettysburg, and by order of General Caldwell, camped in a neighboring field. Shortly after daylight on the morning of the 2d, our brigade moved up upon the field in sight of the enemy's pickets. Our division was placed en masse in columns of regiments, my command being in the front line, stacked arms and ordered the men to rest. We remained in this position during the forenoon. Heavy firing was heard at intervals on our right but everything remained quiet in the vicinity until about three o'clock. At that time musketry commenced on our left, I think about three-fourths of a mile away. The firing had continued an hour when orders came to "fall in". We took arms and were marched, by the left flank, towards the scene of action. After marching about a mile and deploying in line of battle, the division advanced to support, I think, a portion of the Third Corps which was then engaged. Our brigade advanced in line of battle, left in front gallantly led by Colonel Patrick Kelly of the Eighty-eighth New York. As we advanced a portion of the Third Corps retired, passing through the intervals of our line. Having entered a wood we began ascending a hill where large boulders and rocks impeded our progress. Notwithstanding, we advanced in good order. We soon came within sight of the enemy who occupied the crest of the hill, and who immediately opened fire at our approach. Our men returned the fire with good effect. After firing for about ten minutes the order was given to advance, which was done in excellent style, driving the enemy from the position which we at once occupied. We took many prisoners at this point, hundreds of the enemy laying down their arms and going to the rear. We found the position that our foe had occupied a moment before thickly strewn with their dead and wounded. Here we again opened fire, the enemy having again rallied to oppose our further advance. After being engaged about twenty minutes, the enemy having been re-inforced, we began to retire in good order. At this time the division had been completely outflanked by the enemy who had formed a line facing the right flank and rear of our brigade. This line was formed along the edge of a wheat field about a quarter of a mile in our rear. We had to cross the field in getting away and in doing so we encountered the full sweep of the enemy's fire which at this point was most destructive and many of the division fell.

After passing to the rear I found Colonel Brook of the Fourth Brigade forming the division in a field adjoining the Second Division Hospital. He told me that he had orders from General Caldwell to do so, I then halted my regiment and rendered all assistance possible in getting together the members of the Second Brigade. Shortly after dark we were again marched to the front and placed in the same position that we had occupied in the morning. Here we lay on our arms during the night and were awakened at daybreak by the sound of the enemy's cannon.

Major-General Hancock passed along early and moved the line a little forward in order that we might have a better range and our fire be more effective should the enemy attack us. We began entrenching, and by eleven o'clock had quite a formidable breastwork thrown up. All the forenoon we could see the enemy preparing to attack. Batteries were placed in position in our front and everything indicated that an attack was intended. About noon it commenced by a terrific shelling of our lines. After shelling our position for two hours the artillery fire slackened and a heavy force of infantry was seen advancing. At this moment our artillery, which up to this time remained almost silent, opened with terrible effect upon the advancing lines, tearing great gaps in the ranks and strewing the ground with dead and wounded. Notwithstanding the destructive fire the enemy continued to advance with a degree of coolness and bravery worthy of a better cause, until reaching a ravine which ran parallel with our line, about half way between us and their artillery, they halted, being then under cover and no longer exposed to our fire. They halted but to surrender. Finding, I presume, that their ranks were too much thinned to think of charging our works, knowing the heavy loss they would sustain in attempting to reach their own line again, and thinking discretion the better part of valor, they laid down their arms and, almost to a man, surrendered.

Perceiving the failure of their infantry to carry the position the enemy again opened their batteries, but after an hour's firing withdrew, leaving us victors of the field. During the day's fighting the heat was very great and the men being exposed, having neither shelter tents nor water, suffered intensely. The morning of the fourth found us victors of every part of the field. The rain fell in torrents, wetting every one, filling the rifle pits and making us most uncomfortable, but my command was very hopeful and bore the fatigues and sufferings incidental to a great battle with a cheerfulness that ever characterizes the true soldier. We remained in the same position until the afternoon of the same day and then my command, with the division, marched to the village of Two Taverns, where we encamped for the night.

In closing my report I cannot refrain from mentioning the cool and gallant bearing of my command. Of the officers it is almost useless for me to speak. Every one of them did their duty in a manner that excited my warmest admiration and gratitude.

Of the enlisted men I feel happy in mentioning the names of Color Sergeant Abraham T. Detweiler, Sergeant Thos. Detweiler, Company A, and private Jefferson Carl, Company C, as having specially distinguished themselves in the action of the 2d instant.

Respectfully submitted,

Your obedient servant,

ST. CLAIR A. MULHOLLAND,
Major Commanding 116th Pennsylvania Vols.

To CAPTAIN THOMAS W. GREIG,
A. A. A.

NOTES ON GETTYSBURG.

The losses in the battle were, in proportion to the number engaged, enormous, amounting on the Union side to twenty-seven per cent.; and on the side of the Confederates to thirty-five per cent. The number of dead on the official reports represents but about half only of those slain. On the Union side, for instance, there are but 2834 reported killed, while in the National Cemetery alone there are 3575 bodies interred. The names on the official return only include those who were killed dead in action, but takes no account of the vast number who died of wounds within ten days after the battle. If one wants to get at the whole number of men who lost their lives in the Union Army there must be added to the 3575 interred in the National Cemetery, at least 400, buried on different parts of the field, and who were never found or transferred to the cemetery. Four hundred more were taken home by their friends immediately after the battle, and several hundred died soon after of wounds, in the hospital, at Carlisle, Harrisburg and other adjacent points; making in all, about 5000 Union men who lost their lives at Gettysburg, or as the results of that battle. The bayonet, now a weapon almost obsolete in warfare, was used quite freely, many men and officers being killed and wounded in that way. Colonel Jeffers, of the Fourth Michigan, was bayoneted to death in the wheat field, and some fifty-four men fell at that point in the same manner. But it would seem that the soldier of our day prefers to kill his man in some other way.

When the gallant Confederate, General Armistead, leaped over the little stone wall that served as a breastwork for the Philadelphia Brigade, he called to his men to give the Union troops the "cold steel". All in vain, however; within the next five minutes that splendid officer and forty-two of the hundred brave men who followed him over the low wall, were lying dead in their tracks, and all the rest of the noble band were crushed and wounded. The bayonet, in modern warfare, is almost a thing of the past, and the soldier finds but little use for it. Certainly, there were numbers killed by it at Gettysburg, but very few indeed, in comparison to the great number slain by the rifle and artillery.

The sword was also used to a considerable extent. When the lines crashed together in the great cavalry fight on the third day, many men were cut down with the sabre; and General Wade Hampton, now United States Senator from South Carolina had his face split open with a sword cut. But when the infantry came hand to hand, they seemed to rather prefer to club their muskets and dash each other's brains out, than to drive the cold steel into the bodies of their opponents; and many men were killed in this manner. Lieutenant Charles Brockey crushed in a Confederate's skull with a rock, and Lieutenant Worcester, of the Seventh Louisiana Tigers, had his head smashed to a jelly by a hand spike in the hands of one of the gunners.

Several men of the regiment who had been transferred to Battery A, Fourth United States Artillery, distinguished themselves in the battle, and several of them were badly wounded, Michael Hickey, Wm. Miller, Joseph Meander and John McCormick being among the latter. During the last moments of Pickett's charge, when Lieutenant Cushing ordered his last serviceable gun (the third piece) to be run down to the stone wall, Patrick Mullin and Simon Mallinger of the One Hundred and Sixteenth Regiment, together with a man of the battery named McConnell were the three cannoneers who worked the gun until Cushing was killed. He (Cushing) stood with his field-glasses raised, in the act of giving a command (he had been terribly wounded in the groin), when a ball entered his mouth and passing through, broke his neck. The Confederates were then pouring over the wall and placing their flags on the guns, and it became a hand-to-hand fight. When the conflict was over, Mullin, Mallinger and McConnell picked up Cushing's body and carried it to the rear.

GETTYSBURG TO THE RAPIDAN.

Remained in camp at Two Taverns until July 7th, then moved back again to Tawneytown, marching the ten miles on empty stomachs. The trains met the regiment there and rations were issued. July 8th, marched in a drenching rain to vicinity of Frederick and bivouaced within three miles of the town. Here the mail was distributed, the first since leaving Falmouth—nearly a month before. July 9th, resumed the march, passing through the city with colors unfurled, music and drums beating. The inhabitants crowded the streets and cheered the victors of Gettysburg. After passing Frederick struck the Harper's Ferry Road and continued along as far as Jefferson, turned to the right and crossed South Mountain and bivouaced on the heights. Resumed the march July 10th passing up Pleasant Valley and crossing the Antietam battlefield. Towards evening arrived at Jones' Cross Roads and caught up with the enemy. The Union batteries shelled the woods and the regiment threw up breast-works. 11th and 12th strengthened the works and rested, and on the thirteenth marched up the Williamsport Road, sometimes in line of battle, sometimes in column, until reaching the Potomac near Falling Waters and again found the enemy. Passed over the ground where the Fifth Michigan Cavalry had had a fight but an hour before, and there were plenty of indications that the brush was considerable of a row. The enemy's batteries shelled the Union troops vigorously, many of the shells coming from a long distance making a most melancholy, wailing sound, passing close to the men's heads and causing a lot of dodging, fortunately none of the men were hit.

The enemy were found strongly entrenched on the Potomac, their line forming a semi-circle with the ends resting on the river. Next morning, shortly after daybreak, the whole army moved on their line of works, crossed them and found them empty and the army of Northern Virginia gone and all safely across on the other side of the swollen stream. On the 15th, withdrew and moved via Antietam and South Mountain to Harper's Ferry. July 16th, went into camp at Sandy Hook, Md., under the guns of Maryland Heights. Were mustered for pay; made out official reports. 18th, marched at 4 P. M., crossing the Shenandoah River on a wire bridge and encamped at Salem Church. Sunday, 19th, marched from 10 A. M. to 3 P. M. and bivouaced at Woodgrove. 20th, moved to Manassas Gap and found the enemy in possession. After a short fight in which the Second Corps took part, the Gap was captured and held. The march was continued, and on the 25th reached Warrenton; and on the 26th, Warrenton Junction where the regiment went into camp until the 30th, moving on the 31st to Elk Run, and on the 31st to Morrisville where a long halt was destined to be made. The march from Gettysburg, especially after passing Harper's Ferry, will be long remembered for happy days and evenings full of intense enjoyment. Each day's march was rarely of more than eight or ten miles, reaching the ground for bivouac early in the afternoon, and every one fresh enough to enjoy the delightful weather and magnificent scenery of Louden Valley.

Never were the men in such health and spirits. Food was plentiful and even luxuries abundant.

The country was overrun with blackberry bushes, and the fruit, juicy, luscious and ripe, was perhaps the greatest blessing that ever the men came across. The whole army literally feasted on blackberries. The result, health. Every case of diarrhoea disappeared and blackberries saved the lives of hundreds. Blackberries were of more value to the army of the Potomac than all the medical department. If ever there is another war let blackberries be a part of the daily ration. Every man of the One Hundred and Sixteenth will endorse that idea.

Next to the enormous quantities of blackberries in Louden Valley were the numerous swarms of bees. Bees of all sorts—honey bees, wasps and hornets in myriads. On several occasions when marching in line of battle, the command was attacked by the angry swarms. The assault was more difficult to meet and endure than the charge of the Confederates. A cloud of the little pests making a vigorous attack on the men was really something serious. Many a time the ranks were broken, and veterans who would scorn to dodge a shell, quailed before a hornet's sting and fled in dismay when they heard the buzz of a wasp.

The camp at Morrisville was a most happy one, and the evening camp fire recalled many an incident of the great battle just fought. Men told how they had marched through Pennsylvania and had been within ten miles of home. One man had actually stolen out of camp one evening, walked all night and saw his wife and children, rode back in his farm wagon and was in camp before his absence was noticed. One of the men who had been captured and escaped, told of a brave deed of Sergeant Halpin. The Sergeant had been shot through the leg and captured. A day or two afterwards, while on the march for the South, he saw a Confederate guard abusing one of the men who was also a captive. Halpin quickly leaped to his feet and knocked the Confederate down. The other Confederate guards were so charmed with his pluck that they protected Halpin from further insult.

During the cannonading that preceded Pickett's charge, General Alexander Hays was about to visit the skirmish line, a very hot place just at that time; and a little Irishman on a white horse was detailed to accompany him as orderly. The General looked at the diminutive son of the old sod, and judged by his appearance that he might not be very reliable. "Sir", said the General, "are you sure you are brave enough to follow me on the skirmish line?" we may be killed out there. "Gineral", replied the orderly, touching his cap, "go right on, sir; go right on to the line. If yiz is killt out there, yiz won't be in hell five minutes until yiz'll hear me tappin' on the window to get in". With his headquarter flag in his hand, General Hays rode up and down the line, leading it forward and urging on a good fight, and the little man on the white horse stuck to him like his shadow.

Then there was a good story told about an officer of the regiment. On the morning of July 4th the Captain had walked out to a pool of water that was some distance in front of the line (at Gettysburg) for a wash. No sooner had he gotten to work than the Confederate sharpshooters began firing at him. One bullet came very close and caused him to unconsciously shy a little. Some of the others, who were with him, smiled at the involuntary movement. The captain very quietly remarked, "Ah, well, if the Rebs send a ball through my shirt there will be more lives than mine lost!" Considering the three long, warm, summer weeks since anyone had a change of linen, how very true.

The picket line of the Second Corps at Morrisville was remarkable in being very long, at one time running something like ten miles across the country. Of course, the posts were necessarily far apart and in fact, were placed just close enough to allow of the men being seen from one post to the next during the day. Communication was kept up by having a non-commissioned officer and a man or two patroling back and forth. The duty was pleasant and agreeable, but extremely dangerous. At night the bushwhackers would creep through the brush and get close to the line, and when the officer of the day would be passing in the dark, quietly cover him and demand his surrender. Several officers and men disappeared in this way. No matter how vigilant the men were the spies and bushwhackers succeeded in getting to and fro on the line.

LIEUTENANT WILLIAM H. BIBIGHAUS.
Died August 6th, 1863.

One night a rush was made by a party of horsemen who boldly galloped past the picket line. The Union men fired at the sound of horses. A scream was heard, and after searching in the woods for some time, a young lady, daughter of a farmer living near by, was found in the bush where she had fallen from her horse. She was badly wounded, being shot in the thigh and the bone broken. She frankly confessed that she had been piloting a squad of bushwhackers through the picket line.

But while the picket line had its drawbacks and hours of danger it also had its times of merriment and laughter, and the camp at Morrisville was a happy and agreeable one.

August 13th the long expected and much desired order came that was to end the battalion and once more raise the command to a regimental organization. Major Mulholland and a detail of officers were ordered to proceed to Philadelphia and recruit six new companies and fill up the four old ones. He started at once but when they arrived at Philadelphia circumstances prevented the immediate carrying out of the plan, and not until the Wilderness campaign was about to commence was the organization complete.

Lieutenant William H. Bibighaus, Company C, died in June, 1863. He was a brave and estimable young man and an excellent officer, and had greatly distinguished himself at Fredericksburg. He was orderly sergeant of his company at that battle and remained alone, loading and firing by the stone wall after the regiment had fallen back. He was taken sick a few days after the battle of Chancellorsville and sent to the hospital at Washington where he died. His body was brought home and buried in Laurel Hill Cemetery, Philadelphia.

CHAPTER VII.

BRISTOE STATION.

THE regiment remained in camp at Morrisville until August 31st, and the long halt gave opportunity for much needed rest. Brigadier-General William Hays who had commanded the corps during July and August after Hancock was wounded, was relieved on August 12th, by General G. K. Warren, who was assigned to the command while General Hancock should remain absent. On August 31st, the corps broke camp and advanced to the banks of the Rappahannock, but returned in three or four days to the camp at Morrisville without having a fight, remaining until September 12th, when, owing to the Confederate Army being weakened by the sending of nearly the whole of Longstreet's Corps to the West, it was thought a good opportunity to strike a blow, and the Union Army advanced for that purpose, the Second Corps and the cavalry being in the advance. Marched September 12th, to Rappahannock Station, crossed the river, and marched to Culpepper; September 14th, to Slaughter Mountain; 15th, to Racoon Ford on the Rapidan, relieving the cavalry pickets just before dusk. The enemy's pickets could be seen on the other side of the stream and firing began promptly. The Confederates seemed mad and full of fight and blazed away vigorously. The useless firing across a river indulged in by most of the army was never relished by the men of the Irish Brigade, who thought it sheer nonsense to blaze away and keep everybody from enjoying rest and comfort without accomplishing the slightest result. An effort was made at once to have the firing cease and cook supper. Captain Granger, of the Eighty-eighth New York, jumped from cover, waved his sword and stuck it in the ground. The Southern boys understood the signal and inquiring "what troops", found it was the Irish Brigade. A picket truce followed immediately, and all hands settled down to boil their coffee in peace, while for miles to the right and left the useless fusillade was continued far into the night. During the 16th, and 17th, not a man was hit in the battalion, and the picket truce was honorably observed in front of the brigade, but along the balance of the corps front the skirmishing was lively, rendering the outposts most unhealthy. A number of sheep were captured by the men of the brigade, and to show their good feeling for the men on the other side of the river, three or four were sent over. Result, mutton stew on both sides of the stream. Remained on the banks of the river until October 5th, moved to Culpepper and remained until October 10th, when it became apparent that the Confederates were moving around the right of the Union Army. Orders were received to move on what turned out to be one of the most trying campaigns ever experienced by the men. The information obtained by General Meade during the first days of the movement was of so vague a nature that much unnecessary marching, loss of rest and fatigue resulted. With eight days' cooked rations in haversack the battalion marched at 1 A. M., Sunday, October 11th, for Brandy Station, and then on to Bealeton Station on the Orange and Alexandria Railroad, the rear of the corps being covered by the cavalry which had rather a severe fight at Brandy Station. Erroneous information caused General Meade to turn and move back to Culpepper expecting to find the enemy moving on that point, so, on Monday, October 12th, at noon, marched back and recrossed the river on pontoons at Rappahannock Station, and moved on Brandy Station. Shortly after crossing the whole Second

Corps advanced in line of battle across the country, making one of the most beautiful scenes incidental to war, but no enemy was found. On reaching Brandy Station the men were tired and worn, and halted, expecting to pass the night there. Large fires soon blazed on every hill. The coffee boiled and the weary troops sank to a rest that was destined to be of short duration. Hardly had the foot-sore men stacked arms than it was definitely learned that the Confederate Army was passing the right of the Army of the Potomac on a raid towards Washington, and at eleven o'clock at night the worn out troops were on the road once more and had entered upon perhaps the most arduous march ever experienced by the men. Back to Bealeton, thence to Warrenton Junction, to Catlett's Station, Auburn, Bristoe and Centreville, Bealeton Station was reached and found in flames and some of the Union troops busy destroying stores and ammunition. Without a halt the column pushed on to Fayetteville arriving there at six o'clock on the morning of the 13th. A halt of an hour to cook coffee, and the order "Fall in" was heard again. The men had not closed an eye for twenty-four hours and had not even time to cook or eat, but the Confederates were nearing the Capitol, and the army had to be pushed on to outmarch, overtake and pass them. All day long the tired, sleepy, hungry men pushed on, everyone intensely nervous and anxious, for rumors and alarms of all sorts were flying along the marching column and momentary attacks were looked for on the left flank. The Second Corps had the left of the army and brought up the rear making the march all the more fatiguing. At nine o'clock at night the Second Corps bivouaced on Cedar Run near the village of Auburn. It was known that the Confederate Army was marching on a parallel line in a race with the Union Army for Washington. There was no time for rest or delay, and at the earliest dawn on October 14th, the column was on the move again. Fording Auburn Creek or Cedar Run, the men found the water mighty cold, and pushing on a short distance halted, on Auburn Hill, Caldwell's Division stacked arms, gathered sticks and lighting fires began cooking the morning coffee. The culinary duties were never finished, however, for hardly had the men set to work when they were astonished by a Confederate battery, atmost within a stone's-throw, opening with shell, which knocked the coffee pots flying and scattered the fires. For a moment consternation and confusion reigned, but the veteran troops that had often been surprised before quickly ran to arms. Ricketts's Pennsylvania Battery quickly got to work, while General Alexander Hays's division deployed and charged the unknown and unexpected foes, who in a few minutes while the morning mists were still hanging over the scene, limbered up and galloped from the grounds. The sudden and unlooked for attack came from the force of the famous Confederate General J. E. B. Stewart, who had been accidentally caught between two columns of the Union Army, the night before. Hiding his men in the deep woods he remained quiet during the night of the 13th, but when morning broke on the 14th, and seeing Caldwell's men massed upon the exposed knoll, he could not resist the temptation of dosing them with shell from seven guns of Beckham's Battery. His two brigades of cavalry under Generals Gordon and Funsten quickly went to the rear when General Alex. Hays deployed the third division and moved upon the bold cavalryman. The episode of Auburn Hill was a very remarkable one and cost the lives of a dozen men, most of whom were in the Fifty-second New York. They were buried where they fell and within half an hour from the time they were cooking their coffee. The division quickly took up the line of march and entered upon another day of extreme hard work. But no fatigue could daunt the spirit of the men of the Irish Brigade, and as they were filing on to the road they saluted the Corps Commander by going through the manual of arms as they marched. Warren was delighted at the exhibition of pluck and endurance. The day began in sunshine and the morning lovely. Though tired, every one was full of confidence and hope. Before starting on the morning march Lieutenant Sacriste and a large detail was made from the One Hundred and Sixteenth, for picket, skirmishing and flankers, and as the Irish Brigade was rear guard of the whole army, the duties of October 14th, became ardous indeed. Even as the men of Caldwell's Division were lighting the fires on Auburn Hill, Ewell's Confederate Corps was deploying in line of battle to strike and as the rear of the troops passed on towards Catlett's Station, they moved on the Union picket line. Colonel James A. Beaver, of the One Hundred and Forty-eighth Pennsylvania Volunteers, was division officer of the day, and with the picket of Caldwell's division succeeded not only in beating off the attack, but actually held Ewell in check until all the Union troops and trains were passed in safety. Lieutenant Sacriste covered himself, and the men of the One Hundred and Sixteenth, who were with him, with glory, and for the brilliant fight that he made he was afterwards awarded a Congressional medal of honor.

It is as well, however, to let Colonel Beaver and General Warren tell the story in their own way:

"During the retrograde movement of the Army of the Potomac from the neighborhood of Culpepper, Va., to Bull Run, in the autumn of 1863, I was commanding the One Hundred and Forty-eighth Regiment Pennsylvania Volunteers, in the Third Brigade, First Division, Second Corps. Our corps was in the rear during the movement, and on the 13th of October, our division the rear of the corps. After going into camp on the night of the 13th, a heavy detail was made from the division for picket duty, and I was appointed Officer of the Day. On the morning of the 14th of October, after the division had marched, the enemy unexpectedly appeared in the front of our picket line, turning our flank, and attacked the division which had crossed Auburn Creek and was engaged in cooking

MAJOR-GENERAL GOUVERNEUR K. WARREN.
Commanded Second Corps, from August 12th, 1863 to March 24th, 1864

breakfast. The wagon train had not entirely passed, and General Warren, then in command of the Second Corps gave me verbal directions to hold the crest of the hill above the road, at all hazards, until the wagons had all passed. We succeeded in doing this, but by the time the train had passed the ford by which the division and train had crossed, the creek was in the possession of the enemy. When I made the discovery, I had already commenced to withdraw the picket line—a detachment of the One Hundred and Sixteenth Pennsylvania Volunteers, under an officer who I have learned was Lieutenant Louis J. Sacriste had reported to me—and in order to save them and the other detail from destruction or capture, it became necessary to cross the creek south of the ford and march diagonally across the country to rejoin the division.

In order to apprise the officers in command of the detail from other regiments of their danger and of the route of our march, I requested Lieutenant Sacriste to proceed to the line which was then engaged and give direction to them. This service he performed very satisfactorily, and as a consequence we withdrew our line without loss and completely circumvented the enemy in their evident design of capturing our pickets".

JAMES A. BEAVER.
Formerly Col. 148th Reg. P. V. Bvt. Brig.-Gen. U. S. V.

From MAJOR-GENERAL G. K. WARREN:

NEWPORT, R. I., October 8th, 1881.

Colonel Beaver's statements of events are in accordance with my recollections which are very fresh. I witnessed the withdrawal of his pickets, after covering the crossing of both trains and the cavalry (which had also defended the crossing with much gallantry), hard pressed by an overwhelming force of the enemy, who had been held in check by the first division pickets of the Second Army Corps, until we had completed the dispositions of a new line of battle, which the enemy dared not attack. It was one of the finest instances of effective picket and skirmish work I have ever witnessed, and I should accord you all the credit that General (then Colonel) Beaver accords.

Very respectfully,
G. K. WARREN.

The fight of the rear-guard did not end at Auburn, but continued all day and far into the night. All day long the Confederate and Union armies rushed on in parallel lines, in the wild race for Washington, and all day long the fight kept up between the flankers of the two columns on the skirmish line, but in the rear, where the Irish Brigade was covering the retreat, the firing was heavy and continuous. The march of the main column was fully protected by the flankers, and not a wagon, ambulance, mule, or even a harness buckle, was left on the road. Towards four o'clock in the afternoon, ominous sounds were heard from the front and the roar of battle came on the cool autumn air. It was the Confederate corps of A. P. Hill striking the head of the Second Corps column at Bristoe Station in an effort to cut off the rear guard of the army. The fight at Bristoe was short but full of stirring incidents.

The Second Corps of the Union army met and fought and threw back the corps of A. P. Hill, while that of Ewell was preparing to close on the rear and was held back by the skirmish line alone. The One Hundred and Sixteenth Regiment being the extreme rear, reached the field last and was, with the exception of a color guard, at once sent to the skirmish line to join the men of the regiment who had been acting as flankers during the day. The men went out at dusk in a beautiful line and attacked the sharpshooters who were hidden in the trees, and the firing continued until dark. Captain Willauer riding out to visit the picket managed to lose his way and found himself among the Confederate cavalry in rear of their picket line. He quietly rode among them until he got his bearings, and then making a break for his own line, succeeded in getting away safely. In the darkness it was impossible to tell friend from foe, and no one in Confederate ranks suspected for a moment that a Union officer was riding among them.

At midnight the corps having all been withdrawn, the Irish Brigade that had been left alone to hold the picket line for a long time after all had gone, with instructions to bolt in a hurry when they did go, started to follow, falling back from the picket line with great caution and in silence, taking up the double-quick after being clear of the field and keeping it up for an hour. Then the rain began falling and the darkness became intense. All night the march continued and at daylight ended on the heights of Centreville. The race was won and the Capitol saved. The members of the One Hundred and Sixteenth never did harder service than on this short campaign. The fatigue was something extraordinary and the demand on the endurance of the men out of all reason, yet was borne cheerfully. Many fell out of the ranks from sheer exhaustion, were left in the rear and never heard of again. Some were known to have been picked up by the enemy, sent to the southern prisons and died there.

Here is an old letter written by Captain O'Grady, of the Eighty-eighth New York, that sums up in a few words the Bristoe campaign:

CAMP EIGHTY-EIGHTH N. Y. S. V. (IRISH BRIGADE),

NEAR CENTREVILLE, VA., October 16th, 1863.

DEAR DICK: Adventures again. On the 9th we came back from the Rapidan to Culpepper, on the 11th marched back past Culpepper, covered the retreat of the army across the Rappahannock, on the 12th recrossed the Rappahannock, driving the enemy six miles, at 1 o'clock on the morning of the 13th retreated, still last of the army, to Bealeton Station, continued marching to Sulphur Springs, found the enemy there, back to Bealeton, thence to Warrenton, thence to Auburn—a very roundabout course to cover the movements of the other four corps—

some thirty-three miles without a halt. On the 14th were shelled at breakfast by the advance of the enemy, fought six hours in retreat, capturing the first battery by a *coup de main*, encountered them ten miles further on at Bristoe Station, fought, with two divisions, the whole of A. P. Hill's corps, held our position till after midnight, Irish Brigade last, alone and unsupported, till the others were at a safe distance, then a double quick for twelve miles, crossing Deep Run and Bull Run, where we halted, *a march of 76 miles in 56 hours*, fighting two severe engagements in one day, and having to guard the entire baggage and reserve artillery of the army. This is unprecedented in the annals of war, beating the famous march of the Fifty-second to Talavera. *We captured two colors, five guns and four hundred and fifty prisoners, and lost nothing.* Yesterday our pickets were engaged by the advance of the enemy and simultaneously on their right flank, where were concentrated, by easy marches from the Rappahannock, the First, Sixth, Third and Fifth Corps, opened a terrific roar of artillery—we were merely a decoy for them, and were temporarily sacrificed to Meade's plans—in *two hours* this flank and (by this time) rear attack smashed the enemy and they were off routed ; 20,000 cavalry started in pursuit. A congratulatory order was to-day read to the whole army, recounting the exploits of the Second Corps, and thanking us for our endurance, gallantry, etc. When I said we lost nothing, of course there were casualties on both sides, rebels losing six to one, but no baggage, barring a few wagons, that a few negro teamsters deserted, cutting the traces and escaping on the mules ; the wagons and the rebels who took them were recaptured, and the niggers will be shot. The season is getting late and we will, I fancy, go into winter quarters ; the Second Corps after its terrible march will not follow the retreat, besides the others are much nearer the enemy. This is the most decisive campaign of a few days that I believe was ever fought, the rapidity of each blow at the enemy was only equalled by its success. * * * It's pitch dark now and I have no candle * * *

The writer was wrong in some of his conclusions. The army did not go into winter quarters as early as expected, and another short but severe campaign had to be passed through before the long rest.

Before daylight on the morning of the 15th, the men sank on the wet ground at Bull Run and were asleep almost before they touched the earth. They were quickly awakened by the booming of cannon and at six o'clock formed line of battle. Reports were rife about the remarkable way that Meade had drawn Lee away from his base, got in his rear and was pounding the remains of the Army of Northern Virginia. The boys believed the story for quite a while and thought Meade's strategy immense, and the men of the One Hundred and Sixteenth were greatly pleased at the following eulogistic order:

HEADQUARTERS, ARMY OF THE POTOMAC,
October 15th, 1863.
(General Orders, No. 96.)

The Major General commanding announces to the army that the rear guard, consisting of the Second Corps, was attacked yesterday while marching by the flank.

The enemy, after a spirited contest, was repulsed, losing a battery of five guns, two colors, and four hundred and fifty prisoners. The skill and promptitude of Major General Warren and the gallantry and bearing of the officers and soldiers of the Second Corps are entitled to high commendation.

By command of
MAJOR GENERAL MEADE.
S. WILLIAMS,
Assistant Adjutant General.

Having had such a tough time as rear guard, marching and fighting, it was thought that the Second Corps would now be on reserve, but all hands had great hopes that they would be allowed to have a whack at the final victory. These were fairy tales that a few short hours dispelled, and the sad truth dawned that the army had simply fallen back to check-mate a move of the enemy that threatened the National Capital. October 15th, 16th and 17th the army remained at Centreville. The men of the One Hundred and Sixteenth resting, eating and sleeping. Sleeping! Would they ever get enough sleep to make up for the week just passed. One officer was missing from the roll call when the short campaign was ended; Adjutant John A. Dorwart had become panic stricken at Auburn and had fled to the rear when Stewart hurled his shells into the early morning bivouac. He returned to the command some days afterwards, was promptly placed under arrest, court-martialed and dismissed in disgrace. October 19th, marched to Bristoe Station. On 21st and 22d, camped at Auburn, the scene of the early morning alarm. October 23d, moved to Turkey Run, and went into camp near Warrenton, and remained, drilling and recuperating, until November 7th. Broke camp and marched to Kelley's Ford on the Rappahannock, passing en route, through Warrenton Junction, Bealeton and Morrisville. Crossed the river next morning; the Second Corps in support of the Third Corps that had crossed the evening before, securing several hundred prisoners. November 8th, established camp on the north side of Mountain Run on Shakelsforde Farm; and here, on November 9th, General Thomas Francis Meagher visited the camp of the Irish Brigade. He was in citizen's dress. Everyone was delighted to see and welcome their old commander and for several days there was a first class jollification. November 10th, moved to south side of Mountain Run, about four miles from the Rappahannock, where the brigade was reviewed by Marshall Prim of the Spanish army, who expressed his high appreciation of the brigade. He was but repeating compliments that he had given the commander a year previously on the Peninsula. November 15th, orders to be ready to move at a moment's notice. November 19th, orders to draw eight days' rations. and continual rumors and frequent alarms notwithstanding which the pleasant Autumn days were full of enjoyments, and the men of the Irish Brigade indulged in camp sports and horse racing to an unlimited extent. The roads were bad but an excellent track was found on the farm of John Minor Botts. November 25th, broke camp, and leaving horse racing and sport behind, started on the Mine Run campaign. Marched to the Rapidan and crossed at Germania Ford, advanced to Robertson's Tavern and threw up entrenchments on the hills, slept on arms but were not attacked. Roll call at daybreak, November 27th, and after coffee, moved up the road and took up a position in a wood, the edge of which rested on Mine Run, Colonel Peel, of the British Grenadiers, son of Sir Robert Peel, a guest of General Meade, stood by the brigade for an hour or so chatting with the officers, some of whom had good whiskey in their canteens while the Colonel had some excellent cigars, and the interview was enjoyed by all. The fragrance of the consoling weed and an uncorked canteen is calculated to make friends even of hereditary enemies, and the Peelers of the old country were forgotten on the battlefield of the new. A day or two afterwards, on the picket line, Colonel Peel had the visor of his forage cap knocked off by a sharpshooter. November 28th, moved still nearer to the front and spent the day in a drenching rain waiting for orders to attack. Heavy skirmishing all day where the army was massed in front of the enemy's position behind Mine Run. No general attack was deemed advisable as the works of the Confederates seemed impregnable, but General Meade concluded to turn the right of the Confederate line, and after dark the turning column started under command of General Warren. The sixteen thousand men and three batteries moved during the night of the 28th and during the 29th, the roads were heavy, in fact, in a frightful condition, and the progress slow; and it was not until sun-down that the extreme right of the enemy was reached, three miles beyond Hope Church.

The Second Corps found the enemy and at once formed for the attack. Colonel Brynes of the Twenty-eighth Massachusetts in command of the skirmishers of Caldwell's division, pushed his men against a regiment that was deployed to protect the Confederates who were constructing the works, and, with a rush, drove them into their entrenchments, capturing some prisoners. For a short time nearly all of the One Hundred and Sixteenth Regiment and the balance of the brigade were hotly engaged, and had an hour more of daylight been granted to the Union forces, a victory of no small magnitude would have been within reach, but the daylight was almost gone, and the darkness gathered over the field before anything more could be done, other than pushing close to the works that the Confederates were busy strengthening. The night settled down intensely cold, and the men wet to the skin, and their feet soaked, spent a few of the most miserable hours of the whole three years. More deaths resulted from that one night's exposure than were lost in many a battle of magnitude. It was a night of anxiety as well as great physical suffering. Every one expected a bloody sun-rise on the morn, and the dawn was awaited in expectation of the roar of battle beginning with the daylight. Daybreak came, and then full light, but no orders to rush on the opposing line. The cold had steadily increased during the night and the air was biting and piercing. All night long the enemy had labored with zeal to make their works formidable, and the morning found them of such a character that to move against them would be worse than madness; it would be slaughter of men without a shadow of hope of success. With a courage greater than required to attack, General Warren concluded to abandon the attempt and the turning movement in which so much hope was centered, was at an end. It meant the finale of the effort of General Meade to surprise the enemy and nothing was left but to withdraw from his front and go into winter quarters.

REORGANIZATION OF THE REGIMENT.

On November 30th, by special request of General Warren, the Irish Brigade was detailed as guard of the ammunition train, and in the evening started on that duty, marched all night, recrossed the river at Ely's Ford, and went into camp at Mountain Run. After resting here for several days moved to vicinity of Stevensburg, three miles

REORGANIZATION OF THE REGIMENT.

from Brandy Station and began erecting huts for winter quarters. The Bristoe Station and Mine Run Campaigns were movements full of great fatigue and suffering that tested the endurance of the men to the utmost. The loss in battle to the battalion was small but many succumbed to the terrible strain of the long marches and exposure. Quite a number of the men were missing on each campaign who have never turned up again or who were only heard of afterwards as dying in Southern prisons.

At Mine Run, as at Bristoe, almost the entire One Hundred and Sixteenth Battalion was detailed on the skirmish line, and only a guard left with the colors. It was noticed that the Confederate prisoners taken at Mine Run were very young and poorly clad and equipped. They were mostly from North Carolina and many of them seemed almost glad to be captured.

The winter months of 1863 and '64 passed away in picket, drill, reviews and all the other incidents of camp life, each day like the preceding one. Christmas and New Year's came and passed with the usual cheer and boxes of good things from home. February 6th, Captain and Brevet-Major Seneca G. Willauer was transferred to the Sixth Regiment Veteran Reserve Corps and Captain Garrett Nowlen succeeded him in command of the regiment. Major Mulholland was in command of Camp Cadwallader at Philadelphia during the early winter months, and soon after the New Year of 1864 received permission to recruit six new companies and so raise the battalion to a full regiment. Recruiting was actively commenced not only in Philadelphia but in Pittsburg and in Fayette and Schuylkill Counties. Richard C. Dale, of Allegheny County, was appointed by Governor Curtin Lieutenant Colonel, and he took personal charge of the organization of three of the new companies, "H", "I", and "K". The two first were raised in Pittsburg and vicinity, while Company K, was recruited in Uniontown, Fayette County, Company E, was recruited in Philadelphia, and

F, and G, in Schuylkill County. The men enlisted in Philadelphia over and above the number necessary for Company E, were placed in four old companies A, B, C, and D, to fill them up.

On February 25th, 1864, the first detachment of recruits arrived at the Regimental Camp and were assigned to Companies A, B, C, and D, and from that date new men were received daily. Finally on May 3d, the Regimental Organization was completed, and the One Hundred and Sixteenth ceased to be a battalion. The Roster of the Organization was as follows:

ROSTER.

Colonel, St. Clair A. Mulholland . . . . Philadelphia.
Lieutenant Colonel, Richard C. Dale . . . . . . Pittsburgh.
Major, John Teed . . . . Berks County.
Adjutant, Louis J. Sacriste . . . . Philadelphia.
Quartermaster, Richard Wade . . . . Philadelphia.
Surgeon, William B. Hartman . . . . Elk County.
Sergeant, Major William J. Burke . . . . . . Philadelphia.
Quartermaster Sergeant, George McMahon . . . Philadelphia.
Commissary Sergeant, Daniel Reen . . . . Philadelphia.
Hospital Steward, Frederick Wagner . . . . . . Philadelphia.
Principal Musician, T. W. Vanneman . . . . . . Chester County.

COMPANY A.

Captain, William H. Hobart . . . . Montgomery County.
First Lieutenant, George Halpin . . . . Philadelphia.
Second Lieutenant. Vacant.

COMPANY B.

Captain, Francis E. Crawford . . . . Philadelphia.
First Lieutenant, Thomas McKnight . . . . . . Philadelphia.
Second Lieutenant. Vacant.

COMPANY C.

Captain, Henry D. Price . . . . Montgomery County.
First Lieutenant, Abraham L. Detweiler . . . . Montgomery County.
Second Lieutenant. Vacant.

COMPANY D.

Captain, Garrett Nowlen . . . . Philadelphia.
First Lieutenant, Eugene Brady . . . . Philadelphia.
Second Lieutenant. Vacant.

COMPANY E.

Captain, Michael Schoales . . . . Philadelphia.
First Lieutenant, Robert J. Grogan . . . . Philadelphia.
Second Lieutenant, Charles Cosslett . . . . . . Philadelphia.

COMPANY F.

Captain, Wellington Jones . . . . Schuylkill County.
First Lieutenant, Peter H. Frailey . . . . Schuylkill County.
Second Lieutenant, William A. Shoener . . . . Schuylkill County.

COMPANY G.

Captain, Frank R. Lieb . . . . Schuylkill County.
First Lieutenant, Francis McGuigan . . . . Philadelphia.
Second Lieutenant, Samuel G. Vanderheyden . . Schuylkill County.

COMPANY H.

Captain, David W. Megraw . . . . Allegheny County.
First Lieutenant, Robert J. Alston . . . . Allegheny County.
Second Lieutenant, Thompson W. Smith . . . . Allegheny County.

COMPANY I.

Captain, Samuel Taggart . . . . Allegheny County.
First Lieutenant, William O'Callaghan . . . Philadelphia County.
Second Lieutenant, Joseph W. Yocum . . . . . . Montgomery County.

COMPANY K.

Captain, John R. Weltner . . . . Fayette County.
First Lieutenant, James D. Cope . . . . Fayette County.
Second Lieutenant, Zadock B. Springer . . . . . Fayette County.

The regiment started on the campaign of 1864 with but one surgeon, whereas the organization was entitled to three, but doctors were getting scarce after the war had been in progress for three years and the One Hundred and Sixteenth was not the only regiment that had but one. The medical staff were badly needed in the last year of the war, more so than at any other period but the demand had exhausted the supply.

The departure of the new men and companies for the front, gave rise to many of those thrilling heart-rending scenes that were witnessed in every part of the country in the early days of the war. The feeling was more intensified than at first, because the participants had learned, by sad experiences, that for many the parting meant "forever", and those going to the front in 1864 were so young. It was the men who went in '61. The school-boys filled the ranks in '64. The large majority of the new soldiers who filled the ranks of the One Hundred and Sixteenth were innocent of a beard, but they were the bravest and best, and it was so very, very sad for the mother to give them up. She was proud of her soldier boy to be sure, but who can fathom the sorrow of a mother's heart when, kissing her son for the last time, she sends him away to face death in all its various forms. Every one of the new members of the regiment left mothers, sisters and friends behind to pray for them, to weep for them, and cherish forever the memory of those who in many instances never came back. It is not possible to record in these pages all the sad partings incidental to the re-formation of the regiment, but we will speak of one company, a fair sample of all the others, Company K, was recruited in Fayette County, and on a beautiful spring evening the company marched to the railroad depot in Uniontown to take the cars for the seat of the war. The little city had sent hundreds of others during the previous three years, and hardly a family but had passed through seasons of sorrow and the crape had floated from many a door bell for the soldiers who would never return. Nearly every able bodied man was at the front already, and now all the schools were being deserted to swell the army. All the town turned out to see the last company leave for the field. The train was waiting and the local band that escorted the company ceased to play when the depot was reached. The ranks were broken to allow the leave taking, every one of the boys had been loaded with all the tokens of affection and things of usefulness that love could suggest, and all that remained was to exchange the last embrace, the last loving, heartfelt kiss, and say farewell. Then the cars moved off amid sobs and tears, the band played a farewell salute, cheers mingled with the mother's subdued weeping, and the train was soon out of sight. The crowd slowly dispersed, each one going to the lonely home to think of the boy who, living or dead would be, for all time to come, the idol and the hero of the family. Company K, left Uniontown with eighty-one in the ranks. Within one year twenty were killed in battle or had died of wounds. Eight had died of disease and four had died in southern prisons. Thirty-two out of eighty-one were sleeping in soldiers' graves. Of those still alive at the end of the year twenty-two had been badly wounded and four had been transferred to the Veteran Reserve Corps on account of disease.

No wonder that those left behind waited in sorrow for the end. Those who were actively engaged at the front suffered but little compared with those who were left at home.

> The maid who binds her warrior's sash
>   With smile that well her pain dissembles,
> While beneath the drooping lash
>   One starry teardrop hangs and trembles,
> Though heaven alone records the tear,
>   And fame shall never know her story—
> Her heart has shed a drop as dear
>   As e'er bedewed the field of glory.
>
> The wife who girds her husband's sword
>   'Mid little ones who weep or wonder,
> And bravely speaks the cheering word,
>   What though her heart be rent asunder,
> Doomed nightly in her dreams to hear
>   The bolts of death around him rattle,
> Hath shed as sacred blood as e'er
>   Was poured upon the field of battle.
>
> The mother who conceals her grief
>   While to her breast her son she presses,
> Then breathes a few brave words and brief,
>   Kissing the patriot brow she blesses,
> With no one but her secret God
>   To know the pain that weighs upon her,
> Sheds holy blood as e'er the sod
>   Received on freedom's field of honor.

CHAPTER VIII.

THE WILDERNESS.

ON May 1st, a heavy storm of rain and wind swept over the camp at Brandy Station, blowing down the tents and wrecking the winter quarters. Every one set to work to repair the damage but before the tents were well up again orders came to move. Then a day of perfect quiet and rest. Never a day of more portentous and absolute calm in the army than that of May 2d, 1864. No drills, reviews or work of any kind. The lion was about to emerge from his lair and leap upon his foe, and paused to gather strength for the spring; and when the shadows fell on the evening of May 3d the great army silently withdrew from the old camps where it had spent the winter, leaving the camp fires burning, and the long lines moved towards the fords of the Rapidan. Quietly stealing along in the night through the deep forest, the regiment crossed the stream at Ely's Ford, and at noon on May 4th, halted on the open ground around the ruins of the Chancellorsville House where the Second Corps was massed. Pickets were thrown out, a battery placed in position covering the plank road that led to Fredericksburg, arms stacked, the roll called in each company (and not one man was missing), an order from General Meade was read.

ADDRESS OF GENERAL MEADE.

Headquarters Army of the Potomac, May 4th, 1864.

Soldiers: Again you are called upon to advance upon the enemies of your country. The time and occasion are deemed opportune by your commanding general to address

IN THE WILDERNESS—Thirty years after.

you a few words of confidence and caution. You have been reorganized, strengthened and fully equipped in every respect. You form a part of the several armies of your country—the whole under an able and distinguished general, who enjoys the confidence of the government, the people and the army. Your movement being in co-operation with others, it is of the utmost importance that no effort should be spared to make it successful.

Soldiers, the eyes of the whole country are looking with anxious hope to the blow you are about to strike in the most sacred cause that ever called men to arms. Remember your homes, your wives and children ; and bear in mind, the sooner your enemies are overcome the sooner you will be returned to enjoy the benefits and blessings of peace. Bear with patience the hardships and sacrifices you will be called upon to endure. Have confidence in your officers and in each other.

Keep your ranks on the march and on the battlefield, and let each man earnestly implore God's blessing and endeavor by his thoughts and actions to render himself worthy of the favor he speaks. With clear conscience and strong arms, actuated by a high sense of duty, fighting to preserve the government and the institutions handed down to us by our forefathers, if true to ourselves, victory under God's blessing must and will attend our efforts.

       GEORGE G. MEADE,
        Major-General Commanding.

S. WILLIAMS,
 Assistant General.

And then another quiet evening of peace and rest. Hancock, surrounded by his staff, lay under the apple trees in the orchard, on the ground where Leppine's guns stood firing just a year before that very day. The general, tapping his boot with his whip, chatted of the year gone by. Memories, reminiscences, jokes and merry laughter passed the hours away. A gay and happy group it was, full of life, hope and sans souci, as though it were an excursion of pleasure, instead of the most awful and fierce campaign of the war on which they were starting. The Chancellorsville House still lay a mass of unsightly ruins. The debris of the battery still remained scattered over the ground. Broken wheels, shattered poles, pieces of ammunition chests, bursted shells, bones of horses, remnants of blankets, canteens, bits of leather, rotting harness, etc., mingled in dire confusion. In the evening, after resting, when the rations had been distributed, officers and men strolled around examining the ground on which they had been fighting that day a year ago. The apple trees and lilies bloomed again. Pink and white roses struggled to life in the trampled garden of the old homestead and the fragrance of May filled the air. The old members of the regiment took great pleasure in imparting to the new men the particulars of the battle and showing them how the battery was saved. The boys fresh from home, who had not yet heard the sound of a hostile gun were full of curiosity, and took great interest in everything. The evidence of the fight was so strongly visible that the scene impressed them deeply. The burnt and crumbling buildings, trees torn and rent, the ground strewn with debris, told in mute but terribly strong language of the carnage and storm. The shallow graves of the men of the brigade were discovered and, much to the delight of men, were found overgrown with wild flowers and forget-me-nots. When Lieutenant Colonel Dale noticed the profusion of the little blue flower he was deeply effected. He stood gazing upon the ground, wrapped in thought, and spoke in a strangely poetic strain of the goodness of the Creator in covering with beauty and perfume the last resting places of those brave men. He lingered there on that sweet spring evening and talked of the matter for a long time, and finally began writing a letter to a Pittsburg paper, describing the scene and telling of the forget-me-nots. Gentle, noble soul! Within ten days he also filled a soldier's grave, and if the God who sends the flowers in spring casts them over the last resting place of brave men in proportion to the soldier's merits, then indeed the unknown grave of Colonel Dale must be covered with the choicest bloom that nature yields in very great abundance.

Another night of calm and rest, the men sleeping soundly on the graves of their comrades who had been lying there since the battle of a year ago. Reveille awoke the troops for the opening day of the Wilderness campaign. The orders were for the Second Corps to move to Shady Grove Church on the Catharpin Road, but after passing Todd's Tavern orders were received to move to the support of the Sixth Corps. Then several hours of anxious waiting and countermarching. The day became warm and water could not be found. No time for coffee or a halt sufficiently long to allow for cooking. Three o'clock in the afternoon found the command moving on the Brock Road, down which the enemy were reported to be marching.

The country where the regiment was now to fight was very appropriately called the Wilderness, a mineral region where both gold and iron are found, abounding in game and densely wooded. The roads simply consisted of narrow lanes cut through the forests and, in some cases, covered with planks or hewn logs. The Brock Road, where the Second Corps formed line on the afternoon of May 5th, was of this nature, the woods on each side being dense and almost impenetrable. The preparations for the fight were noiseless. The enemy were within sound although could not be seen, and bullets whistled through the trees telling of their presence. Quickly the advance was ordered. Getty's division of the Sixth Corps was already advancing on the right and Hancock was not slow to support him.

The advance in line was more than difficult—almost impossible. The undergrowth was so dense that regimental commanding officers could not see half their own line. One regiment pushed forward and struck the enemy after advancing about three hundred yards. A clash of musketry, and the campaign of '64 began. The ground on which the regiment fought was just to the left of the abandoned gold mines. The decaying timbers of the miners' cabins were scattered through the dense woods, and great cavities still existed showing the position of the ancient mining shafts. In the regimental line there were six hundred new men, or rather should one say, boys, for but few, but very few, bearded faces were seen in the ranks. Fayette, Allegheny, Chester and Schuylkill Counties of Pennsylvania State had emptied their school houses to furnish recruits. Ah, what young, bright, childish faces, full of sweetness, smiles, enthusiasm and hope. Not a cheek blanched, not a coward in all the noble band. Six hundred boys, with less than two months of drill or discipline, in their first battle, yet as steady, confident and reliable as the oldest veterans. The surrounding circumstances were of the most trying nature. The crash of musketry filled the woods, the smoke lingered and clung to the trees and underbrush and obscured everything. Men fell on every side, but still the regiment passed steadily on. One by one the boys fell, some to rise no more; others badly wounded, but not a groan or complaint, and a broad smile passed along the line when Sergeant John Cassidy, of Company E, found fault, because when shot through the lungs, he had to walk off without assistance, some one said to him: "Why, Cassidy, there's a man with all of his head blown off and he is not making half as much fuss as you are"!

The regiment was detached from the Irish Brigade in the first day of the Wilderness and sent to the support of General Miles' Brigade. Towards dusk in returning to join its own brigade and when marching along in column of fours in rear of the line, a gap was discovered in the line of battle and without waiting for orders the One Hundred and Sixteenth promptly moved in and filled it. It was a most important service and recognized as such by

BRIGADIER-GENERAL THOMAS A. SMYTH.

General Barlow. A Confederate force was at the moment moving towards the opening but seeing the well dressed ranks of the One Hundred and Sixteenth halted, and after the exchange of shots, fell back, just as the One Hundred and Fortieth Pennsylvania Volunteers with loud cheers came in to the relief. The fighting ceased with the daylight and when the darkness filled the forest the men were tired, weary and hungry and settled down to sleep supperless. All night long the stretcher-carriers bore the wounded to the rear, and when morning came again the line fell back to the Brock Road and threw up a line of works. When axes and spades had done their work and the revetment had become breast-high coffee and hard tack were in order, the first in twenty-four hours. The first day of the battle of the Wilderness had been an eventful one for the regiment. The command, though composed of more than three-fourths new men who had never been in a fight, had proved not only reliable under the most trying ordeal but full of dash, ardor and the most high courage. Hancock says in his official report of this day's battle: "The Irish Brigade, commanded by Colonel Thomas Smyth and Colonel Brooks's Fourth Brigade, attacked the enemy vigorously on his right and drove his line some distance. The Irish Brigade was heavily engaged and although four-fifths of its members were recruits it behaved with great steadiness and gallantry, losing largely in killed and wounded".

Many narrow escapes were made during the first day's fight. Lieutenant-Colonel Dale was hit in the side, the ball cutting away his undershirt but not breaking the skin. Lieutenant Cosslett was shot in the forehead, the ball cutting through the cap and making a deep flesh wound along the scalp. A young boy, Dan. Chisholm, had the front of his cap shot away, but leaving him unhurt; and so many a close call was talked about before as one by one the tired soldiers sank to rest in the blood-drenched woods. Early on the morning of the 6th, Caldwell's division and that of

General Gibbons's, fell back to the Brock Road. These two divisions, together with a large portion of the artillery of the Second Corps, were placed on the left of the army to meet an expected flank attack of Longstreet's Corps that was reported moving to strike the Union left flank. The regiment lay along the Brock Road near the Trigg House, and while still occupied in building breast-works the whole army, with the exception of the two divisions herein spoken of, moved forward into the deep woods, and the roar of the second day's battle began. It was a morning of intense anxiety to the men. For hours they listened to the continuous roll and the musketry and cheers of the Union Army and they knew that their people were driving everything before them as the huzzas and roar of the firing continued to recede and get further away. But towards noon the Union cheers became less frequent and the firing came nearer. Then the Confederate yell rose loud and wild and the Union line began to come back. The wounded poured out of the woods in streams and everything told of disaster to the Union arms. The victorious enemy halted before reaching the point where the regiment lay and although ready and anxious and more than willing the men did not get an opportunity of firing a shot until towards evening. Towards five o'clock, Captain Megraw, who had been out visiting the picket line, rushed in, tumbled over the breast-work and called out: "They are coming—get ready"! Instantly everyone was in line and very wide awake, although many were resting and dozing a moment before.

A few shots were heard on the picket line which was but a short distance in front, and almost without warning a Confederate line of battle stood within fifty yards of the slight works; they covered the regimental front and began firing. The fight was short and sharp. The men replied vigorously for a few moments, then the breastwork, which was built up with dry fence rails and logs, caught fire. The wind fanned the flames, and soon the whole line in front of the regiment was in a blaze. The smoke rolled back in clouds; the flames leaped ten and fifteen feet high, rolled back and scorched the men until the heat became unbearable, the musket balls the while whistling and screaming through the smoke and fire. A scene of terror and wild dismay, but no man in the ranks of the regiment moved an inch. Right in the smoke and fire they stood, and sent back the deadly volleys until the enemy gave up the effort and fell back and disappeared into the depths of that sad forest where thousands lay dead and dying. Soon the fire communicated to the trees and bush, and in less than an hour, acres of ground over which the armies had struggled and fought during the two awful days, was a mass of fire. This was the saddest part of all the battle. How many poor, wounded souls perished in the flames none but the angels who were there to receive their brave spirits will ever know; but the very awfulness of the situation seemed to call forth renewed evidence of courage, and when volunteers were demanded to rescue the wounded, Lieutenant Cosslett and a score of noble men rushed into the smoke and fire to save them.

The rush of the enemy upon the Union works on the evening of the 6th, practically ended the battle of the Wilderness. During the night of the 6th and all the day of the 7th of May the regiment remained in position along the road, only picket firing being indulged in with an occasional crash from one of the batteries. Owing to the dense timber the sharpshooters had but little chance to work and hence the men behind the breast-works could move about freely and without danger, and the fact of the sharpshooters being unable to ply their vocation made a most remarkable difference in the losses of commissioned officers between the Wilderness and other battles. At Gettysburg, for instance, where the armies fought principally in the open, the losses among the commissioned officers were very great, eight and a half per cent. of all the wounded being of that class, while in the Wilderness but five per cent. of the killed and five per cent. of the wounded were officers. But, if the officers were spared in the first two days of the campaign, they received their full share of punishment during the succeeding fights. An old friend of the writer, Colonel Seymour Lansing, of the Seventeenth New York Cavalry, gave a dinner, just before the Peninsula campaign, to thirteen colonels and their wives, who at the time happened to be visiting the army. Within three months eleven of the ladies were widows. Quite as severe on the officers was this campaign of the Wilderness. The Irish Brigade went into action May 5th with ten field officers. Within six weeks six of them (Colonels Kelly, Byrnes and Dale and Majors Rider, Thouy and Lawyer) were sleeping in soldiers' graves, and the other four were in hospitals seriously wounded.

Here, in the Wilderness, the men of the regiment learned the full value of field works as means of defence and of saving life, and began to realize the fact that the spade and pick were as much and quite as valuable implements of warfare as the musket and bayonet. On the 5th of May began the slashing of timber and digging of earth that ended in leaving whole counties of Virginia crossed and re-crossed in every direction with formidable lines of works, enduring and quite capable of resisting field artillery; and the proficiency attained by the men of the regiment in that direction was indeed wonderful. No sooner was line of battle formed and muskets stacked than everyone was at work, quickly forming squads and moving swiftly, some felling trees and trimming the logs to form the revetment, some driving stakes and others carrying and laying the tree trunks in position. Others with spade and pick, threw up the earth and banked it down, while more dragged the knarled branches and laid them in order to make the abattis. In two hours a line of works would be up and finished sufficiently powerful to resist not only an onslaught of infantry but stop the shells of the heaviest guns then in use. And how cheerfully all hands worked to get under cover. No matter how long the march of the day or how weary and tired the boys might be, there would be no coffee until the works were up and finished, and long before the war had closed every man had become a builder of field-works and an engineer in embryo.

CHAPTER IX.

TODD'S TAVERN OR CORBIN'S BRIDGE.

EARLY on the morning of May 8th, the regiment withdrew from the line of the Brock Road and moved towards Todd's Tavern. The day was warm and the clouds of dust suffocating, rendering the march most oppressive. Water could not be found and the men suffered greatly for the want of it. During a halt in the road General Grant rode past. It was the first time that the men of the regiment had seen the great commander and they had not yet learned to know him. The general rode slowly by, pausing a moment to look at the command while the men gazed with curiosity but without the slightest show of enthusiasm or feeling at the serious, sphynx-like face. He wore the slouch hat and unbuttoned coat and general tout ensemble with which the whole nation has since become so familiar, but on this occasion the ever present cigar was missing. Only one or two staff officers and an orderly was with him and as he rode away in the dust and heat he left an impression never to be forgotten—so calm, quiet and unassuming but the embodiment of stability and firmness.

The Army of the Potomac had found at last a commander worthy to lead it, and on that day he announced to the nation that " to retreat is a memory of the past ", and that " we will fight it out on this line if it takes all summer ".

The regiment was formed in a pleasant wood (at Todd's Tavern), looking out over some open fields, where a few peaceful hours were passed in grateful rest. Miles's Brigade with a battery and some of Gregg's cavalry were

GENERAL U. S. GRANT.

sent out the Catharpin Road towards Corbin's Bridge. In the evening while the force was returning Miles encountered Mahone's Confederate Division and a sharp fight took place. The Irish Brigade was ordered out, double quick, to help. At the moment the order came Colonel Dale was holding a prayer meeting in which the larger portion of the men were participating. The "Amen" was quickly said and in five minutes or less the brigade, with the regiment on the left, was going on a run towards the firing. By the time the command had reached Miles the fight was almost over and he had succeeded in beating off the attack and was falling back in good order. The other four regiments of the brigade fell back with Miles and got away without loss. Not so with the One Hundred and Sixteenth. The regiment had been detached by General Smyth and sent to the extreme right. By the blundering of a staff officer the point of direction was misunderstood and after marching through a dense wood for nearly a mile the command drew up in front of a Confederate line of battle with one of their batteries within a hundred feet. There were no Confederate pickets in their front, but the men of the battery soon discovered the presence of the Union line, and opened a vigorous fire with shell. Fortunately for the regiment, they fired too high and the shells passed over the line. Had the Southern Battery thrown canister instead of shell it would have been a serious matter for the command. While lying here trying to find out the reason of being so placed, a force of infantry was discovered moving through the woods on the right, evidently to get in rear and capture the regiment. A rambling fire of musketry was opened from that column and half a dozen of the men were hit. It was undoubtedly time to leave if the regiment did not wish to spend the summer in the South, so quietly withdrawing, the command moved back into the woods, the battery continuing to throw shells after the retreating line. After an hour of wandering through the forest the way back to the division at Todd's Tavern was found and just at dark the regiment passed through the picket line and entered the camp, much to the surprise of everyone, and was received with demonstrations of gladness and joy. The command had been reported lost and not a soul in the division but fully believed that the One Hundred and Sixteenth Pennsylvania Volunteers—colors and all—was at that moment in the hands of the enemy. It was a strange adventure, a most novel experience, and proved more than one could imagine how perfectly reliable under all circumstances the command was. The Confederate troops who met and fought on the evening were Mahone's Brigade of Hill's Corps and a battery. These troops were en route to Spottsylvania C. H., and the meeting was accidental. The fight at Todd's Tavern took place on a Sunday evening, and the men were summoned from prayer meeting to go to the front. At the time it did not occur to one, but now, when years have passed and we look back we must feel astonished at the high moral standard of the army that fought the war of Secession, and the regiment was second to none in that respect. Seldom was an obscene word or an oath heard in the camp. Meetings for prayer were of almost daily occurrence, and the groups of men sitting on the ground or gathered on the hill side listening to the Gospel were strong reminders of the mounds of Galilee when the people sat upon the ground to hear the Saviour teach. Ofttimes in the regiment the dawn witnessed the smoke of incense ascend to heaven amid the templed trees where serious groups knelt on the green sod and listened to the murmur of the Mass. In the evening Lieutenant-Colonel Dale or Captain Samuel Taggart would hold a meeting for prayer where the larger number of the men would gather in reverence and devotion, while others would kneel around the Chaplain's tent to count their beads and repeat the rosary. Colonel Dale was a man of deep religious thought and feeling, and Captain Taggart was an ordained Minister of the Gospel, both men of great devotion and sincerity, and by their example did much towards making others sincerely good. Both fell early and went to receive their great reward. Saints they were and each died with a prayer on his lips— true to their country and their God.

Through the night of May 8th the picket firing was continuous and indicated a battle next day, as the enemy was thought to be concentrating in front, but the morning of the 9th passed and no attack, although firing was heard to the right and more to the left, and during the day the death of General Sedgwick, commanding the Sixth Corps, was announced. At noon the division was withdrawn from the works that had been erected at Todd's Tavern, and marched to the left about a mile along the Brock Road, then turning to the right crossed the country by a cow path and drew up on the high and open ground overlooking the valley of the Po River. Line of battle was formed along the crest and dinner cooked. During the afternoon a wagon train of the enemy could be seen moving along a road on the other side of the stream and the Union batteries opened upon it with effect. The men looked on and enjoyed the scene greatly as they saw the shells bursting among the mules. The frantic efforts of the drivers to get out of harm's way were most laughable. Towards evening orders came to cross the river and about five o'clock the division moved, Brooks's brigade leading the movement, Birney's division crossing higher up the stream and Gibbons's division below. Brooks drove the enemy back, effected a crossing and was quickly followed by the balance of the division. By the time line was formed, however, the darkness fell, and after advancing into the woods for some distance the division halted for the night.

THE BATTLE OF THE PO.

There was perhaps no more interesting fight in which the men of the regiment were ever engaged or where they played a more important part than that of May 10th, called the battle of the Po. It would be difficult to understand the movement that led to and culminated in this little battle without knowing the lay of the land. The Po, a deep quiet stream, about forty feet wide, after passing the point where the division crossed, makes a sharp turn, and sweeping around towards the south almost doubles upon its course, so that after crossing one could by marching straight forward about a mile, again strike the stream at the Block House Bridge. The intention of the commander-in-chief seems to have been, at first, to send the division over to capture the wagon train that our gunners had shelled with such ludicrous effect, but after the first troops had crossed successfully General Meade seems to have thought it advisable to throw the whole Second Corps across. That having been partly accomplished, the movement quickly suggested the possibility of a turning operation against the left of the Confederate army by again crossing the stream by the Block House Bridge, but darkness checked the advance. No sooner had the line halted for the night in the pitch dark forest, than the regiment was detailed for picket along with several hundred members of a German regiment. The picket force moved very cautiously and were as noiseless as could be until the head of the column reached the bank of the stream at the Block House Bridge. The regiment in perfect silence filed to the right and was deployed along the bank, the officers issuing their orders in whispers and the men groping their way and finding their posts as best they could in the intense darkness. All went well until the picket (composed of the One Hundred and Sixteenth) was in position to the right of the bridge. Every man seemed to instinctively feel the necessity of getting into position without the enemy, who was supposed to be on the other side of the river, being aware of his presence, and the success up to a certain point was remarkable.

But when the German detail filed to the left of the bridge and began deploying in the darkness, matters were very different. Tin cups rattled now and then, and the officers gave their orders in tones loud enough to be heard on the further bank of the stream. Then a man fired his musket. Some one else promptly followed, and the whole detail began blazing away into the darkness. The roar for a few moments was deafening. It seemed impossible to quiet the excited Teutons, and notwithstanding the exertions of their officers, who ran from post to post calling out to stop firing, the noise was continued for ten or fifteen minutes. Not a shot was fired in return, and no sound was heard to indicate that the Confederate pickets were on the other side of the stream, and it is not at all likely that any were there, but the man who fired the first shot on the Union side, and so brought on the trouble, was the direct cause of the failure of all the plans for turning the flank of the enemy's line, for the volleys of musketry echoing through the still woods notified Hill of the presence of the Union Army, and when morning broke, his men were discovered hard at work entrenching and getting artillery in position to cover the passage of the bridge. Hancock and Barlow were on hand early examining the crossing, and at once saw how impracticable it would be to force a passage at that point. Brooks with his brigade crossed the stream lower down, however, and pushing forward half a mile, discovered the left of the enemy's line, and found it strongly fortified, and the movement against Lee's left flank was abandoned. Gibbons's and Birney's divisions were, during the morning, withdrawn and sent to the left to assist the Fifth Corps in an assault on the Confederate line near the Alsop House, and Barlow's division was left alone to hold the advance line across the stream. The entire One Hundred and Sixteenth Regiment was then deployed on the skirmish line to cover the front of Brown's and Smyth's Brigades. The colors were placed with the reserve and the line drawn back somewhat from the stream. All the forenoon the Confederates could be seen working on their fortifications, and but very little firing took place. They seemed to wish to work in peace, and the men were not at all anxious to bring on a fight. A very amusing incident took place during the morning. Lieutenant Springer, of Company K, and another officer, started from the reserve to visit the picket. Strolling along through the woods, their swords over their arms and chatting pleasantly, in some unaccountable manner they passed through the line and were so engrossed with their talk that they were down on the banks of the stream before they were conscious of their whereabouts. The river at this point was quite narrow, and on the further bank stood a Confederate brigade in line and at "parade rest". Pioneers were hard at work throwing a bridge across, that the force might get over on. The two officers, to say the least, were astonished when they saw the long line of gray within thirty feet. The conversation suddenly ceased, and blank amazement succeeded. Our southern friends were just a little more astonished than the two One Hundred and Sixteenth officers. The pioneers dropped their axes and stared. The officers seemed so taken aback by the unexpected apparition of two Union officers in full uniform, quietly standing there looking at them, that for two or three minutes they were too much surprised to speak. Some of them began to draw their swords. The men straightened up, and without waiting for orders, came to "attention." All their faces were full of wonderment. They were evidently thinking of what was to follow the strange apparition. Was there a line of battle coming in rear of these two mild looking men in blue, or what on earth were they doing there anyhow? Soon someone on the other side recovered his senses sufficiently to grasp the situation and called out: "Come over here and give up your swords!" No response from the One Hundred and Sixteenth men. They still continued to gaze and wonder how they were to get out of the embarrassing position. Another order from the opposite side of the creek: "Some of you men, there, go over and bring in those two officers!" Still no response. The party of the first and second part both too much bewildered to act. Third order from the party in gray: "Six of you men from the left of Company B, run over there and catch those two fellows!" Just then a movement was observed at the further end of the two large trees that had been felled across the stream as the six men in question quickly ran to cross. Springer and his friend concluded that it was high time for them to either surrender gracefully or run, and they concluded to chance the latter. Quickly turning, they bolted up the steep bank. The Confederates seeing their prey about to escape, called to the men to fire. The bullets whistled after the fleeing officers, who fortunately got away all safe to live and add, in later times, another tale to the camp-fire stories of hair breadth escapes, and how they walked into a Confederate line. Shortly after noon orders were received to withdraw the division to the north bank of the Po. The movement began about two o'clock, but at the very moment that the Union troops began falling back, the enemy (Heath's division of Hill's Corps) advanced with loud yells to attack. Miles's and Smyth's Brigades and the batteries, with the exception of Arnold's, had already commenced retiring when Heath came forward. The assault was of the most determined character, the enemy pressing close up to the Union line. Brooks's and Brown's men met them with a steady and destructive fire, and the combat became fierce and bloody. A furious artillery duel between the batteries on the north bank and the Confederate batteries on the south bank raging the while, the shells from both sides passing completely over the fighting infantry.

The fight had opened on the right of the regimental picket line, but after the skirmishers of Brown and Brooks were driven in the enemy made their appearance in front of the whole regimental line. Word was passed along to hold the ground even against a line of battle, if possible, and the men of each post, sheltering themselves as best they could behind the trees, did their whole duty nobly.

A portion of Brown's Brigade, in falling back, passed through the line of the regiment, and the retreating troops called to the men that the enemy were right behind them. The woods were on fire and the flames were crackling and roaring. The surroundings were appalling. The men knew that every one was getting to the rear, that soon the bridges would be cut away and their only chance of escape gone, but not a man moved from his place. Examining their pieces and standing at a "ready," they calmly waited for the approaching foe and when the Confederates appeared, poured a steady fire into the advancing line. At last, when all others were gone, the welcome order came to fall back and try to save the regiment. It was almost too late. There was only one avenue, one means of escape. The field officers galloping to the extreme right called to the men on the skirmish line to rally on the left at a run. The reserve with the colors fell back to the road and awaited the assembly of the men from the front. Soon nearly all were gathered up and a hasty retreat made across the open ground to the only bridge left. When safe on the other side, saved almost by a miracle, to look back at the flaming forest and think of the thirty members of the regiment who were still among the blazing trees dead or helplessly wounded, a prey to the pitiless fire! After recrossing the river the line was dressed, and as the darkness was gathering a burst of musketry told of more fighting. Although tired, weary and hungry, the regiment to a man promptly responded to the call to go forward once more, and with a cheer that echoed and rolled along the valley, the command swept forward to meet the foe. But the night was at hand, and the fight of the Po closed with the day.

The reason of the withdrawal from the south bank of the Po was not understood by officers or men at the time, but it was afterwards learned that General Meade did not wish to bring on a general engagement on that side of the river, and had ordered the abandoning of the position and directed General Hancock to personally direct the retirement of the troops. It was at the moment that the movement commenced that the Confederates advanced to the attack, and the line was forced to pause and beat back the assault before retiring. The combat, in the language of General Hancock "was close and bloody. The enemy, in vastly superior numbers, flushed with the anticipation of easy victory, appeared determined to crush the small force opposed to them, and pressing forward with loud yells forced their way close up to the Union lines," delivering a terrible musketry fire as they advanced. The brave troops resisted their onset with undaunted resolution! Their fire along the whole line was so continuous and deadly, that the enemy found it impossible to withstand, but broke and retreated in the wildest disorder, leaving the ground in front strewn with dead and wounded.

Arnold's Rhode Island Battery had been pushed far to the front during the fight, and in the retreat, the horses of one of the guns became terrified by the blazing forest and dragged the piece between two trees, where it became so firmly wedged that it could not be moved. Every exertion was made by the artillerymen and some of the infantry to get it away, but finally it had to be abandoned—the first gun ever lost by the Second Corps. The One Hundred and Sixteenth Regiment performed a brilliant part in this fight, on the south side of the Po, and General Francis A. Barlow personally thanked the officers and men for the great service rendered.

Nothing of importance occurred during May 11th. The men of the regiment rested, and many of them wrote letters home. Lieutenant-Colonel Dale finished and mailed to the Pittsburg papers the letter that he had begun on the morning of May 4th, on the battlefield of Chancellorsville. In the letter he speaks of the fight of the Po as a more important battle than that of the Wilderness. So little did the participants know at the time of what was going on around them, each one seeing and knowing of his own immediate front only. Here is his letter. He tells of the dead and wounded, but of the missing—ah, the missing who disappeared in the flaming woods of the Wilderness and the Po! The missing who were never seen or heard of again, what of them?

Colonel Dale's letter:

HEADQUARTERS 116TH REGIMENT, PENNSYLVANIA
VOLUNTEERS.
May 11, 1864.

DEAR CHRONICLE:

I suppose all who have friends in the army are now anxious to get some tidings of them, knowing that active operations have commenced in earnest. As there are three companies from western Pennsylvania in our regiment, I thought I might relieve the anxiety of some of your readers by sending you for publication, a list of our killed and wounded up to this time. It is possible, however, the list may be lengthened before you receive this, as the fighting is apparently not yet over. I write this upon my knee behind breastworks upon which our men are still at work, while in plain view the "rebs" are also entrenching. We left camp at about eleven o'clock on the night of Tuesday, May 3d, crossing the Rapidan the next morning about seven o'clock, and about noon reached the memorable field of Chancellorsville, where we rested until the next morning. Some of us who had been present at the battle there little thought at the time that we would have returned to the field just one year to the day from our retreat in 1863. You may be sure that we took great pleasure in visiting the spots which were so indelibly impressed upon our memory. I gathered a few flowers as mementoes. By the way, the battlefield is covered with wild flowers, nearly all of a purple color, as though the blood of our brave soldiers had so drenched the soil as to darken the very flowers that grew upon it. Perhaps some who have lost friends at Chancellorsville may take pleasure in thinking that though their dead heroes may sleep in unmarked graves, yet the flowers bloom over them as profusely as if interred in any of our beautiful cemeteries at home.

About four o'clock on Thursday afternoon we became engaged with the enemy about four miles from Chancellorsville, the battle continuing until dark. It was during the engagement that General Alex. Hays was killed. His command was to our right. We have had more or less fighting daily, culminating yesterday in a great battle. Our regiment has lost up to yesterday, forty-two in killed and wounded. In addition to these there are a number missing, but as some of these may turn up again, it is unnecessary to create uneasiness among friends by giving names.

The list is enclosed. I would be glad to have it published.

Very respectfully, your obedient servant,

RICHARD C. DALE,
Lieutenant-Colonel, 116th Penna. Volunteers.

CHAPTER X.

SPOTTSYLVANIA.

MAY 12TH.

THERE was a good deal of picket firing during May 11th, and towards evening a chilling rain set in. Tired and hungry the men shivered around the green wood fires, the fires that when wanted most would never, never blaze or brighten. The wind, raw and sharp, whirled the smoke to the side least expected, and changed its direction every time the audience shifted to avoid having their eyes smoked out of their heads. The same old, familiar smoke that blackened the eyes and dirtied the faces, whose pungent smell lingered so long in the clothes, that in fair weather went straight up to the sky and made the camp fire seem even more inviting and cozy, in the wet and rain clung to the ground, spread itself all over the men, seeking out their most vulnerable parts, bringing tears to their eyes, inserting itself into the deepest and most hidden parts of their lungs, choking and blinding, and causing one to consider whether it would not be better to abandon the effort to secure a little warmth and heat at such a cost and fly to the cold and outer darkness. The men succeeded in coaxing enough blaze to boil the evening coffee, but no blowing or other inducement could raise sufficient fire to fry the pork or stew the moistened cracker; so, cold, cheerless and disconsolate, they sank to sleep in the falling rain, wet to the skin, with their soaked feet to the smouldering embers. But the rest was of short duration, for even as the weary souls were gathering their sodden blankets around them, and trying to find soft spots in the mud, Colonel Comstock, of the Headquarter Staff, and several of the Corps Staff were marking out the line of battle for the morrow; and at 9 P. M. the word came to pack up and march immediately. It did not take long to obey the order; each one had only to rise from the earth, shake himself in a vain effort to get rid of the chills that were ever coursing up and down the spine on nights like this, wring the water out of his shoes, lift the cold, heavy musket from the stack, and all was ready. At 10 P. M. the column was put in motion, Major Mendall, of the engineers, leading the way to Spottsylvania, with orders to attack at daylight. Of all the night marches of the regiment this was the most trying. Through dense woods, in black darkness, the rain falling in torrents, dreary, weary, and in silence, the command tramped through the deep mud, slipping and splashing and falling over tree stumps, with once in a while a long halt, while those in the lead made sure of the way. Sometimes an alarm, sudden and unexpected, would wake up the tired soldiers to wonder and to ask each other: "Where are we going, anyway?" An army pack mule, laden with rattling kettles and pans, carried consternation through the ranks by dashing through the trees, and then an accidental musket shot rang out and startled the marching troops. Shortly after midnight the mystery came to an end, and the head of the column arrived opposite the point to be attacked at daylight. In utter darkness and perfect silence the regiment passed the Brown House, moved out towards the enemy, and formed ready for the assault. The regimental formation was "double column on the centre", the division forming in the clearing to the right of the Landron House. The orders were given in whispers and organizations seemed to find their positions by instinct. It was still very dark when the formation of the attacking columns was completed, and an hour intervened before the time came to rush upon the enemy's works, a heavy fog adding to the density of the darkness. To those who stood there in line, cold, sleepy, tired and weary, a long, long wait it seemed to be. Hancock rode quietly to each command and said a few encouraging words in a low tone, telling the officers in turn to speak to the men and urge them to a brilliant effort. Colonel Dale gathered around him the officers of the regiment and spoke to them of the importance of the coming fight, calling upon them to do their duty well. His last sentence, "Strike for your God and country", were the last words that many ever heard from his lips. He then moved around among the waiting line, speaking words of hope and cheer, and just a few moments before the final move, he stood among a group of officers and spoke, not only of the coming day, but the long eternity that might follow for some who then were full of life. "Gentlemen", said he, "to-day may be for some of us the last on earth. Whilst we are waiting here would it not be well to say a prayer?" Noble soldier that he was, saintly and pure in camp and bivouac, gentle as a lady, setting an example of perfect manhood that influenced the command to the very end. In battle he was a hero of the most exalted type, whose brilliant leadership nerved his men to deeds of fearless daring. The order to move on the salient point at Spottsylvania named four o'clock, but it was dark at that hour and a heavy fog hung over the fields. Hancock, therefore, postponed the time of attack until 4.35, when, day breaking and the mist lifting a little, it became sufficiently light to see dimly. The men were ordered to draw their loads and to use the bayonet only. The division (Barlow's) was formed into two lines, Brooks's and Miles's Brigades in the first, and Smyth's and Brown's in the second. The nature of the ground over which the attacking column was to pass was altogether unknown to every one. General Mott with his division had made an attack on the same spot two days before, but he could give little information as to the twelve hundred yards to be passed over before reaching the works of the enemy. Amid whispered inquiries by the officers as to the work before them and a nervous uncertainty as to what was coming, the order to advance was quietly passed along the line. Without a word louder than an audible whisper of command, the two divisions of the Second Corps, Barlow's and Birney's, moved forward in dead silence. As it was not as yet light enough to see distinctly, the intervals between regiments and brigades were soon lost. Barlow's division having the clear ground to the right of the Landron House to march over, kept somewhat ahead of Gibbons's, but that command, making superhuman exertions, gained the enemy's works almost at the same moment as the former. Not a sound disturbed the moving line. Instinctively every man knew the importance of covering as much ground as possible before being discovered, and not until nearing the Landron House was the advancing force discovered. Then a volley from the Confederate picket reserve was poured into the left of Barlow's line, killing Lieutenant-Colonel David L. Striker, of the Second Delaware, a brave, amiable and most accomplished young officer. No return was made to the fire, but silently pushing on in the gray light of the morning the men caught sight of the red earth of the works, and, with a wild cheer that broke the stillness, they rushed up the sloping ground and in a moment were tearing away at the Abattis, tugging, pulling and dragging the detached branches aside, crawling through and tumbling over the mass of material that was piled in front of the breastworks. The momentary work enabled the brigades of the second line to come up and mingle with those that were in front. All line and formation was now lost, and the great mass of men, with a rush like a cyclone, sprang upon the entrenchments and swarmed over, beating down the defenses and using the bayonet very freely. The surprise was complete. While large numbers of Confederates had already mounted the works and made a brave defense, many of them were still sound asleep, rolled in their blankets and dreaming. A few erected tents were scattered here and there, and in the dim light the inmates crawled out to discover the cause of the noise, to find themselves prisoners. Amid the wild confusion of the glorious success, it was difficult to preserve order. Men became insane with the excitement of victory. Thirty stands of colors, eighteen guns, two general officers and four thousand prisoners captured by two divisions of the Second Corps, and not yet broad day light. While organizations were mixed, and for a short time order was impossible, still the fight went on, the enemy making a most gallant resistance. In squads and singly, every man seemed acting on his own responsibility—the Confederates making a brave effort to stem the tide of Union victory, and the men making the most heroic exertions to make their triumph complete. The men of the One Hundred and Sixteenth were among the first over the works, and the colors of the regiment were in advance. Personal encounters between individuals took place on every part of the disputed ground. Lieutenant Fraley, of Company F, ran a Confederate color-bearer through with his sword; a Confederate shot one of the men when almost within touch of his musket, then threw down his piece and called out, "I surrender", but Dan Crawford, of Company K, shot him dead; Billy Hager, of the same company, ran into a group of half-a-dozen and demanded their surrender, saying, "Throw down your arms, quick now, or I'll stick my bayonet into you", and they obeyed. Henry J. Bell, known as "Blinkey Bell", leaped over the works and yelled, "Look out, throw down your arms, we run this machine now". A large number of the men of the regiment ran forward and took possession of a battery of brass pieces, and turning them around, got ready to open on any force that might appear. Alf. Bales, of Company K, hitched a rope to one of the pieces, and a dozen of the men ran it to the rear. Captain Schoales with a lot of Company E men, ran off with another. The horses of the battery were not visible, but the harness was hanging on the wheels, and everything indicated that the gunners had but a moment before abandoned the guns, or had not time to man them after the first alarm. The prisoners were quickly formed into squads and sent to the rear. Some of them took things very coolly. One big Confederate crawled out from under a tent fly, and when called upon to surrender, stretched himself with great nonchalance and said: "Oh, well, that is all right boys; don't get so excited. Just let us get our coats on, and we will go to the rear." Many trophies were gathered in. Dick McClean, of Company K, relieved General Johnston of his sword, and Dan Sickles, of the same company, captured a regimental flag. Colonel Dale seemed omnipresent, and was everywhere at once, bringing back order and preparing for a further advance, calling the men from the captured batteries and reforming the broken line; then, still crazed with excitement, the line pressing forward through the woods with such men as the division commanders could get together, but still somewhat disorganized and in mass. They were met in front of the McCool House by Johnston's Brigade, of Gordon's division, that had been placed there the evening before. The men, disorganized as they were, made such an impetuous attack on Johnston's men that they broke and fell back through the forest, closely pursued by the victorious troops. That splendid Southern soldier, John B. Gordon, quickly formed the two brigades of Evans and Pegram behind the second line of works, which in anticipation of, and to meet just such an emergency as the present, he had constructed across the salient. The Union men reached this second line and found the front covered by a heavy abattis. They were met by a heavy fire from the two brigades already in line and Johnston's men who had fallen back to this point. The men rushed at the entrenchments with the intention of crossing, the officers vieing with each other in deeds of great personal bravery, but the line of fresh troops, pouring in an extremely heavy fire, threw them back. Already in confusion, the mass of men, many organizations mingled together, and all the commands more or less separated, began to fall back, and then Gordon's line, advancing, struck vigorously and charged with loud cries and cheers. The members of the One Hundred and Sixteenth made a good fight, and were among the last to give ground. Colonel Dale, sword in hand, was ever in the front; and when the retreat began, he lingered behind, with his face to the foe, waving his sword and calling to the men to stand firm. Those of the regiment who saw his heroic efforts, pressed forward to gather round him. Suddenly his sword was seen to drop, his voice ceased and he sank to the earth. At the moment of his falling, the confusion was very great; the Confederates were pressing forward, and the men were giving way. Some men of Company K, who saw him fall, tried to reach him, but were pushed back by the surging mass of fighting, struggling men; the Confederate line swept over his body, and none of his friends or comrades ever saw him again. As the men of Barlow's Division, which had advanced into the angle further than any other troops, began to give ground before the onslaughts of Gordon's Division, the Confederate Brigades of Daniel, Ramseur, Perrin and Harris moved against the Divisions of Birney and Mott that were advancing along the west side of the angle. The troops fell back reluctantly. They did not like to give up the important advantage that they had gained. The Confederate Army was literally cut in two by the early morning rush of the Second Corps, and now to be driven from the position and surrender the ground so nobly won, was too serious to be thought of. Bravely the men fought, but without avail. The momentum of the charge, and the very perfectness of the victory, had destroyed all organization, and Barlow's men were without order or battle formation. It was just as important to the enemy that the angle be retaken and the victors driven out; and the Confederate officers and men rose to the full importance of the occasion. General Lee was in the very front himself, and at one time became so carried away with the intense excitement, that he placed himself in front of one of Gordon's Brigades, and, with hat in hand, was leading the charging line as it swept forward through the woods. The men, recognizing the Commander of their army, burst into prolonged cheers, but refused to allow their leader to expose his life; they calmly, but firmly, requested him to stop, and taking hold of his horse's bridle, forced him to turn back. The men fell back before the vigorous blows of the enemy, leaving behind many of their comrades who fell at every step; finally all were forced out, and took position on the outer face of the angle. Just as the troops were forced out of the salient, the Sixth Corps came to the front and took position on the right of the Second Corps. The men of Barlow's Division were still mixed up to a great extent when they re-crossed the works that they had captured but an hour before. The men of the One Hundred and Sixteenth were scattered in groups along the works, and when, at this point, the all-day fight began, they fought assembled in squads, whenever an officer was found to command them. No sooner were the men over the works than the furious attacks of the Confederates commenced—the assaults that were destined to continue all day and late into the night, and make May 12th the bloodiest day of all the war. Along a mile of the captured entrenchments, the fight went on until midnight. No language can describe this hand to hand fight. The drenching, chilling rain that fell during the day had no effect on the incessant fire. The lines were close together, nothing between them but the log revetment, to which the men were trying to cling, and the enemy endeavoring to shake them off. Men fired into each others faces, were shot through the crevices of the logs, bayoneted over the top of the works. In their wild enthusiasm men would leap up on the works and fire down upon the enemy standing there, while freshly loaded muskets were handed to them, keeping up a continuous fire until they in turn were shot down. The dead and the dying were in piles on both sides of the works, and several times during the day the dead had to be tossed out of the trenches that the living might have a chance to stand. Hancock ran a battery close to the works, and, throwing shells and canister over the heads of the Union troops, swept the ground. The trees were torn in splinters, and one great tree, measuring twenty-two inches in diameter, was cut down entire and fell with a crash, injuring some of the men of McGowan's Brigade. Owing to the all day continuous battle, it was impossible to re-form or get together the members of the One Hundred and Sixteenth, scattered in the charge of the early morning. They fought through the long day with the troops with which they found themselves when they were driven back over the works. Colonel Mulholland was absent, wounded, Colonel Dale was gone, and Major Teed being in a Southern prison, the command of the regiment devolved upon Captain Garrett Nowlen; and when midnight brought the fighting to a close, and the Confederates finally gave up the struggle and fell back, leaving the bloody ground in possession of the Union troops, it became possible to get the command assembled. At daylight on May 13th, Captain Nowlen succeeded in getting the companies and men together, and calling the roll, learned the fate of many a brave and noble soul who would never answer to his name again. The long, bloody day of May 12th did not end until midnight, when the exhausted troops of both armies sank on the wet ground to sleep among the dead and dying, the chilling rain falling on friend and foe alike. After nightfall, heavy details were made for picket, and during the next day the fighting on the skirmish line was quite severe, during which Lieutenant Yocum greatly distinguished himself in leading a charge and forcing the enemy to fall back. Yocum had

LIEUTENANT-COLONEL RICHARD C. DALE.
Killed at Spottsylvania, May 12th, 1864.

gathered up half a dozen Confederate officers' swords during the fight, and selecting the most valuable, gave the others away. It was not known for sometime afterward whether Colonel Dale had been killed or only wounded and a prisoner. He had been seen to fall, but beyond that nothing was certain. Within a few days after the battle, the Government made every effort to learn something of him, even sending a company of cavalry to visit the field and farm houses in the vicinity, thinking that he might be among the wounded and somewhere near the field. Weeks passed away, but nothing definite could be learned until the autumn, when Lieutenant Zadock Springer, of Company K, having been taken prisoner at the battle of Ream's Station, August 25th, and going south on the cars, saw the Lieutenant of a Georgia regiment, who had charge of the party, wearing Colonel Dale's cap and sword. Springer recognized the articles, and was told by the officer that he had taken them from the body of a Union officer who had been killed at Spottsylvania. This Confederate officer's account of Colonel Dale's death coincided exactly with what was known of his fall; he said that he fell while waving his sword and rallying his men, and that he fell by the second line of works. This was the first positive information as to the fate of one of the noblest of men, a man of splendid abilities, virtuous, gentle, brave and accomplished, whose frank and agreeable face and courteous bearing ever cheered his comrades in camp, march and bivouac, and whose bright eye and clear, ringing voice nerved them in battle, a Christian gentleman by instinct and a soldier without a superior. The following biographical sketch is from "Martial Deeds of Pennsylvania":

"Richard Colegate Dale, Lieutenant-Colonel of the One Hundred and Sixteenth Regiment, was born on the 19th of December, 1838, in the city of Allegheny. His father, Thomas F. Dale, M. D., and his mother, Margaret Kennedy Stewart, were both natives of Delaware. He received a thorough English and a partial classical education in his native city. He was, from early youth, characterized by strong individuality. He was engaged for a time as a clerk in commission and manufacturing houses, but finally became an active partner in a mercantile firm. When the war came, he frankly said to his father: 'Mr. Lincoln has called for men. Many, on account of family or other relations, cannot go as well as I. Do not think it is a fit of enthusiasm. I do not imagine it will be any pleasure to be a soldier. His is a life of trial and peril, and I do not know whether my constitution will be strong enough to bear those toils and exposures; but I think it my duty to go.' An only son and carefully reared, it was with great reluctance that the consent of his parents was given to his resolution; but he would listen to no temporizing, and he enlisted as a private in Company A of the Ninth Reserves, in the spring of 1861. In the following August he was detailed from his regiment to serve in the United States Signal Corps. In a School of Instruction for that arm of the service, at Tenalytown, and afterwards as clerk to Major Myers, the commander of the corps in Washington, he was employed till the opening of the spring campaign under McClellan, with whom he went to the Peninsula, and served with fidelity and skill until the final battle at Malvern Hill had been fought. He then received leave of absence for ten days; but in Washington, while on his way home, his furlough was extended by the Adjutant-General, and he was authorized to raise a company for signal duty. He opened a recruiting station at Pittsburg, on his arrival, but having been elected First Lieutenant of Company D, of the One Hundred and Twenty-third Regiment, he accepted the position, and at once entered upon his duties. For four months he served as Adjutant of the regiment, exerting himself to bring the organization up to an efficient standard, when he returned to his place in his company. At the battle of Fredericksburg, he acted with great gallantry, taking command of his company when its leader, Captain Boisol, was wounded, and had his haversack riddled with bullets, though he himself escaped without injury. He was soon afterwards appointed Assistant Adjutant-General of the brigade. A vacancy occurring in the office of Lieutenant-Colonel, he was promptly elected to fill it by the line officers, though the junior Captain among them. So methodical and complete were all his acts, that when notified of his promotion, he was in readiness to turn over his business at the head of the brigade in a finished condition, and at once to assume the responsible one in command of the regiment. He was engaged at Chancellorsville, and when the term of the regiment had expired, which occurred soon afterwards, he returned with it to Pittsburg, where it was mustered out.

"When he heard the intelligence of fighting at Gettysburg, he hastened home, exclaiming, 'Our boys are fighting and falling at Gettysburg, and I am here doing nothing. I cannot stand this!' Gathering up a few articles of clothing, he hurried away to the depot, and reached Harrisburg that night. He immediately reported to the Governor, and asked to be sent to the front, saying: 'I must go. I can at least volunteer as aid to some General, to carry dispatches over the field'. But the Governor could not provide transportation. Indeed, all the avenues were closed—even a private carriage could not be secured, the inhabitants fearing the action of the enemy's cavalry, and refusing every offer, unless bonds were entered for the safe return of the conveyance. Finding it impossible to reach the field, he was obliged, reluctantly, to return home.

"Soon afterwards, General Brooks, at the head of the Department of the Monongahela, offered him the command of a battalion of six months' cavalry. 'I was drilled in cavalry movements when in the signal service', was his response, 'and I shall be glad to serve in any capacity to which you may assign me'. The companies were already recruited and in camp, and fears were entertained that officers who were expecting the command, much older than himself, would object to having a boy set over them. The very troubles arose which were anticipated; but so firmly and judiciously did he suppress the first rising of revolt, and so wisely and well did he enforce his discipline and drill, and instruct his charge, that a large part of the men were desirous of being led by him for a three years' term. He was stationed in Fayette county, and was charged with guarding the border, a duty which he performed to the satisfaction of General Brooks, and, what was more difficult, to the entire approval of the inhabitants among whom he was quartered.

In January, 1864, while General Hancock was engaged in reorganizing the Second Corps, which became famous under his leadership, Dale was offered the position of Lieutenant-Colonel in the One Hundred and Sixteenth Regiment, which was accepted, and he was immediately engaged in recruiting, it having been decimated in previous campaigns while still a part of the celebrated Irish Brigade. In the battle of the Wilderness, where his command was closely engaged, a bullet penetrated his coat, but he escaped. On the 9th of May, his regiment was ordered to the picket line to support General Miles's Brigade, and was under a hot fire of rebel grape and canister. On the following day it was again engaged in a long, hard fight, in which Colonel Mulholland was severely wounded in the head. The command then devolved on Lieutenant-Colonel Dale, and in the assault upon the enemy's works, at the dawn of the 12th, while gallantly leading his regiment into the 'imminent deadly breach', he fell instantly killed or mortally wounded, as is supposed, no tidings having ever been had of him, and no information pertaining to his last resting-place been discovered. When a sufficient time had elapsed to preclude all hope of return, resolutions were passed by his brother officers commemorative of his great ability as a soldier and his many virtues as a man. The colonel of his regiment said of him: 'He

was a man of splendid abilities, virtuous, gentle, brave and
accomplished. He was remarkably calm in battle, and was
very much beloved by his comrades'. His two sisters, who
survive him, say, in closing a communication concerning
him, ' No sisters ever had a more devoted brother ' ".

Lieutenant Henry Keil, of Company E, was killed
during the fight. He was a brave young officer, not more
than eighteen years of age. He joined the regiment as
first sergeant of his company only three months before his
death. He had not yet been mustered in as an officer, and
his commission remained in the adjutant's desk for several
months after Spottsylvania. It was not known at the
time that he was killed, and he was reported " missing ",
but it was afterwards learned that he fell in the battle.

Lieutenants Samuel G. Vanderheyden, of Company G,
and Robert J. Alston, of Company H, were both severely
wounded. The wounds of many of the men were of a
very unusual character. Edward Savage, of Company K,
had both eyes destroyed by the windage of a passing shell.
He was lead from the field, but died in a few hours from
the shock and concussion. A Union officer had both eyes
shot out, the ball passing just back of the eyeballs. He
stood blind and helpless, never uttering a word of complaint, but opening and closing the sightless sockets, the
blood leaping out in spurts. Numbers of men were killed
and wounded by the bayonet, more, perhaps, than in any
other fight of the war ; and facilities for handling the
immense numbers of wounded seemed more inadequate
than usual. Thousands swarmed around the temporary
hospitals, and the woods and the roads in the rear of the
line were filled with stricken men, wandering around in
the drenching rain, seeking assistance. Some few
members of the One Hundred and Sixteenth were sent
back to Army Headquarters with the prisoners ; and they
reported that, during the morning, the four thousand
Confederates had arranged to make a break for liberty, and
to try a rush for their lives. But General Patrick, Provost

Marshal, had defeated and checked the effort. General Johnston and General Stewart were taken at once to the Army Headquarters, and were received with every courtesy and consideration. They were deeply interested, and Johnston eyed General Grant with great curiosity. The meeting was cordial and, on the part of the Union officers, very pleasant.

On the morning of the 13th it was found that the enemy had abandoned the salient and retired to entrenchments, entirely cutting off that portion of their line, leaving great piles of dead and many wounded on the ground on which they had made such a ferocious fight during the preceding day. The picket details from the regiment that had been on duty all the night of the 12th and until four o'clock on the afternoon of the 13th were relieved at that hour, and returned to the regiment exhausted and worn out: They had been under fire continually for thirty-six hours, without food or rest. Lieutenant Yocum received unbounded praise for his action on the skirmish line.

The losses in the regiment during the battle of May 12th could never be actually ascertained. Numbers that were reported missing were afterwards found to have been killed. The total loss of the Union Army on May 12th was: Killed and wounded, 6,020; missing, 800; total, 6,820. The Confederate loss, including the 4,000 prisoners captured by General Hancock and his Second Corps, was between 9,000 and 10,000. The loss to the enemy in general officers was extremely heavy—Brigadier-Generals Daniel and Perrin being killed, and Brigadier-Generals Walker, Ramseur, R. D. Johnston and McGowan severely wounded; and Major-General Edward Johnston and Brigadier-General George H. Stewart captured.

May 14th, under arms at daybreak, but the command was not called upon, and a most welcome rest until 4 A. M., May 15th, when the regiment moved two miles to the left and bivouaced on the Fredericksburg road, resting as best they could, the rain still falling at intervals, and the roads so heavy that it was impossible to move trains or artillery. During the afternoon an order from General Meade was read to the regiment:

HEADQUARTERS ARMY OF THE POTOMAC.
May 13th.

Soldiers: The moment has arrived when your commanding General feels authorized to address you in terms of congratulation.

For eight days and nights, almost without intermission, in rain and sunshine, you have been gallantly fighting a desperate foe, in positions naturally strong and rendered doubly so by entrenchments.

You have compelled him to abandon his fortifications on the Rapidan, to retire and attempt to stop your onward progress, and now he has abandoned his last entrenched position, so tenaciously held, suffering a loss in all of eighteen guns, twenty-two colors and 8,000 prisoners, including two general officers.

Your heroic deeds and noble endurance and privations will ever be memorable. Let us return thanks to God for the mercy thus shown us, and ask earnestly for its continuation.

Soldiers, your work is not yet over. The enemy must be pursued, and if possible, overcome. The courage and fortitude you have displayed, renders your commanding General confident your future efforts will result in success.

While we mourn the loss of many gallant comrades, let us remember that the enemy must have suffered equal, if not greater, losses.

We shall soon receive reinforcement which he cannot expect. Let us determine to continue vigorously the work so well begun, and under God's blessing in short time the object of our labors will be accomplished.

GEORGE G. MEADE,
Commanding-General.

Official—A. Williams, A. A. G.

(Approved.)
U. S. GRANT,
Lieutenant-General Commanding.

Remained on the reserve until the 17th. On the evening of that day, General Thomas Smyth, commanding the brigade, inspected the regiment, and Captain Schoales and Lieutenant Robert J. Grogan, both of Company E, tendered their resignations, which were accepted.

THE BATTLE OF SPOTTSYLVANIA COURT-HOUSE.

MAY 18TH.

During the night the division was moved to the vicinity of the Landron House, and formed for the attack in the line of brigades. It was hoped that by an early attack the enemy might be surprised and his left flank turned. At dawn a general advance was made, but, early as it was, the enemy were found to be wide awake and fully prepared. They were strongly posted in the rifle pits. The ground over which the regiment charged was very rough and broken, and it was with much difficulty that the regimental line was preserved. The command moved forward, however, in excellent order, and held the right flank of the Irish Brigade. No sooner had the charge begun than the movement was discovered by the Confederates, who opened with a musketry fire, in which their batteries quickly joined, throwing shell and canister. It was a hot fire, but failed to break or retard the advancing Union line. Pressing forward and reaching the works to be assaulted, the men were confronted by a deep and heavy abattis that completely covered the Confederate line, the slashing being so dense that all efforts to penetrate were impossible. The Irish Brigade undoubtedly came nearer to getting through than any other, many of the men throwing themselves forward into the tangled wood and branches in their efforts to reach the works. One sergeant of the One Hundred and Sixteenth penetrated the mass for eight or ten feet beyond any of his comrades, and stood there, waist-deep in the abattis, while he loaded and fired three or four times.

SPOTTSYLVANIA—One year after the Battle.

(From a photograph taken at that time.)

Many of the men of the regiment were shot after they became entangled in the brush. The charge was a very noble effort, but absolutely hopeless. The impracticability of reaching the enemy's line, or even piercing the abattis, was soon apparent, and the order to fall back was given, but not a moment too soon. To hold the men in front of the abattis to be shot down would be a useless waste of life. They fell back in excellent order, and, under the circumstances, behaved with wonderful steadiness. Every battle furnishes incidents and strange sights to be talked over by the survivors. Corporals Dick McClean and Daniel J. Crawford, of Company K, were chatting together just as the charge was ordered. "Do you see the Reb works"? said Crawford; "well, I will be killed just as I reach there." And he was. He fell shot through the head as he came to the abattis. McClean lost his arm a moment later at the same spot. As the regiment was falling back, a man of Company G, Franz Poffenberger, received, perhaps, the most awful injury ever received by any man in the command, and still breathed. A solid shot or large piece of shell struck him in the body, literally tearing him to atoms, breaking the large bones and driving them through the flesh. He fell near the colors, and, notwithstanding the fearful injuries received, lived, seemingly sensible, for half an hour. No matter how terrible the surroundings in a fight, there seemed to be a ludicrous incident sure to pop up and cause a smile. One of these was when Robert Glendenning, of Company K, had his wig carried away by a passing shell, and the boys thought his head was gone, but he turned up all right, though very bald. It was a beautiful spring morning when the fight of May 18th took place. The rain had ceased and all nature seemed refreshed; but on the ground occupied and fought over by the regiment on this morning, nothing of charm or beauty was visible. The dead of the 12th were there unburied, and the scene was one of horror, beyond the power of language to describe. The sight was hideous, the stench overpowering and sickening. No sooner was the fight over than almost the entire regiment was ordered out to the picket line, remaining there during all the day and night, and getting a fearful dose of the offensive surroundings. The skirmish line ran over the part of the battlefield where the decaying dead were most numerous. During the day the pioneers did all in their power to cover up the ghastly sight, by digging up the earth and throwing it over the bodies; graves were a luxury not to be thought of. Darkness settled over the scene long before a tithe of the dead could be hidden from view, and the night was passed with the living and the dead mingled together. The men of both armies were so totally exhausted that many slept standing at their posts, and the officers were forced to keep moving along the line during the entire night to keep the men awake. Lieutenant Cosslett and a sergeant, while making the rounds, lost their way in the darkness, and wandered among the pickets of the enemy, whom they found all fast asleep, and hence got back to their own line in safety. Captain Frank R. Lieb, of Company G, was in command of the brigade picket, and received great praise for the tour of duty. It was a night of horror and hardship that will never be forgotten by the members of the One Hundred and Sixteenth. After daylight on the 19th, Captain Lieb was ordered to withdraw the pickets, the corps having moved to the left. He found great difficulty in getting them away, but succeeded in forming and falling back to a wood, pressed by a force of Confederate cavalry that had suddenly appeared. When the captain reached the shelter of the timber, he fully expected to be captured with all his force, but, fortunately, and much to his surprise, he found, just emerging from the forest, a force of Union cavalry, who charged forward and struck the Confederate force in the open. Lieb and his men had the privilege and pleasure of witnessing one of the prettiest and most spirited hand to hand cavalry fights imaginable. It was of short duration, however, the Union men forcing the Confederates back, and allowing the pickets to withdraw. While falling back, one of the men of Company G had his leg cut off by a shell, and Lieb and the men put him in a blanket and carried him for nearly two miles, but were finally forced to leave the poor fellow to die on the roadside. During the night of the 18th, the Second Corps moved to the vicinity of Anderson's Mills, on the Nye River.

The glorious fight made by Captain Frank R. Lieb, on May 18th, calls for more than a passing notice. The brave fight that he made on the skirmish line was witnessed by thousands, and General Hancock personally thanked him, bringing blushes to his cheeks that were almost as red as the blood that was streaming down his face at the moment. No time was lost in acknowledging the gallantry of the captain, and the following was issued a few days after the event:

HEADQUARTERS SECOND BRIGADE, FIRST DIVISION,
SECOND CORPS.

(Orders) June 1st, 1864.

The following is an extract from a communication just received from Headquarters First Division:

"The Brigadier-General commanding division desires that Captain F. R. Lieb, One Hundred and Sixteenth Pennsylvania Volunteers, and Lieutenant Lynch, Company A, Sixty-ninth New York Volunteers, be in some way commended for their gallantry while on duty on the picket line lately.

It is with great satisfaction that the Colonel commanding the brigade communicates the above to the command, and he hopes that for the creditable manner in which those officers have conducted themselves, they may be duly rewarded whenever an occasion may present itself.

By order of COLONEL R. BYRNES,
Commanding Brigade.

(Signed) P. N. BLACK,
Lieutenant and A. A. A. G.

The above bore the following indorsements:

"This is a case worthy of attention. Captain Lieb's recommendations are such that I have no hesitation in endorsing them, and recommend a favorable result to his application. Respectfully forwarded,

WINFIELD S. HANCOCK,
Major-General, U. S. A.

"The within order complimentary to Captain F. R. Lieb, late of the One Hundred and Sixteenth Pennsylvania Volunteers, is heartily endorsed."

U. S. GRANT.

In addition to this the Captain was raised to the rank of Major, by brevet, and all the honors were well deserved, by one of the most unassuming, gentlest and bravest of men. Captain Lieb was not the only one distinguished for bravery on the 18th. Sergeant Alex. Chisholm and private Alfred Bails did a very noble act in rescuing a wounded comrade, 'though of another regiment and corps. After the fight, and when the command had fallen back behind the breast-works, a wounded soldier was seen lying out between the lines among the dead. He was fearfully wounded, and his limbs were crushed. Lieutenant Cope called for some one to volunteer and go out with him to bring the poor fellow in. Chisholm and Bails grabbed up a blanket, jumped over the revetment, ran out to where the man was lying, rolled him over into the blanket and succeeded in getting him in. Fortunately, neither of them were hit, but it was a close call, as the balls whistled wickedly around them; most likely, however, the Confederates fired a little wild, and were not over anxious to kill, like our own men, they admired bravery, and were more than willing to give a gallant soul a chance for life.

The 19th was a quiet day of perfect stillness until about 4 o'clock in the afternoon, when a burst of firing on the right told of a Confederate attack. The assault proved to be an attack by General Ewell, who had struck the right

of the Second Corps on the Fredericksburg road, at that
time the line of supply. The regiment was promptly
under arms, but the attack was beaten off without the One
Hundred and Sixteenth being called out of bivouac.
This attack of Ewell was the reason of the regiment
getting a good night's rest, for had it not taken place, the
command would have marched at midnight, or shortly
after that hour, as the following order had already been
received at Corps Headquarters:

> HEADQUARTERS ARMY OF THE POTOMAC.
> May 19th, 1864, 1.30 P. M.
>
> MAJOR-GENERAL HANCOCK,
> Commanding Second Corps.
>
> The Major-General commanding directs that you move
> with your corps to-morrow, at 2 A. M., to Bowling Green
> and Milford Station, *via*, Guinea Station, and take position
> on the right bank of the Mattapony, if practicable. Should
> you encounter the enemy, you will attack him vigorously,
> and report immediately to these headquarters, which you
> will keep advised of your progress, from time to time.
> Brigadier-General Torbert, with a cavalry force and a
> battery of horse artillery, is ordered to report to you for
> duty. An engineer officer and guide will be sent to you.
> Canvas pontoons will likewise be put at your disposal.
>
> A. A. HUMPHREYS,
> Major-General, Chief of Staff.

On the 20th, General Thomas A. Smyth, who had
commanded the Irish Brigade during the spring campaign up to this date, was assigned to a brigade in the
Second Division. He was succeeded by the senior officer
of the brigade, Colonel Richard Byrne, of the Twenty-
eighth Massachusetts. The departure of General Smyth
was deeply regretted by every one. He was a very handsome man, of commanding appearance, winning and
lovable, a noble soldier of great talent. He had been a

soldier from early youth, having participated in an ill-fated expedition to Central America in 1854, where he saw some hard service. He had entered the field in the very beginning of the war, and rose rapidly to command of the First Regiment, Delaware Infantry. He was mortally wounded at Farmville, Va., a day or two before the surrender of the Confederate Army, and lived until the next morning. General Grant called at the farm house where he was dying and told him of the triumph of the Union cause. He breathed his last a few moments afterwards, cheered by the knowledge that his life was not given in vain. He was, perhaps, the last officer killed in the war; certainly the last general officer. He is buried at Wilmington, Del., on the banks of the historic Brandywine.

Instead of marching at 2 A. M., on the morning of the 20th, the troops remained in bivouac until 10 P. M. of that day, and then marched all night, the men in excellent spirits, having recovered from the fatigue of the 18th by the twenty-four hours' rest; crossed the Fredericksburg and Richmond Railroad, and at daybreak on the morning of the 21st, reached Guinea Station. Here the Union cavalry met and drove in the videttes of the enemy; and after a slight halt on the road, pushed on and reached Bowling Green at 10 o'clock, and Milford Station at about noon. Colonel Mulholland, who was wounded on May 10th, rejoined the regiment on this day.

Here the cavalry under General Torbert had a lively fight with the enemy's infantry that he found entrenched on the north bank of the Mattapony. By a most brilliant dash Torbert captured the rifle pits, taking sixty prisoners of Kemper's Brigade, driving the balance across the river and saving the bridge. Barlow's and Gibbons's divisions crossed the stream promptly. The men of the regiment wading through the water, pushed on for a mile and began entrenching on the high lands on the south bank.

The firing sounded heavy as the enemy retired, but the regiment lost none. Worked on the entrenchments until quite dark and resumed digging early on the morning of the 22d. The day was warm and the work trying. Captain Nowlen, overcome by the heat, fainted in the trenches but refused to go to the rear even for an hour. The works were completed by noon and then a grateful rest, but not without anxiety on the part of all.

The Second Corps occupied a position on the extreme left flank of the whole army, far from supports and no one knew the moment that it might be called upon to meet the attack of a much larger force. However, when the entrenchments were finished, all rested easy, as the works were of the strongest character and were viewed by the officers of the other corps with astonishment and admiration. One could hardly believe that men could construct works of so powerful a nature in so short a time.

May 23d, roll call at day-break, and marched at 9 A. M. as rear guard of the Second Corps. Arrived at the North Anna River near Chesterfield in the afternoon and found the cavalry engaged in trying to drive the enemy across and capture the bridge. The Union artillery formed on the high lands of the north bank and opened fire on the enemy's infantry that could be seen forming on the opposite bank. In the evening the troops charged across the fields and drove the enemy from a small redoubt that covered the bridge, capturing the works, some few prisoners and saving the bridge that the retiring troops endeavored to burn.

The fighting had been severe and the cannonading heavy, but with but slight loss in the regiment during the afternoon. Rested on arms all night and crossed the river early on the 24th on a pontoon bridge that had been laid by the engineers. The firing and fighting was severe during the whole day and the position the regiment had was a very trying one, supposed to be on reserve yet so close to the line of battle that the men were exposed and for a large part of the day were under fire.

The wounded were carried past in great numbers and many of the wounds were of the most ghastly description. Everyone would rather have been in the front line where they could have been firing and join in the excitement of the fray rather than be waiting during the long day under fire and witnessing the depressing scenes in the rear.

The regiment was very fortunate, however, in losing but few men in the fight of the North Anna. The fight continued all day of the 24th and late into the night and was renewed early on the morning of the 25th, lasting all day. The artillery fire was incessant and heavy, but the position occupied by the One Hundred and Sixteenth was sheltered and the fire passed over, the shells exploding far in the rear and hence the loss was light.

May 26th, roll call at 4 P. M. A morning of exciting rumors, and at eight o'clock the regiment was detailed to destroy the tracks of the Fredericksburg and Richmond Railroad near Milford Station. Crossed to the north bank of the river and soon got to work ripping up the track and destroying the rails. Immense fires were made with the ties over which the iron rails were laid and, when red hot, were bent out of shape. A good day's work was done, everyone turning in with a will and enjoying the novelty of the employment.

During the afternoon some of the enemy's cavalry succeeded in getting around in the rear of the Union Army and amused themselves by firing at a very long range at the members of the regiment who were at work. A squadron of cavalry went after them, charged the distant wood that sheltered them and drove them away. After night-fall returned to the brigade, drew rations, returned to the north bank of the river and rested until morning.

May 27th, marched at 10 A. M. A long and trying day, dusty roads, heat oppressive and water scarce, but men cheerful and all filled with hope that soon a great victory would reward the labor and suffering. Passed en route

Concord Church and camped at 10 P. M., within three miles of the Pamunky River.

May 28th, roll call at day-break, marched at 6 A. M. and reached the banks of the river. Crossed at noon at Huntley's, about four miles above Hanovertown, advanced some distance and formed line of battle between the river and Haw's Shop, stacked arms and started vigorously to work digging rifle pits and getting under cover.

Heavy and continuous firing heard in the front, where Sheridan and his cavalry were having a severe fight with the enemy's cavalry reinforced with some of their infantry. Night came and we learned that Sheridan had driven the enemy towards Richmond.

May 29th, completed the rifle pits and at 11 A. M. resumed the march to the front and towards the Totopotomy. The enemy reported close at hand and everyone expected a general engagement. The march was slow, the Irish Brigade and Barlow's Division in the advance, and, after reaching Haw's Shop, saw the evidence of the cavalry fight on the previous day. Dead men and horses were lying in the roads and fields everywhere. The trees were torn by the shells, fences levelled and farm houses and barns filled with wounded.

Barlow's Division met with no opposition until the column arrived at the junction of the Cold Harbor and Hanover Court House roads, when some cavalry disputed the way, but were quickly driven back. On the Totopotomy the enemy were found in force, strongly entrenched, and line of battle was formed. Birney's and Gibbons's Divisions of the Second Corps coming up and forming on Barlow's right and left. The corps' artillery went into position along the ridge, and the prospects were that a great battle was close at hand. Colonel Mulholland was detailed as corps officer of the day, and put in command of the picket line.

May 30th, heavy artillery duel nearly all day, but towards evening the Union guns succeeded in silencing those of the enemy. A delightful summer day, with charges on the enemy's works at intervals. General Brooke with his brigade carried the Confederate rifle-pits in a dashing fight.

May 31st, the battle was continued. Early in the day General Hancock, with the Second Corps, resumed his efforts to force the crossing of the river. The whole corps' line of battle was forced close up to that of the enemy at all points, but the position was found too strong to carry.

The skirmishing and fighting on the picket line was heavy and incessant, and amounted almost to a battle. Colonel Mulholland, in command of the line, was shot through the body, and many men of the regiment, who were on the line, were killed and wounded.

Lieutenant Yocum, with a detail of the command, gained new laurels by charging and capturing a part of the Confederate line, but lost nearly all his men. Two balls passed through the lieutenant's blouse, but he was unhurt. The losses in the Second Corps at the battles of the North Anna, Pamunky and Totopotomy were 1,651 officers and men killed, wounded and missing. The few reported missing were, no doubt, nearly all killed, as but few prisoners were taken by the enemy.

During the battle of Totopotomy an amusing, but rather tragic incident occurred. While a limber chest of one of the batteries was being refilled with ammunition in the yard of a farm house in the rear, a negro woman, crazed with excitement and fright, came out of the kitchen with a shovelful of hot coals, which she emptied into the chest. In the explosion that followed two of the artillerists were killed, while the woman escaped uninjured. A most ludicrous incident of the battle was the cool request, in writing, in language more vigorous than polite, and coming from some ladies living in a house that stood in the line of battle. They desired that General Hancock would change the line of battle so that they would not be disturbed. The general was a very courteous man, indeed, but could not comply with their wishes. He sent an ambulance, however, to convey them to a place of safety. They positively refused to leave the house, and remained in the cellar, while many shells struck the house. They were Confederate missiles, and had the ladies been injured it would have been at the hands of their friends. Nevertheless, they notified the general that "if any of them were killed their blood would rest on his soul forever". Fortunate for all, the ladies lived through the battle unharmed.

June 1st, remained in the rifle-pits all day, the firing being continuous, as the pickets were engaged incessantly. A rigid inspection of the regiment at 5 P. M., and orders to march after nightfall. After dark withdrew from the line of the Totopotomy, and began marching for Cold Harbor. Marched all night and arrived near the coming battlefield on June 2d.

CHAPTER XI.

COLD HARBOR.

THE night march to Cold Harbor was one of the most trying experiences. It was very dark and very warm, the dust stifling and no water to be had. The road was unknown, and Captain Paine, of the Engineers, who was sent to lead the column and show the way, in his efforts to find a short cut, got the troops entangled in by-paths where artillery could not follow and much time was lost. In consequence the head of the Second Corps did not reach Cold Harbor until 6.30 A. M., too late to move to the attack that had been ordered for the morning of the 2d and which was changed to five o'clock in the afternoon.

The men were in an extremely exhausted condition, and the day was spent in throwing up earth-works and in resting. Some firing took place during the day and several of the men of the regiment were wounded. Lieutenant Cosslett was sent with a detail for entrenching tools, and, on returning, the men were seen by the men of a Confederate battery who opened fire and caused the party to run for the shelter of the works. It was a close call but no one was hit.

The regiment held the right of the brigade and rested in an apple orchard, and when the men had an opportunity they would pull the green apples and eat them, from the effects of which it is feared that some of them suffered more than from the bullets of the enemy.

The sharpshooters were vigilant during the day and gave but little chance to climb trees in search of fruit.

Color-Sergeant T. A. Sloan concluded to cook a cup of coffee and, starting a small fire with pieces of cracker boxes, held his tin-cup over the blaze. Just as it was beginning to boil a rifle ball knocked the cup out of his hand and spoiled the anticipated meal.

During the afternoon the order to attack was countermanded and the assault was postponed until day-break next morning. At 5 P. M. the rain began to fall, a great relief from the oppressive dust and heat.

The men of the regiment slept soundly during the night of June 2d. Everyone was so exhausted that they slept even when the artillery was roaring.

Sergeant William Chambers, of Company C, was fortunate enough to possess a blanket, and at day-break the next morning he awoke and remarked to his comrades with whom he had shared the cover: "This is my birthday. I wonder what kind of a present I will receive?" Five minutes afterwards he received a ball in his arm—not exactly the kind of a present he desired. His birth-day was spent in wandering around the field hospitals, trying to get his wound dressed and pouring water over the limb in a vain effort to keep down the inflammation. At night, when he finally found a heap of straw to lay down on, he was astonished to find on each side his two companions of the night before, both wounded, and the same blanket covered the three again.

At 4.30 A. M. the battle of Cold Harbor began by the advance of the Second Corps, Barlow's and Gibbons's Divisions in the front line, supported by Birney's Division. The fight was short, sharp and decisive. It was not the enemy that was surprised this morning, as they were on May 12th, but it was the Union troops that were astonished. No sooner had the attacking party began moving than the enemy opened fire, and a terrible and destructive fire it was, sweeping the ground in all directions. The Irish Brigade was in the second line, but soon caught up with those in the front and joined in the fray.

The Confederates were found strongly posted in a sunken road in front of their works, from which they were driven after a severe fight and followed into their works. Three hundred prisoners, one color and three pieces of artillery were captured in the first rush, but the victory was quickly turned into a most disastrous defeat. Many of the troops succeeded in gaining the main works of the enemy and the men of Barlow's Division exhibited a wonderful persistency in holding to the captured works, but they were soon forced out by the heavily reinforced Confederates and fell back exposed to a severe musketry and artillery fire.

Falling back a short distance the defeated troops halted about seventy-five yards from the enemy's line and quickly covered themselves with rifle pits or took advantage of such shelter as the broken ground afforded. The One Hundred and Sixteenth Regiment was halted and aligned in a ravine, ordered to lie down and had to remain in that position for an hour exposed to not only a direct but an enfilading fire of the batteries, which threw shell and canister. So long as the men could hug the ground the loss was not great, as the pieces could not be depressed sufficiently to strike the line, but when the attempt was made to withdraw from the position the men felt the full force of the fire.

The order was given to go back at a run, but the command had to ascend a hill in the rear and as the men were absolutely without shelter they fell in great numbers. Reaching the crest of the hill the regiment was rallied and aligned, Captain Taggart, Lieutenant Yocum and others of the officers displaying great bravery in reforming, still under a heavy fire.

The Battle of Cold Harbor was less than one hour in duration, yet one of the most bloody battles of the war. The Second Corps lost in a short half hour 3,000 men and officers. Among the latter were many of the most trusted and best brigade and regimental commanders. The One Hundred and Sixteenth lost seventy men and officers, killed and wounded, and among the latter were Captains Lieb, Cosslett and Crawford and Lieutenants Sacriste and Wright. The wound of Captain Frank R. Lieb was of such a severe nature, his foot being destroyed, that he never rejoined the regiment, and the command lost a most gallant and excellent officer. Colonel Richard Byrne (Twenty-eighth Massachusetts Infantry), commanding the Irish Brigade, was mortally wounded and died in the field hospital where he lingered for a few days. He was captain of cavalry in the Regular Army and had been detailed to command the Twenty-eighth Massachusetts Regiment, and as senior colonel was present in command of the brigade. He was strict, reserved and reticent, and one who did not know him would think him severe, but he was a man who did his full duty and expected everyone else to come up to the full measure of all demands. To those who knew him best he was kindly and lovable. A few days before the battle he had some words with Captain Lieb, then commanding the One Hundred and Sixteenth, and may have been a little harsh in his remarks, but when borne to the field hospital and learning that Lieb was there also, he had himself carried to where the Captain was lying and the dying officer apologized in the most courteous manner for anything rude that he might have said.

After the repulse of our army (and that repulse had been uniform along the whole six miles of the battle line) the troops clung tenaciously to the ground. Spade, bayonet, tin-plate and knife, anything that would throw up a little dirt was used to throw up the earth and assist to get under cover. From time to time bursts of firing occurred along the line and the sharpshooters were so vigilant during the 3d and following days that it was impossible to expose even a hand without being fired at. And to show a head meant instant death.

The suffering from thirst was very great, and it was impossible to get water without a serious risk. Corporal Lot Turney, Company E, volunteered to fill some canteens at a spring, but was instantly shot through the head. Another corporal of this company, Aaron Tomlinson, was not so anxious for water as he was for food; his leg was cut off by a shell, and he lay mortally wounded, but positively refused to allow the stretcher carriers to take him to the hospital, unless he was allowed to take his haversack full of crackers along with him. Captain William M. Hobart, Company A, who was serving on the division staff, greatly distinguished himself during the battle by carrying an order to Arnold's Battery that had been accidentally left between the lines. He was so much exposed that his escape from the fire of the enemy's sharpshooters seemed miraculous, his horse being killed. Color Sergeant T. A. Sloan was wounded by a shell when advancing on the morning of the 3d. Then it was that the young boy, Corporal James M. Seitzinger, of Company G, rushed forward and raised the flag, and waving it aloft he called to his father, "Go in, Pap; I'm coming." He was promoted sergeant on the field, and complimented by the colonel commanding.

HEADQUARTERS 116TH REGIMENT, PENNSYLVANIA VOLUNTEERS.

SERGEANT JAMES M. SEITZINGER, Company G:

The colonel commanding directs me to express to you his gratification upon learning of your very gallant and meritorious conduct in bearing the colors of the regiment in the late engagement at Cold Harbor, June 3d.

By order of
COLONEL ST. CLAIR A. MULHOLLAND.

FRANCIS A. MCGUIGAN,
First Lieutenant and Acting Adjutant.

But young Seitzinger was too small and slender to carry the large flag, and he reluctantly surrendered the dangerous honor to Sergeant Peter Kelly, of Company D, who had volunteered.

Dr. Albert W. Hendricks, of Company F, was brigade hospital steward during the Cold Harbor fight, and he afterwards wrote of the day: "From the evening of May 27th, 1864, to the night of June 4th our forces in the hospital departments were busily engaged in performing amputations and dressing the wounded brave men who faced the various charges in the bloody battle of Cold Harbor. As the wounded were brought in on stretchers, or in the ambulance, those of them who could speak were by the surgeons requested to give their names, and the singularity with which the answer came, "The 116th Regiment, Pennsylvania Volunteers," led us to believe a general and thorough decimation of the regiment had taken place. I witnessed their bravery, their fortitude in suffering, and the noble manner in which they sacrificed life and limb in devotion to their country's cause. Oh, how grandly they gave all—even life. Regiment after regiment has its history, brave men their tales of glorious deeds, but no regiment, nor no men can tell with truth its history of battle, its sacrifices or devotion in time of danger, surpassing the One Hundred and Sixteenth Regiment of Pennsylvania Volunteers. On every field of battle in which it was engaged, there remains a monument to its valor in comrades slain".

The regiment remained in the works at Cold Harbor until the night of June 12th, and during the time there was not a moment, night or day, that rest was known. Roll-call was at 3 P. M., and from that hour until darkness came again there was no moment of peace.

On the 5th, the position of the regiment was changed half a mile to the right, and on that evening at eight o'clock the enemy made a vigorous attack, which was repulsed. The dead and wounded of the Union Army remained on the field between the lines until a truce was arranged on the 7th. For five days the thousands of wounded men had been lying under the boiling sun without even a mouthful of water. Many had been killed by the cross fire, and when the truce was declared there were but few left to tell the awful tale of their intense suffering. The details from the regiment for picket were frequent and large, and, once on the skirmish line, there was no chance of being relieved until after dark the following night. Every man had to get under cover, dig a hole the best way he knew how and get into it. The lines were very close, at some places only a few feet separated the men, and while Lieutenant Frank McGuigan was on the line, a Confederate lieutenant walked into his pit and became his prisoner, very much astonished, indeed, that he had wandered from his own line.

On the evening of June 12th, the army quietly withdrew from the works at Cold Harbor and began moving to the left, the regiment marching all night.

When the battle of Cold Harbor closed, within an hour of the first shot being fired, the One Hundred and Sixteenth Regiment had finished the first month of the campaign of 1864. Two officers had been killed, Lieutenant-Colonel Richard C. Dale and Lieutenant Henry Kiel.

Nine officers had been wounded, several of them more than once, Colonel Mulholland at the Wilderness, May 5th; Po River, May 10th; Totopotomy, May 31st. Captains Lieb, Crawford and Cosslett, and Lieutenants Sacriste, Alston, Vanderhyden, Wright, Springer and Yocum. Fifty men had been killed, one hundred and twenty wounded and thirty missing, the larger number of the latter, no doubt, killed, making an aggregate loss during the month of May of two hundred and eleven men.

The regiment had been under fire almost every day of the time in the Wilderness: May 5th and 6th, at Todd's Tavern; May 8th, at Po River; May 10th, at Spottsylvania; May 12th and 13th, at Spottsylvania again; May 18th, 19th and 21st, on the south bank of the Mattopony; May 23d, 24th and 25th, at the North Anna; May 28th, on the south side of the Pamunkey; May 29th, 30th and 31st, on the Totopotomy, and on June 2d, 3d, and 4th, at Cold Harbor, making nineteen days out of thirty-one that the regiment was actually in battle and under fire. No wonder the loss was over two hundred in killed and wounded. It is only remarkable that it was not still greater. These losses, however, do not include Company B, which was at division headquarters, as provost guard, nor those who were sent to the rear sick, many of whom died of the diseases contracted during this month of constant fighting, hardship and exposure. The above figures tell only of the killed and wounded.

Neither was the heavy loss of the One Hundred and Sixteenth Regiment exceptional. All the army had suffered quite as severely, and many regiments had lost more, in proportion to numbers. The Second Corps had been almost annihilated. The official returns of casualties in the Army of the Potomac, from May 5th until May 21st, were 39,791, and these appalling figures do not include the losses of the Ninth Corps, which the writer has no means of ascertaining.

The continuous strain, constant marching, fighting, want of sleep, absence of food and water, sleeping when a chance offered on the ground without even the slight protection of a shelter tent, sometimes in a drenching rain, and most times catching an hour's sleep under the broiling sun—all this was beginning to tell on the strongest constitutions, and even affecting the minds. Lieutenant Peter S. Frailey, Company E, had been one of the bravest in the beginning, but at Cold Harbor his mind gave way, and he was compelled to resign. Captain Michael Schoales and Lieutenant Robert J. Grogan, broke down early in the month and resigned on the 17th.

One officer, Captain Wellington Jones, brought disgrace on himself by resigning in front of the enemy for no other reason than that he could not face the music.

Several other changes took place among the officers during the month. Lieutenant Charles Cosslett was promoted to Captain of Company E, and mustered in June

13th; First Sergeant Henry Kiel, of that company, was commissioned First Lieutenant, but was killed before being mustered in, and Color-Sergeant T. A. Sloan was promoted to Second Lieutenant of Company E.

"Blinkey" Bell, of Company K, who distinguished himself on the morning of the battle of Spottsylvania, was a queer character. He was a veteran when he joined the regiment, having enlisted in the Eighty-fifth Pennsylvania Regiment in the early days of the war. "Blinkey" at first failed to see the necessity of many things in military life, to which, by force of circumstances, he afterwards became reconciled. Guard and picket duty he could not learn for a long time. One evening after dark, while on his first tour of duty, "Blinkey" was marching up and down on his post when the officer of the day approached. Without a salute or challenge "Blinkey" was allowing him to pass. The Lieutenant, disgusted at the seeming ignorance of the sentinel, siezed his musket to show him how he should have acted. "Now, Bell", said he, "walk off a short distance and then approach me, and when I challenge, you must say, 'Friend with the countersign'". "Blinkey" obeyed, and when nearing the officer was confronted with a loud "Halt! who goes there"? and a bayonet leveled at his breast. "Blinkey", to say the least, was astonished at what seemed to him to be a very rude way of greeting an acquaintance, and after catching his breath, exclaimed in a startled voice full of sweet confidence: "Oh! I say, now, look here Lieutenant, don't you know 'Blinkey' Bell?"

"Blinkey" was certainly a little green in those days, but no braver or better soldier died in the Bloody Angle at Spottsylvania than Henry J. Bell.

CHAPTER XII.

PETERSBURG.

AFTER dark on June 12th the Second Corps withdrew in silence from the line of Cold Harbor. Not a sound broke the stillness of the summer night. The men had learned very thoroughly when to make a noise and when to keep still, and on this occasion no extra cautioning of the troops was found necessary.

Every man had his tin cup tied fast and his tin plate, if he was rich enough to have one, safely stowed in his haversack, so when the movement was begun there was not a rattle or a jingle to be heard. The picket was not notified nor relieved until the army had been gone for some hours, and it was thought by almost everyone that the detail would be lost; but a very judicious officer, Lieutenant-Colonel Hammill, of the Sixty-sixth New York, was in command, and he succeeded in quietly withdrawing, with a few exceptions, all the men from the picket line. Forming them in the dark, he moved in quick time after the corps and succeeded in overtaking the main body before noon of the 13th.

Captain Charles Cosslett, of the One Hundred and Sixteenth, was in charge of the detail from the regiment and succeeded in bringing all in safely. It was a narrow escape and all were rejoiced to get away, as they were told when going out on the line that it was to be "killed or captured."

The Second Corps marched all the night of the 12th and reached White Oak Bridge, on the Chickahominy, at daylight on the 13th. Marched all day on the 13th, through White Oak Swamp, and reached Wilcox Landing, on the James River, before sundown. When, on the evening of the 12th, the column of retiring troops had cleared the works and gotten well under way, a thrill of pleasure passed through the ranks, all were so rejoiced to leave the lines of Cold Harbor; and when the men knew that they were far enough away from the enemy not to be heard they burst into song. Many a long march was enlivened in this way. Some musical member would start a patriotic song, and the whole regiment, joining in the chorus, would go swinging along hour after hour, forgetting the fatigue and hardship. "The Sword of Bunker Hill" was a favorite and hundreds of voices would make the Virginia night resound and the dark woods re-echo to the music:

> "The old man died, but in his hand
> His sword he retained still,
> And thirty millions lived to bless
> The sword of Bunker Hill."

It was thirty millions during the war. Now, thirty years after, it is seventy millions; and how many hundreds of millions will in the future bless "The Sword of Bunker Hill"?

The march from Cold Harbor to the James was over historic ground. Two hundred and fifty years before, Captain John Smith, "the father of Virginia," was taken prisoner by the Indians here and surprised his captors by showing his watch and compass, and, after being carried from tribe to tribe as a curiosity, was finally doomed to die. Then it was that the gentle Pocahontas encircled his head with her arms, begging for his life, and induced her father, the Chief Powhatan, to spare the brave Englishman. And here in the forests of the Chickahominy, John Wolfe wooed and won the sweet young Indian maiden and carried her off to England never to return to Virginia again, but in a foreign land to droop and die so young. The blood of the heroine still flows in the land of her childhood, for some of the best known families in Virginia are descended from the one son that was left by the Lady Rebecca, as Pocahontas was called in England.

The peninsula of the Chickahominy had been the scene of fierce and bloody war two hundred years before the Union Army appeared. During the life of Powhatan peace reigned along the valley of the James, but after his death and after the influence and memory of his gentle daughter Pocahontas were forgotten, Opecancanough, the brother of Powhatan, became chief. Observing with sorrow the decline of his people and the encroachment of the whites, he resolved to destroy them. A bundle of arrows wrapped in the skin of a rattlesnake sent to the English Governor was the declaration of war and massacre that continued at intervals for twenty years and ended in the extermination of the red men.

When the Second Corps massed on the banks of the James River it bivouaced on the spot where the foundation and prime reason of the War of Secession was laid in September, 1620. In that month a small Dutch vessel landed here twenty negroes from Africa who were sold to the planters as slaves. Within ten days from the landing of those slaves on the shores of the James River the "Mayflower" landed on the shores of Massachusetts a cargo of very different character—a set of men and women who had fled from slavery and come to the new land in search of freedom. The lowering storm that hung over the bay as the Pilgrim fathers leaped on the Plymouth Rock seemed to herald a life of strife for principle, and a struggle that culminated at Appomattox.

As the years rolled by the people of the South, by force of circumstances, naturally became more attached to the institution of human slavery. It had been shorn of its chief horrors, the slave ship was a thing of history, and in many cases the slaves had come to be regarded as members of the family in which they resided and were often regarded with affection. But to the descendants of the Pilgrim fathers the years failed to soften the hatred of slavery in all its forms. It was so totally in opposition to the Puritan's faith in which all of his descendants and nearly all the people of the North held almost as firmly as the original passengers of the "Mayflower." And so the armies of the North and South were here on the very spot where slavery was founded, and the descendants of the Pilgrim fathers and those who believed with them that human slavery was a crime were there in force and in earnest.

Much has been said and harsh feelings engendered in the two sections of our country endeavoring to fix the blame of originating the war on the North and South, but happily these feelings are becoming less harsh as time rolls on, and now the spirit of mutual love, patriotism and friendship is possessing the whole country. Had that little ship from the Netherlands never brought that cargo of negroes from Africa to the South, we never would have had the War of Secession ; and would it not be a good idea for the future to stop all recrimination and further argument on a subject so harsh and so fruitful of bad humor by putting the blame where it properly belongs—*on the Dutch!*

When, on the evening of the 13th, the regiment reached the north bank of the James, no time was lost in entrenching. The men were tired, but were never too weary to get under cover. When the line of works was finished a grateful night's rest followed. June 14th, the Second Corps began crossing the James River to the south side, but the means of transportation were limited, and the regiment did not cross until the evening. During the day the men rested, and some of them spent a pleasant hour or two in fishing, and were quite successful. All the hardships and fighting of the past two weeks were forgotten in the hunt for fishing tackle and bait, and the fish caught were a treat, for the commissary was very low. At dusk the regiment fell in, marched a short distance to Wilcox Landing, crossed on a ferryboat, and landed on the south side at Windmill Point. Rested until 11 A. M. on the 15th, and took up the line of march for Petersburg, seventeen miles. It was understood that three days' rations would be issued before starting, but no commissary stores arrived, and the Second Corps began the long march in a very hungry condition indeed. The march was severe and trying, the day hot and the water scarce. The route of Barlow's Division, and, in consequence, that of the regiment, lengthened out to twenty miles, and the column did not reach Petersburg until nearly midnight, and were cheered upon their arrival by seeing sixteen field pieces that the negro troops, under General Hincks, had captured during the afternoon.

BATTLE OF JUNE 16th.

Roll call at daybreak, and in the morning moved a short distance, passing the colored division of General Hincks. The negroes had abundance of rations, and liberally shared with the men of the regiment. Never did the army cracker and raw salt pork taste so sweet. No meal prepared by the most accomplished cook could have been relished better than that furnished by the colored troops. About noon, drew full supplies of rations from General Butler's commissary. Built earth-works, and towards evening prepared to advance and assault the enemy's line of works.

Petersburg was defended by a line of entrenchments surrounding the city at a distance of two miles from it. The defences consisted of a series of well-constructed redans connected by infantry parapets with ditches, and nearly all covered by slight abattis.

During the afternoon of the 15th, five of the redans had been taken by the colored troops, but during the night of the 15th, and morning of the 16th, the Confederate troops had been coming up, occupying and strengthening the works; and when, on the afternoon of the 16th, it was finally determined to storm the enemy's line, their works had become too strong to carry by direct assault. The attempt was made, however, and at 6 o'clock in the evening, the Second Corps moved toward the attack. Barlow's Division was on the extreme left of the army, and the weight of the attack fell upon his division and that of General Birney. The regiment charged over broken and open ground near the Hare House, where Fort Steadman was afterwards built. No sooner had the line started than the Confederate batteries opened. The men moved forward steadily in quick time, keeping the alignment beautifully, although exposed to a terrible fire of shell and musketry, and when within a hundred yards of the enemy, took the double quick and went through the slight abattis and over the works at a run. For a few moments, a hand-to-hand fight took place, the bayonet being used. It was soon over, and the Union forces retained possession, capturing guns and prisoners. General Barlow displayed great gallantry in leading the division, cap in hand and cheering the men on. It was the most successful and glorious charge, and resulted in the capture, by the two divisions engaged, of redans 3, 13 and 14, with their guns and connecting works. Among the prisoners were some of the oldest and youngest men as yet seen by the troops; "the robbing of the cradle and the grave", as General Grant afterwards expressed it, had already begun. The regiment lost quite severely in this fight, Lieutenants Detweiler and McKnight being severely wounded, the latter losing his hand. Forty-six enlisted men were killed, wounded and missing. Lieutenant Yocum was knocked senseless by the windage of a passing shell, but recovered sufficiently to report for duty in a couple of hours. The noble commander of the Irish Brigade, Colonel Patrick Kelly, was killed, being shot through the head. He will ever be remembered, by all who knew him, as one of the bravest and most lovable of men. Captain B. S. O'Neill, of the Sixty-ninth New York, was also killed. He was a very handsome man, and much thought of by the men of the One Hundred and Sixteenth. He had left Ireland on the breaking out of the war, and came to America for the sole purpose of joining the Irish Brigade. Every fight seemed to have a ludicrous feature, and the one connected with the 16th of June was a dull-witted son of Ireland in Company I. Daniel Dugan had mysteriously disappeared at the beginning of the charge, and next morning when Captain Taggart charged him with straggling and deserting his command in battle, Dan replied very demurely: "Ah, then, Captain dear, sure its many a poor fellow thats after bein hit on the field lasht noight, an' here oi am shtill aloive"!

"Well", replied the Captain, "if you had been killed you would have lived in the hearts of your countrymen".

"Och, thin", said Dan, "bejabers but its a moighty hard place to live in. I'd sonner be liven' on Uncle Sam's hard tack"!

On June 17th, as on the day before, the regiment was engaged in an assault on the enemy's works. General Barlow led the division in on the right of the Ninth Corps, and lost heavily, the firing continuing until long after dark. The regiment never looked better than when in moving forward in one of the assaults of this day. Not until the men got entangled in the abattis, in front of the enemy's earth-works, did the lines show any signs of breaking an almost perfect alignment. Several of the men succeeded in getting into the works, but were either captured or killed.

June 18th, roll call at daybreak. General Hancock, by reason of his wound breaking out afresh, was forced to relinquish command of the Second Corps, and was succeeded by General David B. Birney. General Birney was a Pennsylvanian, a most gallant soldier, and one of the very best of the volunteer officers, who rose to distinction and prominence during the war, and as such, he was warmly welcomed by the Second Corps. Marched as soon as line was formed, to the right, to participate in a heavy assault on the enemy's position to the right and left of the Prince George Court House Road. Formed behind a hill in double column by division, closed in mass, and moved forward in support of Mott's Division. The result was a bloody repulse. General Gibbons's Division had been repulsed earlier in the day on this same ground, and this fight ended in the effort to carry the entrenched line of Petersburgh by direct assault. On the evening of June 18th, the struggle settled down to a siege operation. The loss of the regiment on this afternoon was slight; three men killed and about a dozen wounded.

June 19th, under arms at daybreak, but no movements of importance during the day. At 10 P. M. the enemy attacked the advance line, but were repulsed.

June 20th, roll call at 3.30 A. M. Moved at 8 A. M. to the rear, and understood that the regiment, with the Second Corps, was on the reserve; but, as a member of the Irish Brigade remarked at Gettysburg, it was "Resarved fur hivy foighting"! Grateful rest during the day and night, although heavy and continuous firing in front and to the right and left.

June 21st, reveille at daybreak. Rest was promised to the troops, but at 10 A. M. the division moved to the left, crossed the Petersburg Plank Road, and advanced several miles in the direction of Reams Station, on the Weldon Railroad, when the regiment was thrown out as skirmishers, and had a severe skirmish fight while the division moved by the right flank, and formed line of battle on the left of the Ninth Corps. Threw up strong entrenchments, and settled down for a night's rest, but the Sixth Corps that was to join on the left failed to connect, leaving a gap of nearly a mile, through which a Confederate cavalry

MAJOR-GENERAL DAVID BELL BIRNEY

force raided during the night, creating alarm and commotion amongst the teamsters, commissaries and hospital attendants.

BATTLE OF WILLIAM'S FARM.
Or, as the Confederates Called it: "Johnston's Farm".
JUNE 22, 1864.

When General Grant finally determined to suspend the direct assaults upon the Confederate's positions and begin siege operations, both armies began entrenching, the right of the Union Army resting on the Appomattox River below Petersburg, and for the purpose of cutting the Weldon and South Side Railroad, and extending the left of the Union line, so as to accomplish that object, and, if practical, to envelope the whole region on the left of the river.

The first extension of the line towards the south was inaugurated during the night of the 21st. The Sixth Corps came up and formed on the left of the Second; and on the morning of the 22d, the Second Corps was ordered to advance, keeping connection on the right with the Fifth Corps, on which the Second pivoted, and on the left with the Sixth Corps, that was moving slowly through the dense woods. Roll call at daybreak, and then rested in the entrenchments until nearly noon, when the advance began; but, owing to the greater distance over which the Sixth Corps had to march, and the difficulty in penetrating the tangled bush of the deep forest, the wheeling movement to the right was necessarily slow. Finally, General Meade, becoming impatient at the progress made, ordered the Second Corps to advance without waiting for the Sixth. General Birney did as directed, and, as he swung forward, the left of the Second Corps left the right of the Sixth Corps far in the rear.

The movement of the Second Corps took place in the woods west of the Jerusalem Plank Road and a little south of Fort Sedgwick, afterwards known as "Fort Hell".

The Confederate line of works running north and south turned abruptly within half a mile of the fort, at an angle of their line known as "Reeves' Salient," and crossing the Plank Road ran directly west. On the 21st of June General Lee, looking across the half mile of open country in front of that line and seeing the dense timberland beyond, anticipated the very movement that Grant had ordered, and on that day he (General Lee) ordered Wilcox to take his division, occupy the woods and feel for the Union line. Wilcox remained in the forest all day long of the 21st and returned to camp in the evening, reporting to General Lee that he had accomplished nothing. On the morning of the 22d, Wilcox was again ordered into the timber with the same instructions. He formed his line in the deep woods south of the Johnston House and seems to have quietly rested without making an effort to ascertain the whereabouts or purpose of the Union troops. When the Second Corps charged front and pivoted on its right, which rested near the Plank Road, the left of the First Division must have actually passed within a few hundred yards of Wilcox's line, the latter evidently taking things easy and not making a very vigorous search for the Union troops, while the left of the Second Corps swung past oblivious to the fact that a Confederate division was there with orders to strike. When the Second Corps had made a half wheel and the line suddenly emerged from the woods and stood at right angles with the Plank Road and was then parallel with and half or three-quarters of a mile distant from the Confederate line that also ran at right angles west from the Jerusalem Plank Road, the men of the Second Corps promptly stacked arms and began entrenching.

It so happened that General Lee was at that moment in a little detached work that had been erected in the field two or three hundred yards in front of his main line. To his astonishment he saw in the distance the troops of the Second Corps vigorously throwing up the dirt at the edge of the wood and prolonging their line in the direction of his right. The ever vigilant and active General Mahone was chatting with General Lee at the time, and seeing a chance to hit the left of the Second Corps, which was then in the air, suggested to him the feasibility of striking with promising results. In a letter from General Mahone he tells of June 22, 1864, in his own way:

PETERSBURG, May 7th, 1895.

DEAR GENERAL MULHOLLAND: I am just in receipt of your esteemed letter of the 30th ult., and it gives me pleasure to comply with your request.

The "occasion" of the 22d of June, 1864, was fought on Johnston's Farm. I enclose a pen diagram of the occasion that you may the better understand this letter. On the morning of the 21st of June General Wilcox was sent out with his division of four brigades, passing on the west side of the Johnston House into the woodland beyond to feel for the left flank of your line, which at that time had not been extended west of the Jerusalem Plank Road, and I was directed to move out of the trenches and co-operate with Wilcox in any attack he should make upon your people, as he should in it uncover my front. General Wilcox went out and returned that night failing to discover your line. On the morning of the 22d of June General Wilcox was again sent out to find the left flank of your army and to strike it a blow, and my instructions were for that day as for the day before. My division occupied the intrenched line from the Reeves Salient to the Ravine of Lieutenant Run. I had gone out to the detached fort in which no artillery had yet been placed as had been previously ordered by General Lee. Then and there I saw the Federal troops moving in orderly fashion across the Plank Road in the direction of the Johnston House, the leading regiment halting, stacking arms and the men going deliberately to intrenching; and the next regiment passing on and, after clearing the leading regiment, halting, stacking arms and then proceeding to intrench. Thus the prolongation of the Federal line west of the Plank Road was commenced and proceeded. I did not see or know of the second line the Federals were projecting until after the engagement which I followed was over. There never was a time in all the siege of Petersburg when the detached fort could have been of any service. Your projecting front line would have been in easy reach of guns in that fort. It was not within practicable range of the artillery in the intrenched line. That detached fort was a blunder and I urged that it should be levelled, that at some time your people would take it and use it as a cover to annoy the entrenched line, and so precisely it came to pass, but my division was not on that front at that time. At this juncture, that is, while you were so deliberately projecting your line, General Lee came upon the ground and expressed a desire that something should be done to arrest the progress of the Federal prolongation. General Wilcox, who was now supposed to be in the very place to deliver a telling blow, had not been heard from. In response to General Lee's expressed desire, I caused the two right brigades of my division to drop quietly to the rear so as to avoid discovery and then moved them up the Ravine of Lieutenant Run, all the way out of view till reaching the open field in front of the Johnston House, and there they were formed in line of battle, a skirmish line put out and the march commenced so as to strike the head of the Federal projecting column. Meanwhile, sending an intelligent staff officer to find General Wilcox and explain to him what I was about and to request that he bear down on my firing, that he was in the right position to take the Federals in the rear. General Wilcox was found resting in the woods and that message delivered, but he did not comply, or, in my judgment, we should not only have swept from the field all the Federal force west of the Plank Road, but materially disorganized your intrenched line east of that road. Meanwhile, my two brigades quickly struck the head of your front projecting column and rolled it up like a scroll until we reached the brush where you were planting four Napoleons. Here I found that my two brigades had been severely depleted in carrying off prisoners, and, after a hurried reconnoissance which disclosed that the Federals were in great force on the Plank Road and that you had a rear projecting column now rapidly falling back on the Plank Road, I determined not to press further.

At this juncture General Wilcox came up, having strangely marched out of the timber and all around the fringe of the woodland to meet me. I urged him to throw in his division and join me with the remnant of my two attacking brigades in a vigorous assault on the Plank Road. He wanted orders from the corps commander, two miles away, so then and there the idea of any further advance on my part was abandoned. I held the ground until daylight next morning when I withdrew my force, meanwhile, repulsing during the night several brisk attacks made by the Federals. The right of my two attacking brigades luckily swept in front of the second projecting column of Federals just far enough away not to be seen, for in sending Major Mills in the midst of the fight with a message to the right of the attacking force, I cautioned him to be careful and not to go too far. I suspected that there might be another line of Federals there. He rode right into the line of that second projecting column.

In this little affair, which might have been turned into a serious disaster to the Federals had General Wilcox borne down on my firing, we captured 1,650 officers and men, a large number of muskets, any quantity of tools and four splendid Napoleon guns.

Here, my dear General, of the "occasion" of 22d of June, 1864, which I hope may interest you. And with best wishes for your every success, I am

Yours truly, MAHONE.

In this characteristic letter General Mahone tells the story of William's Farm, or, as the Confederates knew it, "Johnston's Farm." The attack was to the Union troops more than a surprise. It was an astonishment. It so happened that the One Hundred and Sixteenth Regiment held the extreme left of the Second Corps and, consequently, was the first to receive the assault. Charley Barth, of Company C, had wandered out to the left and was kneeling by some water filling the company canteens when, zip! went a ball into the water. Looking up he saw the Confederates not fifty yards away. As he afterwards remarked, he made "a blue streak for the regiment"!

The startling intelligence he brought could hardly be credited, and Lieutenant Cope and Sergeant-Major Burke started on a reconnoissance to learn the truth. They, too, came tumbling back and had hardly uttered a word of warning when suddenly a heavy musketry fire was opened, not only from the left flank but from the rear as well. The surprise was complete, the attack sudden and totally unexpected. Some regiments of the corps seemed paralyzed, the men running in every direction, and many of them going directly into the Confederate's ranks. The One Hundred and Sixteenth never faltered nor broke, but after receiving the first fire quickly replied and made a noble stand. It was useless, however, and after a ten minutes' fight the order came from the brigade commander to fall back. The regiment moved off by the right flank, leaving behind the dead and wounded. Captains Nowlen, Megraw and Taggart were everywhere on the line, keeping the men together and showing the greatest valor. Lieutenant Henry D. Price, who was then on the division staff, soon learned of the perilous position of the regiment, and galloping down the left where he knew the command was surrounded, he threw himself into the midst of the men, urging them to retire fighting. He exhibited in the hour of trial the highest qualities of the brave soldier that he was. Captain Nowlen was in command of the regiment during the engagement, and he and every one of the officers and men behaved in the coolest manner. The large majority of the men had been in the field but a few weeks, yet they behaved better and exhibited less confusion than many of the regiments that had been two or three years in the service. The excellent conduct of the officers and men was the only thing that saved the organization.

Passing to the right and still firing, the command succeeded in clearing the Confederate line in the rear and moved to a position where the division was being rallied by General Barlow. Lieutenant Yocum was severely wounded, but with twenty of the wounded men got away with the regiment. Tom Scarlett and a dozen or so of the men were for a time completely hemmed in by the enemy, but, hiding in the laurel bushes, they succeeded in evading capture although not escaping the fire. While hiding in the bush the party got foul of a lot of wild hogs, and the grunting and squealing of the animals drew the attention of the Confederate cavalrymen who were riding through the woods in squads picking up prisoners. The cavalrymen fired at the sound and not only hit the hogs but some of the men as well.

Captain Cosslett, Lieutenant Cope and Sergeant-Major Burke were captured and spent many months in Southern prisons. The numbers of dead of the One Hundred and Sixteenth of this fight were never ascertained, as the enemy held the ground. Thirty-five were missing, and a few of them were afterwards heard of as dying in Southern prisons, but most likely the greater part of them still hold the lines where they fell in the forests of William's Farm. A Confederate colonel was captured during the fight. He was mounted on a superb grey horse which General Barlow afterwards purchased and rode in battle. The splendid animal became very fond of the General and would follow him around the camp begging for the lumps of sugar that the General would be pretty sure to have in his pocket with which to treat his equine friend.

The 22d of June was the saddest day ever experienced by the Second Corps. Up to that day the corps had never lost a color and but one gun, but on this occasion the splendid record was lost and the day's disaster cost the Second Corps four guns, one flag and seventeen hundred prisoners that were left in the hands of the enemy. On the morning of the 23d the Second and Sixth Corps moved forward to attack on the same ground fought over the day before, but the enemy had retired into their works and the fighting on the left of the army was ended for a time.

After the fight at William's Farm, sometimes called the "Petersburg Affair," the regiment enjoyed for a few days a well earned rest, if continual digging, intrenching and picket duty could be called by that name; but compared with the long night marches and incessant assaults upon the strong positions of the enemy that occupied every hour of May and June, it was repose and rest of the most welcome character.

Once more the mail was handed around and "news from home" cheered the weary men. But in sorting the regimental mail that had accumulated for weeks, almost half the letters were returned to the writers with the endorsement: "Absent," "Wounded," or, still worse, "Killed."

A few days after the battle of William's Farm General Hancock returned and resumed command of the corps, and on July 11th the corps was withdrawn from the intrenchments that they had erected and went into camp near the "deserted house" on the Norfolk Road.

THE REGIMENT LEAVES THE IRISH BRIGADE.

The regiment remained here for two weeks and during this time was transferred from the Second (Irish) Brigade to the Fourth Brigade. The transfer of regiments and consolidation of brigades was rendered necessary at this time by the heavy losses of men and officers. In some brigades not a field officer remained to take command. The Irish Brigade was commanded by a captain. Six of the ten field officers who had started with the campaign on May 5th had been killed and the other four severely wounded.

The members of the regiment left the Irish Brigade with regret. They had participated in all the glories and triumphs of that famous brigade for two years, and although the One Hundred and Sixteenth was composed almost entirely of American born citizens, the men had learned to love and esteem the men of the Emerald Isle. The brigade to which the regiment was assigned was in no way less brave than the one from which it was parting. It was the brigade of General John R. Brooke, one of the bravest and best of officers, who had commanded the brigade with great honor to it and to himself. He had been wounded on several occasions, and when the regiment joined the Fourth Brigade the gallant soldier was absent, suffering from a wound received at Cold Harbor. The members of the One Hundred and Sixteenth soon felt at home, for the men form friendships quickly when under fire and sharing each other's dangers. Every regiment in the brigade with which the command was for the future to be associated were veteran organizations that had been tried on every field from the very beginning of the war. The regiments composing the brigade were the Fifty-third, One Hundred and Forty-fifth and One Hundred and Forty-eighth Pennsylvania; Second Delaware; Sixty-fourth and Sixty-sixth New York, and Seventh New York Heavy Artillery, acting as infantry. The arms of the regiment were changed at this time. The old pattern smooth bore musket, with a ball and three buck shot, calibre 69, was withdrawn and the Springfield, calibre 58, with a rifle barrel, substituted. It was a welcome change, for, while the old weapon with the buck and ball was an excellent one at close quarters, the men felt that the new rifle piece was far superior, especially on the skirmish line.

Towards the end of June and during July the siege of Petersburg was pressed along the whole line, from the right on the Appomattox River to the left near the Jerusalem Plank Road, and the spade and pick were in active use by night and day.

Redoubts and siege batteries rose in rapid succession, and nearly all the men became quite expert in forming fascines, gabions, sap-fagots and all the paraphernalia incidental to siege works. A siege train arrived on the ground, and thirty-pounder Parrott guns soon added their thunder to the general roar. Ten-inch mortars and several batteries of Coehorn mortars were placed at intervals along the line and rained vertical fire upon the enemy. To the Confederates this sort of dropping fire from heaven, as it were, was a surprise. It was so unexpected and astonishing. They were not prepared for a fire of this nature, and for some days suffered heavily without being able to give adequate reply; but they quickly built strong bomb-proofs and in a short time had lots of mortars themselves sending showers of iron down into the camps when the Union people worried them in like manner. To the men on the main line of battle the mortar firing seemed to matter but little, as they learned to scuttle into the bomb-proofs and thus find security and shelter; but to the men on the picket and reserve the fire of the mortar batteries was a serious matter. The mortars were not fired singly but in volleys. Half a dozen mortars would be fired at once, and six immense shells would fly skyward in a bunch and, slowly curving high above the camps, would begin their downward course, gaining speed at every foot and, finally, with a scream and a rush, drop among the men, bursting and scattering death in all directions. As these ponderous shells descended in groups, it was impossible to avoid them, although after dark one could see the streaming fire from the burning fuse as the shells ascended and fell; but as running from one meant simply running into another, it was felt that trying to avoid them was useless. Just to stand and take the chances was all that could be done.

The danger from the mortar shells was not confined alone to the picket or main line of works, but sometimes the shells would reach to the camp of the army reserve, far away from the main line, and men were frequently killed while sleeping in what they fancied was perfect security. As a member of the Irish Brigade remarked, that he "never knew when he went to sleep at night whether he would not wake up dead in the morning". Eleven men were killed in a Michigan regiment at one discharge of a Confederate mortar battery, and it was said that thirty-one men were killed in a Confederate regiment when a shower of mortar shells from one of the Union batteries fell among them. This mortar business, raining down shells from the clouds at all hours of night and day was, perhaps, the most annoying feature of the siege. As General Humphreys remarked: "It was depressing"; and that was putting it very mildly. It certainly was depressing.

CHAPTER XIII.

FIRST DEEP BOTTOM; OR, STRAWBERRY PLAINS.

TOWARDS the end of July, General Grant determined to send a force of infantry and cavalry to the north bank of the James River, to make a dash on Richmond and destroy the railroads to the north of the city, and also for the purpose of drawing away from the defences of Petersburg, and to the north bank of the James a portion of the Confederate Army. General Sheridan was placed in command of the cavalry, and the whole expedition was under General Hancock.

At 4 o'clock on the afternoon of July 26th, the Second Corps left camp near the "Deserted House", marching for Point of Rocks. Just after dark, the corps crossed the Appomattox River on the pontoon bridge at Point of Rocks, and continued the march during the night by way of Jones Neck. The night was warm and very dark, but by order of General Butler, small fires had been lit at intervals along the route which aided much in getting along. The James River was reached about 2 A. M. on the morning of the 27th, and crossing on the pontoons, the corps was massed in the woods to await daylight. As soon as it was sufficiently light to see, the advance was ordered, Barlow's Division leading. The regiment was commanded by Captain Garrett Nowlen, and he handled it beautifully. No sooner had the line begun moving forward than the skirmishers of the division became engaged, and with a rush, they captured the works of the enemy, with four twenty-pound Parrott guns and a lot of prisoners.

MAJOR-GENERAL FRANCIS C. BARLOW.

FIRST DEEP BOTTOM; OR, STRAWBERRY PLAINS.

The Twenty-eighth Massachusetts was one of the regiments that fought on the skirmish line, and when the four large guns with the caissons were hauled to the rear, the men of the One Hundred and Sixteenth seemed almost as glad to witness the glory of the regiment with which they had been associated so long, as though they had made the capture themselves. The regiment met with a heavy fire while passing over the plain, but finally reached the Confederate works without serious loss. The fire of the enemy was diverted and rendered less destructive by the firing of the gun-boats which threw their immense shells over the heads of the men and into the works of the enemy. These tremendous hundred-pound shells made a sound that was awe-inspiring, and when they burst in the timber, they tore the giant trees into ribbons.

During the 27th and 28th, Barlow's Division did heavy marching and entrenching, moving far out to the right, trying to find the enemy's flank, but without avail. The whole movement, so far as making a dash on the Confederates' Capital, failed; but the second object for which the expedition had been organized—the drawing of a large part of the Confederate Army to the north bank of the James River in order to leave an opening for a successful assault on Petersburg—had been successful. Five-eighths of the whole of Lee's army had hastily concentrated in front of Hancock.

As soon as it was dark, on the evening of the 29th, the return march to Petersburg was commenced, and the whole force got back in time to see the explosion of the mine in front of the Ninth Corps, and witness the miserable fiasco that cost the Union Army four thousand men. The Second Corps returned to the camp near the "Deserted House", and the One Hundred and Sixteenth Regiment enjoyed another rest of two weeks. Picket duty, however, was always in order, and the loss of men on the outer line was frequent.

SECOND DEEP BOTTOM.

Early in August, General Grant deemed it advisable to again send a strong force to the north bank of the James to threaten Richmond. General Hancock was again selected to command the movement, and in order to deceive the enemy the troops were ordered to march to City Point and embark on steamboats, to give the Confederates the impression that the expedition was destined for Washington; then sail up the river by night and land at Deep Bottom by daylight, ready for the attack.

At noon on the 12th of August, the corps marched to City Point, and on the following day began embarking on the fleet of steamers that had been gathered there. Not only was the enemy deceived by the movement, *via* the boats and river, but also the men who composed the force. No sooner had they begun marching on board the steamers than their spirits rose, and "On to Washington"! was the cry.

As night settled down the surmise deepened into a certainty, and laughter and happiness prevailed to an extent altogether beyond reason. The men of the One Hundred and Sixteenth shared in the good feeling, and when, at 10 o'clock at night, the steamboats pulled out into the stream and the voyage began, general hilarity and wild delight took possession of every one. Songs were started in which all joined, and "The Sword Of Bunker Hill" was sung with an enthusiasm that was universal. It was a lovely night on the water. The stars never looked so bright, or the river so calm and beautiful. No one thought of sleep. There was no time to even doze while the boys were having such a good time. Were they not on their way to the North! With the tolling of the midnight hour came a sad ending to the Washington dream. The steamer on which the One Hundred and Sixteenth was rejoicing and having such a jolly time, slowed up, and a tug came alongside with the orders. In five minutes every man knew that it was Deep Bottom and a fight in the morning, instead of Washington and a trip to the North. The singing quickly died away. The river did not seem half so beautiful nor the stars half so bright. Quickly everyone lost interest in the passing shores. The silence of disappointed hope settled over the men, who at once felt tired and sleepy instead of wide-awake and full of happy song. The steamer went ploughing through the water, and soon all hands were slumbering. It was a cruel disappointment, to be sure.

The sleep of the men was ended in a couple of hours, and before daylight the troops disembarked and massed on the shore. At 5 o'clock the firing commenced, and the sun had risen on the hottest day ever experienced by the members of the One Hundred and Sixteenth Regiment. As Colonel Walker, Adjutant-General of the Second Corps, remarked: "The rays of the August sun smote the heads of the weary soldiers with blows as palpable as if they had been given with a club." Hundreds of men of the army fell during the awful heat of this day. During this, the 14th of August, the regiment marched, intrenched and counter-marched from sunrise until dark and participated in the assault made by General Barlow at 4 o'clock in the afternoon near Fussell's Mill, which was unsuccessful, and at dark the division was massed at the junction of the Darby and Long Bridge Roads.

The 14th of August will long be remembered by every member of the One Hundred and Sixteenth Regiment as one of the most intense suffering. Not one of them will ever experience a warmer day in this world or, let us hope, in the next. Certainly not if they have done their duty in the Union Army and have an honorable discharge.

The 15th of August passed with the picket fighting and intrenching. General Birney, with his Tenth Corps, was moving to find the enemy's left, and it was almost night before he found a place to attack. A day had been lost without anything gained.

During the 16th the Union cavalry, supported by Miles' Brigade, advanced up the Charles City Road and drove the Confederate cavalry as far as White's Tavern, within seven miles of Richmond, but were compelled to fall back again.

General Chambliss, the Confederate cavalry commander, was killed during the fight. His body was lying on a stretcher on the roadside as the regiment passed. He was a handsome man, extremely neat in dress, his mustaches nicely waxed and pointed. He looked as trim and neat as though just fresh from the barber shop. A small Testament found in his pocket testified as to his identity. On the fly leaf was his name and the words: "A gift from his mother".

Towards evening the Fourth Brigade, to which the One Hundred and Sixteenth was now attached, was ordered to reinforce General Birney at Fussell's Mill.

During the 17th there was heavy skirmishing along the whole line of the Second Corps and the men of the regiment suffered severely. From 4 until 6 o'clock on the afternoon of this day a truce was declared for the purpose of removing the dead and wounded from between the lines. The body of General Chambliss, that had been buried within the Union lines, was taken up and delivered to his friends.

On the morning of the 18th General Barlow was compelled to relinquish for a time the command of his division by reason of his wounds and disease. He was a man absolutely without fear, and was succeeded by General Nelson A. Miles, a brilliant and fearless soldier.

With the exception of picket firing the day was uneventful until 5.30 in the afternoon, when the enemy came out of their works near Fussell's Mill and attacked the line of General Birney's Division. General Miles moved forward with the First and Fourth Brigades and struck the flank of the attacking column. For half an hour the roar of musketry was tremendous, and at the same hour a heavy attack was made on the Union cavalry.

Everything indicated a battle of some magnitude, but while the Union cavalry were driven back, the attack on the lines at Fussell's Mill failed and the Confederates were driven back, leaving the field covered with dead and wounded. The One Hundred and Sixteenth Regiment participated in the movement on the enemy's flank and did noble service in pouring in a most destructive fire.

During the 19th and 20th nothing but heavy picket firing occurred, the regiment furnishing large details for the skirmish line; and on the night of the 20th the whole force was withdrawn from Deep Bottom and began the return to Petersburg. The march of the regiment was another of the many disagreeable incidents of the campaign. It was a terrible night. The rain fell in sheets and the roads were in a frightful condition in the ink-like darkness. The thunder rolled and lightning flashed incessantly. As the pickets were being withdrawn, the storm's fury seemed to be concentrated on the picket line. The thunder pealed through the woods and the lightning flashed among the rain-soaked men. Several large trees were struck and torn to ribbons, and while the storm was at its height the army withdrew.

Returning by way of Point of Rocks, the regiment reached the old camping ground early on the morning of the 21st. The casualties of the regiment during the second Deep Bottom campaign are not known to the writer and cannot now be ascertained. The men who were missing were never heard of again and most likely all were killed.

The casualties of the Second Corps were nine hundred and fifteen, more than one-half of which were in the First Division, to which the One Hundred and Sixteenth Regiment was attached. When "arms were stacked" in camp once more, it was thought by everyone that after the fearful fatigues of the last week a rest of a few days would be given to the exhausted troops who had participated in the Deep Bottom campaign, but no such good luck was in store for them. Despite the fearful condition of the worn-out men, they were allowed to remain just long enough to cook their coffee and then ordered to the vicinity of the Strong House to slashing and work on the intrenchments. It was more than human nature could endure and, although the distance was short, many of the men fell on the way utterly unable to move, and, worse still, as soon as the weary and foot-sore men arrived at the first point of destination, they were ordered to continue the march to the Gurley House, on the Weldon Railroad, several miles further. Slowly dragging their weary limbs along through a steady and pouring rain, they finally reached their position late in the afternoon. Too weary and tired and without life or spirit enough to even light a fire, the men of the One Hundred and Sixteenth Regiment sank on the wet ground and slept in the softest of Virginia mud.

The morning of August 22d broke grey and wet. The men made coffee with water thick with clay from the muddy streams, and many of the stragglers who had fallen by the way the day before came in and joined their companies.

At noon the First Division was set to work destroying the Weldon Railroad. All the afternoon of that day and all day of the 23d the work went on. It was not the first experience of the regiment in this line of business, and when the fatigue of Deep Bottom wore off the men rather enjoyed the work. It was certainly better than building breast-works with the sharpshooters cracking at the workers, and the roaring fires of the railroad ties at intervals along the line, on which the rails were bent and roasted, looked cheerful and gave the boys a chance to dry their clothes after the rain.

During the afternoon several miles of the railroad were effectually destroyed and on the 23d the work was continued. On the evening of that day the First Division reached as far as Reams Station and the regiment was placed in intrenchments there.

CHAPTER XIV.

BATTLE OF REAMS STATION.

ON the morning of August 24th, the First Division was relieved by the Second, and proceeded in the work of destroying the railroad beyond the station. The advance of the working party was covered by Colonel Spear with two regiments of cavalry; while General Gregg's Division of cavalry held all the roads by which the enemy could approach from Petersburg or Dinwiddie. During the day, Spear had a brush with the enemy's cavalry, but with the assistance of some of the infantry of the First Division, drove them off. General Barlow was again forced, by reason of his wounds, to relinquish command of the First Division on this day, never to return, and was succeeded by General Nelson A. Miles. It was not without regret that the men of the One Hundred and Sixteenth saw General Barlow take final leave of the division. He was a fearless officer, perfectly reckless as regarded his own person, and in spite of wounds and disease stuck to the work, and remained with the command long after a man with less force of character would have given up the struggle.

During the day the working party succeeded in destroying the railroad to a point three miles beyond and to the south of the station, to a place known as Malone's Crossing. At dark the division returned to the intrenchments at Reams Station. The members of the regiment were in good spirits, and, after cooking coffee, sat around the camp-fires for awhile, enjoying the usual smoke and chat that almost invariably marked the close of a day like this.

The night of the morrow and the regiment would be stealing away in the darkness from the bloody field, leaving many members, the dead of August 25th, to hold the works forever.

Orders were issued for the Second Division of the corps to move out and resume the destruction of the railroad on the morning of the 25th, but at midnight a dispatch from the headquarters of the army, notified General Hancock that a force of the enemy, estimated at eight to ten thousand, had been seen leaving their works at Petersburg, moving south, and cautioning him to look out for them. This Confederate force was afterwards learned to be a very heavy column of infantry and cavalry (the numbers have never been ascertained), under command of General A. P. Hill, consisting of nearly all of his own corps, Anderson's Brigade of Longstreet's Corps, and two cavalry divisions under General Hampton. This force began to develop in Hancock's front early in the forenoon of the 25th; and, in consequence, the Second Division, that had started to destroy the track, was at once recalled and placed in the intrenchments.

The pickets of the Second Division, who had been on duty during the night, were relieved by those of the First Division shortly after daylight, and a large detail of the One Hundred and Sixteenth went out on that duty. The line of works into which the two divisions of the Second Corps had retired to await the assaults of the Confederate column were slight and faulty in construction. They had been constructed in June by some of the cavalry. They ran along the railroad for some ten or twelve hundred yards, having a return almost at right angles at each end, of about the same length, and were thrown up in such a way that the troops occupying them would be exposed to an enfilading fire.

The First Division, to which the One Hundred and Sixteenth was attached, commanded by General Nelson A. Miles, occupied the right half of these intrenchments,

MAJOR-GENERAL NELSON A. MILES

and Gibbons's Second Division the left. The pickets were thrown well out into the woods in front, and towards noon they felt the approach of the enemy.

In front of that part of the line there was open ground of about one hundred and fifty yards to the timber, and in this wood the picket ran in a line parallel with the works.

At noon the Confederates advanced along the Dinwiddie Road and struck the picket of the First Division, driving in the picket line and taking possession of these woods, the sharpshooters occupying every tree and available spot along the front of the Union line.

At one o'clock an attempt was made to drive the Confederates back into these woods and reform the picket line, and the regiment went out to support the movement, leaving the colors with a guard in the works, but the effort was not successful. In this fight, which was at very close quarters, the regiment lost some good men but did effective work. Sergeant Edward S. Kline behaved nobly and was severely wounded. Sergeant T. A. Sloan, while in the act of loading his rifle, was ordered by a big fellow to surrender. Sloan had just got his load down but the ramrod stuck and he could not withdraw it, so he let him have it, ramrod and all. When it came to a question of surrender Tim Sloan was ever ready to enter a very earnest protest.

At about 2 o'clock the Confederate General Wilcox made a very determined and spirited attack on that part of the Union line held by the First Division, but each time was driven back with great loss. A second attack was made and was vigorous and close, many of the men falling within musket reach of the Union works. Captain Garrett Nowlen, then in command of the regiment, stood up in front waving his sword and cheering on the men. At that moment a ball pierced his heart. For an instant he was motionless, then turning quickly to where the men of his own company were in line, he looked towards them and waved his hand.

"Good-bye, boys, good-bye—good-bye." He was falling when he repeated the last words, and when he struck the ground he was dead. Captain Sam'l Taggart then took command of the regiment. A few minutes elapsed and Taggart, passing down the line (it is thought for the purpose of seeing Nowlen's body), crossed an opening in the line. He walked slowly, knowing no fear. As he approached the spot that was so exposed to the fire some of the men called out: "Hurry, Captain; they may kill you, too." But the brave soul never hastened a step, and as he reached the spot where Nowlen fell he was shot through the body. The men ran forward and carried him behind the works and laid him beside Nowlen. He was perfectly sensible and tried to speak but could not. He turned his head a little and smiling on the men who had gathered around him and who loved him tenderly, he awaited death, calm, serene and fearless, as became the gallant martyr that he was. He lived fifteen minutes after he was struck, the smile never leaving his face for a moment, and his pure spirit ascended to heaven, bright with the light of battle and radiant with the light of a stainless life.

As the hours passed in the afternoon the position of Hancock's forces became extremely critical, the enemy concentrating for a tremendous onslaught and no forces to which Hancock could look for assistance within supporting distance. At 5 o'clock the enemy inaugurated the final attack by a very heavy artillery fire that demoralized to a great extent many of the recruits and substitutes who had recently joined the Second Corps. The shelling continued for about fifteen minutes, and then the whole Confederate force, led by Heth's Division, assaulted the Union line. The principal attack was made on Miles's First Division and on that part of the line held by the Fourth Brigade.

The men of the One Hundred and Sixteenth stood shoulder to shoulder, pouring in their fire on the advancing hosts, and had the other troops of the corps made as noble a fight as the Fourth Brigade, Reams Station would have been a great Union victory. But it was not to be.

While the brigade was hurling death into those in the front, two New York regiments on the right gave way and went to the rear. The victorious enemy poured through the opening, capturing flags, guns and prisoners. Hancock and Miles were everywhere, cheering, rallying and urging the men, but the break was too great to repair and the line was forced back. Fighting on and contesting the ground inch by inch the regiment fell back, but not until the works on the right were in the hands of the enemy and they were receiving on the left an enfilading fire of the most destructive character. The line gradually fell back across the space enclosed by our works until the men of the regiment found themselves fighting among the troops of the Second Division, who, in turn, were forced out of their works and were obliged to occupy and fight from the reverse side of their own intrenchments.

To go into further details of the Battle of Reams Station is not necessary in a regimental history. Suffice to say that the fight continued until dark and then both sides in the struggle withdrew from the field. The loss of the regiment was never actually known. After the command returned to Petersburg and the members compared notes, the names of seventeen men killed and ten wounded were all that could be accounted for, but there were thirty-one missing. Only four or five were ever heard of again and they were heard of as dying in southern prisons. The others were undoubtedly killed.

Captain Francis E. Crawford and Lieutenant Zadock Springer were taken prisoners. Notwithstanding the crushing defeat sustained by the two divisions of the Second Corps and the terrible loss in the ranks of the One Hundred and Sixteenth, the regiment never broke once during the afternoon and the men never abandoned the bodies of the two dead captains whom all had loved so dearly; and when darkness fell and the retreat began the bodies were placed on stretchers and carried mile after mile through the gloomy forest back to the camp at Petersburg, then embalmed and sent home.

It is difficult to understand the reason for the battle and disaster of Reams Station. It was known to the commander of the army the night before that a large force had left Petersburg for the purpose of attacking either Hancock or Warren's Fifth Corps, which was five miles on his right and between Reams Station and Petersburg. At 9 o'clock on the evening of the 24th General Warren telegraphed to General Meade that he felt certain that the force of Confederates had gone out to interfere with General Hancock and added: "They cannot do anything with me here." It would seem that it should have been determined then to either reinforce Hancock that he might fight to win a victory and beat back the column sent against him and then continue the destruction of the railroad, or, if that was not considered of sufficient importance to make a fight for, then to have called him back and abandon the work without risking a battle. But no doubt General Meade thought that General Hancock and the two divisions of the Second Corps were fully able to hold the ground and render a good account, and so they would had it been the same Second Corps that charged Marye's Heights at Fredericksburg or held the Brock Road in the Wilderness. Death had been busy in the ranks and but few men of the early part of the year's campaign were left. All the brigade and regimental commanders had fallen in the first three months of the campaign. All had been replaced, not once nor twice, but several times. At least thirty brigade commanders had fallen during the three and one-half months ending at Reams Station; and at the latter end of October thirty-seven brigade commanders had been killed and wounded, an average of three to each of the brigades in the Second Corps in this one summer campaign of less than six months. The men, too, had gone down in brigades and regiments, and the veterans of the Peninsula and Antietam had been largely replaced by recruits and substitutes who had but little heart in the work.

The number of Confederates engaged in the battle has never been ascertained. The force that Hancock fought with consisted of 8,000 infantry and cavalry, of which he lost 2,400 killed, wounded, and prisoners. The loss of officers in the Union ranks was out of all proportion. The Confederate sharpshooters picked them off, as in the case of Nowlen and Taggart. Captain E. P. Brownson, of Hancock's staff, was among the killed. He was a brave and handsome young officer, and fell while leading forward some troops to the attack. Colonel Francis A. Walker, also of the staff, in his daring got into the enemy's line and was captured.

Just before the fight commenced General Hancock placed Tom Scarlett, of Company A, on the Spires House as a safe-guard. Tom climbed to the top of the carriage house to watch the fight, but the bullets came so lively around the spot that he thought it judicious to get down and forego sightseeing. But he found it not less dangerous on the ground. A negro and dog were wounded in the garden. The family retired to the cellar and left Scarlett in sole possession. So well did he do his duty that Mrs. Spires not only kept him safely concealed during the next day when Hampton's Confederate cavalry surrounded the house, but after dark crammed his haversack with all the good things she could raise, and then personally conducted him through the lines and put him on the road back to his own camp. Sergeant James Cavanaugh, of Company B, distinguished himself greatly by defending one of the guns of Battery B, First Rhode Island Artillery. When the enemy rushed over the works Cavanaugh lost his musket in the struggle, but seizing a spade he fought like a tiger until knocked down, overpowered and taken prisoner.

A letter from General Heth, who commanded the last charge on the Union works, is of interest:

WASHINGTON, May 13th, 1895.

GENERAL ST. CLAIR MULHOLLAND,
  Philadelphia, Pa.

Dear General: Yours of May 1st was duly received. I am afraid I cannot give you the information you most desire in reference to the Reams Station fight, August 25th, 1864.

I have, assisted by Mr. Kirkly, one of the board compiling the official records of the Union and Confederate Armies, examined the records, hoping to find some data which would give us the information as to the strength of the brigades that carried your works on August 25th, 1864. I am sorry to say that there is absolutely nothing that throws any light upon this subject.

On the 25th of August, 1864, General A. P. Hill, with Wilcox's Division, or a part of it, and two brigades of my division, took up the march to Reams Station, where General Hancock with his corps, or a part of it, was engaged in destroying the Weldon Railroad.

Wilcox's Division was in the advance, and on reaching Reams Station was ordered to attack the works held by Hancock's troops. He attacked and was repulsed. My two brigades, commanded by Generals Cooke and McRae, North Carolina troops, arrived, and I was ordered by General Hill to carry the works. Lane's North Carolina Brigade, of Wilcox's Division, was assigned to my command to assist in the attack. The works I was to attack ran parallel with the railroad in front of quite a deep cut. A heavy body of woods was in front of the works I was to attack, with an open field between the woods and the works. Probably the distance across this open field was two hundred yards, more or less. I formed my command for the attack in these woods, as near to the open field as possible without being exposed to view and parallel to your works, Cooke or McRae on the right and Lane on the extreme left. I placed two or more batteries under Colonel Pegram, commanding, in a good position still

CAPTAIN AND BREVET MAJOR GARRETT NOWLEN.
Killed at Reams Station, August 25th, 1864.

further to the right, having an oblique fire on your line of works and your artillery in rear of the works. Adjusting our watches so that they indicated the same time, Pegram was ordered to open all of his guns and fire as rapidly as possible at the works and at your artillery. At the end of thirty minutes he was to cease firing, when the infantry would charge the works. Pegram's fire was wonderfully accurate and effective. Some of your guns were dismounted, caissons blown up and many horses killed. His fire had a demoralizing effect temporarily upon the troops behind the works, and before they had time to recover their normal status my infantry was in possession of the works. My loss in crossing the field was very small. The left brigade met with abattis in front of the works it was to carry and sustained greater loss. The number of prisoners, guns, etc., captured by my command in this fight will be found in the Official Records, Vol. 42, Part 1, page 851.

General Lee says in a dispatch, dated August 26th, 1864, to Hon. Jas. A. Seddon, Secretary of War: "Cooke's and McRae's North Carolina Brigades, under General Heth, and Lane's Brigade, under General Conner, with Pegram's artillery, composed the assaulting column. Seven stands of colors, 2,000 prisoners and nine pieces of artillery are in our possession. The loss of the enemy in killed and wounded is reported to be heavy, ours relatively small."

Thirty years have elapsed since this fight. All my papers and retained returns were destroyed at Appomattox, April 9th, 1865, so any estimate of the attacking force under my command when your works were carried August 25th, 1864, would be merely guesswork. I should say that the attacking force was between 4,000 and 4,500 strong.   Very truly yours,   H. HETH.

REAMS STATION.

Captain and Brevet Major-General Garrett Nowlen, who fell in the battle and died so heroically, was born in Philadelphia, on March 6th, 1835. He entered the army as second lieutenant of Company G, August 2d, 1862, and was promoted to first lieutenant and adjutant, March 1st, 1863; to captain of Company D, November 21st, 1863; to brevet major, August 25th, 1864. He was severely wounded at Fredericksburg, December 13th, 1862, the ball shattering his hip bone. He was a man delicate by nature, thoughtful and studious, of liberal education and a graduate of the Philadelphia High School; most generous, unselfish and self-sacrificing. Simple and gentle as a boy, with a high sense of honor and truth that directed every action of his life. His body was embalmed and brought to Philadelphia and buried at Laurel Hill, on the banks of the beautiful Schuylkill where he had often played in childhood's happy days. He is interred among the friends of his youth who loved him in life, and he sleeps in good and honorable company. By his side lies General Meade, the Commander of the Army of the Potomac; General Mercer, who fell at Princetown; General Hector Tyndale, who died of wounds received at Antietam; Colonel Sargent, who fell at Petersburg, and young Colonel Dalgren, who went down in front of Richmond, and many another patriot and hero. Some loving friend has marked on his tomb the words: "Oh, brave heart!" Truly a loyal and noble heart was stilled when Garret Nowlen fell.

A letter written by Lieutenant Frank McGnigan, a few days after the battle, tells in graphic language how Captain Nowlen fell:

HEADQUARTERS 116TH REGIMENT, PENNSYLVANIA VOLUNTEERS.

In the field near Petersburg, Va.

September 9th, 1864.

MAJOR CHARLES W. MATTHEWS, Philadelphia, Pa.

Dear Sir: Yours of the 4th instant has been received. It was my intention to write to the relatives of the late Captain Garrett Nowlen and give them a history of the sad event, but owing to circumstances over which I had no control I was unable to do so.

Captain Nowlen was killed at the battle of Reams Station, on the afternoon of August 25th. Our regiment had been on picket duty for several days previous to the fight. On the evening of the 24th our brigade was withdrawn from the left of the line and fell back about two miles to the breastworks at Reams Station, on the Weldon Railroad. Nothing unusual occurred during the night. The next morning we received orders to strengthen the works. The men had scarcely begun to work before orders came to march the brigade to the left into a large cornfield. We did not remain in the latter position long, but advanced into the main line of works where we remained about half an hour and were again ordered to move. This time only our regiment was ordered to move. We then deployed our line as skirmishers and at once advanced on the enemy.

The regiment had gone but a short distance when the enemy opened with a heavy fire of musketry which made our line give ground for a moment, but they soon rallied and returned the compliment. At this moment the support, composed mainly of dismounted cavalry, broke, which compelled our line to fall back. At this time Captain Nowlen gave us another proof of his bravery and coolness in time of danger. He succeeded in bringing his regiment out with comparatively small loss and gained the shelter of the works without personal injury. But a few moments only elapsed before the enemy advanced in great numbers and charged our line. They were driven back with terrible loss of life during this charge. Captain Nowlen was at his post cheering his command and exposing himself to great danger. After the latter charge an interval of about half an hour occurred, nothing of any consequence going on except now and then a shell from our batteries would fall among the Rebs and make them stir.

About 3 P. M. the enemy began to show signs of moving, and not many minutes elapsed before they began to advance in our front from the woods in great numbers with the evident intention of charging our works again. We were not kept long in suspense as they at once advanced three "lines of battle deep." Our men (but two small divisions) remained firm and held their fire until the word was given, when they opened on the enemy volley after volley of musketry. But still the enemy advanced, the fire of our men staggering them somewhat, but not breaking their lines. At this moment Captain Nowlen sprang up from behind the works and, waving his sword, cheered the men. It seemed but an instant he stood and the next he fell, shot through the heart by a minie ball, the brave soldier and courteous gentleman who had won the confidence and esteem of every officer and man in his command. His loss is deeply felt by every member of the regiment, more especially by the old officers of the regiment who have been his companions in arms for more than two years.

With the assistance of three of the men I had his body carried off the field and conveyed to the rear. Next morning, with the help of the quartermaster of our regiment, I had the body removed to City Point, where it was embalmed and from thence sent home to his relatives. All the effects that were on his person at the time of his death will be sent to you in his valise at the earliest opportunity.

Enclosed you will find the blank you sent to be filled as the questions required. I did as you requested, but thinking a detailed account would be more satisfactory, I have taken the liberty to write the above.

    Yours respectfully,
      Francis A. McGuigan.

Captain and Brevet Major Samuel Taggart.

It is difficult to find words in which to describe the high and lofty character of Samuel Taggart. It is rare, indeed, that we meet in life with a human being so replete in every good attribute that adorns a life or forms a perfect man. As a soldier he was "sans peur et sans reproche".

He was born in Pittsburg, Pa., on the 10th of May, 1841. He received his early education in the Second and Sixth Ward schools of his native city and was among the first to enter the High School on the opening of that institution in 1855. He graduated therefrom in February, 1860, and entered the Western University for the purpose of preparing for college. After continuing at the University for six months he taught a public school near Woodville, Allegheny County, Pa., the term commencing in September, 1860, and ending the following March. In the fall of 1861 he entered Westminster College, New Wilmington, Lawrence County, Pa., from which he was graduated in June, 1862. He entered the United Presbyterian Theological Seminary, Allegheny, Pa., in the spring of 1863, and continued there for one year.

Under the first call of Abraham Lincoln for troops he felt a strong desire to enter the service, and joined a company organized at that time, but there being no scarcity of recruits, he yielded to the persuasion of friends and applied himself to preparing for the ministry, having early resolved to make that profession his calling in life.

After graduating at Westminster he enlisted in Company H, One Hundred and Twenty-third Regiment, Pennsylvania Volunteers, and was appointed first sergeant of his company. He participated with the regiment in the battles of Antietam, Fredericksburg, and Chancellorsville, and was mustered out in May, 1863, the regiment having been organized under the call for nine months men. Shortly after this he entered the Theological Seminary. While a student at the seminary in the winter of 1863, he laid aside his books and organized a company of infantry which was assigned as Company I, of the One Hundred and Sixteenth, Pennsylvania Volunteers. Of his services in that regiment his surviving comrades need not be reminded. He was a young man of spotless character, brave heart, brilliant mind, and genial temperament.

The following fitting tribute to his worth is from the pen of an intimate friend and classmate at High School and College:

"He was my intimate and beloved friend for years, and his death has been to me a life-long regret. I never can restrain my tears when I think it. The pure-minded boy, the faithful friend, the gifted student, the manly man, the devoted christian, the patriotic soldier. No costlier sacrifice was ever laid on the altar of the country, than when that precious life went out on the battlefield of Virginia. The church was looking forward to his useful services as a minister. Teachers and classmates at the school and college expected and predicted great things for him. His talents and temperament would have given him an honorable place anywhere, but he cheerfully gave all. Youth, strength, education, prospects, he gave all to the cause of his country. It is only when we think of him and thousands who, like him, counted not their own lives dear to them, that we can realize what the preservation of the Union cost. It would take not a hasty sketch, but a volume to do justice to his memory".

The writer, who has seen Major Taggart on the battle-field and in camp, and who loved him as a brother, joins in every word of praise offered in his saintly memory. A soldier of the most exalted type, and a man whose daily life was a sermon on Christianity. He met death with the most serene composure, and a smile that betokened the eternal bliss that awaited his pure and noble soul. He is buried in Allegheny Cemetery near Pittsburg, and the ground where he rests is a sacred spot.

CAPTAIN AND BREVET MAJOR SAMUEL TAGGART.
Killed at Reams Station, August 25th, 1864.

"How glorious fall the valiant, sword in hand,
In front of battle for their native land."

A few days after the battle General Gibbons, commanding the Second Division of the Second Corps, issued an order depriving several regiments of their colors on the ground that their conduct at Reams Station had rendered them unworthy to carry them. The order was approved by General Meade, but General Hancock felt that the action taken was unjustly severe and entered his protest against it in a strong letter to General Grant. In this communication the commander of the Second Corps tells in plain language the eloquent story of that organization:

HEADQUARTERS SECOND CORPS,
September 28th, 1864.

LIEUTENANT-GENERAL U. S. GRANT,
Commanding Armies of the United States.

General: I have the honor to solicit your attention to the enclosed copy of an order published by Major-General Gibbons, of the 30th ult., with my endorsements thereon; and to the printed order of the Major-General commanding the Army of the Potomac, confirming and approving General Gibbons's order.

It will be seen that General Gibbons deprived three (3) regiments of his division of the privilege of bearing colors, they having lost their colors at the battle of Reams Station, August 25th, that I approved of the principle but requested that if it was adopted the rule might be made general and affect other corps as well as my own, and, finally, that General Meade overruled my suggestion and singled out these regiments, the Eighth New York Heavy Artillery, One Hundred and Sixty-fourth New York Volunteers and Thirty-sixth Wisconsin Volunteers, to be published to the army as having rendered themselves unworthy to carry colors. This without regard to the fact that in the same action other divisions of my command lost colors and that but a few days before several regiments of another corps had met with the same misfortune. Under the circumstances I respectfully submit that these regiments have been proceeded against with unnecessary severity and a slur cast upon the corps which I have the honor to command, which, in view of the past, might well have been omitted. It is, perhaps, known to you that this corps has never lost a color or a gun previous to this campaign, though oftener and more desperately engaged than any other corps in the army or, perhaps, in any other in the country. I have not the means of knowing exactly the number of guns and colors captured, but I myself saw nine in the hands of one division at Antietam and the official reports show that thirty-four fell into the hands of the corps at Gettysburg. Before the opening of this campaign it had captured at least over half a hundred colors from the enemy and never yielded one, though at a cost of over twenty-five thousand (25,000) casualties. During this campaign you can judge how well the corps has performed its part. It has captured more guns and colors than all the rest of the army combined. Its reverses have not been many and they began only when the corps had dwindled to a remnant of its former strength; after it had lost twenty-five brigade commanders and over one hundred and twenty-five regimental commanders and over twenty thousand men.

I submit that with the record of this corps it is in the highest degree unjust, by a retrospective order, to publish a part of it as unworthy to bear colors. It is not necessary, perhaps, to speak more particularly as to the injustice done these regiments, the principle discussed covering their case. I may say, however, that these regiments first appeared at the battle of Spottsylvania. At Cold Harbor the colonel of the Thirty-sixth Wisconsin—as gallant a soldier as ever lived—fell dead on the field, as did the colonel of the Eighth New York Heavy Artillery. The colonel of the One Hundred and Sixty-fourth fell mortally wounded beside his flag on the breastwork of the enemy. These regiments have since that action suffered severely, one of them, at least, having lost two commanding officers.

I respectfully request that these colors may be returned to them. They are entitled to the same privileges as other regiments—that is, the right to strive to avoid the penalties of General Order No. 37, current series, headquarters Army of the Potomac.

I am, General, your most obedient servant,

W. S. HANCOCK.
Major-General Commanding Second Corps.

In compliance with this request the colors of the regiments named were afterwards restored to them.

HEADQUARTERS OF THE ARMY OF THE POTOMAC.
November 7th.

The Eighth New York Heavy Artillery, One Hundred and Sixty-fourth New York Volunteers and the Thirty-sixth Wisconsin Volunteers, having been reported to the major-general commanding as having behaved with distinguished bravery during the engagement of October 27th, 1864, on Hatcher's Run, he takes pleasure in restoring to these gallant regiments the right to carry the colors of which they were deprived by his General Order No. 37, of September 23d, 1864.

By command of Major-General Meade.

S. WILLIAMS,
A. A. General.

CHAPTER XV.

PETERSBURG.

AFTER the battle of Reams Station the regiment remained on the reserve for two or three weeks, moving from one point to another in rear of the line, but furnishing full details for picket and being constantly exposed to the fire of the enemy's batteries, if not under that of the infantry.

In September the command moved into the front line and then remained in the trenches for two months, a continuous battle night and day. A letter of General Hancock to the commander of the army tells in pathetic words the story of this time:

HEADQUARTERS SECOND CORPS,
November 10th, 1864.

BRIGADIER-GENERAL S. WILLIAMS,
Assistant Adjutant-General, Army of the Potomac.

General: I have the honor to invite the attention of the major-general commanding to the following remarks:

General Mott's division, of my corps, took up the intrenched line near Petersburg from near the Norfolk Railroad to the left on the 20th of August. On the 24th of September the other two divisions relieved the Tenth Army Corps, holding the line from the Norfolk Railroad to the river. My corps has held the centre line from Battery No. 24 to Redoubt Converse since that time, Mott's division having been withdrawn on one occasion for a few days, Mott and Gibbons for a few days during the operations of October 26th, 27th and 28th, and Miles's division for two days after the return of Mott's and Gibbons's divisions.

With these exceptions when the troops were withdrawn to participate in movements against the enemy, my command has been under fire in front of Petersburg for two months and a half, holding the only part of the lines of the army in close proximity to the enemy. They have been subjected night and day to the fire of artillery, and have frequently been engaged in considerable picket skirmishes.

I have about two thousand men on picket daily, and 1600 of these are in action, it may be said, day and night.

The troops in the enclosed works and rifle-pits are subjected to a constant fire from the enemy's mortars, and are obliged to live in underground holes and bomb-proofs, and are called upon almost nightly to get under arms and to be in readiness to resist an attack. They cannot even walk about in safety in their own camp on account of the danger of stray bullets, mortar shells or the fire of sharpshooters. They have no opportunity for drill or instruction.

My command is composed largely of new men.

From the left of my corps to the left of the army, I believe there is hardly a place where the enemy are in sight. The troops are not harassed by being called up in the night, or by constant skirmishing during the day, and their camps are not disturbed by the enemy's artillery. They are comfortably camped by regiments and brigades, with abundant opportunity for exercise, drill and instruction.

I submit that my command has been a long time without rest and in a state of constant and wearing strain, and has been very disadvantageously situated in every respect, compared with the other corps.

I do not speak of it complainingly, and do not know that there is any remedy for it, but consider it a proper matter to lay before the Major-General commanding the army. I am General,

Very respectfully, your obedient servant,

WINFIELD S. HANCOCK,
Major-General of Volunteers.

During the whole time of the siege there were continual fights betwen the pickets. Frequently whole brigades and divisions would be drawn into these affairs which would result in serious loss. After dark the attacks and counter-attacks were of nightly occurrence, and sometimes the firing of a single picket would quickly develop into an engagement extending for a mile along the line. The lines were very close at places, and the intervening space between them would be frequently swept by fire from dark to sunrise. Even when peace would reign for a short time, and not a sound be heard in front, half the picket would be standing at a "ready", and at the slightest sound would begin firing, and then blaze away for hours lest some force might be moving to the attack. The more intense the darkness the heavier the fire, and brigades would fire twenty or thirty thousand rounds of ammunition during a single night. Morning and daylight would reveal the same open spot just as it was the evening before, without a single indication that anyone had been moving over it during the darkness. A load of powder and ball had been expended and nobody hurt; no, not even kept awake or disturbed in their slumbers by the noise, for everyone became accustomed to the row and would dream in perfect peace, if not in security, even when siege guns, mortars, musketry and all were blazing away for miles along the line.

But danger was ever present on the picket line at Petersburg. Many a night, from sundown to sunup the next morning, the dead were almost as numerous as on some of the celebrated battlefields of the world's history. as many as twenty bodies have been carried in from the front before daybreak in the Fourth Brigade alone. The line of newly made graves would be extended and reach a little further, that was all. Before dinner time the incident would be forgotten and life go on as usual.

ON THE PICKET RESERVE.

The lines were so close at many points that the men could have reached over and touched the muzzle of each other's muskets, and the line of earth-works occupied by each line was almost as heavy as the usual field works that sheltered a line of battle.

Thousands of ever wakeful eyes were watching and thousands of ears were constantly listening. Thousands of rifles were continually pointed through chinks in the log revetment, and the vigilant sharpshooter, finger on trigger, was ever ready to draw a bead on any moving object, not only on the picket line, but, by using the telescope affixed to the barrel, on moving figures a mile in the rear. To expose a head on the picket line meant instant death, and many points far in rear of the main line of battle were so acutely covered by the sharpshooters that it was almost impossible to pass without being hit. These dangerous places soon became known to everyone, and when it became necessary to cross, one had to dash past on a run. But no matter how great the speed, half a dozen bullets would sing around and urge still more rapid flight. The relief went out in the dark, as changing in the sunlight was out of the question. The relief that went on before dawn in the morning had to remain on the line until after dark in the evening, but the firing was principally at night and was then continuous.

It is questionable if there was a single hour from the first shot fired at the siege of Petersburg until the Confederates evacuated the works ten months afterwards, that there was not firing on some part of the line. It might be on the immediate front, or on the right or left, or maybe miles distant, but night or day, listen when one would, the firing could be heard.

The reserve of the picket was sometimes quite a comfortable place, and although out in front was less exposed to danger than the main line of works. Generally in a hollow of the ground or otherwise sheltered, the men could be quiet, and pass the day well enough, but it was necessary to keep very still, and in daylight all communication with the line in the rear and the picket in front was impossible. The hours seemed long, but sometimes the shelter afforded a chance to rise from a reclining posture sufficiently to allow a game of cards. Where that was not possible the men hugged the ground and chatted, bantered jokes and took a whiff of the pipe, provided the enemy would not see the smoke. Stories were told and every incident was seized upon for pastime. While the nervous tension of being constantly exposed to danger was very great, yet as the months passed away everyone became in a measure reconciled to the situation and found pleasure in the most trivial things of life.

A group of soldiers on the reserve lying on their stomachs, chin resting on the hands and elbows on the ground, found entertainment in watching a tumble-bug rolling before him a ball of earth three times as large as himself, and admired the perseverance of the little insect in doing his work all over again every time the men would set the ball back a foot. A stunning hour's amusement was furnished by a battle royal between two colonies of ants who advanced in lines and fought just as the men were fighting here, the only difference being in the size of the combatants and the arms used. The ants tore each other's limbs off and left lots of dead in the field, just as men do, and as someone remarked: "No doubt they are fighting for some principle just as we are." "With this difference," said another, "that a storm may come up in an hour and a flood will wash away the sand bank. The ants, their principles and quarrels will all be swept away together and that will be the end, while the principle for which we are fighting will remain forever, even if we to a man are swept away in the storm of battle." "Well, it is only a question of time," put in a third. "The day will

LIEUTENANT GEORGE HALPIN.
Died at close of War of disease contracted in Prison.

come when all men, their ideas and principles will have passed away as completely as these ants." "That all may be," said another, "but men do not end with this life and maybe what we do here will have an influence on the hereafter. Who knows?"

"Well," said Lieutenant Halpin, "I will tell you what I know. I know that there is a hereafter for I once saw the ghost of a soldier."

"Oh, I say, that is something worth listening to," cried one of the men. "Tell us about the ghost."

"Be quiet, then, and I will relate an incident that occurred to me in India."

HALPIN TELLS A GHOST STORY.

"I had the military fever ever since I was able to stand, and when I was a bit of a chap in Ireland I remember sideling up to every red-coat I met in the street to look at the little cap on the top of his head and make mental calculations as to how long it would be until I was big enough to enlist. Time passed, however, and one day I found myself quite tall enough to don the red cap, so I took Her Majesty's shilling and for a week stalked around the country with a bunch of ribbons flying from over my left ear, mighty proud of all my new fixings and, bidding all my friends good-bye. I was soon off for the East Indies, for the regiment in which I enlisted was under orders for that sweet clime when I took the shilling. I need not tell you of my two years' experience up to the time I saw the ghost, but will come right to the point and place at once. I just arrived in India as the murmuring of the great mutiny of '57 was being heard, and soon the storm broke in all its fury. It offered a splendid opportunity for death or promotion. The fighting, to be sure, was not so vigorous as we have it here, but the men who were not hit by the Sepoys were pretty sure to catch the cholera, so the chances were about even. Lots of fellows went down in the regiment to which I was attached and half the non-commissioned officers and men were laid away in the gullies and jungles as we marched from one place to another under the hottest sun that a man ever endured. Promotion was rapid in consequence, and I wore sergeant's stripes before the mutiny was well under way. Now, the ghost I am going to tell you about was not of our people, but a native, and maybe one of the fellows that we shot away from the cannon, only he was not in two pieces as a ghost of that kind would naturally be. It happened at the siege of the ancient city of Delhi. The Sepoys got possession of that place early in the trouble, and we had a mighty big time getting it back. The whole country for miles around the city is covered with palaces, mosques and splendid ruins of the tombs of emperors and princes of the Mogul dynasty, and near the Cashmere gate the bungalows of the English residents cover the hills. I was sergeant of a picket reserve, and instead of lying out on the ground as we do here, the reserve occupied the second story of a large stone building near the English settlement. It was a quiet moonlight night and red hot. My relief had come in and, piling up their arms in a corner, they dropped on the floor and in half an hour every man was fast asleep. I did not feel like sleeping and, lighting my pipe, I sat myself on a large table in the centre of the floor in the immense room to enjoy a smoke. While sitting there I heard a step ringing on the stairway and it became more distinct every moment as it neared the top. I naturally looked towards the opened door and was astonished to see a Hindoo walking in. He was turbaned and draped in white, with the saddest, queerest eyes I ever saw. As he entered the room I jumped from the table and called to him, demanding his business. He looked straight at me with those infernal queer eyes and walked right into the room, moving as though he would walk around the table and avoid stepping on the sleeping men. When he had almost completed the circuit of the room and was abreast with me I yelled at him to halt, but he still kept staring at me with those coal black eyes and moving right on. I made up my mind that he would not leave the room until I knew what his business was, and grasping my sword—the sergeants at that time carried a short, thick weapon, like the old Romans used to do—I ran to the door, and as he approached I ordered him to halt or I would run him through. The sinner never took his terrible eyes off me nor stopped for a moment, and when he came close I could stand it no longer but involuntarily stepped aside to let him pass, and as he did so I once more screamed at him to halt. He did not obey, so I ran my sword right through him, but there seemed to be nothing there and the phantom Hindoo was going down the steps with a stately, even tread. I then called down to the sentinel at the door to stop that man, but the sentinel saw no one pass either going in or coming out. Gentlemen, that is my ghost story. It ain't much, to be sure, but it is true."

"Very good, Halpin, but what was in the canteen that night before you saw the spectral form?"

"Not a blessed thing but water, and the water from the Jumna is not fit to drink, either."

"Now", put in Lieutenant Brady, "let me tell you a story of a real Christian ghost, and a soldier at that. You all remember that on Saturday evening, May 2d, at Chancellorsville, the fight was pretty hot for a while, and a good many of our people dropped in the woods on the right of our line? Well, it is of one of them that I will tell you. There was an old lady living at that time in the little village of Hockendaque, on the Lehigh River, who had a son in the Eleventh Corps. On Sunday morning, May 3d, the old lady crossed the river to Catasaqua, a village just opposite to where she lived, and called upon the pastor of a church, with whom she was acquainted. She told him that her son was home and walking around the streets, but he would not speak to her. 'Last evening (Saturday)', said she, 'I was washing out some things, the door was open, and who should walk in but my son John.

I did not expect him, and I was so astonished for a moment, I did not realize his presence, then quickly drying my hands on my apron, I ran towards him. Would you believe it, he never offered to come towards me, but giving me such a sad, strange look, and without uttering a word, he turned and walked up the stairs. As soon as I could come to my senses I ran after him, but he was gone. The window was open and he must have climbed down the trellis work that the grape-vine clings to, and so left the house. I lay awake all night thinking, and expecting him to come back, but daylight came and no John. I got the breakfast and started out to hunt him up, and as I was walking along the street I saw my son just in front of me. I ran to catch up but he turned a corner, and when I reached there he was gone. I dare say he went into one of the neighbor's houses, but which one I could not find out. Now, sir, you can see that my son is evidently angry at something and will not speak to me. Won't you come over to Hockendaque to see him, and find out what is the matter'? The reverend gentleman, pitying the poor woman, returned with her to her home, hoping to find her boy and have mother and son reconciled. He hunted everywhere through the village, but could learn nothing of the soldier. No one had seen him but his mother. On Tuesday morning, May 5th, a letter came saying that the boy had been killed on Saturday evening, just at the time that he walked in to see his mother. Gentlemen, that is a true story of a Christian soldier in full uniform and in broad daylight, and no sad-eyed Hindoo prowling around at midnight dressed in white, like Halpin tells about."

"It's my turn now", said another officer, "and I, also, will tell of a Union soldier who fell at Chancellorsville. You all recollect Captain Harry G ———, of the Seventy-third Pennsylvania Volunteers. He was a frequent visitor in the camp of the One Hundred and Sixteenth, and we all loved him. He was one of the best and most lovable men in the army. I remember that he spent Sunday before the fight with us. Well, on that same Saturday evening that the dead boy went home to see his mother, Captain G—— was killed during the charge of Stonewall Jackson on our right. Within a very few minutes of the time he fell his family heard his footsteps walking up the stairs and into his own room in his home in Philadelphia. The foot-fall was a heavy one, made by an army boot, and his sister remarked at the time: 'That is Harry's wraith'"!

"Very good", chimed in Captain McGraw. "Now, I will tell you of a ghost in Ireland, who galloped on horseback on certain nights of the year".

"Oh, no"! chorused everyone, "no Irish ghosts to-night, especially midnight shadows on horseback. That fellow must have belonged to the cavalry. Give us plain United States broad-daylight spectres. None of those dressed-in-white-midnight gentlemen who only appear in India or Ireland."

"But what puzzles me", said another, "is how Captain G—— got his boots home. We can understand how a man can get through space himself, when a piece of shell or minie ball releases him from his earthly tenement, but how he can take his army boots along! That is the mystery". No reply greets this psychological query, however, for it is getting dark, and the firing is getting brisk on the picket line. It is almost time for the relief to go out, and who knows but that some of us will be ghosts before morning.

It is dark enough now to creep out to the front without being seen, and here is the detail with the canteens refilled; but, before we go, maybe Halpin will give us a song".

"Well, I don't mind", says Halpin, "but one has to be careful to sing in a low tone, or our friends on the other side of the works might hear. I will give you a new song, just out, and by a namesake of mine, Colonel Charles G. Halpin. It is a mighty fine thing, and written by a good soldier and an able all 'round man":

THE OLD CANTEEN.

There are bonds of all sorts in this world of ours,
Letters of friendship and ties of flowers,
   And true lovers' knots I ween;
The girl and the boy are bound by a kiss,
But there's never a bond, old friend, like this—
   We have drank from the same canteen.

It was sometimes water and sometimes milk,
And sometimes applejack, fine as silk;
   But whatever the tipple has been,
We shared it together in bane or bliss,
And I warm to you, friend, when I think of this—
   We have drank from the same canteen.

The rich and the great sit down to dine,
And they quaff to each other in sparkling wine
   From glasses of crystal and green;
But I guess in the golden potations they miss
The warmth of regard to be found in this—
   We have drank from the same canteen.

We have shared our blankets and tents together,
And have marched and fought in all kinds of weather,
   And hungry and full we have been;
Had days of battle and days of rest,
But this memory I cling to and love the best—
   We have drank from the same canteen.

For when wounded I lay on the outer slope,
With my blood flowing fast, and but little hope
   Upon which my faint spirit could lean;
Oh, then, I remember, you crawled to my side,
And, bleeding so fast it seems both must have died,
   We drank from the same canteen.

"Beautiful, beautiful. It is dark enough now and we had better get the men out on the line before the moon comes up."

"Second relief, fall in!"

Many an amusing incident and many a narrow escape occurred during the siege. One day while occupying the line in front of Fort Steadman, Wm. J. Curley, drummer boy of Company E, came from the fort across the field and above the rifle pits, looking for his company. Lieutenant

Brady, of Company D, seeing his danger, called to him to jump into one of the rifle pits. Before he had time to do so, however, a Johnny let go and sent a ball through the head of Curley's drum.

Curley was almost a child, but the youngest member of the regiment was a drummer boy of Company H, Christopher H. Moore, who enlisted when he was nine years and eight months old. Christopher was much better at foraging on the enemy than in getting music out of his drum. Because of his ability in preying upon the country he was nick-named "Mosby", after the celebrated cavalryman. If there were any chickens left on the line after the musician of Company H had passed along it was not his fault. "Mosby" seemed to have but one tune on his drum, but the music he gave the farmers when he was hustling for something good to eat was of many kinds and full of melody and sweetness.

About October 1st the regiment moved from the left to the right of Fort Steadman, a position which the colored troops had occupied previously. The regiment got into position somewhat earlier than our colored friends expected. Consequently they did not get all their commissary stores packed up as quickly as they should have done. The boys of the regiment were out of rations and very hungry. Private Caldwell, Company E, known all over the regiment as "Big Jim", was one of the company cooks. He had a plan to get a supply without waiting for the commissary. He asked two men to go with him on a foraging expedition, and he did not have to ask twice. Away they went and in less than an hour they returned with sixty pounds of smoked bacon, two bags of beans, three boxes of hard tack and one jug of molasses. The colored boys had to suffer the loss, to be sure, while the boys of the regiment were swimming in bean soup for a week.

In a letter written by Charley Barth we learn in his own language of an incident in the trenches: "About the first week in October we lay in front of Fort Steadman in the extreme outer works (the same that the regiment leveled to the ground later on). There was nothing between us and the enemy, two hundred yards away, and we were in full view of each other. If you showed your head you could hear the "zip" of the ball from the sharpshooters' rifles. One day, about 4 P. M., the Confederates began to cheer along their whole line, and about 5 P. M. Sergeant McElroy said : ' Barth, you will report for special duty.' In a short time I was called in line with about thirty or forty of our regiment. An officer called, "Attention!" we were counted off in fours and a sergeant placed in command of each group of four. (The sergeants were from the Sixty-fourth New York, I think. They were not of our regiment.) Then he gave us our instructions that after dark the sergeants were to take their men over the works and try to get close enough to the Johnnys to find out what they had been cheering about, but to be sure and come in before daylight as it would be sure death to remain out longer. Well, to say that I was scared is putting it very mildly. I looked over that corn field that lay between us and the enemy, and they had full command of the field. The sergeant was to do the advancing and we were to support him. Well, after dark we went over the works and on our hands and knees crawled towards the enemy. Oh, how still we were and how careful not to break a stalk of corn! Finally, we came to a small pit, dug, no doubt, by one of our pickets before the lines were made. Here the sergeant told us to remain until he came back as he was going on further. Well, that was the last we saw of him. In a short time the Johnnys opened on us, and how we four did hug the sacred soil of Virginia! What a rattling the balls made among the cornstalks and what a long night that was to us! I can remember the name of but one of our group, Daily, of Company A or B. Well, no one heard what the Johnnys had been cheering about but one, and he was captured. He was a member of Company G, I think."

During September and October the regiment was moved from one part of the line to another, but always in the trenches—sometimes in Forts Morton and Rice, again in Forts Haskell or Steadman, but always under fire.

Colonel Mulholland returned October 15th, having been absent, suffering from wounds, from June 1st, and assumed command of the brigade, relieving Lieutenant-Colonel Glenny, Sixty-fourth New York.

CHAPTER XVI.

PETERSBURG.
TURNING MOVEMENT AGAINST LEE'S RIGHT.

OCTOBER 27TH.

AS the end of October approached General Grant, wishing to make a vigorous effort to capture Petersburg or, at least, to seize the Boydton Plank Road and South Side Railroad before the bad weather set in and compelled the suspension of active field operations, sent the larger part of the Second, Fifth and Ninth Corps to find and strike the right of the Confederate line.

The expeditionary party marched during the night of October 26th and fought the battle of Boydton Plank Road on the 27th. The withdrawal of so large a force from the works in front of Petersburg necessarily left but a very thin line in the intrenchments. The First Division, Second Corps, commanded by General Nelson A. Miles, then numbering about 6,000 men, was spread out so as to occupy the whole line from the Appomattox River on the right to Battery 24, half way between the Jerusalem Plank Road and the Weldon Railroad.

The Fourth Brigade of the Division, then commanded by the writer, occupied the line immediately opposite the Crater, where the mine explosion of July 30th had taken place. The left of the brigade occupying Fort Rice and the right extending towards Fort Steadman.

The One Hundred and Sixteenth Regiment was stationed in the intrenchments near Fort Haskell. The picket firing was brisk during the day and rumors of the battle, which was then in progress on the left, were flying, and an anxious spirit was manifest among the men in the works.

Towards evening, General Miles, wishing to deceive the enemy as to the force then holding the Union line, ordered an attack on the works in front to be made by a small party from each of the two brigades commanded by Colonel McDougal, and the writer who, being one of the principals in the affair, will tell the story of the event as it occurred to him personally.

About 5.30 P. M., I received an order from General Miles to take one hundred men and make a demonstration on the enemy's works. Believing it quite possible to capture one of the forts in my front, I selected for the attempt one hundred men of the One Hundred and Forty-eighth Pennsylvania Regiment. I took the men from this organization because I could not withdraw the One Hundred and Sixteenth from the position occupied without endangering that important point in the line, and I knew the men of the One Hundred and Forty-eighth Regiment to be excellent and reliable, and a big consideration was that they were armed with the Spencer magazine rifle, capable of firing seven shots without reloading.

The storming party was under command of Captain J. Z. Brown, Lieutenant P. D. Sprankle and Lieutenants Alexander Gibb and John F. Benner.

Addressing the men, I told them of the desperate nature of the duty required, and I said that no one need go unless willingly. Every man was not only willing but anxious to go. As it was impossible to reach the picket line (from which the attack was to be made) in a body since the sharpshooters were vigilant, and covered the ground between our main line and the picket, I ordered the party to break ranks and go out individually, taking different routes and creeping through the low brush, be able to assemble at a point indicated without being seen by the enemy. In fifteen minutes every man of the party met me as ordered. We were within fifty yards of the object of attack, and, so far, all had gone well. Forming the party into two sections, I ordered one, under Captain Brown, to run around the right of the fort and enter the sally port, while the second section was to charge up the face of the Banquet slope and, gaining the crest, pour their fire down into the works.

Ten of the men were given axes instead of rifles, and were to run ahead, cut the wires that joined the chevaux-de-frise together, and open a section for the storming party to get through. The twilight was gathering by the time all was ready, and the orders were to "make the demonstration at 6 o'clock". As I was about to give the order to charge, I looked back and saw a horseman galloping rapidly towards me. He was coming from the direction of Division Headquarters, and thinking that he might be bringing some last order, I paused until he came up. It was Captain Henry D. Price, my Adjutant-General. He threw himself from his horse and said: "Colonel, what's up? I have been at Division Headquarters, and heard that you were going to make an attack. I am going along"

I did not wish him to go, but he insisted upon it, and knowing his value, I finally consented with much reluctance. He drew his sword, unbuckled the belt and handing it, together with the scabbard, to Lieutenant Tom Lee, one of my aides, he said: "Tom, if I am killed, send these to my mother".

I gave the order, and the gallant little band, leaping over the slight earth-works of the picket line, ran direct for the enemy's fort, not fifty yards distant. With a few blows the axe-men cut the fastenings that lashed the chevaux-de-frise together, dragged out a section, and the party ran through.

The attack was a complete success, Brown entering the fort from the rear and Price mounting the slope in front.

CAPTAIN AND BREVET MAJOR HENRY D. PRICE.
Killed at Petersburg, October 27th, 1864

The defenders for a few moments made a gallant defense, but in vain. In ten minutes from the starting on the charge, the fort was carried, and all in it was in our possession. It was getting quite dark when the rush was made, and Captain Price disappeared from my view. I could not see him after he reached the crest, but I heard his voice as he called to the men to follow him, and then I heard him directing their fire. Suddenly his voice ceased, and I felt sure that he had fallen.

As soon as the fort was won, the prisoners were sent into our lines, and an effort made to bring in or destroy the artillery, but little could be accomplished with the latter, as the noble band that had done so well were now few in number. There was no possibility of getting re-enforcements. None could be spared from the thin line that held the Union works, and after holding the Confederate fort for twenty minutes, I very reluctantly gave the order to abandon it, and return to our own line, and not a moment too soon, for the enemy had begun concentrating a force to recapture the works and their forts, and from the right and the left of the one captured, there poured in a terrible fire on the little band of Union men then in possession.

The following account of the action is from the Philadelphia "Press" of November 1st, 1864:

Special correspondence to the "Press".

From General Grant's Army—Brilliant affair on the centre—Capture of a Rebel Fort and fifty prisoners—The garrison was completely surprised—A Confederate Colonel in our hands—Important information gained—The enemy's line very weak—Their picket line cut into for several hours.

(Mr. C. Edmund's Despatches).

Before Petersburg, October 28th, 1864, 9 P. M.

The tremendous artillery firing which took place last evening, commencing about 9 o'clock and continuing until past midnight, turns out not to have been altogether without cause. One of the most brilliant affairs in which the Second Corps has participated has just been enacted by a portion of the Fourth Brigade of the First Division. About one hundred and fifty yards beyond our picket line and scarcely a fourth of a mile from the famous mine which was exploded by the Ninth Corps under Burnside some months ago stands one of the strongest and best constructed fortifications in the enemy's outer line. It is an earthwork, with bomb proofs, and is environed with abattis of novel construction. Between this fort and Fort Rice, held by one brigade, is a ravine which the adjacent enemy's forts may sweep. The order for the assault was issued by General Miles, who intended the affair mainly as a reconnoissance, having no idea that the enemy could be so easily caught napping. To Colonel Mulholland, One Hundred and Sixteenth Pennsylvania Volunteers, the general management of the works was intrusted. Much against the wishes of the colonel, Captain Henry D. Price, of the same regiment, volunteered to lead the charge, and a detachment of one hundred men from the One Hundred and Forty-eighth Pennsylvania Regiment also volunteered. Shortly after 5.45 P. M. the brave little band passed out from the defences and silently formed inside our picket lines. Colonel Mulholland instructed Captain Price as to the method of removing the abattis and directed the men not to fire a shot but to use the bayonet. They were likewise ordered not to cheer unless they should succeed in entering the fort, when a single cheer would be a sufficient signal for sending forward reinforcements. About 6 o'clock the men started forward on double-quick. It was raining at the time. The evening was dark, and they had almost reached the fort before the enemy perceived them. Still no shot was fired. They sprang over the earthworks and before the garrison could recover from its surprise the victory was ours. The Confederates made some little resistance, but they had been taken completely by surprise and, save a few who effected their escape, the garrison, numbering about fifty men, were taken prisoners. We succeeded in taking the following officers: Colonel Harrison, Forty-sixth Virginia Regiment, commanding the fort; Lieutenant-Colonel Wise, Forty-sixth Virginia Regiment; Lieutenant Bylen, Thirty-fourth Virginia Regiment; Lieutenant Coxe, Forty-sixth Virginia Regiment, and about forty private soldiers. Colonel Harrison could not at first be induced to believe that he was a prisoner, so astonished was he at the audacity of the enterprise, and pronounced the affair to be a "d——d Yankee trick."

We learned from the prisoners that Wise's Brigade, Bushrod Johnson's Division of General Anderson's Corps, together with Ransom's and Finnegan's Brigades, held the line opposite us. In addition to the prisoners taken, numbers of the enemy were killed and wounded in the trenches, refusing to surrender. Colonel Harrison admits that if our assailing party had been supported by two hundred men they could have maintained their position in the fort. But this was not to be. As soon as we took the fort our men gave a cheer as a signal, and Colonel Mulholland despatched his aides to the adjacent fortifications to obtain the needed reinforcements. It was in the plan of arrangements that the Twenty-sixth Michigan should be held in reserve. But this regiment did not arrive upon the grounds in time and no available troops could be got ready to send forward for half an hour. In the meantime the enemy rallied about seven hundred strong and drove out our men. About fifty men out of the hundred are missing, the majority being wounded. Captain Price, the leader of the charge, was the only officer killed. His body is still in the enemy's possession. A complete list of the casualties is subjoined. During the fighting which this rencontre led to neither side used artillery, each fearing that it might inflict more damage upon its own men than on the enemy. But immediately upon the return of our assaulting party with their prisoners all our forts in this vicinity opened upon the Confederate forts a terrific cannonade, to which they responded with equal vigor. The firing commenced about 9 o'clock, as I have stated, and lasted until 1 o'clock this morning. During the whole time the rain was falling.

[From the Philadelphia "Press" of November 2d, 1864.]

The body of Captain Price has been recovered. A flag of truce will be sent for it in a day or two. A couple of deserters who came in last night state that they saw the body of a captain lying in a trench fronting the fort, and from their description there can be no doubt that it was the body of the lamented officer referred to.

The Colonel Wise captured turns out to be a nephew of ex-Governor Wise. He was in Philadelphia at the breaking out of the war and was a student in the office of one of our most eminent members of the bar. At the time of his capture Governor Wise was in the fort but escaped by concealing himself in one of the bomb proofs. He had just despatched a courier to one of the adjacent regiments with a circular. The courier was taken but chewed up the missive in such a hurry that its contents are unknown. All the prisoners admit that their line was weaker than it had ever been before since the campaign commenced. They say that if we had had one regiment in reserve to reinforce the storming party we could have held the fort permanently, and with this fort we could have swept the whole outer line of their works. No better evidence of the weakness of Lee's army is needed than this fact.

As soon as the storming party returned to our own line all the forts on both sides opened a terrific fire that continued until midnight. The rain fell and the darkness became intense. The One Hundred and Sixteenth Regiment stood in line during the fight, ready to move forward if ordered to do so. When the men learned of the death of Captain Price there was many a tear shed for the gallant boy whom we all loved so much. Lieutenant P. D. Sprankle, of the One Hundred and Forty-eighth Regiment, was severely wounded and left in the hands of the enemy, as were nearly all the wounded of that regiment. In the darkness and confusion it was impossible to remove them.

I have said that I selected the men of the One Hundred and Forty-eighth Regiment for this affair because I believed them to be reliable. I will add that I now think that in point of discipline, material of which it was composed, gallantry and every quality necessary to make a perfect organization that regiment had no superior and but few equals in the army. The article taken from the Philadelphia "Press" and quoted here does an injustice when it says that the storming party was led by Captain Price. The attack was led by Captain J. Z. Brown and Captain Price was with the party as a staff officer but took a very active part until he fell. I had the very great pleasure of recommending Captain Brown for the brevet rank of major and also a Congress medal of honor for his distinguished bravery and excellent conduct on this occasion, and I rejoice that the well-deserved honors were accorded him.

A few days after the fight a flag of truce went out, and the body of Captain Price recovered. We learned that on the morning after the assault, an Irishman of a Georgia regiment had seen the body and recognized it by the number of the regiment as a former member of the Irish Brigade. He had tenderly wrapped him in a blanket and carefully buried him. When the body was brought into our lines, it was embalmed and sent home. The ball that killed him had entered his forehead just above the eye. When he was embalmed he looked smiling and natural, his lips partly open, showing his beautiful teeth, and so died one whom we all loved and knew as "Little Pricey". Only a boy, just from school, but a hero and a veteran, gentle and unassuming, but brave as the bravest. How his boyish laughter would ring through camp! Even in battle his face would wear a smile. He sleeps by the Schuylkill on whose banks Meade and Hancock and a host of his comrades rest, and among the thousands who fell in the great struggle, none are more worthy of honor than the noble boy who died so bravely, and whose memory will ever be cherished.

A few days before the death of Captain Price, as he and I were passing along the works, we noticed a mass of roses in an old garden. I accidently expressed a desire to have one. The autumn had lingered long that year, and it was remarkable that the rose tree was in bloom. The bush was growing on a rise of ground, lately the garden of the Hare House, but where Fort Steadman had been built. The spot where the roses were blooming was exposed to the fire of the sharpshooters, and to pull a rose would seem like courting instant death. When, in passing, I had admired the flowers, Harry had said nothing, but in half an hour afterwards he came into my tent with an armful of roses. He had exposed himself to the fire until he had pulled every one from the bush. I could not help but admire his utter want of fear and reckless daring, although condemning the useless risk he had taken. As he was standing in the tent-door, with his arms full of flowers, and laughing as if the whole thing were a great joke, one of the boys of his company came up to bid him good-bye, as he was just starting for home on a twenty days' furlough. As I knew that the young man lived quite near the Captain's home, I quickly tied up a large bunch of the roses and told him to deliver them to Captain Price's mother.

A few months after the close of the war, I visited the family, and I found Mrs. Price to be a sweet old lady. As she sat in the parlor, talking of her dead boy, I noticed hanging on the wall above her head a garland of roses under glass.

When I inquired where they came from, Harry's sister said that "he had sent them home to mother a few days before being killed". I then remembered the circumstances, and tried to tell the family how they came to be there, but found it impossible. Every time I essayed to speak, my feelings overcame me. If Mrs. Price is still living she may learn, for the first time, from these pages, the story of her son's roses.

The captured work was known as Davidson's Salient, and stood about fifty yards to the left (the Union left) of the Crater. A dark, rainy night followed the fight, and when morning broke, the men of the One Hundred and Forty-eighth eagerly scanned the fort that they had so gallantly captured the evening before, and which was now again in the hands of the enemy, and saw some bodies lying around the work. One with upturned face to the falling rain was recognized as that of Captain Price. The men composing the storming party of the One Hundred and Forty-eighth were heartily congratulated by their comrades, and the following order was issued from Brigade Headquarters:

(General Orders. No. 31.)

HEADQUARTERS FOURTH BRIGADE, FIRST DIVISION,
SECOND CORPS.

October 28th, 1864.

The Colonel commanding the brigade takes pleasure in congratulating the detail of the One Hundred and Forty-eighth Pennsylvania Volunteers for the gallantry displayed in the assault and capture of the enemy's fort, on the evening of October 27th, 1864. Captain Jerry Brown, Lieutenants Sprankle, Gibb and Benner deserve special mention for their bravery and skill in leading the charge.

He deeply regrets the loss of Captain Henry D. Price, One Hundred and Sixteenth Pennsylvania Volunteers, Acting Assistant Adjutant-General, Fourth Brigade, who fell nobly sustaining the proud name he had won by his valor in the field, and sympathizes with the brave men who were wounded.

By order of Colonel Mulholland,

J. WENDEL MUFFLY,
Lieutenant and A. A. A. G.

The Confederate account of the affair is given by General B. R. Johnson, and is most interesting. He states that the Confederates took fifteen prisoners, including one Lieutenant. He also accounts for Captain Price, whom he mentions. As thirty-three of the One Hundred and Forty-eighth were missing, it would seem that seventeen of them must have been killed or left between the lines too severely wounded to get away.

HEADQUARTERS JOHNSON'S DIVISION.
Petersburg, Va., October 28th, 1864.

Lieutenant: About 10 o'clock on yesterday morning, I moved Wallace's Brigade to the right, and relieved Saunder's and Harris's Brigades in the trenches. Wise's Brigade was moved from reserve into the position on the front line vacated by Wallace's Brigade. My right now rests at Battery No. 30.

About dark last evening a force from the One Hundred and Forty-eighth Pennsylvania Regiment, Fourth Brigade, First Division, Second Corps, perhaps one hundred strong, advanced without support upon the battery on our front line to the right of the Baxter Road, known as Davidson's Battery. It was the usual hour for posting and relieving pickets, and the division officer of the day, who happened to be passing at that point, mistook the force for pickets returning to the line, and gave orders to sentinels not to fire. By others this force was regarded as deserters coming to our lines. This impression was communicated by the orders on the infantry line to the gun in rear of the Crater, which bore on the ground over which the force

MAJOR-GENERAL ANDREW A. HUMPHREYS.
Commanded Second Corps, November 25th, 1864 to June 28th, 1865.

advanced. A light fire was, however, opened by our infantry to the right and left of Davidson's Battery. With axes the little force opened a passage through our chevaux-de-frise, and entered Davidson's Battery and mingled with our men. Their hostile character having been ascertained, troops of Wise's Brigade charged them and drove them out, capturing one Lieutenant and fourteen men, who report that a number of their men were wounded and killed in the advance, among the latter a Captain of the One Hundred and Sixteenth Pennsylvania Regiment.

About 10 P. M. the enemy advanced upon and drove out men from a portion of the picket line on the right of Rive's house, occupied by troops of Wallace's Brigade. General Wallace promptly threw out a force and reoccupied the line. During these events the mortar and cannon firing were heavy, especially from Colquitt's Salient to my right. Later in the night there was considerable artillery firing on my right. During the latter part of the night, Brigadier-General Ransom, whose brigade is on my left, and extends to the river, reported that the enemy's troops were seen to be moving to our left. It was thought they might be massing in his front.

Respectfully, your obedient servant,

B. R. JOHNSON,
Major-General.

LIEUTENANT McWILLIE,
A. A. A.-G.

On the 26th of November, General Winfield S. Hancock left the Second Corps and proceeded north to organize a new corps to be composed entirely of veterans. To try to express in words the sorrow of officers and men at parting with the great soldier with whom they had been so long associated, would be a useless effort. The new commander of the corps was General Andrew A. Humphreys, like Hancock, a Pennsylvanian and a brilliant soldier.

During this month, Major John Teed was released from prison. He had been captured at Gettysburg, nearly a year and a half before. He returned broken in health and unable to perform field duty, and resigned as soon as he reached the regiment.

Towards the latter end of November, the Second Corps was relieved from duty in the forts and works that were so continually exposed to the fire of the enemy, and was moved to the left where the lines were further apart, and, owing to the woods, were often not even in sight of each other. The relief to the men of the regiment was very great, and after the severe strain of being two months and a half under fire, night and day, they enjoyed the relaxation more than words can express. But even then it was not all rest and peace. No hour was free from care, and the sudden call to arms was frequent. The regiment occupied the works on the Peebles' Farm, and from this point made several rapid marches to different parts of the line.

One Sunday afternoon, when the sun was shining, the Chaplain holding services, and the voice of prayer and hymn of praise ascending among the autumn trees, the long roll was heard, and in ten minutes the division was on the march. Arriving at a place on the extreme left of the Union lines, the Confederates were seen busily engaged throwing up works and putting batteries into position. The Union troops were not slow to follow, and picks and spades were handled deftly. Before the works were half completed, firing began, and a score of men of the division who had been enjoying the sunshine, and joining in the afternoon prayer, were buried as the sun went down.

December the 9th, the division, commanded by General Miles, went on a reconnoissance to Hatcher's Run and had a sharp fight, carrying some works and capturing some prisoners. The regiment in this affair did not lose a man, being with the brigade held in reserve. They bivouaced in the woods, and returned to camp at the Peebles' Farm next day.

Christmas, 1864, the third and last Christmas in the army, was enjoyed by all in camp—the same games and the same efforts to force amusement. Boxes from home with plenty of good things, enough and to spare for a good dinner to everyone. Happiness and goood cheer reigned for the time, but while all was pleasant in the camp in front of Petersburg, Christmas was an extremely sad day for those of the regiment who were captives in Southern prisons. It would seem as though the thoughts of home and the dark surroundings of the day had a fearfully depressing effect on the prisoners. Of forty-five men of the regiment who died in Andersonville and other Southern prisons, several died on this Christmas day. No doubt but that the surroundings hastened the end, but we can fondly hope that, after all, it was a happy Christmas for them. They were home indeed, and their marches and battles ended. The regiment was commanded during the winter by Major David W. Megraw, who had been promoted from Captain of Company H, Colonel Mulholland being in command of the brigade.

On the morning of February 5th, 1865, the Second Corps started on a reconnoissance to Hatcher's Run, four or five miles to the left of the Union Army. At about noon, the enemy's skirmishers were discovered and driven across the stream. Towards four o'clock, the regiment crossed the stream in line, the men wading through the ice-cold water. Several were hit while in the act of crossing, and several men in the corps were drowned. After reaching the further bank the firing became heavy, and the fighting close and severe. The Confederates made a stubborn resistance, but were gradually forced back into their intrenchments, leaving several hundred prisoners, mostly North Carolinians, in the Union lines. The regiment remained in front of the Confederate works until after dark, when the whole force was withdrawn and returned to camp. During the fight, and long into the night, a terrible storm of snow, sleet and rain prevailed, and the men suffered greatly from the wet and cold.

In the early spring orders were issued authorizing the names of battles to be inscribed on the colors of the regiment:

> HEADQUARTERS, ARMY OF THE POTOMAC.
> March 7th, 1865.
>
> (General Orders, No. 10.)
>
> In accordance with the requirements of General Orders, No. 19, of 1862, from the War Department, and in conformity with the reports of boards convened to examine into the services rendered by the troops concerned, and by the authority of the Lieutenant-General Commanding Armies of the United States, it is ordered that there shall be inscribed upon the colors or guidons of the following regiments and batteries, serving in this army, the names of the battles in which they have borne a meritorious part, and as hereinafter specified, viz.:
>
> ONE HUNDRED AND SIXTEENTH PENNSYLVANIA VOLUNTEERS.
>
> | | | | |
> |---|---|---|---|
> | Fredericksburg, | Wilderness, | Cold Harbor, | Todd's Tavern, |
> | Chancellorsville, | Po River, | Petersburg, | Auburn, |
> | Gettysburg, | Spottsylvania, | Strawberry Plains, | Pamunky, |
> | Bristoe Station, | North Anna, | Deep Bottom, | William's Farm. |
> | Mine Run, | Totopotomy, | Reams Station, | |
>
> By command of Major-General Meade:
>
> GEORGE D. RUGGLES,
> Assistant Adjutant-General.

CHAPTER XVII.

GRAVELLY RUN AND FIVE FORKS.

MARCH, 1865.

HAPPY spring time again! The woods animated with the renewed life of another year; blossoms and budding leaves; the mating birds busy with household cares; the laughing streams once more free from wintry chains, rushing towards the sea. All nature gave charm and health to the army, bidding renewed hope and the last strong, earnest efforts to ultimate success and final victory.

Towards the latter end of March, all being ready, the great struggle began. The thirteen days campaign that was to end the war was severe, and the marching and fighting was without rest or interruption. During the night of March 28th the Second Corps withdrew from the intrenchments in front of Petersburg and on the 29th moved to the left, crossing Hatcher's Run by the Vaughan Road. Shortly after noon fighting commenced to the left of Dabney's Mill, and was sharp and earnest. The rain fell in torrents, flooding the low, swampy country into which the troops of the Second Corps were advancing, but the storm had but little effect in delaying the end.

During the 30th the fighting and skirmishing in front of the regiment was continuous and the fire seemed to come from all sides. There was no chance to cook, eat or sleep, and even when darkness fell there was no opportunity to prepare coffee. The rain extinguished most of the fires and those that did burn were soon made targets for the enemy's fire, which spilled the coffee and knocked over the cooks.

The regiment lost some of the best men during the evening of the 29th and on the 30th. Early on the morning of that day the First Division, Second Corps, had moved still further to the left and joined the force of General Sheridan.

MARCH 31st.

The battle of March 31st and April 1st was of the most sanguinary nature and the One Hundred and Sixteenth Regiment did noble work, but at a fearful cost. Lieutenant Eugene Brady was killed, and Major David W. Megraw and Adjutant Thos. Ewing wounded. The losses among the enlisted men were heavy, and as the dead were left where they fell the extent of the loss was never known.

During the fight of March 31st General Lee commanded the Confederates in person. The attack of the enemy on Ayer's Division of the Fifth Corps was of so courageous and impetuous a character that the line gave way. The commander of the Second Corps (General Humphreys), seeing Ayer's men going to the rear, quickly ordered in the First Division. General Miles led it forward with a wonderful dash and hurled back the Confederate brigades of Wise and Hunton, capturing a flag and many prisoners and restoring the Union lines.

Lieutenant Eugene Brady, who was killed on this day, was a brave and most excellent officer and an estimable man. He seemed to have a premonition that he would be killed, and on the expiration of a short furlough, some months before his death, he bade his friends good-bye and told them that he would not see them again. Captain Nowlen, who was home at the same time, remarked to him: "Yes, Brady, we will say farewell to our friends, for we will both be killed in the coming campaign." Unhappily, his words came true. Sergeant Edward S. Kline, in a letter to a friend, tells the story of Lieutenant Brady's death. He says: "I remember distinctly, after wading across a creek, that the enemy had some rifle pits on a hill in a

LIEUTENANT EUGENE BRADY.
Killed at Five Forks, March 31st, 1865.

field and Lieutenant Brady said, 'Let us go for that pit.' Together with four or five other men I joined him and we succeeded in gaining possession of the pit, but the enemy soon had a flank fire on us. I think I was the only survivor. Lieutenant Brady was killed first. He made some remark about a Confederate color-bearer shaking his flag at us from behind a tree some hundred yards distant when he was hit right in the forehead. He fell against me and died instantly. The rest of my comrades were all silent and, I think, all dead, so after relieving Lieutenant Brady of his shoulder straps and memorandum book, thinking he would be captured, I made a very narrow escape back to the regiment, which was under cover of the hill. The enemy was afterwards charged and driven back some distance, after which I was sent back with a detail and put Lieutenant Brady and his effects in charge of the regimental surgeon, Dr. Wm. B. Hartman."

The body of Lieutenant Brady was taken home to Philadelphia and buried in the Old Cathedral Cemetery in that city.

During the entire day of April 1st the firing was almost incessant. General Miles, ever vigilant, made frequent dashes on the Confederate works and the regiment was always in the front. On the evening of that day General Grant ordered the commander of the Second Corps to throw forward his left and, by seizing the White Oak Road, prevent the enemy from sending troops against Sheridan at Five Forks.

Miles's Division was assigned to the work, and it held the road until after dark when an order came to assault the enemy. A furious artillery fire preceded a rush on the Confederate works. Moving in the dense darkness over brush and tangle wood, the regiment struck the enemy's skirmishers, drove them back into their works and advanced into the slashing. The position could not be carried and the firing died away, but hardly had the fight been ended when Miles, with the First Division, was ordered to push the enemy wherever found. On the morning of April 2d, moving out the Claiborn Road, he came in contact with four brigades under General Cook. General Miles promptly attacked and, after the most severe fighting, carried the position at 3 o'clock, capturing guns, colors and prisoners.

During one of the charges of this day Color-Sergeant Peter Kelly fell wounded. Sergeant Edward S. Kline rushed forward and quickly raised the flag and carried it to the end of the fight. Sergeant Chas. Maurer, of Company F, was then appointed color-sergeant and carried the flag to the end.

One of the men killed in this fight was more than usually beloved by his comrades—John S. Lagnin, Company B. He was the life of the company, full of good humor and fun, and brave as he was good. His comrades buried him tenderly by the side of a little school house, and thought so much of him that after the war closed they sent a committee down to Virginia to bring the body home.

Whilst Miles was fighting so fiercely at Sunderland Station on this Sunday of April 2d the whole Union line had advanced and captured all the works around Petersburg and Richmond, with the exception of a few detached forts, and those cities were at the mercy of the Union Army. The end was near at hand, and as Mr. Davis, the President of the Southern Confederacy, knelt in prayer in St. Paul's Church, a messenger from General Lee informed him that all was over and that the Confederate Army would at once evacuate the works still remaining in their possession and retreat towards the South.

APRIL 3RD.

There are hours in the life of all men that are filled with a joy so great that nothing can add to or increase it. The morning of April 3d, 1865, was an occasion of this nature, giving to each and every tired and weary soldier a meed of happiness and a thrill of joyful emotion the like of which he might never experience again. Richmond and Petersburg taken and the Confederate Army in full retreat was the news that flashed through the ranks. All fatigue, sufferings and trials were on the instant forgotten, and exhausted men who were scarcely able to drag their limbs along leapt with delight and felt fresh and strong enough to start in immediate and rapid pursuit of the flying foe. Without waiting for rations or further rest the march began: all day long, tramp, tramp, tramp, in an effort to catch up to and capture or destroy the still large and formidable army which during the night of April 2d, had abandoned the long line of works that encircled the Confederate Capitol and Petersburg and passing around the left flank of the Union Army was escaping towards the South.

The men of the One Hundred and Sixteenth Regiment were hungry and tired, but hunger and fatigue were alike forgotten as mile after mile was passed. When evening fell, the Second Corps bivouaced on Wintercome Creek. The sleep was short but sound, and on the morning of the 4th, the march was resumed. Another day of hope and expectation, hard and rapid marching and extreme fatigue. The roads were heavy with rain, but the men were buoyed up with excitement of the chase. Evening again, and a short rest at Deep Creek, when the corps halted at 7 P. M. On the road again at 1 A. M. of the 5th, and another day of marching with hardly any rest, reaching Jettersville late in the afternoon. During the night it was learned that the Confederate Army had concentrated around Amelia Court House, within three miles or less, and at 6 A. M. the Second, Fifth and Sixth Corps moved to the attack, but as the line approached the Confederates' position, their troops were seen in full retreat around the left flank of the Union forces. The flight of the enemy was first discovered by the Second Corps, and the artillery dashed into position and opened upon the moving columns. After some sharp fighting the whole Union force abandoned the movement on Amelia Court House, and took up the pursuit of the retreating foe. In the wild race of this 6th of April, all fatigue, hunger and hardship was forgotten. It was anything but a demoralized army that was making for the South. Although beaten and driven from the works they had held so gallantly and well, the Confederates were still as brave and defiant as on the first battlefield of the war. But as the miles rolled away under the swift feet of the men, evidences of the final breakup became more apparent every hour. Hundreds of totally exhausted Confederates were found by the way and became prisoners. Ambulances, tents and baggage of all descriptions littered the road.

The Union artillery marched in the van, and wherever it was possible to strike the rear or flank of the enemy's columns, the batteries would rush for a position, line of battle would be formed on a run, and a fight would be on. The Confederate General, John B. Gordon, commanded the force immediately in front of the Second Corps, and on this day he still further added to his reputation as a great soldier, if that were possible.

The last stand of the day was made at Sailor's Creek, where a severe and stubborn fight resulted in another Union victory, and the trophies of the Second Corps were four guns, thirteen flags, two thousand prisoners and an immense supply train. The men of the One Hundred and Sixteenth helped themselves liberally to the contents of the wagons. New Confederate uniforms took the place of worn out Union clothes. Never were the blue and grey so mixed up as on this occasion. Tired and hungry, but very happy, the men sank to sleep. The morrow would see the last battle of the long and bloody war.

FARMVILLE.
APRIL 7TH.

Marched at 5 A. M., and when High Bridge, on the Appomattox, was reached, the enemy was discovered

MAJOR-GENERAL PHILIP SHERIDAN.

making an attempt to destroy the bridges, all having escaped to the other side of the river. By a vigorous attack the enemy was compelled to retreat, and the bridges were saved. The Second Corps crossed and again took up the pursuit, and at 1 o'clock came up with the enemy, who were strongly intrenched. General Humphreys promptly attacked and kept up an almost continual series of assaults until dark, the indomitable Miles, with the First Division, making the last attack of the day. Farmville was a bloody fight for the First Division, 424 officers and men falling on that day. In the Second Division, General Thomas A. Smyth, the noble officer who commanded the Irish Brigade in the first days of the Wilderness Campaign, was killed. He was a typical soldier, handsome, fearless and beloved, and was the last general officer to fall during the war.

APRIL 8TH.

Daybreak revealed the Confederate works in front of the Second Corps evacuated, and the enemy gone. At 5.30 A. M. the troops were again on the road in hot pursuit. All day long a continuous rapid march. Hundreds of the best men fell by the way exhausted. Human nature had reached the extreme limit of endurance.

The One Hundred and Sixteenth Regiment suffered in this way as well as other commands, but not to the same extent. The men of the regiment did nobly, and but few were missing when, at midnight, the column halted, and they were allowed to fall on the ground to instantly sink to sleep.

Both Generals Grant and Meade accompanied the column of the Second Corps during the day's march; while Sheridan, with the cavalry and the Fifth and Twenty-fourth Corps, was pushing on to head off the enemy at Appomattox.

APRIL 9TH.

Rations were issued at daylight, and the troops of the Second Corps did not get on the road until 8 o'clock, but when they did fall in and start after the enemy, it was with as much vim and ardor as characterized the first day's march.

Towards noon, the advance struck the skirmishers of the Confederates, and General Humphreys promptly formed line and moved forward to attack when the welcome news arrived that negotiations, looking to a surrender of the enemy, were in progress, and the firing was stopped. Then came a few anxious hours of waiting, gazing across at the narrow strip that divided the two lines, and wondering whether the move would be to attack and slay, or cross and shake hands. At 4 o'clock in the afternoon, the glad news swept through the lines: "Lee and the Confederate Army have surrendered", and glorious and final victory, and a country saved were the great rewards of four years of the most awful and sanguinary war that mankind had ever witnessed.

Of the scenes following the surrender, it is superfluous to speak. All men have learned how nobly, and with what tender regard, the commander of the Union Army treated the gallant foe. How the members of the two armies mingled together, and how the Union soldier shared with the men in grey his ration and his blanket. Foemen yesterday, brothers to-day, with not a whit less of love for the Union, or a particle less determination to preserve it, the soldiers who had fought so bravely and long for the salvation of the Republic could not but admire the superb heroism of the men who had just grounded their arms and rolled up their flag which was never to be unfurled again. The men of the North can never admit the justice of the Southern cause in the great war, but every man who participated in the fight, or witnessed the Confederate troops in battle, is willing to acknowledge their magnificent bravery. They were Americans, and fought as only Americans can, and none but Americans could have conquered them. No wonder that Grant said to them: "Keep your swords and your horses and return to your homes, and you will not be disturbed by the United States so long as you observe your parole and the laws", and the soldier, through his blinding tears of joy, saw now, in his late enemy, only a brother, a friend and a countryman, and shook hands and parted, one towards his Southern home, the other towards the North. Appomattox was a reunion: peace after the war, calm after the storm. When each combatant shall reach home once more, and look across the crimson fields of blood and carnage that lie between the North and South, where hundreds of thousands of the blue and gray sleep in death together, may each one ever pray that God bless the Union ; and the blood of the North and South that has been so freely shed will be only another sacred tie to bind the nation together in harmony, good will and peace, with one destiny and one flag.

> Between the lines the smoke hung low,
> And shells flew screaming to and fro,
>   While blue or gray in sharp distress
>   Rode fast, their shattered lines to press
> Again upon the lingering foe.
>
> 'Tis past—and now the roses blow
> Where war was waging years ago,
>   And naught exists save friendliness
>   Between the lines.

It will ever be a proud thought to the men of the One Hundred and Sixteenth Pennsylvania Volunteers, and a proud boast of their descendants, that the regiment was present, and in the very front when the surrender of General Lee and the army of Northern Virginia took place; and it so happened that the news of the surrender was first communicated to the command by General Meade in person.

It is interesting to read the letters and memoranda written by officers and men during the last campaign. In the diary of Captain Yocum we read: "Received orders to march 28th of March, 1865. Broke camp March 29th and moved to the left. 5 P. M. met the enemy, stacked arms for the night. Situation, swamp; weather, rainy. March 30th, moved by the flank to the left and to the front, as skirmishers met the enemy's skirmishers and charged, driving them to their works. 5 P. M., supported a battery under a heavy artillery fire, threw up works and remained in this position until March 31st, when we moved to the left to support the Third Division, Fifth Corps. The latter were repulsed when our brigade forded Hatcher's Run and charged. The fighting was very severe as the enemy was in good positions. In consequence of brigade on our right not supporting in time we were compelled to fall back. Reformed and advanced a second time, driving the enemy at all points. Lieutenants Brady, of Company D, and Condy, Company E, were killed. Major Megraw and Adjutant Thos. Ewing were wounded, and the loss among the enlisted men was severe. Threw up works and held the position. April 1st, supported battery, after which marched and countermarched in keeping up connections with Fifth Corps. Cavalry on the left and corps to the right. April 2d, severe fighting. Brigade charged, capturing two pieces of artillery, five hundred prisoners and the South Side Railroad. The color-bearer, Sergeant Peter Kelly, was wounded and several others killed and wounded. April 3d, supported battery and skirmished. April 4th, advancing, supporting battery and skirmishing. April 5th, skirmishing. April 6th, captured baggage teams. April 7th, severe fighting; brigade lost heavily. Brigade bugler killed. April 8th, heavy skirmishing. April 9th, halted, cooked coffee and received the glorious news of the surrender."

In a letter to a friend Sergeant-Major S. D. Hunter gives a vivid description of the last day:

FARMVILLE. 313

"April 9th, 1865, found us again on the go at early morn, our regiment supporting the skirmish line with balance of brigade closely in our rear. It was about 9 o'clock when we halted on an elevated position. I was ordered to see that the men had their canteens filled with water. I made a detail from each company. When I was asked by some what it meant I told them it looked as if we would have a little "hell" soon and they had better be prepared. Soon we heard the artillery coming up and getting into position, with two pieces in the road and another to our left. The firing had ceased on the skirmish line. We could see the Johnnies in large numbers behind their breastworks. But what did all this mean? We remembered the heavy fighting of the night before in Lee's rear until long after dark. What great anxiety spread through the ranks! Was it to be General Lee's one, last, great struggle? We all felt tired and hungry, so many lay down to sleep, some to crack jokes, others to read their bibles, when by and by a flag of truce comes from the Johnnies' lines and with all possible speed goes back to Meade's headquarters. Soon this was followed by a four-mule stage coach, in which it was said was Commissioner Orr, of Lee's army, going back to our rear. It was impossible to imagine what was going on. Officers and men would ask each other, but all were in total ignorance. Some seemed to think they were trying to compromise without any more fighting, not thinking of an absolute surrender on the part of Lee. It was the opinion of many that before Lee would do so he would make one grand rally and die at the head of his army which he had led forth in so many battles. In the midst of all these conjectures we heard cheering coming towards us and soon we saw that modest hero of Gettysburg, General George G. Meade, and staff coming up on a gallop, passing through our lines and over into the enemy's stronghold. Now for surmising! It has full sway. Surrender or be annihilated, which will Lee do?

"We were now flushed with victory, having kept the Johnnies on the run from early morning till late at night. We had had nothing to eat but a little fresh meat, sassafras and sour grass, and what we lost in coffee, pork and hard tack was more than made up by the continual excitement and battles which had lasted for eleven days. We were unanimous in hoping that Lee's star was on the wane and that the war would soon be over. What great suspense now hung over us! We talked of nothing but the return of our great leader, Meade. Soon an officer from Meade's staff came into our lines and galloped back to headquarters. Soon after the order was given to fall in. We marched to within one hundred yards of the rebels' breastworks, our regiment on the right. We halted when the command 'Front' was given. 'Two paces to the rear. March!' When the regiment was properly aligned another regiment was placed on the opposite side of the road in like manner, and so it continued until the entire corps or back to the rear had been reached. Standing at 'Attention', we 'Order Arms'. Could it be that Lee was going to surrender? Were they going to march him at the head of our vanquished foe through our lines that we might see the remnant of that once brave and fearless army which we had fought on so many disputed battlefields? But, no, all this ceremony was for the purpose of announcing to that wing of the army under General Meade the news of Lee's surrender.

"It was about 4 o'clock in the afternoon when we heard the clatter of horses coming from within the Johnnies' lines. The order 'Attention, carry arms!' was given and we awaited their approach. As General Meade, accompanied by his staff, stopped in front of our One Hundred and Sixteenth Regiment, Pennsylvania Volunteers, no salute was given except the dipping of the colors. Taking his cap in his hand he bowed and announced to us: 'General Lee has surrendered to General Grant!' Turning to the regiment on the opposite side of the road, he repeated the message, and so on. With his own lips he proclaimed to the army which he had led forth to victory the news of Lee's surrender. It now seemed as if by the hand of God life had been suspended for several minutes. Not a word was spoken, not a movement was made. Officers and men stood like regiments of statue-soldiers in the perfect silence. Then like an electric shock broke forth one grand shout and cheer after cheer rent the air. The Lynchburg Plank Road became one swaying mass of joyful Yankees. The delirious shouts were soon taken up by the Johnnies, and never before and never again will the hills and valleys around Appomattox in old Virginia resound with such soul-inspiring shouts as came from the conquerers and the conquered as they blended their voices together on that afternoon of the 9th day of April, 1865.

Thus ended the career of the glorious and heroic One Hundred and Sixteenth Regiment, Pennsylvania Volunteers, which had marked the trail of the Army of the Potomac with the blood of its hundreds of killed and wounded, from Fredericksburg to Appomattox. With depleted ranks it had now reached the pinnacle of its glory. It was the first regiment to receive the official announcement from General Meade of Lee's surrender."

Charley Barth, of Company C, writes about this campaign :

"Well do I remember the morning of the 28th of March, 1865, when we left our winter quarters for the final campaign of the war. Although this campaign was not so long as the one of the year before, yet what an amount of hunger and fatigue we passed through in those thirteen days. I shall never forget it. On the morning of the 29th our regiment was sent on the skirmish line. What a day this was, raining as we advanced through the woods, sometimes in water up to our knees. Then over brush and fallen trees, halting to re-form and then advancing again, and so we went on until night came, when we halted in a swamp with the water up over our shoe tops. Here an amusing incident occurred which I think is worth mentioning. The Fifty-second New York was right in our rear with the rest of the line of battle and for some cause they did not stop with them but came on and would have passed had they not been stopped, as it was then so dark that one object could not be distinguished from the other. This made considerable confusion. If you remember, the Fifty-second New York were nearly all Germans, and such a time as their officers had getting them all together again. Shouting: 'Dis way, fifty-two mans!' And they would come up to some of us and say: 'Be you a fifty-two mans?' Finally, they got back to their line again. We remained on the skirmish line until the next day, the 30th, when we were relieved and went back to our brigade. The next day, the 31st, we fought the battle of Gravelly Run; and so we continued marching, fighting and skirmishing every day and night until the end came on the 9th. But what I started to write about was an incident that happened on the 8th. This will illustrate and confirm what I said in my letter to you that my thoughts were on how I should get enough to eat and enough sleep. We had been marching all day until about 2 o'clock, when we stopped at a place called New Store. I was tired and hungry, as I had nothing in my haversack but a small piece of pork. At this place I was fortunate enough to get a little flour. Soon the bugle called forward, and then it was tramp, tramp again. Oh, how tired I was! How I would look ahead to see if the head of the column would file to the right or left, which I knew would mean rest. Well, just as it was growing dark I saw the head of the column file to the left into the woods. Then came the vision of the nice cake I would make out of the flour and piece of pork, and what a nice sleep I would have. But how often our brightest hopes are blasted. Scarcely had we halted when we were ordered out as flankers with orders to make no fire. This meant to me no cake, no sleep. Finally, after the line was established, we concluded to make a fire and I began to bake my cake, and as the under side became hard I turned it over. A few minutes later we could hear firing in front of us. It was Sheridan who had blocked the way in front of the Johnnies. Just then the order came to fall in. Now the question was, what shall I do with my half-baked cake? I dumped it into my haversack. Then we went on to the road again for a four mile tramp. Well, as the cake cooled I ate it, although it was half dough. As I pulled it from my haversack it would stretch from there to my mouth, but it helped to fill me. That night the supply train came up, and the next morning, that ever welcome day of the 9th, I had a feast on coffee, hard tack and pork, and I was contented and happy because my stomach was full. Could I have known then what this day was to still bring forth my enjoyment would have been much greater. It was then I felt proud that I had done some little towards the overthrow of the Rebellion."

The surrender of the other armies of the Southern Confederacy followed rapidly upon that of General Lee, and it only remained for the Union troops in Virginia to turn their faces toward the North and home and await the muster out and disbanding of the armies. So on April 13th the last march began. Leisurely and without war's rude alarms, it was a joyful march, indeed. Reaching Farmville, the men were gladdened by the return of four officers who had been captives in Southern prisons for months and who had just been released. All had much to tell of the hardships endured. Captain Cosslett is still on earth as this book is being written and his story of prison life in the South is interesting.

Reminiscence of Prison Life in the South

By

CHARLES COSSLETT,

Brevet Major, United States Volunteers.

DURING the campaign of 1864, when the army reached the fortifications before Petersburg, our regiment had lost by death, wounds and sickness a great many men; there were no field and but few line officers left for duty.

On the morning of June 22d, being still quite lame in my right knee and thigh from rheumatism contracted in the trenches at Cold Harbor and suffering from a long and severe attack of diarrhœa, Dr. Hartman gave me a pass to go to the hospital. Whilst waiting for an ambulance Captain Nowlen, who was in command of the regiment, came to me and said we had orders to move and that we were likely to have another dust with the Johnnies. There was no officer in his company and as I was the only one in mine, which was on his left, he told me to take the two companies into the fight and when we came out I could go to the hospital. I said to him: "I may not come out; I may be killed." "Charlie," replied he, in his off-hand, jocular way, "if you are killed you won't want to go to the hospital." Noble, generous, brave Nowlen! That was our parting joke; shortly after you gave your life for your God and country.

When I went back to the regiment one of my men, Michael Cavanaugh, came to me with one hundred and fifty dollars which he wished me to send to his people, he having an idea he was going to be killed. I answered that my risk was as great as his and advised him to give the money to Father Ouellet, the Chaplain of the Sixty-ninth New York Regiment, which he did.

Early in the morning of the 22d of June, Wilcox's Division of Hill's Corps moved from their quarters on the lines of Petersburg and, crossing the works to the right of the Tannahill House, followed the line of the Weldon Railroad. Wilcox's instructions were to find the Union column and drive it back to the Jerusalem Plank Road. About 9 A. M. his troops were beyond and to the right of the Johnston House. The leading brigades were halted and formed in line of battle, facing the Plank Road. General Mahone, who, from a small and unoccupied fort in advance of his line, had been watching the Federal troops marching into position, stacking arms and throwing up breastworks, quietly withdrew Wright's Virginia Brigade and Saunder's Georgia Brigade of his division out of the main works about 2 P. M., and filing through a deep ravine in the direction of the Johnston House, and thence into a field near a skirt of woods where he formed a line of battle, he at once advanced, struck the flank of the Union line, rolled it up and captured four guns, eight stands of colors and over seventeen hundred prisoners. Before General Mahone commenced the movement he sent Captain Girardey over to General Wilcox to say he would attack the Union troops as soon as he could reach the head and flank of their column and that all he, Wilcox, had to do was to bear down towards Petersburg to effect a co-operation with Wright's and Saunder's Brigades in the proposed attack. Captain Girardey, on his way, met General Hill at the Davis House on the Weldon Railroad and to him communicated the message. General Hill replied that Wilcox would be informed at once of General Mahone's request. However, Captain Girardey, fearing a delay, immediately galloped over to Wilcox and told him that Mahone was ready to strike the Union line as soon as he, Wilcox, was prepared to co-operate with him. The Confederate advance on the Plank Road was instantly arrested and two brigades were ordered to move in the direction of Petersburg. At this time Wilcox was to the left and rear of the Union troops, but failed to join General Mahone until the fight was over.

On that fatal day the Second Corps moved forward, pivoting its right on the left of the Fifth. The Sixth Corps, being on the left of the Second, was to move with it, but, having a greater distance to traverse in the wheeling movement, it could not keep up with the Second Corps, and therefore, General Meade ordered General Birney, who was that day in command of the Second Corps, to advance without waiting for the Sixth. When the Confederates struck the Union line the Second, or Irish, Brigade was on the left of the Second Corps and our regiment was on the left of the brigade.

After passing through some woods we halted at the top of a ravine. Four or five of the men took a number of canteens to fill at the rivulet, but in a few minutes came running back and said the Johnnies fired at them from the opposite side. The men who had been quietly resting quickly formed line. By this time the bullets were coming thick and fast and killed and wounded quite a number, amongst the latter Captain Yocum. Captain Nowlen sent Lieutenant Cope and Sergeant-Major Burk to the left of the line to see if the enemy were flanking us. In a very short time they returned in hot haste and reported the Confederates marching in column of fours past our left. This was about 3 o'clock in the afternoon.

Not long after, by General Barlow's orders, a brigade covered our flank, but it was soon on the run past the rear of our line. When the enemy found our left uncovered and the Sixth Corps far behind, they struck our flank and pushed with great vigor into our rear. The front line, finding itself exposed and likely to be captured, hastily fell back. Being lame I could not get along very fast and when I got out of the woods and walked over a field I came to a partly constructed breastwork. I crossed over this into another wood with dense brush so thick I could not see through it.

Here I met about thirty men from different regiments. They were listening to the sound of voices which came from our rear but could not see anyone. Some thought they were our men who were talking, but others said they were Johnnies. However, no one seemed inclined to find out the real state of affairs. At last a young sergeant in a New York regiment volunteered to accompany me for the purpose of solving the problem. After pushing through the brush we reached an open space where we were surprised to see, not six paces from us, a line of battle. When we found they were Confederates our first thought was to run. About a dozen rifles were pointed at us and the Johnnies told us to come in, saying: "It is no use trying to get away; we have been going behind you fellers for two hours."

We were sent under guard to the rear. On our way we saw one of our guns which they had captured and quite a number of our dead. In a narrow road at the edge of the woods lay a Union officer who had been shot in the thigh. We made a stretcher with a blanket and some rails and carried him to the Johnston House where the doctors were attending to a number of wounded men. On the way I saw a general who, I was told, was Mahone and that it was his command which captured us.

A regiment going to the front passed us. Their salute was: "How are you, blue bellies? How do you like your new quarters?" etc. Just before dark we were taken to a clearing in the woods. In it were assembled sixteen hundred men and sixty-five officers. There I met Lieutenant Cope, Sergeant-Major Burk and a number of men of our regiment. Before we left this place a staff officer rode in with some of our flags tied on his horse.

After dark we were removed and camped on the side of a hill for the night. Lying on the cold ground, without any covering, I suffered severely from diarrhœa. In the morning John M. Wiley, one of my men, gave me a tablespoonful of black pepper mixed in water, after which palatable dose I was greatly relieved. Another of my men, Albert Nelson, handed over to me his gum blanket.

He said the Johnnies were going to take from them their haversacks, canteens, etc., but he thought they would leave me in possession of the blanket.

In the forenoon the enlisted men were separated from the officers and we were then taken to the cars and sent to Richmond. On our arrival, under a strong guard, we were marched through the streets to Libby Prison. When we passed into the commandant's office our names, rank, regiment and address were entered in their books. We were next thoroughly searched for money, and if any was found, it was very kindly placed to our credit. The officials promised to return it when we left the prison, but when we did leave, by some oversight on their part, we were obliged to go without it. They took from us everything in our possession, haversacks, canteens and blankets. One officer had a few hardtack in his haversack. Its contents were dumped on the floor, then there was a scramble for the pieces. I was fortunate enough to get a handful of crumbs, the first thing I had had to eat for two days.

After this incident we were taken upstairs to the second floor and put in a large room in which were already about fifty officers. I took up my quarters under the window on Twentieth Street, nearest to Carey and directly over the office. The enlisted men were confined in six rooms in the centre and east of the building. At 9 o'clock every morning and at 4 in the afternoon we had roll-call. Prison Clerk Erastus W. Ross, or "Little Ross", as he was designated because of his small stature, accompanied by a guard under the command of Sergeant George Stansil, of the Eighteenth Georgia Regiment, would come up and count us off, fearing some would be missing.

Every day at 11 A. M. rations were brought up. Stalwart negroes carried in two tubs, made of a barrel cut in two, with rope handles, full of what the Confederates called pea soup. It was a composition of horse beans with a piece of some kind of meat boiled in water. No one knew whether the meat was cow, pig or horse flesh

Every man received three-quarters of a pint of soup, some beans, a piece of meat about the size of two fingers and three-fourths of a pound loaf of coarse corn bread without any salt in it, and these were all the rations we were given in twenty-four hours. Some of the men would eat their allowance all at once and then lie on the floor until 11 o'clock next day, not daring to walk about, fearing it would increase their hunger.

I divided my portion and enjoyed three short meals daily. We formed squads of twenty, and any man who was fortunate enough to possess a tin cup would drink his soup and then lend the cup to another. It was amusing to hear some of the prisoners talking about what good things they would like to eat, and if they were only at Delmonico's or some first-class restaurant they would order a dinner fit for a "city councilman".

The third day we were at Libby Adjutant Latouche sent up one old army blanket for each man, which answered for both bed and bedding and was the only donation we received during our long confinement. On that day came an exchange for some doctors who lay in the corner next to me. After they left prison early the next morning I found an old tin cup which it seems they had promised to a cavalry officer. About an hour afterwards he came around hunting for the cup. Of course, he could not find it, but he swore rather loudly and said if he knew the man that took it he would wring his neck. However, I was not foolish enough to tell him.

On the floor I found a piece of old canvas. I borrowed a thread and needle from one of the prisoners and made of it a very good haversack, and with that and the tin cup I set up housekeeping. The same evening an officer gave Lieutenant Cope some tea. The latter with his knife cut a few chips from the rafters and built a fire on the floor, and in my cup we made our first tea, which, though having neither sugar nor milk, tasted so good that we boiled the leaves three times over.

The only furniture in the room was a long, pine-board table. In the southwest corner were two old bath tubs and a good supply of water. The windows were without glass, but instead had heavy iron bars. Shortly before I went to Libby Captain Forsyth, of the One Hundredth Ohio Volunteers, was shot dead by a sentinel while standing at one of the windows, the guards having instructions to shoot any one putting his hands on sill or bar.

Libby Prison was a large, three-story brick building, divided by heavy walls into three sections. It stood on a hill which descended to a street by the side of the canal. The building contained nine large rooms, each 105 x 45 feet. The slant of the hill gave an additional story on the south or Dock Street side. The prison fronted on Carey Street and was bounded on the west by Twentieth and on the east by a vacant lot. The west room on the first floor was the commandant's office and it was also used as sleeping quarters for the prison officials. The centre room was the kitchen and the east one served as a hospital. On the second floor the west room was called "Milroy's Room"; the middle one was named "Lower Chickamauga Room", for there were a large number of Chickamauga prisoners in it; the east room was known as "Lower Gettysburg Room". The west room on the third floor was called "Streight's Room"; the centre room, "Upper Chickamauga Room", and the east room, "Upper Gettysburg Room". The basement on Dock Street was divided into west cellar, middle cellar, or carpenter's shop, and the east cellar, generally called "Rat Hell".

Libby Prison was built in 1852 by John Enders, a Scotsman. He was a prominent tobacco manufacturer, and Libby was one of the several large warehouses he had constructed in Richmond. In 1854 he leased the building to Luther Libby, who used it in the ship chandlery and commission business. On the northwest corner hung a sign which read: "Libby and Son, Ship Chandlers and Grocers". The son, George W. Libby, was admitted as a partner in 1860 and served in the Confederate Army during the war.

The first Union prisoners arrived in Richmond July 23d, 1861, followed in a few days by others captured at Bull Run. The first building used as a military prison was a tobacco factory on Main Street, between Twenty-fifth and Twenty-sixth Streets. General John H. Winder, who was in command at Richmond, finding it impossible to accommodate all the prisoners in the Liggon Building, took possession of Libby and Son's warehouse. The first commandant of this prison was the notorious Henry Wirz, who was not long in charge before being sent to Andersonville, where his cruelty to the unfortunate captives caused him to be hanged after the war. He was succeeded by Major T. P. Turner, who, when the war was over, practiced dentistry in Memphis, Tenn.

In October, 1861, Lieutenant Thomas P. Turner, generally called "Dick" Turner, was promoted to the rank of captain and ordered to report for duty at Libby, (He was no relative of Major Thomas P. Turner.) After the war he had a saw mill in Isle of Wight County, Va. Chief Clerk Ross was burned to death in the Spotswood House, Richmond, Va., in 1873. Adjutant John Latouche died in Richmond, October 4th, 1890, aged 70.

Nearly sixty thousand prisoners were confined in Libby during the war. On the night of February 9th, 1864, one hundred and nine officers, including eleven colonels, seven majors, thirty-two captains and fifty-nine lieutenants, made their escape through the tunnel. Forty-eight of them were recaptured. Colonel Streight and several officers were concealed for a week by Miss Bettie Vanlew, a Union sympathizer. She was afterwards appointed postmistress of Richmond by President Grant. Captain Gates, of the Thirty-third Ohio, was the only one recaptured inside the city limits.

For several days after the escape great numbers of citizens wandered around Libby. One of them happened to remove a plank in the yard back of the office of the James River Towing Company and the secret was revealed. A dog was dropped into the hole and he made his way to "Rat Hell".

After the evacuation of Richmond the Union troops were placed on guard through the city. Samuel E. James, a private in Colonel Brady's Regiment, the Two Hundred and Sixth Pennsylvania Volunteers, claimed to have taken the key of Libby Prison from a colored man who had attempted to make off with it. James ran after the negro and took it from him. It was an iron key about six inches long with a flange about an inch wide. James lived for a time in Kittaning, Armstrong County, Pa.

All the old prisoners were removed from Richmond early in May, 1864, and those who were captured during May and June were taken to Libby. About the first of July orders came to send all officers to Macon and the enlisted men to Andersonville. Early one morning we were taken from Libby, marched over to Manchester, on the south side of the river, put on board passenger cars and began our journey. At some of the stations where we stopped for wood and water several officers lost their head gear by a little Southern strategy. After the train started some Johnnies would create an excitement on the platform. Our men would naturally look out to see what was the matter, and if a good hat was seen on any of them some enterprising Confederate would snatch it off and very politely throw back his old one with many compliments.

Our first landing place was Lynchburg, where we were put in a field near the river. The Johnnies had captured one of our supply trains and for rations gave us our own genuine hardtack and good, fat Yankee pork, which was a great treat.

Our guard at this place was composed of about seventy men who had belonged to an Irish regiment in Stonewall Jackson's Brigade. They told us their regiment had been so reduced in numbers that they were taken from the front and put on guard duty.

When we left Lynchburg we were started on a four days' tramp to Danville. General Averill with his cavalry had torn up part of the railroad, so we had to foot it all the way. We marched in column of fours, officers on the right, and had two regiments of home guards to look after our welfare. At some places along the road the women would bring us out buckets of cool spring water and often a corn cake, which was very acceptable.

On the second night of our journey we camped on the border of a small stream. Having obtained permission from the guards to take a bath, some of the men indulged in the unusual luxury of a swim. Meanwhile, I found a one dollar Federal note, which proved its great value early next morning when a young Johnny came into camp with a basket of onions. In exchange for my one dollar he offered me four dollars in Confederate money or three large onions. I chose the latter, knowing that if I ate them they would agree with me and not being quite sure that I could digest the dirty, ragged Confederate scrip.

Sunday, July 3d, as we passed a church on the roadside, the congregation came out and some of the women wept bitterly when they saw our miserable condition. A woman's heart will always bleed for suffering humanity.

> "Honored be woman! She beams on the sight,
> Graceful and fair, like a being of light;
> Scatters around her wherever she strays
> Roses of bliss on our thorn-covered ways;
> Roses of Paradise, sent from above,
> To be gathered and twined in a garland of love!"

At Danville we were quartered in a large warehouse at the east side of the town, with Major Moffart in charge. We there drew a day's rations—half a loaf of corn bread, a quarter of a pound of bacon and a pint of soup. We were told not to go near the windows, for the guards had orders to shoot us if we did.

Next morning we were loaded into cattle cars. Four sentinels were placed at the doors inside and six or eight on the top of each car to guard the fifty men which it contained. We stopped at Greensborough for a short time, then started for Charlotte, where we arrived the subsequent evening. Our next halt was at Columbia, where we got some corn bread and bacon, and were then taken to Augusta. The home guard under command of Provost-Marshal Bradford, a son of Governor Bradford, of Maryland, had charge of us at that place. Early next morning we were sent to Macon, which city we reached the following afternoon.

We were received by Dick Turner, who had been sent on from Libby, and a regiment of Georgia militia and marched into Camp Oglethorpe. (The camp was named for the Governor of Georgia.) It was about a quarter of a mile east of the city. Some three acres were enclosed by a stockade fence sixteen feet high. On the outside of the fence, four feet from the top, was a platform on which the guards were stationed and from which they had a good view over the camp. Inside the stockade and about twenty feet from it was a picket fence four feet high called the "dead line". No one was allowed to go over or touch this line.

The morning we entered the camp our first salute from the old prisoners was cries of "Fresh fish", "Give him air", "Don't take his tooth-pick", "Close up", etc. Near the gate stood Captain George Halpin, who was captured before me. He called out: "Is there any one from the One Hundred and Sixteenth Pennsylvania?" When I answered "Yes", he took my hand and put his arms around me and said he was glad and yet sorry to see any one from the old regiment. He led me to his quarters and gave me a portion of his dinner, which consisted of a piece of corn bread and a cup of coffee made of burnt meal scalded with water, and he regretted very much that he could not entertain me better; but I was exceedingly thankful to have my hunger thus far appeased.

A few days after I entered the prison pen I accidentally put my hand on the dead line, when some officers called out: "Take your hand away, take your hand away!" which I quickly did, as the sentinel had his rifle already aimed at me. On the evening of the 11th of June Lieutenant Otto Grierson, Forty-fifth New York Volunteers, while near the spring was shot and mortally wounded by a guard, although at the time he was some distance from the line.

There were twelve hundred prisoners in the pen when we went there. In the centre of the camp was a large wooden warehouse, which had been used as a hospital for Confederate soldiers, but as many of our officers as could get in made it their sleeping quarters. Early one morning I went into the building, and, seated on the floor were a great number of them with their shirts off, performing a very necessary act before making their morning toilet, as the building was swarming with vermin. In those days there was an open market in all Southern prisons for the vender of insect powder.

To the prisoners who were in the stockade previous to our arrival the authorities had given lumber with which they built open sheds for themselves and fixed up bunks, and it was in one of these that Captain Halpin and Lieutenant John McGovern, of the Seventy-third Pennsylvania Volunteers, had their quarters. When our squad of one hundred and twenty arrived there was no room in the sheds for us, so we had to bunk outside. I took up my quarters near the spring, which was situated about thirty feet from the dead line.

Our contingent was divided into squads of twenty, each squad being furnished with a camp kettle and an iron skillet. We formed messes of five and arranged to have the cooking utensils turn about. Rations were drawn every five days, our daily allowance being one pint of corn meal, one ounce of rice and a quarter of a pound of fat bacon. Sometimes in place of rice we received beans. Every ten days they gave us a tablespoonful of salt, every three weeks two ounces of soft soap with which to wash our ragged clothes, and each morning the authorities sent in a wagon load of fire-wood for cooking purposes. The second week I was there Captain Halpin fell insensible in the yard and was carried to the hospital. I did not see him again for two months. During the first six months of prison life we were called "fresh fish"; the next four months, "suckers"; the next two months, "dry cod"; after that, "dried herring", and after exchange, "pickled sardines".

When General Johnston was retreating towards Atlanta before the victorious army of Sherman, Governor Brown, of Georgia, ordered every man capable of bearing arms to the front, and transferred the State militia, under the command of Major-General G.W. Smith, to the Confederate service to defend the bridges across the Chattahoochee River for the safety of the important city of Atlanta. From an elevation in the prison yard we could see regiments of boys, some of them not fifteen years of age, marching past. They looked full of fight and quite proud of being soldiers.

A great many of the prisoners were afflicted with "chronic diarrhœa" and about four hundred had "scurvy". Those with the latter disease would put earth on their sores to check its ravages. Another beneficial remedy was to eat raw potatoes steeped in vinegar. These luxuries the negroes would sometimes bring into the prison. Growing inside the stockade were two old white oak trees, the bark of which was stripped off and chewed by some of the men, while others boiled it and drank the water as a cure for diarrhœa.

One day the Confederate sutler brought in provisions in a large box. When it was emptied Lieutenant Wilson,

Fifth United States Cavalry, got into it. The negroes, wishing to aid his escape, fastened the lid temporarily on the box, which was placed on the wagon and driven out of the prison pen. After going some distance away the negroes removed the precious load from the wagon, took off the lid and the lieutenant made his way to a negro hut. While washing and making his toilet the patrol came up and asked him if he was a Union prisoner. Rather than tell a lie he acknowledged that he was, and, as a result, was brought back the same day to the pen. I thought that under the circumstances, when he had a chance of making his escape, he deserved great praise for telling the truth, which proved that he did not forget the good advice of a noble mother.

For amusement those who were strong enough would play base ball; others would spend their time with checkers, chess and dominoes; but a pack of cards, the soldier's prayer book, was always in demand. Crib, faro and poker were the favorite games. Very often Captain Irsch, a German, of the Forty-fifth New York Regiment, and Captain Rompé, a Swiss, would entertain us with the sword exercise performed with wooden foils which they made for the purpose. The Swiss officer, whose real name was known to few, was generally called Rompé, a French word which he frequently used while fencing.

July 27th Captain Gibbs, commandant of the prison, received orders to count out six hundred prisoners to be sent to Charleston, as the Confederates, knowing that Sherman was on his way to Atlanta, feared a raid of Union troops to release the prisoners. Some of our men were in hopes of exchange, but they soon found they were to be confined in Charleston to protect that city from the fire of our guns on Morris Island. We were told we would not be allowed to take the cooking utensils with us. The guard at the dead line would not permit Lieutenant McGovern to take even a skillet with him, so he handed it over to me. Next evening the second six hundred were called out to go to Savannah. I tied up the skillet in my old blanket, put it under my arm and, when my name was called, stepped over the line. We were guarded by the Fifth Georgia Regiment, marched to where the box cars were and remained there during the night. We knew by the hurried movement of troops and placing of artillery in position there was some trouble brewing for the Confederacy.

At break of day we left Macon and reached Savannah about 5 P. M. The guards told us that General Stoneman with his cavalry cut the road at one station half an hour after we passed it. Stoneman attacked Macon, was repulsed and taken prisoner with part of his command, July 31st, at Clinton, about six miles north of the city. At the time he was on a raid to release the Union prisoners in Macon and Andersonville.

Our prison in Savannah was a lot adjoining the Marine Hospital and surrounded by a stockade fence. It was called "Camp Davidson", for its first commandant. The city authorities who had charge of us were very kind and did all they could for our comfort. They gave us tents and boards to make bunks, also cooking utensils and bricks to build ovens in which to bake our corn bread. We built the ovens oval on top and stuck the bricks together with mortar made of clay. The bread we made by stirring corn meal in water and baking in the skillets.

Colonel Miller, One Hundred and Forty-seventh New York Volunteers, acted in the prison as commandant. Through him all our requests were made known to Captain Davidson. Our guards, the First Georgia, a number of whom had been prisoners of war, thought we deserved good treatment, as they had received it at the North.

Our tents were pitched in regular military order and the streets were swept every day. For our rations we were given each morning half a pound of meat, a pint of rice, half a pint of meal, and every four days a tablespoonful of salt. The water we used came from a well near the hospital fence. It was clear and cold but so offensive to both taste and smell that some of the prisoners told the authorities they would like it cleaned out, for they were sure there was a dead dog or nigger in it. Next day a detail came in and gave it a thorough cleaning, but only a few leaves and twigs were found in it, and not till then did we know it was a very strong sulphur spring. A few days after a long wooden trough was made and a supply of city water turned on. Fires were kept burning all night inside the pen, so that the sentinels could see all our movements.

In the tent in rear of mine a cavalry officer dug a well about six feet deep, from the bottom of which he started a tunnel about two feet six inches in diameter. It was carried under the stockade with the intention of running it beyond what was thought to be a second line of sentinels. The work was completed on the morning of August 22d, and on the afternoon of the same day a cow, walking over the tunnel, broke through. The guards saw her floundering in the hole and with great difficulty released her. A detail was sent at once into the pen to locate the tent and fill up the hole. The officer was taken to the Confederate headquarters and sentenced to severe punishment, but came back next day in good condition.

August 26th, the ladies of Savannah gave a picnic to the Confederate soldiers stationed in the city and we could hear their voices and the music distinctly. On the same day, Captain W. McGinnis, Seventy-fourth Illinois Volunteers, died. Our officers asked permission from the new Confederate commandant of the camp, Colonel Wayne, to give the Captain a decent burial, but he positively refused. In the evening, we received a note from the ladies in the city stating that, with profound sorrow, they had heard of Colonel Wayne's answer to our request and that they would purchase a burial lot where, under their care and direction, the Captain's remains would be properly interred.

Early one morning a chicken flew into the pen and, for a while, there was a lively time, as about fifty men were after it. Finally, Lieutenant Allen caught it, and with some rice we made our first and last pot of chicken broth.

Being very weak from a long attack of diarrhœa, I went to the doctor for some medicine. He gave me three pills and told me to keep quiet, adding that our people had the coast blockaded, the physicians in the South could obtain no drugs and that was all he could do for me. With few exceptions, the Confederate doctors were humane and kind and, with the means at their disposal, did all they could for our comfort and relief.

August 30th, an exchange came for all chaplains and doctors; they were sent in the evening to Charleston to be taken north on the flag-of-truce boat.

On the afternoon of September 11th, the order came for the rest of the prisoners to "pack up". My outfit consisted of a ragged coat and pants, a worn-out hat and an old blanket. Having neither shoes nor shirt, but in possession of my tin cup and skillet, it did not take long to get ready to move. We sat up all night making snap-jacks and corn bread to last us on our journey. At 6 o'clock on the morning of September 12th, under guard of the Second Georgia Regiment, we were marched out of camp and turned over to a regiment of state militia. We remained for several hours in the streets before we took passage in the cattle cars. We knew then we were to be taken to Charleston and placed under the fire of our guns. When we stopped at a station on our way for wood and water, one of our men asked leave from a guard to step out of the car for a few minutes; another guard saw him and, thinking he was trying to escape, shot at him; fortunately he got back without a Southern keepsake.

We reached Charleston in about ten hours and the citizens, white and black, turned out in force to look at the "Northern Blue Bellies". Under a strong escort we were marched through the streets to the jail, which was situated in the southeastern part of the city—it could be seen from Morris Island, where our batteries were. The jail was a large octagonal building, four stories, with a tower forty-five feet high. The yard was surrounded by a strong wall, and on the outside was the platform for the sentinels to walk on. The water we had to use was brackish and came from a covered well in the centre of the yard. Not far from it, on the south side, stood the gallows, a pleasant reminder of what might be our last hitching-post.

Outside and near the prison wall were two large buildings, the Roper Hospital and the Work House. Both being full of prisoners, we could not be admitted and were put into the jail yard, the latter, having been occupied by convicts and prisoners for some time, was in a very filthy condition,—the ground having a moving crop of vermin. Near the south wall stood a few old tents which were of no use for shelter, the prisoners who had been there before us having cut out and carried away large pieces of the canvas to make shirts and other wearing apparel of which they were sadly in need.

Lieutenant J. Ogden, First Wisconsin Cavalry, composed the following verses while confined in the Roper Hospital:

> Oh, thou doomed city of the evil seed,
> Long nursed by baneful passion's heated breath!
> Now bursts the germ, and lo, the evil deed
> Invites the sword of war, the stroke of death!
> Suns smile on thee, and yet thou smilest not
> Thy fame, thy fashion, are alike forgot.
> Consumption festers in thy inmost heart;
> The shirt of Nessus fouls thy secret part
>
> Lo, in thy streets—thy boast in other days—
> Grim silence sits, and rancorous weeds arise!
> No joyous mirth, nor hymns of grateful praise,
> Greet human ears nor court the upper skies;
> But deadly pallor, and a fearful looking for
> The hand of vengeance and the sword of war.
> Thy prayer is answered, and around, above,
> The wrath of God and man doth hourly move.

Thy foes are in thy heart, and lie unseen;
They drink thy life-blood and thy substance up;
   And though in pride thou usest to sit a queen
Justice at last commands the bitter cup.
   The blood of slaves upon thy skirts is found;
   Their tears have soaked this sacrilegious ground.
The chains that manacled their ebon arms
Now clank about thine own in dread alarms.

   Thy sanctuaries are forsaken now;
Dark mould and moss cling to thy fretted towers;
   Deep rents and seams, where straggling lichens grow
And no sweet voice of prayer at vestal hours;
   But voice of screaming shot and bursting shell,
   Thy deep damnation and thy doom foretell.
The fire has left a swamp of broken walls,
Where night-hags revel in thy ruined halls.

   Oh, vain thy boast, proud city desolate!
Thy curses rest upon thy guilty head!
   In folly's madness, thou didst desecrate
Thy sacred vows to holy Union wed.
   And now behold the fruit of this, thy sin:
Thy courts without o'errun, defiled within;
   Gross darkness broods upon thy holy place;
   Forsaken *all*, thy pride in deep disgrace.

   Wail, city of the proud palmetto-tree!
Thy figs and vines shall bloom for thee no more!
   Thou scorn'dst the hand of God, that made thee free,
In driving freemen from their native shore.
Thy rivers still seek peacefully the sea,
Yet bear no wealth on them, no joy for thee.
   Thy isles look out and bask beneath the sun,
   But silence reigns—their Sabbath is begun!

   Blood! Blood is on thy skirts, oh, city doomed!
The cry of vengeance hath begirt thee round;
   Here, where the citron and the orange bloomed,
God's curse rests on the half-forsaken ground!
   Thy treason, passion-nursed, is overgrown—
   Thy cup of wrath is full, is overflown.
   Repent, for God can yet a remnant save,
   But traitors and their deeds shall find the grave!

CHARLESTON, S. C., September 25, 1864.

September 20th, about noon, a terrible thunder-storm came on and it rained incessantly all day and night. There were two inches of water over the yard and we could not get the fires to burn. Wet, cold and without shelter, we made application to get into the jail, but did not succeed, as at that time it was full of prisoners of various grades. On the first floor were the civil convicts; the second story was occupied by Confederate officers and soldiers under punishment for military offences; the third story, by negro prisoners; and the fourth, by deserters from both the Confederate and Union Armies. In the yard were a number of negro prisoners who had been captured at the assault on Fort Wagner. As they received for rations nothing but corn meal, it was said they suffered so much from hunger that they would catch the rats, skin, roast and eat them.

September 22d was very warm and our boys on Morris Island made it hotter for the enemy, for during that day and night, about one hundred shot and shells were thrown into the city. We would watch "Foster's Messengers", as we called them, screeching over our heads and hear them crash into the houses; then followed the rumbling of the engines and the shouts of the firemen on their way to extinguish the flames.

About noon, on September 24, we were startled by the sound of a musket shot. On running to the jail door, we found that a sentinel had killed a negro boy, a prisoner, who had run into the main corridor. The guard ordered him to return, but the boy, not retreating quickly enough, was shot and died instantly.

In the evenings, the negro prisoners would entertain us by singing songs. The one which they seemed to like best was composed by Sergeant Johnson (colored) of Company F, Fifty-fifth Massachusetts Infantry. The song was as follows:

When I enlisted in the army,
　　Then I thought 'twas grand,
Marching through the streets of Boston
　　Behind a regimental band.
When at Wagner I was captured,
　　Then my courage failed;
Now I'm lousy, hungry, naked,
　　Here in Charleston jail.

CHORUS.—Weeping, sad and lonely—
　　Oh! How bad I feel;
Down in Charleston, South Carolina,
　　Praying for a good "square meal".

If Jeff Davis will release me,
　　Oh, how glad I'll be;
When I get on Morris Island
　　Then I shall be free;
Then I'll tell those conscript soldiers
　　How they use us here;
Giving us an old "corn-dodger"—
　　They call it prisoner's fare.

We are longing, watching, praying,
　　But will not repine
Till Jeff. Davis does release us,
　　And sends us "in our lines".
Then with words of kind affection,
　　How they'll greet us there!
Wondering how we could live so long
　　Upon the "dodgers fare".

CHORUS.—Then we will laugh long and loudly—
　　Oh, how glad we'll feel,
When we arrive on Morris Island
　　And eat a good "square meal".

September 30th a great many shells were thrown into the city. A piece of one struck the west end of the Roper Hospital, and another piece dropped into the jail yard near where I was standing. I picked it up and brought it home with me when paroled, as a fond remembrance of prison life. The guards told us that a shell killed the Provost-Marshal whilst standing at a table in his office issuing orders to his Lieutenant, who was also killed. A few nights after, an Irishman and his wife, whilst sleeping, met their death in the same manner.

As the Union officers were taken to Charleston to save the city from the fire of our guns on Morris Island, General Foster, in retaliation, placed an equal number of Confederate officers on transports in front of his works to prevent the enemy from firing on him. Foster's gunners knew our whereabouts and took good care not to plant a shell amongst us.

On October 2d, the Confederate Captain commanding the prison and his adjutant died of yellow fever. Many of the guards, some of our officers and a large number of enlisted men, brought from Andersonville, also died of the disease. The Sisters of Charity were allowed to enter the jail yard and hospitals to visit our sick soldiers. I have seen them bend over and speak words of hope and comfort to our fever-stricken boys, and give with loving hearts and kind hands grapes, wine or any little delicacy they could obtain. All over the South they ministered to the wants of both Confederate and Union soldiers and, without any hope of reward, risked health and life in those loathsome, fever-stricken hospitals.

"Where the fateful war cry sounded,
 Echoing through valleys fair,
From each verdured mount resounded,
 Rousing hearts to do and dare;
There her noble mission leads her
 Where relentless Death is near,
But the wounded soldier needs her
 And her brave heart knows no fear.

Like a radiant sunbeam straying
 Through the ward where sufferers lie,
Her soft touch the pain allaying,
 Her sweet smile forbids the sigh.
When the soldier feels Death near him,
 Naught of dread appalls his soul
With her gentle voice to cheer him
 Onward to the Heavenly goal.

Then! behold her, where privation
 Frets the spirit of the brave,
Where the fever and starvation

  Lead from prison bars to grave;
Breathing words of pity tender,
  Soothing oft the throbbing brow,
Still no selfish fears attend her
  For the captive needs her now.

How she casts a glow about her,
  Gladd'ning all o'er-freighted hearts!
'Twould be wondrous dark without her,
  While her spotless soul imparts
To her face such noble beauty,
  That the soldier grows more brave,
Fearless treads the path of duty—
  Seeking but the Flag to save!

Truly, soldiers, may you love her
  For the deeds performed so well;
No one knows but Him above her
  In her task what hardships dwell.
Weave your tenderest thanks around her
  For her help in bitter need.
True and tried, you've ever found her,
  Through the strife a friend indeed!"
—GEORGINA ST. CLAIR GARTLAND.

October 3d and 4th, our batteries gave the city a good shelling. Some of the missiles exploded very near the jail, but without injury to us. On the evening of the 4th we heard from Charleston Race Course, where a number of our enlisted men were confined, a great many of whom were dying from the ravages of scurvy and yellow fever.

Early on the morning of the 5th the Confederate authorities told us to pack up, saying we were to be removed for fear the yellow fever would carry more of us off. Captain Mobly, of the Thirty-second Georgia Regiment, informed us that we were to go to Columbia.

At 9 A. M. we were taken out of the yard, marched through the streets, escorted by the Thirty-second Georgia Regiment, packed into cattle cars and started on another trip and, the rolling stock being nearly worn out, we only made about fifteen miles an hour. Some of the prisoners cut holes in the bottom of the cars and at night, when we came to a stop, would drop out, crawl from under the cars into the brush and make their escape. An officer, in going through one of these holes, was shot in the leg, which had to be amputated. Another plan to escape was to slip the cap from the gun when the guard was not looking, put a splint in the cone, jump out of the door and make for the woods. During the trip, about a dozen prisoners made their escape in this way.

We arrived at Columbia in the midst of a rain storm and camped all night in a field on the north side of Bridge Street. We suffered greatly, the ground being flooded with water, while our only covering was the old blankets we had brought from Libby. We were closely guarded by two regiments of infantry and had four pieces of artillery trained on us. Next morning the Confederate authorities offered us our parole, but not to go beyond a specified range. Under these conditions, we would not accept it, for it would release two regiments of guards who would be sent to the front.

That afternoon, a German baker brought a wagon-load of bread into the camp. Men who had money bought a few loaves and thus engaged the attention of the baker, while other less fortunate prisoners took possession of the wagon and, before the guards came up, every loaf was gone.

Later, on the same day, Lieutenant H. L. Clark, Second Massachusetts Artillery, approached the fence to receive some bread from a citizen, when a sentinel stabbed him in the back with a bayonet. Though seriously wounded, the Lieutenant recovered.

On the opposite side of Bridge Street, near the railroad station, was a large warehouse filled with hams and bacon. Lieutenant Cooper and I tried to hook some through the barred windows with a piece of fence-rail but without success, as one of the guards caught us at our honest employment and, at the point of his bayonet, drove us back into camp.

In the evening, after receiving a ration of corn meal and sorghum molasses, we were marched over the bridge to the south side of the Congaree River. Our new camp was in an open field two miles from the city. The water supply was a small creek at the lower side of the field; our couch was the cold, damp earth; our covering, the blue sky above.

A dead line, made of stakes, was established about thirty feet inside of where the sentinels walked. We were guarded by two regiments of infantry and a battery of artillery, and called our new quarters "Camp Sorghum".

October 8th we received from the sanitary commission boxes of clothing and drew lots for the various articles. Some of the prisoners got undershirts; some, socks; others, drawers, etc. I was very lucky, for I drew a woman's cotton morning gown, which, by wonderful tact and mechanical ability, I made into a spring overcoat.

A box of clothing was sent to me from home, but I never got it. Both gold and notes were sent by mail, but not a dollar did I receive. One day the Confederate adjutant handed me a letter that had contained money and said it was open when they received it from the flag of truce boat. However, no money was in it when delivered to me.

There were about fifteen hundred prisoners in camp at this time, and, as the presidential election was soon to take place, it was proposed to have one in the pen on October 16th. The votes were taken by the senior officer of each State and sent to a general officer. We wrote our ballots and deposited them in a meal bag. We also had a telegraph office and bulletin board and published sham returns every hour. In the evening when the returns were all in and the count was finished, the result was one hundred and forty-three votes for McClellan and ten hundred and twenty-four for Lincoln.

Every five days we drew rations—half a pint of rice, one pint of sorghum molasses and five pints of meal, and every two weeks, half a pint of vinegar and a tablespoonful of salt. Some men would eat their share in three days and go begging for the other two. We were never given any vegetables and, for nearly five months, not a particle of meat.

A sutler's shop was started by three or four of our officers, between whom and the Confederates an arrangement had been made by which bread, meat and vegetables were brought into the pen. Some prisoners received money from home, and others who had watches, rings, knives or buttons would sell them to the Johnnies and, with Confederate scrip, buy what they wanted at the following prices:

Potatoes, per bushel	$40.00
Flour, per quart	4.00
Milk, per quart	3.00
Onions, three for	1.00
Wheat Bread, small loaf	2.00
Butter, per pound	10.00
Lard, "	8.00
Coffee, "	10.00
Tea, "	12.00
Eggs, per dozen	6.00

These prices were in Southern money. At that time one dollar, Federal money, was worth twenty-two dollars of Confederate.

October 18th two Confederate officers came into camp, inquiring for Lieutenant-Colonel Dale, of the One Hundred and Sixteenth Regiment Pennsylvania Volunteers, as our government made a request to find him if possible, not knowing at the time that he was killed at Spottsylvania.

Every ten days we were mustered into squads of twenty, given two axes and taken out to chop wood for our fires. Before going each one was expected to take the following parole: (but when the ceremony was being performed I always managed to be absent and so was free to escape whenever I got the chance)

CONFEDERATE STATES MILITARY PRISON.

COLUMBIA, S. C., October —, 1864.

I, ———, prisoner of war, confined near the city of Columbia, S. C., Confederate States of America, do pledge my parole, as a military man and a man of honor, that I will not attempt to escape from the prison authorities nor pass beyond the prison limits more than three-quarters of a mile, and that at the expiration of the time named in the parole I will return promptly to the adjutant's office and have the same revoked.

It is understood by me that this parole is involuntary on my part and that it is given with a view to securing privileges which cannot be otherwise obtained.

(Signed) ———.

In the mess with me were Lieutenants Robert Allen and Richard Cooper, Seventh New Jersey Volunteers; Charles Stallman, Eighty-seventh Pennsylvania, and Henry F. Anshutz, Twelfth West Virginia Volunteers. The first time our party went out we cut some poles, and, with an old piece of canvas and a blanket, we fixed up a tent in the camp. At night we spread one blanket on the ground, lay down spoon fashion and pulled the other three old ones over us. Sometimes it would be so cold we would have to sit by the fire or walk about all night to keep warm and then sleep in the sun during the day.

To shelter themselves from the cold winds hundreds of the men dug graves to sleep in. Often heavy rains which lasted for two or three days would come on and fill the graves with water. When the rain was over the grave diggers would recommence their dismal occupation and make a new resting place.

October 18th, after nightfall, three officers made their escape down by the creek. The guards fired a number of shots at them, but, fortunately, none took effect.

On the 19th General Winder paid a visit to the prison and promised to send us straw with which to make beds, but we never got it. Shortly after we heard that he dropped dead in Richmond.

About 9 o'clock on the evening of the 20th Lieutenant Young, of the Fourth Pennsylvania Cavalry, while seated at a little fire talking with some officers, was shot through the body by a sentinel and only lived a few moments. The guard said his gun went off by accident, but the prisoners had their doubts about that.

October 23d our squad went out for firewood. Lieutenant Allen hid behind a large tree and made his escape. The guards, being careless or stupid, did not miss him. Just before we were to return to camp I saw a good chance, and, taking advantage of it, pushed through some brush and got into the woods without being seen. Until dark I searched for Allen but could not find him, so I took up my quarters under a large tree and fell fast asleep. Next day I walked as well as I was able, but, having no shoes and my feet being bruised, torn and very sore from the underbrush and briars, I did not make much headway. That night I slept the best I could beside a little stream. Early next morning, being very hungry, I crossed a road and went to what I thought was a negro cabin; a big dog came barking at me and in a few moments two men on patrol duty came up. By noon they had me safely lodged in my old quarters. Three days after Allen was recaptured and once more joined our mess.

Almost every night prisoners would escape, but nearly all were recaptured. Captain Halpin was out for five days at one time, and on the night of October 30th ran over the line again. On this occasion he was out three weeks, and when brought back had on a new suit of Confederate clothes. He told me that when re-captured he was taken to a farmhouse. The family said they would like to let him go but were afraid the neighbors would inform on them. He was kindly treated and at night slept in the best bed in the house. In the evenings, when the young people went to little parties given by their friends, he was taken along and had a good time, which only made the sufferings of prison life harder to endure on his return to camp. November 1st a mail from the North arrived and long-looked-for letters were distributed.

November 14th a large wild boar ran into camp. Cooper, Allen and I were going to the brook for water when he ran past us. Cooper dropped the kettle and grabbed the hog by a hind leg. By that time Allen had his clasp-knife open and in a few seconds had cut the whole ham off the hog. In five minutes not a trace of that lively porker could be seen. When fifty hungry men were fighting for a share—one having hold of his ear, another his tail and another a leg—it did not take long to get away with Mr. Hog. When our ham was boiled it was so rank you could have smelt it a square away. One of our mess had to stand guard over it night and day till it was all eaten, fearing some of our friends would be tempted to dine on it.

On the 29th of November, Captain John Taylor, of the Second Pennsylvania Reserves, made his escape by running past the sentinels who fired several shots at him, but before they could reload the Captain was in the woods. The Confederates thought he looked so lonely and forlorn traveling about in a strange country that they very kindly gave him a military escort, and in three weeks had him again amongst his friends in prison. This was the third or fourth time he had made his escape and been recaptured.

One morning two blood-hounds came into camp, and, not being looked upon as friends of the prisoners, they were taken to a gravel pit and an artillery officer killed them with an axe and then buried them. Next day they were dug up by the Johnnies, who, to be revenged on us for slaying their dogs, said they would put the bodies in the brook above where it entered the camp, but I do not think the threat was carried out. It was reported that

Lieutenant Parker, who made his escape, was so badly bitten by blood-hounds that he died the day after his recapture.

December 1st, 1864, about 9 o'clock in the morning, whilst walking near the dead line I heard a shot, and, looking around, saw Lieutenant Turbayne, of a New York infantry regiment, just falling to the ground. The ball entered his back, passing through his lungs, and he lived but a few moments. He was walking on a path near the line when a sentinel, by the name of Williams, of Newbury Court House, S. C., ordered him to go back. He turned and had only taken a few steps when fired upon. After the guard was relieved by the officer of the day we made a complaint to Major Griswold, the commandant of the prison, but he would not give us any satisfaction. That evening the murderer was back again on duty and next morning was paraded through camp escorted by a strong body guard, fearing if he came alone our officers would take revenge and kill him, as they threatened to do if they got an opportunity. Only a few nights after Lieutenant T. K. Eckings, Third New Jersey Volunteers, was shot dead as he ran past the sentinels at the guard line whilst trying to make his escape.

On the 9th of December an exchange came for about fifty prisoners and one for an officer by the name of Cooper, who was not in the pen, he having made his escape. Lieutenant Richard Cooper, of our mess, said he would personate the absent officer and get exchanged. When the name was called and he had passed over the line to the place where the other officers were assembled, one of them told the Confederate officials he was not the right man. Cooper was immediately sent back to camp, and when he gave the name of the officer who informed on him the prisoners swore if they ever got North they would kill that "son of a gun".

On December 12th we were removed to Camp Asylum. The stockade enclosed part of the insane asylum grounds, and in it was a frame house which was used as a hospital for our sick officers. We were given lumber to build sheds and bunks, which, when finished, only held about one-half the prisoners. Each of the ten sheds was to accommodate fifty men, so we drew lots for a berth and I was fortunate enough to secure a place in one of the sheds. More lumber was to be sent but it did not come, so about six hundred men had to fix up sleeping quarters the best they could with their old blankets and some boards which they found in the stockade. Between scanty clothing, short rations and the intensely cold weather we had a hard time trying to keep warm.

One day the Confederate sutler brought in a load of meal for our rations. When the negroes dumped it in the bin I watched my chance and stole an empty bag. By cutting a hole in the bottom for my head and one on each side for my arms, that evening on the promenade I sported a very stylish new shirt.

Captain Fischer, an artist, obtained permission to go outside and make a sketch of the camp for the Confederate authorities. He also made a note of the formation of the ground outside the fence for us that we might know the best point for tunnelling. Lieutenant McNiece, of the Seventy-third Pennsylvania Volunteers, had one dug from his shanty nearly to the fence when one morning the Johnnies came in and filled it up. How they found it out he never could tell, for no one in camp knew he was making it. Tunnels were then the order of the day. We commenced one in the shed I was in. Every man was sworn to secrecy, and at night a detail of five was made to work in the tunnel. One man would dig, another pull the earth out in an old box and the others would pack it under the bunks and scatter it about the prison grounds to conceal all traces of the work. Unfortunately, we were moved from the camp a few nights before its completion.

Early in January a French captain was sent to command the prison. He was a good natured fellow and promised to send in plenty of straw with which to make beds. Captain Henry Ritter, Fifty-second New York Volunteers, and some others were good at faro. The Frenchman thought he would soon "break the bank", but in two days our boys had him cleaned out of funds. A few days after he went on a big spree and was dismissed, so we had to do without the straw.

Most of the time a number of our officers were at headquarters. It was said they were clerking for the Confederate officials, and they allowed they were justified in saving their lives by so doing, for they received more and better food than was given them in the camp. I thought they should have remained in the prison, taking their chances with the rest of us, and not aided the Confederates in any way.

It was while we were at Columbia that Adjutant S. H. M. Byres, Fifth Iowa Volunteers, wrote "Sherman's March to the Sea", and Lieutenant Rockwell composed the music.

For several days the negroes were telling us that Sherman was on the march from Charleston. On the afternoon of February 14th, we were told to make ready to move and, that evening at 5 o'clock, we were marched out and put into box cars. We got under way and, in the early part of the night, it became very cold. A severe storm of rain and sleet came on, and when about thirty miles on the way the last car, in which I was, caught fire from warm boxes. The hind truck and bottom were nearly destroyed before the engineer stopped the train. Some of the guards on the tops of the cars were frozen stiff and had to be lifted down. We built fires with fence rails to keep ourselves warm whilst waiting for the Confederates to prepare another car which, when ready, was placed next the engine. We had not gone far on our journey when this car began to stretch. The engine in front and the weight of the train behind had nearly pulled the old box car in two, when the guards on the top, seeing the danger we were in, called to the engineer who hastily brought the train to a standstill. The old wrecked car was removed from the track and, as there was no other to replace it, they were obliged to crowd us in with the other prisoners.

In the evening of the 15th we reached Charlotte, remained there over night and, next day, were removed to Raleigh, where we were placed in a field near the railroad. Here we were given our parole and had hopes that we would be allowed to enter the town and enjoy a little bit of civilized life. But we were mistaken for, in a few hours, we were put on a train made up of flat and box cars and started on our way to a new camp. When about a mile from town, a broken switch threw the engine and five or six cars off the track. They ran over the ties for about a hundred yards when the engine plunged down a high embankment. Fortunately, the coupling broke or the cars would have gone over and the loss of life would have been very great. Some of the prisoners said it was done with the intention to kill us, but others thought that, as the Confederate captain in command was on the engine, he would not risk his own life and the lives of the engineer and fireman for the satisfaction of killing us.

The evening we left Columbia, there not being enough room in the cars for all the prisoners, several hundred were left in the camp and next day forwarded to Charlotte on another made-up train of box cars. During the trip, Captains Meany, Thirteenth Pennsylvania Cavalry, Durborough of New York, Evans of Ohio and Gilbert, One Hundred and Thirty-second New York Volunteers, cut a hole in the bottom of the car they were in with a saw which, by the help of an old file, they had made out of a table knife. After dark, the train ran into a herd of cattle that was being driven out of the reach of Sherman's Army. When the train came to a stop, Captain Evans dropped out to reconnoitre. He returned and reported to the boys that all was favorable for escape but, as he lowered himself through the hole the second time, the guards saw him and several shots were fired, one ball passing into his stomach. He also received a bayonet wound. Captains Meany and Gilbert pulled him into the car and did what they could for their wounded friend, but he died in a few minutes.

From Raleigh, many prisoners made their escape, amongst the number Captain Halpin, who safely reached Sherman's lines. The guards at this place knowing we were on our way to be exchanged seemed to have no wish to prevent our escape. Quite a number of them being Union sympathizers allowed us every chance to get away.

After being eight days at Raleigh we were removed to Goldsborough. Here, there were thousands of prisoners encamped who had been brought from Andersonville to be exchanged. I spent a day amongst them and will never forget the awful scenes I witnessed ; men worn to skeletons from disease and want of proper nourishment, as black as negroes from sitting over the pine-wood fires and not being washed for months. Some wandered about as if demented ; a great many were in their last agony ; and a number of the dead were lying on the roadside, having been carried out of camp when their sufferings were over. Our officers gave their old blankets and what clothing they could possibly spare for the comfort of their wretched fellow-soldiers.

February 28th, we were paroled and had to give our word of honor to the Confederates not to reveal in the North what we saw on the way to Wilmington. They took good care, however, that we should not see the fortifications for, when it became quite dark, we were crowded into and on top of cars and started on our last, but most welcome, journey.

We stopped about eight miles from Wilmington, where we met Major Mulford, the Northern and Captain Hatch, the Southern Commissioner of Exchange. A Union guard was stationed on one side of the line and a Confederate one on the other. When we passed into our lines the Federal guard presented arms. Then went up a hearty cheer and old meal bags, tin cups and skillets went flying in all directions. Some colored troops, who were quartered in the vicinity, gave us a rousing welcome. We then partook of a "good, square meal" of coffee, meat and bread, which sumptuous repast made some of us exceedingly ill, not being used to such high living. The very sick were taken on a steamboat to the city. As there were no other means of conveyance, the rest had to walk all the way along the railroad track. In the evening we had supper, and for the night were quartered in a Methodist Church. In the morning, I was physically much refreshed after the good night's sleep I had had in an uncushioned pew and, mentally and spiritually, I was much revived from having spent so many hours in such a sanctified place. That day we had a good breakfast and dinner and, in the evening, were put on board a steamboat and taken to Annapolis. When we arrived there we went to some clothing stores and, by giving our name, rank and regiment, got all the clothes we wanted on credit. We were then taken to the bath house, discarded our old rags with much pleasure, had a thorough wash, donned our new suits and every man thought he was himself again. We slept that night in a government building and, next day, the doctor sent me to the Naval Academy Hospital, where I remained for two months.

In the hospital we were given good, nourishing food, so that gradually our systems were brought back to their normal state. We were not allowed to take any kind of spirituous liquors but at dinner, if we wished it, we were permitted to have one glass of beer.

There was a captain of cavalry in the same ward with me. Thirteen of his men who had been in Andersonville, but were then in Camp Parole, got a thirty days' furlough to go home and see their families; they came to bid their captain good-bye. All were cleaned up, had on new clothes and looked very well. When their time was up only two came back. Eleven had died from being overfed and having too good a time with their friends. The doctors at Annapolis said there were few, if any, who spent six months in prison, who were not afflicted with some disease and the system could not stand the sudden change of diet. Of the nine men in my company who were captured, only three lived to return, the others having died in less than three months after being taken.

When we were given notice of our exchange, I requested and received my discharge from the hospital and joined my regiment after an absence of nearly a year.

One of my men, Sergeant Thomas Lacompte, who had been a prisoner in Andersonville, gave me a copy of the following verses composed by a Union captive after he was paroled:

UNION PRISONERS FROM DIXIE'S SUNNY LAND.

Dear friends and fellow-soldiers brave, come listen to our song,
About the Rebel prisons, and our sojourn there so long;
Yet our wretched state and hardships great no one can understand,
But those who have endured this fate in Dixie's sunny land.

When captured by the chivalry, they strip't us to the skin,
But failed to give us back again the value of a pin—
Except some lousy rags of gray, discarded by their band—
And thus commenced our prison life in Dixie's sunny land.

With a host of guards surrounding us, each with a loaded gun,
We were stationed in an open plain, exposed to rain and sun;
No tent or tree to shelter us, we lay upon the sand—
Thus, side by side, great numbers died in Dixie's sunny land.

This was the daily "bill of fare" in that Secesh saloon—
No sugar, tea or coffee there at morning night or noon;
But a pint of meal, ground cob and all, was served to every man,
And for want of fire we ate it raw in Dixie's sunny land.

We were by these poor rations soon reduced to skin and bone,
A lingering starvation—worse than death—you can but own,
There hundreds lay, both night and day, by far too weak to stand,
Till death relieved their sufferings in Dixie's sunny land.

We poor survivors oft were tried by many a threat and bribe,
To desert our glorious Union cause and join the Rebel tribe,
Though fain we were to leave the place, we let them understand,
We had rather die than thus disgrace our flag! in Dixie's land.

Thus dreary days and nights roll'd by—yes, weeks and months untold,
Until that happy time arrived when we were all paroled.
We landed at Annapolis, a wretched looking band,
But glad to be alive and free from Dixie's sunny land.

How like a dream those days now seem in retrospective view,
As we regain our wasted strength all dressed in "Union Blue".
The debt we owe our bitter foe shall not have long to stand;
We shall pay it with a vengeance soon in Dixie's sunny land.

The dreadful monotony of prison life was hard to endure; day after day, week after week and month after month, the same scenes over again. When a few men would meet, the general conversation would be about home and family. The prospects were that the war would last so long they would not live to see the end, and that they would never be exchanged, and what then would become of their wives and children. I have seen some men so worried and despondent with these thoughts they seemed to be demented and their hair, dark and glossy when captured, would be in a few months turned to gray or white.

It is impossible for anyone, who has not been a prisoner, to realize the privation and suffering those unfortunate men had to endure. With few exceptions, their clothing was worn to rags; a great number were without shoes or shirt, and they had nothing but their old blankets to cover them in the cold, frosty nights; for months at a time lying on the bare, damp ground with no shelter; the rations, scant and miserable; and night and day constantly tortured with vermin from which no one could keep free. Is it any wonder that loathsome diseases should prevail, or that welcome death should end the earthly sufferings of so many thousands who went to that blessed land above that they might receive their Martyr's Crown?

RETURN MARCH TO WASHINGTON.

AS the army moved towards Appomattox through that portion of Virginia where hitherto but few of the Union troops had been seen, the slaves on the plantations watched the passing columns with great interest, some showing their white teeth in a broad smile, whilst others looked grave. They all seemed to feel that their fate rested with the boys in blue, but the war was not yet ended, and they knew not whether they were to remain in bondage or breathe the air of freedom.

The majority of the men had already gone North or had left for Alexandria, but the women and children all remained and swarmed to the road-side to see the army pass, all willing and anxious to give information of the flying Confederates. But when, after the surrender, the army passed over the same road, on the way back, the situation was different. Every soul of them had become aware of the Union triumph, and knew that, as a consequence, the chains had fallen from their limbs. Old and young wanted to abandon the homestead at once and follow the victorious army. The roads were soon filled with the poor things, each with a little bundle containing their all hung on a stick (just as the woodcuts of runaway slaves used to look in the newspapers in ante-bellum times), each one laughing and happy, all tramping towards the North, not having an idea where they were going, but each thinking that Father Abraham would care for them somehow.

For them the days of the lash and task-master were over, but the future was a blank. Now and then one would be encountered who had some definite object in leaving the plantation.

One old darkey who paused in front of some officers began talking to them of the necessity of saving their souls and preparing for the great hereafter. A strange character he was, who could neither read nor write, but knew almost every word of the Bible by heart. He had been the local preacher of the plantation, and when one of the officers asked him if he believed in "Virtue, Liberty and Independence", he promptly replied: "I don know, massa, I don know. I neber hear ob dat ligeon, but I bleve dat a man got to be bawn again if he specks to be saved". Abraham, for that was the old man's name (and as he said himself, "he neber had no names ceptin jus Abraham") remained with the regiment until it was mustered out. He was going to Alexandria to find his wife and child, who had been sold to some one near that city twenty-four years before. He had never heard of them during all that time, but his heart was true to the wife of his youth, and his newly found freedom was made sweeter by the hopes of finding once more his early partner and his child. Abraham held a prayer-meeting and preached a sermon every evening before "Taps", and the negroes would gather around and enjoy it. The soldiers were at first disposed to laugh at the crude theology and uncouth oratory of the old slave, but they soon ceased to ridicule, and then listened with interest.

Poor old Abraham! I wonder if he ever found his lost bride and his little baby. He must be very old now, if he is still alive, and no doubt he is still searching for his lost love, if he has not already found her. If he has been "bawn agin" he has certainly met her, for as he said (after learning the meaning of the words), "he bleved in de vartue, but dint know so much about de Liberty an' Independence". Let us hope that he enjoys all three in the Land of the Blessed.

Perhaps one of the most interesting and remarkable things witnessed in connection with the homeward march was the late Confederate soldiers busy working on their farms. The very hour after the surrender they hastened to their former homes, and within twenty-four hours many of them were eagerly at work getting the neglected farms in order. As the Union Army had halted at Burkville for two weeks, the Virginian had time to reach his home and get to work before the returning victors passed his way, and in every case the ex-Confederate was found hard at work fixing up his fences or laboring in the field with the horse that General Grant had so wisely allowed him to keep when surrendering. Sensible and practical as well as brave, when they laid down the musket, they went back without delay to the ploughshare, and all along the road the ex-Confederate soldier was seen leaving his plough or harrow for a time and standing by the roadside to greet with a smile and pleasant word his foes of but a few days before.

The regiment encamped at Burkville Junction during the remainder of the month of April, and on the evening of the 15th the sad news of the assassination of President Abraham Lincoln was received. When the dispatch was read the regiment was just forming for dress-parade. The adjutant quietly removed his coat, and, ripping out the black lining, used it to drape the colors. The dress-parade that followed was silent and sad, the men looking towards the heavily draped flag and wondering what it meant. When the adjutant read the orders, and then, with tears streaming down his cheeks, and choking voice, read the announcement of the murder, the effect was indescribable. When arms were stacked the men gathered in little groups in the company streets and spoke in low tones of the martyred President, whom they loved so tenderly.

It happened that Lieutenant Wm. H. Tyrrell, of Company C, was on duty in Washington, and was "officer of the day" in the city when the assassination of the President took place. The lieutenant's account of the eventful evening is interesting. In his diary we read:

"Friday, April 14th, 1865. Was detailed as "officer of the day" at Washington. A gentleman came very hurriedly to headquarters, between 10 and 11 P. M., with the intelligence that the President had just been assassinated at Ford's Theatre, and informed General Augur in an excited manner, as nearly as he could, of the occurrence. The play was "The American Cousin," and was going along smoothly when the whole audience was startled by a pistol shot in the President's box. A man sprang from it onto the stage, brandishing a large knife, and, shouting "Sic semper tyrannis"! rushed across the stage and disappeared. The audience was terror-stricken. Some shouted that it was Booth. Others said no; that it was only a subterfuge to shield the real assassin. General Augur ordered me to take a guard, go to the National Hotel and arrest Booth, anyhow. Went there, and was told he was not in. Went up to his room; found everything there as though he expected to return soon.

I returned to headquarters and reported. By this time it developed that an attempt had been made on Vice-President Johnson, and that Secretary Seward was also almost killed. I was ordered to return to the hotel and bring any papers or anything else which I thought likely to throw any light on the case. Brought some papers which led to the arrest of Atzerof and Herold; also, two pairs of handcuffs which I found in his trunk. Reported at headquarters. Found great excitement there. Secretary of War Stanton, Adjutant-General Townsend and others were there. They did not then know the extent of the plot, and seemed to think that the provost marshal's headquarters was a place of refuge.

It then developed that the original plot was to capture Lincoln and Seward, get them across the line, hold them as hostages, and then make their own terms. The handcuffs were intended to be used on the occasion. There

CARD PHOTOGRAPH OF WILKES BOOTH, LEG IRONS AND HAND-CUFFS INTENDED FOR PRESIDENT LINCOLN. THESE ARTICLES WERE TAKEN OUT OF THE TRUNK OF THE ASSASSIN BY LIEUTENANT TYRRELL.

was an old mansion on Seventeenth street, about two squares below the White House, where the conspirators had a secret room fitted up for the reception of their distinguished captives. They could thus have been concealed a few minutes after their abduction, and no one would have thought of looking for them so near at hand. After the excitement was over they were to be taken over to Moseby's lines, and then to Richmond, but as that plan was evidently abandoned, the assassination followed.

The excitement in Washington was intense. The people were ready for any extreme. On the Sunday afternoon following, April 16th, a Confederate colonel was brought to the provost marshal's office. An immense crowd of people gathered and wanted to hang him. While Colonel Ingraham, the provost marshal, was talking and trying to quiet them, the prisoner colonel was hurried out the back way and driven in an ambulance to the old Capitol Prison. Monday morning, April 17th, at 3 A. M., an orderly came to my house with orders to report at headquarters. On my arrival found that they had Payne, the man who had cut Secretary of State Seward's throat. He was a large, muscular man, and had his hands handcuffed behind him. He was captured by the detectives who were in Mrs. Surratt's house, on H street, near Sixth. He came to the door, and, as he had lost his hat, had taken the lower part of his trousers and made a cap of it. He had a spade in his hand and claimed to be a workman. Lieutenant Sharp and myself took him in an ambulance, with two guards walking outside to keep off intruders. Orders were to let no one know who it was. If it were known, a regiment of soldiers could not have taken him down to the Navy Yard. When we arrived there the gates were closed, and the major in command turned out the whole guard, about twenty-five men, and put him in the centre until we arrived out on one of the ironclad monitors, where he was securely confined. It was thought necessary to do so, as no ordinary prison would have been safe from the populace, so intense was the public feeling.

The following Wednesday, April 19th, Colonel Ingraham ordered me to take a guard and proceed to the Baltimore and Ohio Depot. He met us there, and as soon as the train arrived put a guard on each door, and would allow no one out until the general who commanded the Department of Maryland came out with three prisoners, who were escorted to the large bus of Willard's Hotel. We all got in, and drove rapidly to the Navy Yard. No one on the train had suspected who the prisoners were, or they never would have reached Washington alive. They were Atzerof, Herold and Arnold. The former was the one who was to have assassinated Vice-President Johnson at the Kirkwood House, but he weakened at the last moment. Booth, after entering the passage leading to the President's box, secured the door on the inside, and, advancing, shot the President from behind. The pistol was a small Derringer, single barrel, about 42 calibre. Mr. Rathbone, the President's private secretary, tried to detain Booth, but brandishing a large knife, he leaped from the box. In doing so, one of the spurs which he had on caught in the flag in front of the box, and threw him on the stage. In the fall he broke his ankle, but got up and drove the terror-stricken actors before him. He rushed out the back way into an alley, where he had a horse saddled, mounted it and escaped.

Thursday, April 20th, Dr. Mudd was brought to headquarters. It was at his place, down in Maryland, that Booth in his terrific ride stopped and had his broken ankle dressed, and received the carbine which had been previously left there by Mrs. Surratt. He then continued his journey until surrounded in a barn and shot by Boston Corbett while the barn was all ablaze.

Mudd was also put aboard the ironclad."

During the homeward march a halt of a couple of days was made at Manchester, within a few miles of Richmond, and while there a platform was pointed out upon which it was said the slaves were stood to be auctioned. The men of the regiment took it down and cut it into small pieces, and fired the pile with a show of ceremony. It seemed like a burnt offering on the altar of Liberty. The platform was of no further use. No man, no matter what his color, would ever again be bought or sold in all the land.

While encamped at Manchester orders came to prepare for review in Richmond, and a busy day was spent cleaning up. Guns and equipments were made to shine, and when the troops passed through the late Capital of the Southern Confederacy they never looked so well. The white citizens were not backward in giving to the victorious army a welcome and a cheer, whilst the colored people seemed fairly crazed with joy. To them it was "Kingdom come", the day of jubilee longed for and prayed for. The column passed in review by the equestrian statue of Washington, in the Public Square, and the Father of his country seemed to smile in gladness on this happy day.

The march continued through Hanover Court House, and then to Fredericksburg, and on to Alexandria, where a halt was made long enough to make out the muster-out rolls.

In the last grand review, in Washington, May 23, 1865, the One Hundred and Sixteenth Regiment marched on the right of the Fourth Brigade, First Division, Second Corps. The regiment on that occasion was commanded by Lieutenant-Colonel David W. Megraw, Colonel and Brevet Major-General St. Clair A. Mulholland being in command of the brigade. A few days afterwards the Philadelphia companies of the regiment started for that city, and were finally mustered out on June 3d. The remaining companies were mustered out at Pittsburg, July 14, 1865, and the regiment passed out of existence.

The members returned to their homes to be welcomed by their friends and fellow-citizens, to lay aside forever the uniform that they had honored, and to become once again a part of the people—a good citizen because a good soldier.

The regimental flags, four in number, shattered, bullet-torn and blood-stained, were deposited in the State Capitol at Harrisburg, where for generations to come the descendants of the members of the regiment can with reverence look upon the sacred standards, the only remaining emblems of a gallant command that upheld them in storm of battle, carried them to victory, and returned them to the State with honor.

Of the officers of the regiment eight were killed in battle, two died of gunshot wounds, one died of disease, and one of disease contracted in Southern prisons. Thirty-one were wounded, and seven were for months prisoners in the South. Of the original officers who left Philadelphia with the regiment, September 2, 1862, only one, Colonel Mulholland, returned with the command at the close of the war.

THE LAST MUSTER.

On the 11th day of September, 1889, the last reunion of the regiment took place when the survivors met at Gettysburg to dedicate a monument to the command. Post 51, Grand Army of the Republic, paraded as an escort, the battery of the post firing the salute, the first gun being fired by John W. Emsley, the son of an officer who never missed a fight or a battle, and, with sounding artillery, and speeches by Major Chill Hazard, General Thomas J. Stewart, Lieutenant Edmund Randall, General Mulholland and others, the splendid memorial was fittingly dedicated.

MONUMENT OF THE REGIMENT AT GETTYSBURG

General Mulholland, on the occasion, delivered the following address:

IN all the four years of its existence the men of the Army of the Potomac never hailed an order with more delight than that one which withdrew us from before Fredericksburg and sent us north. When on that lovely summer evening in June, 1863, we looked for the last time on Marye's Heights and the monument of Washington's mother, which had been shattered and broken by the shells of both armies, and stood out there on the plain back of the city as though protesting against this fratricidal strife, a mute and sorrowful Niobe weeping for the misfortunes of her children, every heart beat with a quickening throb, and all the men rejoiced to leave the scenes of the last six months. We withdrew from the line of the river after the shades of night had fallen over the landscape, and it seemed to be an appropriate hour, for had not the great army while here been in shadow, without a ray of sunshine to gladden our souls, and we had been here so long that we were beginning to be forgotten as the Army of the Potomac, and letters came to us marked "Army of the Rappahannock".

As we marched away in the darkness our joy was not unmingled with sorrow, for was there a veteran in the ranks who did not leave behind the graves of noble and well-beloved comrades who had fought beside him from the beginning of the great struggle? We did not march away with all the army, for when our camp-fires—which on this night burned with unusual brightness—went out and left the valley of the Rappahannock in darkness, the living army was gone to be sure, but twenty thousand of our members lay over on the other side of the river —the heroes of Fredericksburg and Chancellorsville. An army of occupation indeed, the corps of honor, forming a great and permanent camp—the bivouac of the dead.

Thoughts of sadness soon gave way to those of a more buoyant nature; we felt, when the head of the column turned toward the Capital, that the road we trod would lead to victory. The march to Gettysburg was one of the longest and most severe we had yet experienced. In thinking of war we are apt to look only at the battles ; to hear the dread sound of strife; see the deadly, gaping wounds, and are ready to crown the survivors or give honor to those who fell; but the hardships of the march, the heats of summer, the colds of winter, the entire absence of every comfort and luxury in active service is overlooked or forgotten by those who do not participate. Napoleon, when retreating from Moscow, lost many of his men by the excessive cold; directly opposite was our experience on the way to Gettysburg. On one day, I think the second out from Falmouth, our corps lost more than a dozen men from sunstroke—they fell dead by the wayside. On another day we crossed the battlefield of Bull Run, where the year before Pope had met with disastrous defeat. No effort had been made to bury the dead properly; a little earth, which the rain had long ago washed away, had been thrown over them where they fell, and their bodies, or rather their skeletons, now lay exposed to view. In some parts of the field they were in groups; in other places singly and in all possible positions. One cavalryman lay outstretched with skeleton hand still grasping his rusted sword. Another, half covered with earth, the flesh still clinging to his lifeless bones, with hand extended as if to greet us. We rested for a short time on the field, and one of the regiments of our brigade (the Twenty-eighth Massachusetts), halted on the very spot on which they had fought the year previously, and recognized the various articles lying around as belonging to their own dead.

The route of the Second Corps to Gettysburg was over two hundred miles in length. Some days we marched fifteen, on others eighteen miles, and one day (June 29) this corps completed the longest march made by infantry during the war, leaving Frederick City, Maryland, in the morning, and halting at 11 o'clock P. M. two miles beyond Uniontown, a distance of thirty-four miles. When I look back over the almost score of years to this march of the Second Corps, and think of the perfect discipline in the ranks, the cheerfulness with which the enlisted men, with their heavy load, musket and ammunition, knapsack and cartridge box, shelter tent and blanket, canteen and rations— trudged along under the broiling sun of the hottest month of the year; how bravely they struggled to keep up with their regiments lest they should miss the fight, and how, while on the march no act was committed which could bring dishonor upon them as men, as citizens or as soldiers, my heart fills with admiration, and I offer a flowing measure of praise to my comrades who are yet alive and to those who are no more. There is not an inhabitant on all that line of march who can tell of a single act of vandalism by any of the men, such as we are wont to hear of other armies. In the rich and cultivated country through which we passed life and property were respected as much as though we were in the halcyon days of peace. Old and young came to the roadside to see the army pass, and knew they were safe from insult or molestation. The fields of ripening grain waved untrampled when the corps had gone by, the men even going out of their way to avoid the gardens, lest they should step upon the flowers. The perfection of discipline in the army at this time was extraordinary. The armies that fought the war of 1861 differed very widely from the armies of other nations. We had no hordes of Cossacks, no regiments of Bashi-Bazouks to burn and destroy, to insult the aged or crush the defenseless.

When Hancock, at Williamsburg, said to his brigade, "Gentlemen, charge", he did not call his troops out of their name. Our army was literally an army of gentlemen.

And so we passed on to Thoroughfare Gap, to Edwards' Ferry, to Frederick, Maryland, to Uniontown and Taneytown, where, on the morning of July 1, the Second Corps was massed and where General

Meade's headquarters had been established. While the corps were filing into the fields to the right and left of the road and settling down for a rest and to wait for orders, General Hancock rode over to General Meade and entered into conversation with him. As they were talking a mounted officer dashed up bringing the intelligence that fighting had begun at Gettysburg—thirteen miles distant. The news was meagre—only that there was fighting, that was all; yet it caused a general surprise, unaware as we were of the near proximity of the enemy, and was enough to send a thrill throughout the veteran ranks. The road that leads to Gettysburg is scanned with anxious eyes and soon, away in the distance, rises a cloud of dust, which comes nearer and nearer, and another messenger from the front is with us. He tells us that Reynolds is killed and that the First and Eleventh Corps are fighting and the battle is against us. It is now 1 o'clock, too late for the Second Corps to reach the field that day to take part in stemming the tide; but not so with its commander. Meade orders Hancock to proceed to the front and take command of all the troops there assembled. This was 1.10 o'clock, and within twenty minutes Hancock, with his staff, was on the road to Gettysburg. He goes like Dessaix at Marengo, to snatch victory from the jaws of defeat. (A strange coincidence related to me by General Hancock himself, nearly a century before the grandfather of General Hancock, then a soldier of Washington's army, started from this same little village of Taneytown to escort some of the prisoners of Burgoyne to Valley Forge.) The Second Corps promptly followed General Hancock, and it required no urging to keep the men up. The regiments moved solidly and rapidly and not a straggler was to be seen. Men never covered thirteen miles so quickly; but as they hurried along a halt was ordered, the ranks opened, and an ambulance passed containing the dead body of the heroic General John F. Reynolds. Then the corps pushed on to within a short distance of the battle ground, where it camped that night and arrived on the field early the next morning.

As General Hancock proceeded to the front, he rode part of the way in an ambulance so that he might examine the maps of the country, his aide, Major Mitchell, galloping ahead to announce his coming to General Howard, whom he found on Cemetery Hill, and to whom he told his errand. At 3 30 o'clock, General Hancock rode up to General Howard, informed him that he had come to take command. Howard answered, "Hancock, go ahead". At this moment our defeat seemed to be complete. Our troops were flowing through the streets of the town in great disorder, closely pursued by the Confederates, the retreat fast becoming a rout, and in a very few minutes the enemy would have been in possession of Cemetery Hill, the key to the position, and the battle of Gettysburg would have gone into history as a Confederate victory. But what a change came over the scene in the next half hour. The presence of Hancock, like that of Sheridan, was magnetic. Order came out of chaos. The flying troops halt and again face the enemy.

The battalions that were retreating down the Baltimore pike are called back, and with a cheer go into position on the crest of Cemetery Hill, where the division of Steinwehr had already been stationed.

When order had taken the place of confusion, and our lines once more intact, he sent his senior aide, Major Mitchell, back to tell General Meade, that in his judgment, Gettysburg was the place to fight our battle. Major Mitchell found General Meade in the evening, near Taneytown, and communicated these views. General Meade listened attentively, and on these representations he fortunately concluded to deliver the battle at Gettysburg, and turning to General Seth Williams, his adjutant-general, he said: "Order up all the troops, we will fight there!"

The morning of July 2, and the second day of the battle dawned clear and bright, and found Hancock posting the Second Corps on Cemetery Ridge. As yet, no one in that corps, with the exception of the general and his staff, had heard a shot fired. As we approached Gettysburg the day before, the sounds of the fight, owing to the direction of the wind or the formation of the country, were wholly inaudible. Those who came upon the field after nightfall, had no idea of the whereabouts of the enemy, but as the daylight increased and objects became visible, we saw their lines nearly a mile distant on Seminary Ridge, and away to our left rose Little Round Top, and still farther on Round Top. As the day wore on and not a shot or a hostile sound broke the stillness of the morning, it became evident that the enemy were not yet ready to renew the fight. Our corps had got into position (not on the eastern slope of Cemetery Ridge as now marked, but directly on the crest some fifty yards forward) and in a woods just back of our line the birds carolled and sang. Our horses quietly browsed in the rich grass, and the men lay in groups, peacefully enjoying a rest after the rapid march of the day before. The troops that arrived on the field or changed their position, did so leisurely and unmolested. Sickles came up and went into position on our left, and Geary took his division over to Culp's Hill. About 10 o'clock A. M., picket firing was heard out towards the left beyond the Emmitsburg pike, continuing at intervals until long after noon, at times becoming quite sharp. But 3 o'clock came and still no signs of the general engagement.

The boys had partly recovered from their fatigue and were actually beginning to enjoy life; some of them indulged in a quiet game of euchre, while others toasted their hardtack or fried a little bacon at the small fires in the rear of the lines. Shortly after 3 o'clock, a movement was apparent on our left. From where we (Caldwell's Division) lay, the whole country in our front and far to our left, away to the peach orchard and to Little Round Top, was in full view, the country not then being so grown up as at this day. Our division stood in brigade columns, and when it became evident that something was going to take place, the boys dropped their cards, regardless of what was trump, and all gathered on the most favorable position to witness the opening of the ball. Soon the long lines of the Third Corps are seen advancing, and how splendidly they march. It looks like dress parade, a review. On, on they go, out toward the peach orchard, but not a shot fired. A little while longer and some one calls out "there," and points to where a puff of smoke is seen arising against the dark green of the woods beyond the Emmitsburg pike. Another and another until the whole face of the forest is enveloped, and the dread sound of artillery comes loud and quick, shells are seen bursting in all directions along the lines. The bright colors of the regiments are conspicuous marks, and the shells burst around them in great numbers. The musketry begins, the infantry becomes engaged and the battle extends along the whole front of Sickles's Corps. (The writer, in company with General Hancock, who, a few minutes before, had ridden up to the right of the Second Brigade and dismounted, General Caldwell, Colonel Kelly of the Eighty-eighth New York, Colonel Burns of the Twenty-eighth Massachusetts, and several other field officers, who had sought that eligible locality to view the contest, were grouped together. Hancock was resting on one knee, leaning upon his sword; he smiled and remarked: "Wait a moment, you will soon see them tumbling back.") Now the sounds come from Little Round Top, and the smoke rises among the trees, and all the high and wooded ground to the left of the peach orchard seems to be the scene of strife. An hour passed and our troops give way and are falling back, the odds are against them and they are forced to retire.

A staff officer rides up with an order to the commander of the Second Corps to send a division to report to General Sykes on the left. Hancock quietly remarks, "Caldwell, get your division ready." "Fall in," and the men run to their places, "take arms," and the four brigades of Zook, Cross, Brooke and Kelly, although small in numbers, are ready for the fray. There is yet a few minutes to spare before starting, and the time is occupied in one of the most impressive religious ceremonies I have ever witnessed. The Irish Brigade, which has been commanded formerly by General Thomas Francis Meagher, and whose green flag has been unfurled on every battle in which the Army of the Potomac was engaged, from the first Bull Run to Appomattox, and now commanded by Colonel Patrick Kelly, and to which our regiment was attached, formed a part of this division. The brigade stood in column of regiments closed in mass. As a large majority of its members were Catholics, the chaplain of the brigade, Rev. William Corby, proposed to give a general absolution to all the men before going into the fight. While this is customary in the armies of the Catholic countries in Europe, it was, perhaps, the first time it was ever witnessed on this continent, unless, indeed, the grim old warrior, Ponce de Leon, as he tramped through the everglades of Florida in search of the Fountain of Youth, or De Soto, on his march to the Mississippi, indulged in this act of devotion. Father Corby stood upon a large rock in front of the brigade. Addressing the men, he explained what he was about to do, saying that each one could receive the benefit of the absolution by making a sincere act of contrition and firmly resolving to embrace the first opportunity of confessing their sins, urging them to do their duty well, and reminding them of the high and sacred nature of their trust as soldiers and the noble object for which they fought, ending by saying that the Catholic church refuses Christian burial to the soldier who turns his back upon the foe or deserts his flag. The brigade was standing at "order arms," and as he closed his address, every man fell on his knees, with head bowed down. Then, stretching his right hand toward the brigade, Father Corby pronounced the words of the general absolution, "*Dominus noster Jesus Christus vos absolvat, et ego, auctoritate ipsius, vos absolva ab vinculo excommunicationis et interdicti in quantum possum et vos indi;etis, deinde ego absolvo vos a peccatris vestris in nomine Patris, et filis, et Spiritus Sanctus.* Amen!" The scene was more than impressive, it was awe-inspiring. Nearby stood Hancock, surrounded by a brilliant array of officers, who had gathered to witness this very unusual occurrence, and while there was profound silence in the ranks of the Second Corps yet over to the left, out by the peach orchard and Little Round Top, where Weed, Vincent and Hazlett were dying, the roar of the battle rose and swelled and re-echoed through the woods, making music more sublime than ever sounded through cathedral aisles. The act seemed to be in harmony with all the surroundings. I do not think there was a man in the brigade who did not offer up a heartfelt prayer. For some it was their last, they knelt there in their grave clothes—in less than half an hour many of them were numbered with the dead of July 2d. Who can doubt that their prayers were good? What was wanting in the eloquence of the good priest to move them to repentance was supplied in the incidents of the fight. That heart would be incorrigible indeed, that the scream of a Whitworth bolt, added to Father Corby's touching appeal, would not move to contrition.

The maps published by the Government made the time of Caldwell's Division moving to the left at 4 o'clock. I think this is a mistake. I believe it was nearly five o'clock before we started. The division moved off by the left flank and marched rapidly. We had hardly got under way when the enemy's batteries opened and shell began falling all around us. The ground on which this division faced the enemy on the afternoon of the 2d had already been fought over, and the fields and woods were strewn with killed and wounded.

Our division moved from its position on Cemetery Ridge without change of formation, each brigade being in column of regiments, the One Hundred and Sixteenth Pennsylvania being the rear or left of the column forming the Second or Irish Brigade, each regiment of course moving by the left flank. We soon descended to the low ground, skirted a small run and on reaching the plowed land near Trostle's

FATHER CORBY GIVING GENERAL ABSOLUTION ON THE BATTLEFIELD OF GETTYSBURG.

house received a fire of solid shot from the enemy's guns then in position near the peach orchard, for by this time all that ground had been cleared of our troops and guns; still moving to the left the division reached the spot now known as "The Valley of Death" in front of Little Round Top. As we passed the road to the north of the wheat-field, General Hancock sat upon his horse looking at the troops. As Colonel Cross of the Fifth New Hampshire Regiment passed by, he said to him, "Cross, this is the last fight you'll fight without a star." Without stopping Cross replied, "Too late, too late, general, this is my last battle." Ten minutes afterwards the country lost one of the best soldiers in the army. Cross was dead, shot at the head of his brigade leading them to the charge.

When we reached Little Round Top the division was deployed double-quick. Cross's Brigade deployed to the left of the wheat-field and moved forward as did each brigade without waiting for the other brigades. Up to this moment, strange to say, not a shot was fired at our regiment (or more properly battalion, for we had been consolidated into four companies). Suddenly some one in the ranks cried out "there they are!" Sure enough, not forty feet from us up towards the crest, behind the trees and big rocks covering that ground, was the enemy; no orders were given, but in an instant every musket on the line was at its deadly work. The enemy having to rise to fire over the rocks, their shots for the most part passed over our heads, but as they exposed themselves to our men at such close quarters, armed with smooth-bore muskets firing "buck and ball" (one large ball and three buck shot), the effect of our fire was deadly in the extreme, for, under such circumstances, a blind man could not have missed his mark. The officers too joined in the fray, each one emptying his revolver with effect. For ten minutes this work went on, our men seeming to load and fire twice as fast as the enemy. Now the voice of Kelly is heard ordering the charge; with a cheer, a few quick strides, and we are on the crest among the enemy.

Here took place a rather extraordinary scene. Our men and their opponents were mingled together. In charging we had literally ran right in among them. Firing instantly ceased, and we found there were as many of the enemy as there were of ourselves. Officers and men of both sides looked for a time at each other utterly bewildered; the fighting had stopped, yet the Confederate soldiers stood there facing us, still retained their arms and showing no disposition to surrender. At this moment I called out, "Confederate troops, lay down your arms and go to the rear!" This ended a scene that was becoming embarrassing. The order was promptly obeyed and a large number of what I think were men of Kershaw's Brigade became our prisoners; they held the left flank of their line. In front of our brigade we found that the enemy had suffered much more than we had. When engaged, our line was below theirs, as they stood on the crest of the hill. They fired down while our men fired upward and our fire was more effective. On their line we found many dead, but few wounded—they were nearly all hit in the head or upper part of the body. Behind one rock we counted five dead bodies. This was some of the most severe fighting our division had ever done. During the fight our regiment held the extreme right of the division, and from where we stood we could see the peach orchard, and none of our troops were between that point and us—a distance of an eighth of a mile.

Some fifteen minutes after the fighting had ceased we dressed line and our men, awaiting the next event, the One Hundred and Fortieth Pennsylvania Volunteers of Zook's Brigade was placed in the rear and at right angles to my command, and about the same time I noticed what I believed to be a column of the enemy passing through the peach orchard and to the rear of our division. I reported the matter to the brigade commander (Colonel Kelly), but I could not convince him that the column in question was a Confederate force, the smoke and distance preventing our seeing accurately. Feeling, however, uneasy and anxious in regard to the character of the troops I requested him (Colonel Kelly) to relieve me from command of my own regiment and allow me to take the One Hundred and Fortieth Pennsylvania Volunteers over the fields and ascertain the nature of the column. He at once told me that I could do so. Placing Captain Garrett Nowlen in command of my regiment, I went back to where the One Hundred and Fortieth stood in line, told the officers and men my mission, learned from them that Colonel Roberts had been killed and that there was no field officer present with the command. Pointing to the column that for full ten minutes had been passing to our rear, I asked the regiment to follow me out to the peach orchard that we might learn what troops it was composed of. The duty demanded was of the most desperate nature. The command had just lost its heroic colonel and on another part of the field fifty of its members lay dead and two hundred wounded, and now an officer who was a stranger to almost every man in the ranks, asked them to go forward and attack, if necessary, a whole brigade of the enemy. Yet every man in that most noble command responded to the call and promptly followed me toward the advancing hosts. We had only marched some fifty yards when the flags unfurled in the breeze and we saw distinctly that the moving column consisted of Confederate troops. Further advance was useless. I then requested the senior officer of the One Hundred and Fortieth Pennsylvania Volunteers to place his command on my right and so prolong our line. He started to do so, and moved his regiment over towards the grove (since cut down) on my right flank, while I walked back to my own command. At that moment a staff officer ran up from our left and in a very excited manner called out " that we were surrounded and to fall back and save as many of our men as possible." Looking to the left I discovered that, with the exception of the One Hundred and Fortieth and the men of my own regiment, all the division had gone.

Whilst the One Hundred and Fortieth Pennsylvania Volunteers deserves the highest praise for volunteering in a most desperate duty, yet the truth of history compels me to record the fact that that regiment did not fight on the right of the division, neither did it hold the right of the division line for a single instant during the fight. When the regiment came up and went into position to my rear (the spot is marked by a monument erected by the survivors some years ago) the firing had been over for at least fifteen minutes and the prisoners sent to the rear. Not a shot was fired on that part of the field after the One Hundred and Fortieth came there and when, by my request, the command moved over to the grove (since cut down) on my right, there was no division there, as at that moment everything had gone to the rear except that regiment and my own. We were still on the ground because we happened to be the last to receive the orders to retreat.

I have thought proper to make this statement about the One Hundred and Fortieth Pennsylvania Volunteers because a second monument has been recently erected on the field of the second day's fight, which purports to mark the spot where it fought, but it is as far from correct as the inscriptions upon it.

When I got back to my own command I quickly told the men of the danger and for each one to look to his own safety, pointing out the direction they were to take towards Little Round Top. I rolled up the colors and with some thirty men ran down through the woods and into the wheat-field; here we were in a trap, a line of the enemy was advancing on the wheat-field from the south and Wofford's Brigade, the column I had seen marching around the peach orchard and into our rear, was closing in from the north, we caught it from both sides, the slaughter here was appalling, but we kept on, the men loading and firing as they ran, and by the time we had reached the middle of the field the two lines of the enemy were so close that for a few moments they ceased firing on us, as they fired into each other. Then I heard voices calling out, "come here, run this way;" a few seconds more and I was over a low stone wall and among Sweitzer's Brigade, about ten of my command were with me, other were saved, many by running into Ayres's Division as it advanced. I went back to the Taneytown road, I there found Colonel Brooke, Fifty-third Pennsylvania, commanding brigade, sitting on his horse, he was all alone; he asked me where the division was. I could give him no information. He directed me to plant my colors there in a field so the division might be collected together which was done, and the remnants of "Caldwell's Division" again got into fighting shape.

I am aware that this is not a pleasing narrative of the withdrawal of the First Division from the second day's fight at Gettysburg, nor is it in accord with the numerous "official" regimental reports, which speak of "retiring in good order," "slowly falling back," and other such terms, more flattering than truthful.

Passing through this alley of death in the wheat-field, where the bullets came in showers, we got away with a large part of the division, but the loss was terrible. In the half hour we were under fire fourteen hundred men were lost. Of the four brigade commanders, two were killed—General S. K. Zook and Colonel E. E. Cross. Zook fell almost at the first fire and Cross a few minutes afterwards.

Some of the men who fell in the wheat-field during the retreat of this division and were forced to lie there between the two fires, fared badly. One man of our regiment fell shot through the leg, and while he lay there was hit five or six times. When it became evident that we had to fall back, our wounded, with visions of Belle Isle and Libby before them, begged piteously to be taken along—many of them keeping with us wholly unaided.

General Buford says of the first day's fight: "There seemed to be no directing head." This might be applied to the fighting on the left on the second day. If there was any directing head it was not especially visible. Until toward dark the fight had certainly gone against us, and the battle had extended along the line to the right, almost half way to the cemetery. The evening and our prospects grew dark together. The Third Corps had been driven back, broken and shattered, its commander wounded and carried from the field, the troops that had gone to its support fared no better, and every man felt that the situation was grave.

However, all was not yet lost. Meade had again thought of Hancock, and, as yesterday he sent him to stop the rout of the First and Eleventh Corps, so to-day he orders him to assume command on the left. Once more he is in the field. A half hour of daylight yet remains, but it is long enough to enable him to rally some of our scattered troops, face them once more to the front, gather reinforcements, drive back the enemy and restore our broken lines. At Waterloo, Wellington petitioned God for " Night or Blucher". At Gettysburg, on this evening, we had no Blucher to pray for. Our whole force was up; but, while omitting the last part of the great Englishman's prayer, we had every reason to adopt the first portion. As the fight was closing upon the left of our army Ewell was striking a terrific blow on the right. As we reformed our division on the Taneytown road, and we had some difficulty in getting things in shape after the rough handling we had received, we heard, away to the right and rear, the yells of Ewell's men as they rushed over our works at Culp's Hill. This was the most anxious hour of all. We had been driven on the left, and on the right the enemy had effected a lodgment in our works, in one of our strongest positions, and were, in fact, in our rear, without any adequate force to oppose them. Another hour of daylight and, unless some miracle had intervened, we would most likely have left Gettysburg without waiting to bid the inhabitants good evening. But, fortunately for us, there was no Joshua around Lee's headquarters, so the sun went down on almanac time, utterly regardless of the little troubles we were trying to settle. Darkness fell upon the scene and prevented the Confederates from taking further advantage of their success, giving us chance to repair our disasters.

Few of us slept during that night. Our division went back and was put in position on Cemetery Ridge by General Hancock, who, all the night long, labored to strengthen this line. The men gathered rocks and fence-rails and used them to erect a light breastwork. Had the necessary tools been distributed to the troops, we could have intrenched this line and made it formidable, but we could not find a pick or a shovel, and the works that we did attempt were very light, scarcely sufficient to stop a musket ball. During the whole night mounted officers galloped to and fro, and troops were hurried to important points. At the first faint gray of the morning of July 3 the fight was resumed on Culp's Hill, where darkness had interrupted it the night before, and from then until about 11 o'clock the fire was heavy and incessant. We knew that Slocum was trying to drive the enemy out of our works which they had slept in and occupied without invitation the night before. Culp's Hill was about a mile from where we lay, and we could hear the cheers of Geary's men, which came to us on the morning air, mingled with bullets which had missed the mark for which they were intended and, almost spent, went singing over our heads. As the day advanced sounds of the artillery mingled with the musketry, and we knew that a hard fight was in progress. The men of our line almost held their breath with anxiety. About 11 o'clock the firing suddenly ceased. A tremendous cheer went up, and a minute later every man in the army knew we were again in possession of Culp's Hill. Then came two hours of peace—a perfect calm.

It was a warm summer day and from Round Top to Culp's Hill hardly a sound was heard, not a shot fired. The men rested after the fighting of the previous evening, no troops were moving to or fro, the only activity seen was the stretcher-bearers taking the wounded to the field hospitals, but during those two hours we could see considerable activity along Seminary Ridge. Battery after battery appeared along the edge of the woods. Guns were unlimbered, placed in position, and the horses taken to the rear. Our men sat around in groups and anxiously watched these movements in our front and wondered what it all meant. Shortly after 1 o'clock, however, we knew all about it. The headquarters's wagons had just come up and General Gibbon had invited Hancock and staff to partake of some lunch. The bread that was handed around—if it was eaten—was consumed without butter, for, as the orderly was passing the latter article to the gentlemen, a shell from Seminary Ridge cut him in two. Instantly the air was filled with bursting shells; the batteries that we had been watching for the last two hours going into position in our front did not open singly or spasmodically. The whole hundred and forty-seven guns which now began to play upon us, seemed to be discharged simultaneously, as though by electricity. And then for nearly two hours the storm of death went on. I have read many accounts of this artillery duel, but the most graphic description by the most able writers falls far short of the reality. No tongue or pen can find language strong enough to convey any idea of its awfulness. Streams of screaming projectiles poured through the hot air falling and bursting everywhere. Men and horses were torn limb from limb; caissons exploded one after another in rapid succession, blowing the gunners to pieces. No spot within our lines was free from this frightful iron rain. The infantry hugged close the earth and sought every shelter that our light earthworks afforded. It was literally a storm of shot and shell that the oldest soldiers there—those who had taken part in almost every battle of the war—had not yet witnessed. That awful rushing sound of the flying missiles which causes the firmest hearts to quail was everywhere.

At this tumultuous moment, we witnessed a deed of heroism, such as we are apt to attribute only to knights of the olden time. Hancock, mounted and accompanied by his staff, Major Mitchell, Captain Harry Bingham, Captain Isaac Parker and Captain E. P. Brownson, with the corps' flag flying in the hands of a brave Irishman, Private James Wells, of the Sixth New York Cavalry, started at the right of his line where it joined the Taneytown road, and slowly rode along the terrible crest to the extreme left of his position, while shot and shell roared and crashed around him, and every moment tore great gaps in the ranks at his side. It was a gallant deed, and withal not a reckless exposure of life, for the presence and calm demeanor of the commander, as he passed through the lines of his men, set them an example which, an hour later, bore good fruit and nerved their stout hearts to win the greatest and most decisive battle ever fought on this continent. For two hours our batteries replied vigorously and then ceased altogether; but the Confederate shells came as numerously as ever, then, for ten minutes, not a soul was seen stirring on our line—we might have been an army of dead men for all the evidence of life visible. Suddenly the enemy stopped their fire, which had been going on for two hours without intermission, and then the long lines of their infantry—eighteen thousand strong—emerged from the woods and began their advance.

At this moment silence reigned along our whole line. With arms at a "right shoulder shift", the division of Longstreet's Corps moved forward with a precision that was wonderfully beautiful. It is now our turn, and the lines that a few moments before seemed so still now teemed with animation. Eighty of our guns open their brazen mouths, solid shot and shell are sent on their errand of destruction in quick succession. We see them fall in countless numbers among the advancing troops. The accuracy of our fire could not be excelled, the missiles strike right in the ranks, tearing and rending them in every direction.

The One Hundred and Sixteenth Regiment was supporting Sterling's Second Connecticut Battery, the men lying in front of and between the pieces; it was marvelous, the rapidity and accuracy with which these guns were served. The ground over which the enemy have passed is strewn with dead and wounded. But on they come. The gaps in the ranks are closed as soon as made. They have three-quarters of a mile to pass, exposed to our fire, and half the distance is nearly passed. Our gunners now load with canister and the effect is appalling, but still they march on. Their gallantry is past all praise—it is sublime. Now they are within a hundred yards. Our infantry rise up and pour round after round into these heroic troops.

At Waterloo the Old Guard recoiled before a less severe fire. But there was no recoil in these men of the South—they marched right on as though they courted death. They concentrate in great numbers and strike on the most advanced part of our line. The crash of the musketry and the cheers of the men blend together. The Philadelphia Brigade occupy this point. They are fighting on their own ground and for their own State, and in the bloody hand-to-hand engagement which ensues the Confederates, though fighting with desperate valor, find it impossible to dislodge them—they are rooted to the ground. Seeing how utterly hopeless further effort would be, and knowing the impossibility of reaching their lines, they attempt to retreat, and the battle is won. To the left of the Philadelphia Brigade we did not get to such close quarters. Our eager gaze was upon Pickett and his murderous reception by the Philadelphia Brigade, but now right in our own front Wilcox's and Perry's Brigades are seen coming straight for our line, every musket is tightly grasped and our men become impatient to begin their work, but the orders are to hold the fire, and it took all the officers could do to keep the men from firing. But the enemy are coming nearer, and as the welcome order is sounded down the line "ready", the air becomes filled as though by a great flock of white pigeons; it was the fluttering of hundreds and hundreds of white rags, the tokens of surrender, and Wilcox's and Perry's men throw down their arms and surrender; as the mass of the enemy come into our lines, some few spirits, bolder than the rest, run back to their own lines, our men being prevented from firing on them for fear of killing the prisoners.

Five thousand prisoners were sent to the rear, and we gathered up thirty-three regimental standards in front of the Second Corps. The remaining hours of daylight during this day were occupied in caring for the wounded, looking over the field and talking over the incidents of the fight. Many noble officers and men were lost on both sides, and in the camp hospital they died in hundreds during the afternoon and night. The Confederate General Armistead died in this way. As he was being carried to the rear he was met by Captain Harry Bingham, of Hancock's staff, who, getting off his horse, asked him if he could do anything for him. Armistead replied to take his watch and spurs to

General Hancock that they might be sent to his relatives. His wishes were complied with, General Hancock sending them to his friends at the first opportunity. Armistead was a brave soldier with a chivalric presence, and came forward in front of his brigade waving his sword. He was shot through the body and fell inside of our lines. Some of the wounded Confederates showed considerable animosity toward our men. One of them, who lay mortally wounded in front of the Sixty-ninth Pennsylvania, sullenly refused to be taken to the hospital, saying that he wanted to die right there on the field where he fell. The scene after Longstreet's charge was indescribable. In front of the Second Corps the dead lay in great heaps. Dismounted guns, ruins of exploded caissons, dead and mutilated men and horses were piled up together in every direction.

Out on the field where Longstreet's Corps had passed thousands of wounded were lying. We had no means of reaching these poor fellows, and many of them lay there between lines until the morning of the 5th. The Confederates could be seen moving around on Seminary Ridge. Welcome supplies came up and were issued. All hands felt cheerful, but a degree of uncertainty as to whether the battle was over or whether the enemy were getting ready for some new movement, prevented us from celebrating the national anniversary in a proper manner. Once in a while the sharpshooters would try their skill on some of our people to let us know they were still there. The stench from the dead became intolerable, and we tried to escape it by digging up the ground and burying our faces in the fresh earth.

On the morning of the 5th we found the enemy had gone, and then what a scene. I think the fact was first discovered by the troops on Culp's Hill, and what a cheer went up; a cheer that swelled into a roar and was taken up by the boys on Cemetery Hill, rolled along the crest to Round Top and then back again. Cheers for the Philadelphia Brigade that stood a living wall against which the hosts beat in vain. Cheers for Meade, the soldier "without fear or reproach," who here began with a great victory his illustrious career as commander of the Army of the Potomac. Cheers for Hancock, who had stemmed the tide of defeat on the first day and selected the ground on which this glorious victory was achieved, who, on the second day had again stopped the tide of defeat and restored our shattered lines, and on the third day had met and repulsed the final assault on which Lee's all was staked, and won the battle that was the death-blow to the Rebellion.

On the morning of the 5th of July, I went out in front of our line to wash at a small run when I came across our picket line; they were New York troops, I think the One Hundred and Eleventh Regiment; about forty of them lay dead in a regular line, just as they had been posted, caught between the two fires, not a man seems to have escaped.

In the battle of Gettysburg we were but a small battalion of one hundred and sixty-five officers and men, and lost thirty-seven killed and wounded; most of these were lost on falling back through the wheatfield on the evening of the second day's fight, but in that fight the dead and wounded Confederate troops found lying behind the rocks when we charged and captured the wooded crest, proved to us that we inflicted a much greater loss upon them than they upon us.

ADDRESS OF LIEUTENANT EDMUND RANDALL.

COMRADES: Twenty-seven years ago this month we "broke camp" for the first time. As we filed out of those beautiful woods to the Lancaster Pike, just beyond Hestonville on the outskirts of Philadelphia, with light hearts and elastic steps we started on that eventful three years' march, our destiny and destination then unknown. Kind Providence hid from our sight the bloody tracks we were to make over many fields in Virginia, Maryland and Pennsylvania. Our death roll was started ere we left the precincts of our deserted camp, and, oh, how quickly it was filled; that holocaust at Fredericksburg on December 13, 1862, added to it the names of forty-four gallant comrades, the first to receive their furloughs on the battle-field, which truly took them home.

Some of us fell out of the ranks early on this march. Some, driven by distress, sought the shelter of the hospital, from which they emerged broken down, a few of them still stalking among us like living wrecks; some weak and exhausted returned to their homes, others among you with stout hearts tramped the unmeasured miles of that great march which led you through Charlestown, through the dismal and bloody fields of Fredericksburg and Chancellorsville, where your hearts sickened by defeat and misfortune almost to despair, to the glorious field on which we now stand. Oh, what memories cluster around this hallowed spot! Here in July, 1863, you planted your standard, and, like MacGregor of old, your "foot was on your native heath," and you could not be conquered; from here still onward you marched; never again defeated, though sometimes repulsed, receiving heavy blows and many bloody wounds, until April, 1865, brought you out of the dismal woods, and you at length beheld the glorious sunrise at Appomattox shed her golden rays upon your tattered standard crowned with victory. Oh, what a victory, the like of which the world had never witnessed, a victory shared even by our enemies, for with them have you shared its fruits, a country, saved and united. How different would it have been had we failed at Gettysburg. Georgia, New York, South Carolina, Virginia and Pennsylvania, would have been, if not hostile, at least foreign States and strangers to each other. This would have been a continent of inharmonious States, and not an American citizen upon it. We took no prisoners, inflicted no punishments, but having triumphed, invited our foes to sit with us and enjoy the banquet our valor had prepared. Where in history can such magnanimity be paralleled?

Comrades, we would not now change this condition of affairs if it were possible, yet, standing here upon this historic spot, to dedicate this monument to the memory of our comrades who paid the forfeit of their lives that our country might not perish, let us not forget that there is unhappily in some parts of this land a feeling ripe that would belittle your victory here by undue praise of your foes, whom, in the charity of our hearts, we have forgiven. Yet look you around here at these stones and tree stumps, behind which, on July 2, 1863, lurked armed enemies who shot the life of many of our comrades away, comrades to whom this day we dedicate this granite monument. Forgive them we do, and time's merciful hand may even blot their crime from memory. Yet praise them never, while this monument tells of martyred men and the glorious cause for which they died.

Comrades, there were many others who started with us on that march from Jones's woods who neither left the ranks nor yet returned with you to Philadelphia in June, 1865, when you furled your colors and returned them, unsullied, to the State which gave them in your keeping three years before. Where are these comrades? The good, the brave, the best of all; they fought the good fight through, stripped off their armor and stepped behind the veil that hides us from our God. Yea, on every field, from Fredericksburg to Appomattox, our comrades of the One Hundred and Sixteenth Regiment can be found sleeping beneath the sod.

Here we are to-day, comrades, twenty-seven years older than when we started on our three years' march, the designs of Providence now unfolded, and we alone of that strong column are left surviving, it may be questioned whether our lot has been the happiest. Our comrades went down in honor, how grand was the fate of those who gave up their lives for their country. Generations yet unborn shall sing their praises. So long as this country shall exist, so long shall the memory of our dead comrades be honored and glorified. Without the blood of our forefathers in 1776, this free country would never have sprung from the womb of time. Without the blood of our comrades, its life would have been trampled out by the Rebellion of 1861.

How happy should we feel that we have been spared to assemble here to-day to dedicate this monument to the memory of the fallen brave; it is the last and only act we can do for them.

Comrades, our work is done; yet a little while longer we must linger here in camp, watching and waiting day by day, as one or the other of us weary of this life's long march, unsling our knapsacks and fall out to rest with our comrades sleeping here. It will be but for a day in time's calendar when the adjutant of the Lord shall sound the last call which will assemble us all together again to hear the Lord of Hosts call the roll of the just. Oh, comrades, may we be all upon the right hand and hear the voice of our great Captain, Christ, proclaim "all present and accounted for."

And now, during this Christmas time of 1895, the writer brings the record of the One Hundred and Sixteenth Pennsylvania Volunteers to a close.

His heart goes out to every member of the regiment, living or dead; to every lonely grave on the Blue Ridge and on the Rappahannock's banks where angels guard the mouldering form of the hero who still remains at his post, and whose sacred ashes mark the line of the picket where he stood on guard, and fell, the true and faithful sentinel of thirty years ago.

His heart is filled with sweet recollections of all the dear comrades, memories sad and tender of those who are no more and happy in the warm affection of those who are still enjoying the blessings of the land they helped to save.

In the fond hope of meeting one and all again, "farewell", or, rather, "good night", for believing that He who even "marks the fall of a sparrow" will grant great reward to everyone who did well in helping to preserve the Union of States, thus saving the American Continent to freedom and liberty, the writer lives expecting to meet again with all the noble souls who marched and fought in defense of the flag of the One Hundred and Sixteenth Regiment; and so, as the evening of life draws near, the shadows fall, and the hour approaches for the final "taps". In the hope of the glory of that last reveille which shall find us united in an eternal bivouac, my comrades, one and all, "good night".

It is to be greatly regretted that this roster of the regiment is very incomplete; more than four hundred names will be found unaccounted for. Many of these were killed, others died of disease or wounds or in Southern prisons. Every effort has been made by the writer to complete the record of each man, but the only source from which the information could be obtained is closed, as the following letter will show, and there is no other means available. The roster, as it appears here, was made principally from memory of those present at the muster out of the command and was hurriedly made more for the purpose of mustering those present at that time than accounting for those absent.

WASHINGTON CITY, June 19th, 1893.

To THE ADJUTANT-GENERAL
    OF THE STATE OF PENNSYLVANIA,
        Harrisburg, Pa.

SIR: Referring to your letter of the 14th inst., received to-day, in which you enclose rolls of the One Hundred and Sixteenth Pennsylvania Volunteers, and request that such information relative to the final record of the members of said regiment as is lacking from those (some three hundred in number) whose names appear on said rolls, be supplied from the official records on file in this Department, for use in publishing a history of that command, I am directed by the Secretary of War to invite your attention to the enclosed copy of orders dated February 17th, 1892, which sets forth the rule of the Department relative to requests of this nature. Under this rule it becomes necessary to deny all requests for information for personal or historical purposes, and it is regretted that the information you desire cannot, therefore, be furnished.

The rolls submitted by you are herewith returned.

    Very respectfully,

        F. C. AINSWORTH,
          Colonel United States Army,
            Chief Record and Pension Office

ROSTER

116TH REGIMENT, PENNSYLVANIA VOLUNTEERS.

FIELD AND STAFF OFFICERS.

NAME.	RANK.	DATE OF MUSTER INTO SERVICE.	TERM—YEARS	REMARKS.
Dennis Heenan	Colonel	Sept. 1, 1862	3	Wounded at Fredericksburg, Va., Dec. 13, '62—honorably discharged by reason of consolidation of regiment to a Battalion of four companies, Jan. 27, 1863.
St. Clair A. Mulholland	Colonel	Sept. 1, 1862	3	Lieut.-Col., Sept., 1862—Major of Battalion, Feb. 27, 1863—Col. of reorganized regiment, May 3, 1864—Brevet Brig.-Gen. for services in Wilderness campaign—Brevet Maj. Gen. for capturing Confederate fort in front of Petersburg, Oct. 27, 1864—Congress medal of honor for distinguished services on the picket line at Chancellorsville, May 4, 1863—wounded at Fredericksburg, Va., Dec. 13, 1862, at Wilderness, May 5, 1864, at Po River, Va., May 10, 1864, and at Totopotomy, Va., May 31, 1864—honorably disch. by reason of termination of war, June 3, 1865.
Richard C. Dale	Lieut. Col.	April 14, 1864	3	From Lieut.-Col. 123d Regiment, Pa. Vols.—killed at Spottsylvania, May 12, 1864.
David W. Megraw	do	April 14, 1864	3	From Capt., Co. H, to Major, Jan. 28, 1865, to Lieut. Col., June 6, 1865—wounded at Five Forks, Va., March 31, 1865—honorably discharged by reason of termination of war, July 14, 1865.
George H. Bardwell	Major	Sept. 1 1862	3	Brevet Lieut. Col. and Brevet Col. for services at Fredericksburg, Va., Dec. 13, 1862—wounded at Fredericksburg, Dec. 13, 1862—honorably discharged by reason of consolidation of regiment into battalion, Jan. 27, 1863.
John K. Miles	Adjutant	July 3, 1862	3	Wounded at Fredericksburg, Dec. 13, 1862—resigned Feb. 16, 1863.
Garrett Nowlen	do	Aug. 2, 1862	3	Promoted from 2d Lieut., Co. G, Feb. 27, 1863, to Capt., Co. D, Nov. 21, 1863, Brevet Maj.—wounded at Fredericksburg, Va., Dec. 13, 1862—killed at Reams Sta., Va., Aug. 25, '64.
Louis J. Sacriste	do	March 1, 1863	3	Promoted from 1st Lieut., Co. D, Nov. 21, 1863, to Capt., Co. D., Sept. 22, 1864—wounded at Cold Harbor, Va., June 3, 1864. Brev. Maj. for gallant service during the war—Congress medal of honor for distinguished service on the picket line at Bristoe Station, Va., Nov. 14, 1863—transferred to Regular Army at close of the war.
Thomas S. Ewing	do	Oct. 15, 1864	3	Wounded at Five Forks, Va., May 31, 1865—mustered out with regiment at close of war.
David S. Bunnell	Q. M.	June 20, 1862	3	Resigned January 26, 1863.
Richard H. Wade	do	Aug. 8, 1862	3	Promoted from Quartermaster Sgt., Jan. 27, 1863—mustered out with the regiment at close of war.
John P. Ashcom	Surgeon	Sept. 1, 1862	3	Honorably discharged March 19, 1863.
William B. Hartman	do	March 9, 1862	3	Promoted from Asst. Surgeon, July 4, 1863—honorably discharged at close of war.
John W. Rawlings	Asst. Surg.	July 15, 1862	3	Promoted to Surg., of 88th Penna. Infantry, Feb. 3, 1863.

386   THE STORY OF THE 116TH REGIMENT.

NAME.	RANK.	DATE OF MUSTER INTO SERVICE.	TERM-YEARS.	REMARKS.
Philip A. Boyle	Asst. Surg.	Sept. 1, 1862	3	Resigned February 28, 1863.
D. S. Cunningham	do	Oct. 1, 1864	3	Resigned October 18, 1864.
Rev. Edward McKee	Chaplain	Sept. 24, 1862	...	Resigned December 24, 1862.
Rev. Bernard McCollum	do	Nov. 18, 1864	3	Honorably discharged at close of war.
William J. Burk	Sgt. Maj.	Aug. 14, 1862	3	Promoted to 1st Lieut., Company C.
George M. Book	do	Sept. 5, 1862	3	Promoted to 1st Lieut., Company B.
George Roeder	do	Aug. 30, 1862	3	Promoted to 2d Lieut., Company A.
Samuel D. Hunter	do	Aug. 5, 1862	3	Promoted to 2d Lieut., Company F.
George McMahon	Q. M. Sgt.	Aug. 14, 1862	3	Promoted to 2d Lieut., Co. B, April 8, 1864—prisoner of war from May 10, 1864 until Feb., 1865—honorably discharged at close of war.
Francis E. Crawford	do	July 19, 1862	3	Promoted to 1st Lieut., Co. B, March 7, 1865.
John Lutton	do	Feb. 13, 1864	3	
Daniel Reen	Com. Sgt.	July 16, 1862	3	
Patrick Costello	do	June 22, 1862	3	
Charles Shelly	do	Feb. 20, 1864	3	Honorably discharged at close of war.
Frederick Wagner	Hos. Std.	June 16, 1862	3	
T. W. Vanneman	Prin. Mu.	Aug. 18, 1862	3	

COMPANY A.

NAME.	RANK.	DATE OF MUSTER INTO SERVICE.	TERM-YEARS.	REMARKS.
Patrick Carrigan	Captain	Oct. 25, 1862	3	Discharged by special order, Jan. 27, 1863.
Seneca G. Willauer	do	Aug. 20, 1862	3	Wounded at Fredericksburg, Va., Dec. 13, '62—promoted from 1st Lt. Co. C, March 1, '63—transferred as 1st Lieut. to 9th reg. Vet. Res. Corps, Feb. 5, '64—to 6th reg., April 25, '64—promoted to Capt. 11th reg., Dec. 3, '64—Brev. Maj., March 13, '65—discharged October 30, 1867.
William M. Hobart	do	June 11, 1862	3	Promoted from 1st Lieut., March 1, 1864—discharged Jan. 2, 1865.
George Halpin	do	Aug. 30, 1862	3	Wounded at Gettysburg, Pa., July 2, 1863—prisoner from July 2, '63, to April 11, '65—promoted from 1st Sgt. to 1st Lieut., April 14, '65—to Capt., May 15, '65—mustered out with company, June 3, 1865.
Christian Foltz	2d Lieut.	Sept. 5, 1862	3	Promoted from Sergeant, Oct. 25, '62—killed at Fredericksburg, Va., Dec. 13, 1862.
George Roeder	do	Aug. 30, 1862	3	Promoted from Sgt. Major, March 1, 1863—Oct. 28, 1863, dismissed.
Thomas Detweiler	do	Aug. 4, 1862	3	Wounded at Petersburg, Va., June 16, 1864—prom. from Sgt.—com. 1st Lieut., Jan. 23, '65 mus. out with company, June 3, '65.
William Emsley	do	Aug. 13, 1862	3	Promoted from 1st Sgt. June 1, '65—mustered out with company.
Ambrose O. Wilson	Sergeant	June 24, 1862	3	Mustered out with company, June 3, 1865.
Josiah C. Randolph	do	July 16, 1862	3	Mustered out with company, June 3, 1865.
Samuel Llewellyn	do	Aug. 14, 1862	3	Promoted from Corp., May 1, '65—mustered out with company, June 3, 1865.
Charles Gallagher	do	July 29, 1862	3	Not on muster-out roll.
Matthew Murray	do	July 26, 1862	3	Wounded at Gettysburg, Pa., July 2, 1863—discharged October 13, 1863
James McCready	do	Aug. 11, 1862	3	Detailed on staff of Gen. Meagher—mustered out with company.
Dougherty, Thomas	do	Aug. 28, 1862	3	Drowned in Acquia Creek, Va., May 1, '64.
William Nichols	Corporal	June 30, 1862	3	
Nathan Adams	do	July 29, 1862	3	
Mathias Landrican	do	July 25, 1862	3	Mustered out with company, June 3, 1865.
Daniel Price	do	Aug. 2, 1862	3	
Thomas Scarlett	do	June 18, 1862	3	Promoted to Corp., May 1, '65—mustered out with company, June 3, 1865.
Jacob A. Coble	do	Sept. 5, 1862	3	Not on muster-out roll.
William C. Andress	do	July 31, 1862	3	Wounded at Fredericksburg, Va., Dec. 13, '62—not on muster-out roll.

THREE YEARS' SERVICE. 387

NAME.	RANK.	DATE OF MUSTER INTO SERVICE.	TERM—YEARS.	REMARKS.
James F. Duffey	Corporal	July 31, 1862	3	Wounded at Gettysburg, Pa., July 2, '63—not on muster-out roll.
Philip Clause	Musician	July 7, 1862	3	Absent, sick, at muster out.
Robert Henry	do	June 28, 1862	3	Mustered out with company, June 3, 1865.
Ahem, Daniel	Private	Aug. 11, 1862	3	Mustered out with company, June 3, 1865.
Allingham, Robert	do	June 28, 1862	3	Deserted July 7, '63—returned May 1, '65—transferred to Co. K, June 2, '65.
Arms, John W	do	Aug. 4, 1862	3	Not on muster-out roll.
Altimus, John S	do	Aug. 14, 1862	3	Died December, 1863, of wounds received at Gettysburg, Pa., July 2, 1863.
Butters, Thomas	do	Aug. 8, 1862	3	Mustered out with company, June 3, 1865.
Bock, George M	do	Sept. 5, 1862	3	Promoted to Sergeant Maj.—date unknown.
Bidding, Augustine	do	Aug. 12, 1862	3	Not on muster-out roll.
Beale, James	do	Feb. 29, 1864	3	Transferred to V. R. C.—disch. by G. O.—date unknown.
Brocklehurst, Robert	do	July 8, 1862	3	Discharged for wounds received at Gettysburg, Pa., July 2, 1863.
Conway, John	do	Aug. 28, 1862	3	Mustered out with company, June 3, 1865.
Cole, John	do	July 14, 1862	3	Mustered out with company, June 3, 1865.
Carroll, Alexander	do	Aug. 18, 1862	3	Not on muster-out roll.
Cummings, John	do	Aug. 10, 1862	3	Not on muster-out roll.
Corloy, John	do	Aug. 16, 1862	3	Captured at Bristoe Station, Va., Oct. 13, '63—died in prison, Belle Island.
Clark, Hugh	do	May 12, 1864	3	Not on muster-out roll.
Deihl, Jacob H	do	Aug. 21, 1862	3	Mustered out with company, June 3, 1865.
Dunn, John	do	Aug. 28, 1862	3	Wounded at Gettysburg, Pa., July 2, 1863—mustered out with company, June 3, 1865.
Devonshire, Jeremiah	do	Aug. 4, 1862	3	Wounded at Gettysburg, Pa., July 2, 1863—transf. to 51st Co., 2d batt. V. R. C., Nov. 15, '63—disch. Aug. 5, '65—exp. of term.
Douglass, Robert	do	Aug. 28, 1862	3	Wounded at Chancellorsville,Va., May 3, and at Gettysburg, Pa. July 2, '63—disch. by General Order, June 26, 1865.
Dobbins, John W	do	Aug. 18, 1862	3	Not on muster-out roll.
Dyson, Freeman	do	Aug. 6, 1862	3	Died at Petersburg, Va., Oct., 1864.
Engle, Peter	do	Aug 15, 1862	3	Mustered out with company, June 3, 1865.
Edwards, Thomas	do	Feb. 20, 1864	3	Transferred to Co. K, June 2, 1865.
Eisenhower, Fred	do	July 31, 1862	3	Mustered out for disability, Dec., 1863.
Foltz, Samuel	do	Sept 5, 1862	3	
Gravell, George	do	Aug. 1, 1862	3	Mustered out with company, June 3, 1865.
Giltman, John	do	July 21, 1862	3	Discharged by General Order, Nov. 14, 1865.
Goldy, John	do	June 13, 1862	3	Wounded at Gettysburg, Pa., July 2, 1863—died Nov. 2, 1864,—buried in Poplar Grove, National Cemetery, Petersburg, Va., div. D, sec. C, grave, 80.
Geiger, John	do	Aug. 13, 1862	3	Mustered out with company, June 3, 1865.
Harman, Wm. H	do	June 15, 1862	3	Mustered out with company, June 3, 1865.
Handline, George	do	Aug. 12, 1862	3	Mustered out with company, June 3, 1865.
Hibbs, Joseph H	do	Aug. 12, 1862	3	Transferred to 53d company, 2 batt. V. R. C.—disch. by General Order, Nov. 22, 1865.
Howe, Wm. H	do	Aug. 8, 1862	3	Executed—date unknown.
Hart, John	do	Feb. 28, 1864	3	Transferred to Co. K, June 2, 1865.
Hendricks, Jonas M	do	Aug. 18, 1862	3	Wounded at Gettysburg, Pa., July 2, 1863—not on muster-out roll.
Hauck, Daniel	do	Aug. 23, 1862	3	Not on muster-out roll.
Hutchinson, Wm	do	June 24, 1862	3	Wounded at Gettysburg, Pa., July 2, 1863—transferred to Co. D, 11th reg. V. R. C.—discharged by General Order, June 28, 1865.
Hartnett, James	do	Mar. 25, 1864	3	Not on muster-out roll.
Jones, Charles	do	Aug. 14, 1862	3	Not on muster-out roll.
Johnson, Charles	do	April 6, 1864	3	Not on muster-out roll.
Kite, Wm. S	do	Aug. 19, 1864	3	Transferred to V. R. C.—discharged by General Order, June 27, 1865.
Keim, Ephraim	do	Feb. 24, 1864	3	Transferred to Co. K, June 2, 1865.
Kearns, John	do	Feb. 24, 1864	3	Transferred to Co. K, June 2, 1865.
Lawson, Jacob	do	Aug. 20, 1862	3	Discharged by General Order, June 9, 1865.
Lick, Jacob	do	Aug. 5, 1862	3	Mustered out with company, June 3, 1865.

NAME.	RANK.	DATE OF MUSTER INTO SERVICE.	TERM—YEARS.	REMARKS.
Lynch, Joseph	Private	Aug. 21, 1862	3	Not on muster-out roll.
Moser, William	do	Aug. 22, 1862	3	Absent, sick, at muster out.
Mosley, John	do	June 13, 1862	3	Wounded at Gettysburg, Pa., July 2, 1863 absent, in hospital, at muster out.
Mills, Charles	do	Aug. 22, 1862	3	Discharged by General Order, June 26, 1865.
Murray, James	do	Mar. 1, 1864	3	Transferred to Co. K, June 2, 1865.
Michael, Charles	do	Aug. 30, 1862	3	Not on muster-out roll.
Mickle, John B.	do	July 30, 1862	3	Not on muster-out roll.
Marshall, Samuel	do	Aug. 19, 1862	3	Not on muster-out roll.
Moxley, Wm.	do	July 31, 1862	3	Killed at Gettysburg, Pa., July 2, 1863.
McNamara, Matthew	do	July 29, 1862	3	Mustered out with company, June 3, 1865.
McDonald, John	do	Mar. 1, 1864	3	Discharged by General Order, June 26, 1865.
McCarter, Wm.	do	Aug. 23, 1862	3	Wounded at Fredericksburg, Va., Dec. 3, '62—mustered out with company.
McNulty, Bernard	do	Aug. 30, 1862	3	Not on muster-out roll.
McSorley, Patrick	do	July 9, 1862	3	Not on muster-out roll.
Oxenford, Henry	do	Aug. 8, 1862	3	Wounded at Fredericksburg, Va., Dec. 13, 1862—not on muster-out roll.
O'Harra, Henry	do	July 7, 1862	3	Not on muster-out roll.
Pennypacker, S.	do	Aug 23, 1862	3	Not on muster-out roll.
Porter, Charles	do	Aug. 29, 1862	3	Mustered out with company, June 3, 1865.
Rodormell, Chas.	do	Aug. 12, 1862	3	Wounded at Gettysburg, Pa., July 20, 1863—mustered out with company, July 3, 1865.
Ryan, Isaac I.	do	Feb. 12, 1864	3	Transferred to Co. K, June 2, 1865.
Ryan, John	do	Mar. 8, 1864	3	Transferred to Co. K, June 2, 1865.
Sacriste, Sebastian	do	July 30, 1862	3	Wounded and captured at Gettysburg, Pa., July 2, 1863—ab. at Camp Parole, Annapolis, Md., at muster out.
Sickles, Charles	do	Aug. 18, 1862	3	Mustered out with company, June 3, 1865.
Smith, James	do	Aug. 4, 1862	3	Wounded at Fredericksburg, Va., Dec. 13, 1862, and at Gettysburg, Pa., July 2, 1863—mustered out with company, June 3, 1865.
Smith, Benjamin	do	Aug 12, 1862	3	Wounded at Fredericksburg, Va., Dec. 13, 1862, and at Gettysburg, Pa., July 2, 1863—not on muster-out roll.
Strechaboe, Jacob	do	Aug. 30, 1862	3	Not on muster-out roll.
Smith, Josiah	do	June 16, 1862	3	Not on muster-out roll.
Stephenson, Robert J.	do	Aug. 9, 1862	3	Wounded at Gettysburg, Pa., July 2, 1863—not on muster-out roll.
Twelves, Stephen	do	Aug. 16, 1862	3	Discharged by General Order, May 27, 1865.
Toner, John	do	Feb. 17, 1864	3	Transferred to Co. K, June 2, 1865.
Taylor, Francis	do	June 13, 1862	3	Not on muster-out roll.
Turner, George	do	Aug. 22, 1862	3	Killed at Gettysburg, Pa., July 2, 1863.
Verill, John	do	Aug. 20, 1862	3	Not on muster-out roll.
Wadsworth, Job	do	July 26, 1862	3	Mustered out with company, June 3, 1865.
Whitaker, Warren	do	Feb. 8, 1864	3	Transferred to Co. K, June 2, 1865.
Webb, Wm. H.	do	Aug. 22, 1862	3	Not on muster-out roll.
Wade, Richard H	do	Aug. 8, 1862	3	Promoted to Q. M. Sergt—date unknown.
Woodward, John	do	Aug. 16, 1862	3	Missing in action, Oct. 12, '63—died in prison at Belle Island.

Company B.

Thomas A. Murray	Captain	Sept. 1, 1862	3	Discharged by General Order, Jan. 27, 1863.
Francis T. Quinlan	do	Sept. 1, 1862	3	Promoted from 1st Lieutenant Co. H, Mar. 7, 1863—discharged April 15, 1863.
Francis E. Crawford	do	July 19, 1862	3	Promoted from Q M Sergeant to 1st Lieutenant, Mar. 7, 1863—Captain, Nov. 25, 1863—wounded at Cold Harbor, Va., June 3 1864—captured at Reams Station, Aug. 25, 1864.—mustered out with company, June 3, 1865.
John McNamara	do	Aug 23, 1862	3	Resigned March 7, 1863.
Timothy J. Hurley	1st Lieut.	Aug. 5, 1862	3	Discharged Oct. 6, 1862.

THREE YEARS' SERVICE.   389

NAME	RANK	DATE OF MUSTER INTO SERVICE.	TERM—YEARS	REMARKS.
George M. Book	1st Lieut	Sept. 5, 1862	3	Promoted from Sergeant Major, Nov. 1, 1862—discharged Jan. 26, 1864.
Robert T. Maguire	do	Aug. 23, 1862	3	Promoted from 2d Lieutenant, Mar. 7, 1863—discharged Mar. 10, 1863—died of wound received at Fredericksburg—date unknown.
Thomas McKnight	do	July 12, 1862	3	Promoted from Sergeant, February 3, 1864—discharged July 30, for wounds with loss of hand, received at Petersburg, Va., June 16, 1864—re-commissioned Dec. 1, 1864—mustered out with company, June 3, 1865.
Henry D. Price	2d Lieut	July 5, 1862	3	Promoted from 1st Sergeant to 2d Lieutenant, Sept. 2, 1862—to 1st Lieutenant Co. C, Mar. 1, 1863.
Thomas A. Dorwart	do	Aug. 21, 1862	3	Promoted to 2d Lieutenant, Mar. 19, 1863—cashiered Jan. 7, 1864.
Wm. O'Callagan	do	Aug. 15, 1862	3	Promoted from Sergeant to 2d Lieutenant, Mar. 1, 1864—to 1st Lieutenant Co. I, May 2, 1864.
Thomas J. Murtha	1st Sgt	July 24, 1862	3	Mustered out with company, June 3, 1865.
Benjamin F. Groves	Sergeant	Aug. 4, 1862	3	Commissioned 2d Lieutenant Co. E, June 1, 1865—not mus.—mustered out with company, June 3, 1865.
John H. McCullough	do	Aug. 15, 1862	3	Mustered out with company June 3, 1865.
James E. Craig	do	July 22, 1862	3	Commissioned 2d Lieutenant company G. June 1, 1865—mustered out with company, June 3, 1865.
Daniel Connelly	do	Aug. 12, 1862	3	Discharged by General Order, May 18, 1865.
Daniel Keen	do	July 16, 1862	3	Promoted to Com. Sergeant, Jan. 29, 1863.
Augustus Lindsay	do	Aug. 12, 1862	3	Transferred to U. S. Navy, Mar., 1864.
Charles Bishop	do		3	Wounded at Cold Harbor, June 3, 1864—mustered out with company, June 3, 1865.
James Davies	Corporal	July 21, 1862	3	Mustered out with company, June 3, 1865.
Lawrence J. Coates	do	Aug. 29, 1862	3	Mustered out with company, June 3, 1865.
Jacob W. Adams	do	Aug. 18, 1862	3	Wounded at Cold Harbor, Va., June 2, 1864—mustered out with company, June 3, 1865.
James A. Carlin	do	Aug. 18, 1862	3	Wounded at Reams Station, Va., Aug. 25, 1864—mus. out with company, June 3, 1865.
John H. Rowen	do	Aug. 6, 1862	3	Mustered out with company, June 3, 1865.
James M. Moore	do	Aug. 16, 1862	3	Promoted to Corporal, Jan. 1, 1865—mustered out with company, June 3, 1865.
John Farley	do	Aug. 14, 1862	3	Promoted to Corporal, Jan. 1, 1865—mustered out with company, June 3, 1865.
Henry Adams	Musician	June 26, 1862	3	Mustered out with company, June 3, 1865.
Charles Porter	do	Aug. 29, 1862	3	Mustered out with company, June 3, 1865.
Anderson, S. P.	Private	July 5, 1862	3	Disch'd on Surgeon's certificate, May, 1864.
Austin, Charles	do	July 7, 1862	3	Not on muster-out roll.
Anderson, William	do	July 10, 1862	3	Transferred to Co. C, Jan. 26, 1863.
Bishop, Charles	do	June 30, 1862	3	Wounded at Fredericksburg, Va., Dec. 13, 1862, and at Five Forks, Mar. 31, 1865—ab. in hospital at muster out.
Brown, William H.	do	Aug. 7, 1862	3	Wounded at Spottsylvania C. H., Va., May 12, 1864—discharged on Surgeon's certificate—date unknown.
Bentley, George W.	do	June 27, 1862	3	Transferred to Vet. Res. Corps—date unknown
Bennett, James	do	Aug. 2, 1864	3	Transferred to Co. H, June 2, 1865.
Birely, Isaac	do	Aug. 28, 1862	3	Disch'd on Surgeon's certificate, Dec. 1863.
Bagshaw, Walter	do	Aug. 18, 1862	3	Disch'd on Surgeon's certificate, Feb. 7, 1863.
Blackburn, John	do	Aug. 12, 1862	3	Transferred to Co. C, Jan. 26, 1863.
Brooks, William H.	do	Aug. 12, 1862	3	Disch'd on Surgeon's certificate. Nov., 1864.
Black, Theodore	do	Aug. 27, 1862	3	Not on muster-out roll.
Bowlin, Michael	do	Aug. 23, 1862	3	Wounded at Fredericksburg, Va., Dec. 13, 1862—transferred to Co. C, Jan. 26, 1863.
Brennan, Dom. C.	do	Aug. 28, 1862	3	Pr. to 1st Lieut. 69th Pa. Vols., June, 1863.
Chambers, William	do	Aug. 13, 1862	3	Wounded at Wilderness, Va., May 3, 1864—mustered out with company June 3, 1865.
Cannon, Bernard	do	Aug. 4, 1862	3	Mustered out with company, June 3, 1865.
Cummings, James	do	Aug. 24, 1862	3	Mustered out with company, June 3, 1865.

NAME.	RANK.	DATE OF MUSTER INTO SERVICE.	TERM—YEARS	REMARKS
Clark, William	Private	Aug. 7, 1862	3	Absent, in hospital, at muster out.
Carter	do			Buried at Winchester, Va.
Collar, John	do	Aug. 18, 1862	3	Mustered out with company, June 3, 1865.
Collins, Henry M	do	Aug. 13, 1862	3	Mustered out with company, June 3, 1865.
Clifford, Charles	do	Feb. 23, 1864	3	Transferred to Co. H, June 2, 1865.
Clements, William	do	Aug. 23, 1862	3	Disch'd on Surgeon's certificate, May, 1863.
Carroll, James	do	Feb. 18, 1864	3	Killed at Petersburg, Va., June 16, 1864.
Clause, Philip	do	July 7, 1862	3	Transferred to Co. C, Jan. 26, 1863.
Collins, Charles	do	July 22, 1862	3	Transferred to Co. C, Jan. 26, 1863.
Cocklin, William	do	Aug. 9, 1862	3	Not on muster-out roll.
Casey, Patrick	do	Aug. 7, 1862	3	Not on muster-out roll.
Campbell, James	do	Aug. 9, 1862	3	Not on muster-out roll.
Coggins, Bartholomew	do	Aug. 25, 1862	3	Not on muster-out roll.
Clark, John	do	Aug. 29, 1862	3	Wounded at Fredericksburg, Va., Dec. 13, 1862—discharged—date unknown.
Cummings, Benjamin	do			Died Sept. 3, 1864—buried at Cy. Hill Cemetery, L. I.
Chambers, William	do	July 9, 1862	3	Mustered out with company, June 3, 1865.
Chambers, James	do	Feb. 9, 1864	3	Not on muster-out roll.
Davison, George	do	July 9, 1862	3	Mustered out with company, June 3, 1865.
Daisley, Thomas	do	July 14, 1862	3	Wounded at Cold Harbor, Va., June 2, 1864—discharged by General Order, June 29, 1865.
Delaney, Matthew	do	Aug. 13, 1862	3	Disch'd on Surgeon's certificate, Mar., 1863.
Dennison, Edmund	do	June 28, 1862	3	Not on muster-out roll.
Deener, Henry	do	July 5, 1862	3	Transferred to Co. C, Jan. 26, 1863.
Dugan, Hugh	do	July 14, 1862	3	Transferred to Co. C, Jan. 26, 1863.
Daley, James	do	July 29, 1862	3	Not on muster-out roll.
Doublebower, F. T	do	Aug. 21, 1862	3	Not on muster-out roll.
Delaney, Fenton	do	Aug. 21, 1862	3	Transferred to Co. D, Jan. 27, 1863.
Deveney, Michael	do	Aug. 23, 1862	3	Not on muster-out roll.
Dempsey, John	do	Aug. 23, 1862	3	Wounded at Fredericksburg, Va., Dec. 13, 1862—discharged April 19, 1864.
Decamp, William	do	Aug. 30, 1862	3	Not on muster-out roll.
Elliott, George	do	Aug. 2, 1862	3	Mustered out with company, June 3, 1865.
Ellieman, Philip H	do	Aug. 11, 1862	3	Mustered out with company, June 3, 1865.
Erwin, Edward	do	Aug. 10, 1862	3	Not on muster-out roll.
Emrich, Harry	do	Aug. 22, 1862	3	Not on muster-out roll.
Fisher, Andrew	do	June 14, 1862	3	Absent, in hospital, at muster out.
Fagan, Edward	do	Aug. 23, 1862	3	Killed at Spottsylvania C. H., Va., May 18, '64—wounded at Fredericksburg, Dec. 13, '62.
Frise, John	do	July 29, 1862	3	Wounded at Fredericksburg, Va., Dec. 13, '62—not on muster-out roll.
Gasper, Henry	do	Aug. 14, 1862	3	Mustered out with company, June 3, 1865.
Gibbons, Richard	do	Feb. 4, 1864	3	Transferred to Co. H, June 2, 1865.
Gilbert, Stephen	do	Jan. 28, 1862	3	Not on muster-out roll.
Gibson, William	do	July 7, 1862	3	Transferred to Co. C, Jan. 26, 1863.
Gray, James	do	July 14, 1862	3	Not on muster-out roll.
George, John	do	July 17, 1862	3	Not on muster-out roll.
Gray, Thomas	do	Aug. 7, 1862	3	Transferred to Co. C, Jan. 26, 1863.
Gaffney, Francis	do	Aug. 18, 1862	3	Not on muster-out roll.
Hughes, Lewis W	do	June 14, 1862	3	Mustered out with company, June 3, 1865.
Hill, John	do	Aug. 13, 1862	3	Mustered out with company, June 3, 1865.
Hunt, David M	do	Sept. 3, 1864	3	Mustered out with company, June 3, 1865.
Hamsbury, Joseph S	do	Feb. 5, 1864	3	Transferred to Co. H, June 2, 1865.
Henderson, Joseph	do	Feb. 21, 1864	3	Disch'd on Surgeon's certificate, Feb. 1, 1865.
Hevener, Jonas D	do			Wounded at Spottsylvania C. H., Va., May 18, 1864—discharged on Surgeon's certificate, Feb. 10, 1865.
Haley, James	do	July 11, 1862	3	Not on muster-out roll.
Haas, Henry	do	July 23, 1862	3	Not on muster-out roll.
Higgins, James B	do	June 25, 1862	3	Transferred to Co. C, Jan. 26, 1863.
Haley, William	do	July 26, 1862	3	Not on muster-out roll.
Hurley, Dennis	do	Sept. 28, 1862	3	Transferred to Co. C, Jan. 26, 1863.
Isaacs, George	do	May 9, 1864	3	Not on muster-out roll.
Jones, William S	do	July 22, 1862	3	Not on muster-out roll.
Joyce, Patrick	do	Aug. 25, 1862	3	Transferred to Co. C, Jan. 26, 1863.
Jordan, James	do	Aug. 25, 1862	3	Not on muster-out roll.

THREE YEARS' SERVICE.   391

NAME.	RANK.	DATE OF MUSTER INTO SERVICE.	TERM—YEARS	REMARKS.
Jones, Francis	Private	Aug. 30, 1862	3	Not on muster-out roll.
Keenan, Francis E.	do	Aug. 19, 1862	3	Discharged by special order, June 17, 1864.
Kelly, John	do	Aug. 12, 1862	3	Not on muster-out roll.
Klyse, Henry	do	Aug. 13, 1862	3	Transferred to company C, Jan. 26, 1863.
Keyser, Charles	do	Aug. 23, 1862	3	Not on muster-out roll.
Lincke, Henry	do	July 22, 1862	3	Wounded at Gettysburg, Pa., July 2, 1863—mustered out with company, June 3, 1865.
Lutz, Jacob	do	Aug. 15, 1862	3	Mustered out with company, June 3, 1865.
Little, William H.	do	July 7, 1862	3	Captured at Spottsylvania C. H., Va., May 12, 1864—absent, at Camp Parole, Annapolis, Md., at muster out.
Lenci, Augustus	do	Aug. 12, 1862	3	Transferred to U. S. Navy, April 12, 1864.
Laudenschlæger, G.	do	Mar. 22, 1864		Transferred to Vet. Reserve Corps, Apr. 15, '65—discharged by General Order, July 22, '65.
Leguin, John S.	do	Aug. 19, 1862	3	Killed at South Side R. R., Va., April 2, '65.
Landrican, Matth's	do	July 25, 1862	3	Transferred to company A—date unknown.
Lehman, John	do	July 22, 1862	3	Transferred to company C, Jan. 26, 1863.
Mooney, Owen J.	do	Aug. 20, 1862	3	Mustered out with company, June 3, 1865.
Murray, John	do	Aug. 14, 1862	3	Mustered out with company, June 3, 1865.
Monahan, James	do	Aug. 20, 1862	3	Mustered out with company, June 3, 1865.
Manneeley, Wm.	do	Aug. 9, 1862	3	Wounded at Cold Harbor, Va., June 2, and at Reams Station, Aug. 25, '64—mustered out with company, June 3, 1865.
Mabuerry, Isaac M.	do	Aug. 18, 1862	3	Discharged on Surgeon's certificate, Mar. '63.
Mink, Andrew J.	do	Jan. 13, 1864	3	Transferred to company H, June 2, '65.
Mallon, Daniel	do	July 11, 1862	3	Not on muster-out roll.
Morrow, Robert	do	July 21, 1862	3	Not on muster-out roll.
Melville, Wm. B.	do	Aug. 11, 1862	3	Not on muster-out roll.
Marks, James	do	Aug. 11, 1862	3	Not on muster-out roll.
Mooney, Wm. W.	do	Aug. 14, 1862	3	Transferred to company C, Jan. 26, '63.
Martin, Manuel	do			Died at Philadelphia, Pa., July 19, '63.
M'Mullin, John R.	do	Aug. 29, 1862	3	Wounded at Cold Harbor, Va., June 3, '64—absent, in hospital, at muster out.
M'Mahon, George	do	Aug. 14, 1862	3	Promoted to Q. M. Sgt., Jan. 27, '63.
M'Hugh, James	do	July 2, 1862	3	Died at Frederick, Md., July, 1863—burial record.
M'Cuen, John	do	June 21, 1862	3	Not on muster-out roll.
M'Grath, John	do	July 5, 1862	3	Not on muster-out roll.
M'Coy, James	do	July 5, 1862	3	Not on muster-out roll.
M'Cann, Bernard	do	July 28, 1862	3	Transferred to company C, Jan. 26, '63.
M'Gurk, William	do	Aug. 6, 1862	3	Not on muster-out roll.
M'Guigan, Francis	do	Aug. 12, 1862	3	Promoted to 1st Lt. company G, April 4, '64.
M'Laughlin, Pat.	do	Aug. 23, 1862	3	Not on muster-out roll.
M'Nulty, Michael	do	Aug. 23, 1862	3	Transferred to company C, Jan. 26, '63.
M'Millin, John	do			Wounded at Wilderness, May 5, '64.
Oliver, Abraham	do	Aug. 14, 1862	3	Mustered out with company, June 3, '65.
Porter, William	do	Aug. 20, 1862	3	Wounded at Gettysburg, Pa., July 2, 1863—mustered out with company, June 3, '65.
Parker, John	do	July 18, 1862	3	Absent, in hospital, at muster out.
Pilkington, John	do	Aug. 12, 1862	3	Absent, in hospital, at muster out.
Porter, Aubrey Sr.	do	Sept. 15, 1862	3	Wounded at Five Forks, Va., March 31, '65—discharged by General Order, May 3, '65.
Polly, John	do	Apr. 14, 1864		Wounded at Wilderness, Va., May 5, 1864—transferred to company H, June 2, '65.
Pilgen, Adam	do	July 23, 1862	3	Not on muster-out roll.
Pryor, Michael	do	July 29, 1862	3	Not on muster-out roll.
Price, Daniel	do	Aug. 2, 1862	3	Mustered out with company, June 3, '65.
Price, William	do	Aug. 18, 1862	3	Transferred to company C, Jan. 26, '63.
Parker, William	do	Aug. 18, 1862	3	Not on muster-out roll.
Ryan, John	do	Aug. 18, 1862	3	Absent, in hospital, at muster out.
Rutherford, Thos.	do	Aug. 14, 1862	3	Discharged on Surgeon's certificate, Mar. '63.
Richmond, Samuel G.	do	Aug. 18, 1862	3	Missing in action at Spottsylvania Court House, Va., May 12, '64.
Russell, John	do	June 24, 1862	3	Not on muster-out roll.
Rogers, John	do	June 14, 1862	3	Killed at Fredericksburg, Va., Dec. 13, '62.
Ryan, James	do	May 9, 1864		Not on muster-out roll.
Sally, Patrick	do	July 7, 1862	3	Wounded at Cold Harbor, Va., June 2, '64—mustered out with company, June 3, '65.

NAME.	RANK.	DATE OF MUSTER INTO SERVICE.	TERM—YEARS.	REMARKS.
Search, Francis,	Private	July 24, 1862	3	Mustered out with company, June 3, '65.
Sperling, Frederick	do	Aug. 13, 1862	3	Mustered out with company, June 3, '65.
Shields, James,	do	Aug. 15, 1862	3	Mustered out with company, June 3, '65.
Stokes, Charles,	do	July 14, 1862	3	Mustered out with company, June 3, '65.
Scott, Patrick,	do	Aug. 13, 1862	3	Tr. to 115th reg. Ohio Vols., Feb. 13, '63.
Shields, John,	do	Mar. 26, 1864	3	Transferred to company H, June 2, '65.
Steenbury, Charles,	do	Feb. 1, 1865	3	Transferred to company H, June 2, '65.
Smith, Dixon,	do	Mar. 29, 1864	3	Discharged by General Order, June 7, '65.
Stewart, Robert,	do	Apr. 15, 1864	3	Wounded at Totopotomy, Va., May 31, '64—transferred to company H, June 2, '65.
Sharpe, Morris,	do	July 18, 1862	3	Transferred to company B, 22d reg. Vet. Reserve Corps—wounded at Fredericksburg—discharged by General Order, July 3, '65.
Standring, John,	do	July 21, 1862	3	Not on muster-out roll.
Stein, Louis,	do	July 1, 1862	3	Not on muster-out roll.
Stein, John,	do	July 12, 1862	3	Not on muster-out roll.
Smith, William S.,	do	July 28, 1862	3	Transferred to company C, Jan. 26, '63.
Smith, Thomas,	do	July 21, 1862	3	Transferred to company C, Jan. 26, '63.
Spain, Patrick,	do	July 31, 1862	3	Transferred to company C, Jan. 26, '63.
Scott, James,	do	Aug. 2, 1862	3	Not on muster-out roll.
Sanderton, Benj.	do	Aug. 14, 1862	3	Not on muster-out roll.
Spence, Michael,	do	Aug. 30, 1862	3	Transferred to company C, Jan. 26, '63.
Thomas, Alonzo C.	do	Apr. 14, 1864	3	Transferred to company H, June 2, '65.
Tracy, Francis,	do	Aug. 19, 1862	3	Transferred to Battery A, 4th U. S. Artillery
Vaughan, Joseph,	do	Aug. 6, 1862	3	Mustered out with company, June 3, '65.
Vanderslice, And.	do	Aug. 18, 1862	3	Mustered out with company, June 3, '65.
Vanloan, George W.	do	Feb. 4, 1864	3	Wounded in action, Sept. 25, '64—discharged by General Order, May 15, '65.
Watling, Charles,	do	Aug. 6, 1862	3	Died at Beverly, N. J., April 14, '63.
Wright, John,	do	Aug. 7, 1862	3	Transferred to Co. C, Jan. 26, '63.
Whiklin, Matthew	do	Aug. 9, 1862	3	Not on muster-out roll.
Wells, Edward,	do	Aug. 22, 1862	3	Not on muster-out roll.
Wilbur, Oscar	do	Aug. 30, 1862	3	Not on muster-out roll.
Young, William,	do	Aug. 29, 1862	3	Transferred to Co. C, Jan. 26, '63.

Company C.

NAME.	RANK.	DATE OF MUSTER INTO SERVICE.	TERM—YEARS.	REMARKS.
John Teed	Captain	Aug. 26, 1862	3	Captured at Gettysburg, Pa., July 2, 1863—com. Major, April 8, 1864—not mustered—hon. disch. on acct. of disability, Nov. 28, '64
Henry D. Price	do	July 5, 1862	3	Pr. from 2d Lieut. Co. B, to 1st Lieut. Co. C, March 1, '63—to Capt., Co. C, April 8, '64—Brev. Maj.—kil'd at Petersburg, Oct. 27, '64
William J. Burk	do	Aug. 14, 1862	3	Captured at William's Farm, Va., June 22, '64—promoted from Sgt. Maj. to 1st Lt., Jan. 28, '65—to Capt., Feb. 13, '65—mustered out with company, June 3, '65.
Seneca G. Willauer	1st Lieut.	Aug. 26, 1862	3	Wounded at Fredericksburg, Va., Dec. 13, '62—promoted to Capt. Co. A, March 1, '63.
Thomas Gray	do	Aug. 2, 1862	3	Wounded at Gettysburg, Pa., July 2, 1863—promoted from Sgt., Feb. 13, '65—mustered out with company, June 3, 1865.
John B. Parker	2d Lieut.	Aug. 26, 1862	3	Resigned March 21, 1863.
Wm. H. Tyrrell	do	Aug. 12, 1862	3	Promoted from Sgt. Co. K, May 1, 1863—transferred to Vet. Res. Corps, Aug. 12, '63—wounded at Fredericksburg.
Abraham L. Detweiler	do	Aug. 11, 1862	3	Pr. to Cor.—to Sgt.—to 2d Lt., Nov. 9,'63—com. 1st Lt., April 8,'64—wd. near Petersburg, Va., June 16,'64—disch. Dec. 23, '64.
Wm Chambers	1st Sgt.	July 9, 1862	3	Wounded at Cold Harbor, Va., June 2, '64—com. 2d Lt., June 1, '65—not mustered—absent, in hospital, at muster out.
Wm. H. Bibighaus	do	Aug. 15, 1862	3	Promoted to 2d Lt. Co. D, March 1,'63—died Aug. 6, 1863.

THREE YEARS' SERVICE.

NAME.	RANK.	DATE OF MUSTER INTO SERVICE.	TERM-YEARS.	REMARKS.
Francis Malin	1st Sgt.	Aug. 13, 1862	3	Killed at Gettysburg, Pa., July 2, 1863.
Jacob Carl	Sergeant	Aug. 11, 1862	3	Wd. at Spottsylvania C. H., Va., May 12,'64—disch. by General Order, June 13, '65.
Jefferson Carl	do	Aug. 14, 1862	3	Promoted from Corporal, Dec. 1, 1863—mustered out with company, June 3, 1865.
Henry McElroy	do	July 31, 1862	3	Wounded at Reams Station, Va., Aug. 25, 1864—promoted from Cor., Feb. 13, 1865—mustered out with company, June 3, 1865.
Anthony Matter	do	Aug. 11, 1862	3	Wounded at Fredericksburg, Va., Dec. 13,'62—mustered out with company, June 3, 1865.
Thos. M. Rowland	do	July 12, 1862	3	Killed at Fredericksburg, Va., Dec. 13, 1862.
Wm. H. Stewart	do	July 12, 1862	3	Not on muster-out roll.
Elhannan W. Price	do	Aug. 1, 1862	3	Killed at Fredericksburg, Va., Dec. 13, 1862.
Franklin B. Missimer	do	Aug. 1, 1862	3	Killed at Fredericksburg, Va., Dec. 13, 1862.
George K. Bryan	Corporal	Aug. 12, 1862	3	Discharged by General Order, June 3, 1865.
Wm. Anderson	do	July 10, 1862	3	Mustered out with company, June 3, 1865.
Andrew McLaughlin	do	Aug. 19, 1862	3	Mustered out with company, June 3, 1865.
William Price	do	Aug. 18, 1862	3	Mustered out with company, June 3, 1865.
Willoughby F. Bickle	do	Aug. 12, 1862	3	Prisoner from Aug. 25, '64, to May 17, '65—mustered out with company, June 3, 1865.
John Eckart	do	Aug. 22, 1862	3	Mustered out with company, June 3, 1865.
John Blackburn	do	Aug. 12, 1862	3	Mustered out with company, June 3, 1865.
Henry Marshall	do	Feb. 12, 1864	3	Wounded at Cold Harbor, Va., June 3, 1864—transferred to Co. E, June 2, 1865.
William H. Brooks	do	Aug. 12, 1862	3	Not on muster-out roll.
James E. Stout	do	July 29, 1862	3	Wounded at Fredericksburg, Va., Dec. 13, 1862, and at Gettysburg, Pa., July 2, 1863—missing at Gettysburg.
William Reynolds	do	July 29, 1862	3	Not on muster out roll.
William E. Martin	do	Aug. 5, 1862	3	Died Dec., 1862, at Falmouth, Va.
Samuel J. Willauer	do	Aug. 11, 1862	3	Killed at Fredericksburg, Va., Dec. 13, 1862.
Henry C. Roberts	do	Aug. 13, 1862	3	Not on muster-out roll.
Michael B. Schaffer	do	July 23, 1862	3	Not on muster-out roll.
James Stewart	do	Aug. 18, 1862	3	Not on muster-out roll.
John Lehman	Musician	July 22, 1863	3	Mustered out with company, June 3, 1865.
Philip Clause	do	July 7, 1862	3	Transferred to Co. A—date unknown.
T. W. Vannaman	do	Aug. 18, 1862	3	Promoted to Principal Mus.—date unknown.
Lewis Ritch	do	Aug. 12, 1862	3	Wounded in action, Oct. 1, 1862—discharged—date unknown.
Albright, Charles	Private	Aug. 8, 1862	3	Mustered out with company, June 3, 1865.
Bowlin, Michael	do	Aug. 25, 1862	3	Mustered out with company, June 3, 1865.
Branson, Samuel	do	Aug. 22, 1862	3	Absent, sick, at muster out.
Barth, Charles G.	do	Feb. 11, 1864	3	Transferred to Co. E, June 2, 1865.
Braddish, Stephen	do	Mar. 29, 1864	3	Transferred to Co. E, June 2, 1865.
Byarly, James	do	Mar. 17, 1864	3	Transferred to Co. E, June 2, 1865.
Biddle, George W.	do	Aug. 5, 1862	3	Killed at Fredericksburg, Va.
Bartle, Lewis	do	Aug. 13, 1862	3	Not on muster-out roll.
Blankanbiler, George	do	Aug. 15, 1862	3	Not on muster-out roll.
Collins, Charles	do	Aug. 12, 1862	3	Mustered out with company, June 3, 1865.
Curran, Patrick	do	Feb. 16, 1864	3	Wounded at Five Forks, Va., March 31,'65—transferred to Co. E, June 2, 1865.
Cosgrove, Edward P.	do	Sept. 25, 1863	3	Drafted—wd. at Five Forks, Va., March 31, 1865—transferred to Co. E, June 2, 1865.
Curry, Richard	do	July 25, 1862	3	Not on muster-out roll.
Cauler, William	do	Aug. 4, 1862	3	Killed at Fredericksburg, Dec. 13, 1862.
Dehaven, William	do	Aug. 12, 1862	3	Discharged by General Order, June 9, 1865.
Deener, Henry	do	July 15, 1862	3	Absent, sick, at muster out.
Donald, George	do	Apr. 5, 1864	3	Transferred to Co. E, June 2, 1865.
Dugan, Hugh	do	July 14, 1862	3	Missed in action at Fredericksburg.
Davisson, Theo. H	do	Aug. 28, 1862	3	Not on muster-out roll.
Davis, Richard W.	do	July 25, 1862	3	Not on muster-out roll.
English, John	do	Feb. 9, 1864	3	Discharged by General Order, July 24, 1865.
Fulton, Robert A.	do			Died Dec. 25, '64—buried in U. S. Hospital Cemetery, Annapolis, Md., grave 139.
Ginther, Joseph	do	Aug. 14, 1862	3	Wounded at Gettysburg, July 2, 1863—transferred to Co. B, 18th Reg., V. R. C.,—discharged by General Order, June 17, 1865.

NAME.	RANK.	DATE OF MUSTER INTO SERVICE.	TERM—YEARS.	REMARKS.
Gibson, William	Private	July 7, 1862	3	Mustered out with company, June 3, 1865.
Gallagher, William	do	Aug. 6, 1862	3	Died Dec. 29, of wounds received at Fredericksburg, Va., Dec. 13, 1862—buried in Military Asylum Cem., D. C.
Gliden, John	do	Aug. 2, 1862	3	Not on muster-out roll.
Gosser, John	do	Jan. 20, 1865	3	Not on muster-out roll.
Higgins, James B	do	June 25, 1862	3	Wounded at Fredericksburg, Va., Dec. 13, '62—absent, in hospital, at muster out.
Heinman, William	do	Aug. 25, 1862	3	Mustered out with company, June 3, 1865.
Hurley, Dennis	do	Aug. 26, 1862	3	Not on muster-out roll.
Haney, Cornelius	do	July 30, 1862	3	Not on muster-out roll.
Harrison, Glenn	do	July 30, 1862	3	Killed at Fredericksburg, Dec. 13, 1862.
Heffner, Anthony	do	Aug. 2, 1862	3	Killed at Gettysburg.
Hendricks, A. S.	do	Aug. 5, 1862	3	Died in camp after battle of Fredericksburg, Dec. 13, '62.
Hunter, Samuel D.	do	Aug. 5, 1862	3	Promoted to Sergeant-Major, Jan. 28, '65.
Houp, John	do	Aug. 27, 1862	3	Killed near Deep Bottom, Va., Aug. 14, '64.
Joyce, Patrick	do	Aug. 25, 1862	3	Mustered out with company, June 3, '65.
Jones, James L	do	Mar. 18, 1864	3	Tr. to V. R. C.—disch. by G. O., June 7, '65.
Jefferson, F. A.	do	Aug. 23, 1862	3	Wounded at Fredericksburg, Va., Dec. 13, '62—not on muster-out roll.
Kollar, John	do	Aug. 28, 1862	3	Wounded at Fredericksburg, Va., Dec. 13, '62—absent, in hospital, at muster out.
Klyse, Henry	do	Aug. 13, 1862	3	Wounded at Fredericksburg, Va., Dec. 13, '62—absent, in hospital, at muster out.
Kramer, Charles	do	Mar. 16, 1864	3	Wounded at Spottsylvania C. H., Va., May 12, '64—transferred to Co. E, June 2, '65.
Kelly, Joseph	do	Apr. 17, 1864	3	Wounded and missing in action at Spottsylvania C. H., Va., May 12, '64.
Kane, Thomas J	do	Aug. 5, 1862	3	Not on muster-out roll.
Kelly, William	do	Aug. 13, 1862	3	Not on muster-out roll.
Lubeck, Henry	do	Aug. 27, 1862	3	Mustered out with company, June 3, '65.
Litch, Benjamin	do	July 29, 1862	3	Not on muster-out roll.
Laudenberger, A.	do	Aug. 2, 1862	3	Killed at Fredericksburg, Va.
Landis, Allen	do	Aug. 4, 1862	3	Died at Philadelphia, Pa., Oct. 2, '64.
Landis, Aaron, J.	do	Aug. 11, 1862	3	Killed at Fredericksburg, Va., Dec. 13, '62.
Mooney, William W	do	Aug. 14, 1862	3	Mustered out with company, June 3, '65.
Marquett, Mahlon	do	Aug. 5, 1862	3	Wounded at Fredericksburg, Va., Dec. 13, '62—not on muster-out roll.
Major, David E	do	Aug. 18, 1862	3	Died sud'ly near Falmouth, Va., Nov. 17, '62.
McNulty, Michael	do	Aug. 23, 1862	3	Mustered out with company, June 3, '65.
McCann, Bernard	do	July 28, 1862	3	Discharged by General Order, June 17, '65.
McCall, Andrew	do	Aug. 18, 1862	3	Transferred to Co. B, 12th Reg., V. R. C.—wounded at Fredericksburg—discharged by General Order, June 28, '65.
McGranahan, James	do	Feb. 14, 1864	3	Wounded at Wilderness, Va., May 5, '64—transferred to Co. E, June 2, '65.
McBride, James	do			Mustered out with company.
McGinn, John H	do	Feb. 17, 1864	3	Transferred to Co. E, June 2, '65.
McLamara, Patrick	do	July 29, 1862	3	Not on muster-out roll.
Neander, Joseph	do	Aug. 18, 1862	3	Trans. to Battery A, U. S. Art'y—wounded.
O'Rourke, Francis	do	Feb. 25, 1864	3	Wounded at Spottsylvania C. H., Va., May 12, '64—transferred to Co. E, June 2, '65.
Patrick, John M	do	Aug. 23, 1862	3	Mustered out with company, June 3, '65.
Parker, John B., 2d	do	July 12, 1862	3	Not on muster-out roll.
Palmer, Wm. R	do	Aug. 18, 1862	3	Not on muster-out roll.
Phillips, Frederick	do	Apr. 12, 1864	3	Transferred to Co. K, 11th reg. Vet Reserve Corps—disch'd by Gen'l Order, Aug 18,'65.
Ramick, Jacob	do	Aug. 8, 1862	3	Mustered out with company, June 3, '65.
Reinhart, David	do	Aug. 8, 1862	3	Mustered out with company, June 3, '65.
Rhoads, John C	do	Aug. 11, 1862	3	Mustered out with company, June 3, '65—captured at Gettysburg.
Roxburgh, T. W.	do	Aug. 16, 1862	3	Wounded at Chancellorsville, Va., May 3, and at Gettysburg, Pa., July 2, '63—absent, in hospital, at muster out.
Rodgers, John	do	June 14, 1862	3	Mustered out with company, June 3, '65.
Rhoback, David	do	Aug. 18, 1862	3	Wounded at Fredericksburg, Va., Dec. 13, '62—absent at muster out.

THREE YEARS' SERVICE.

NAME.	RANK.	DATE OF MUSTER INTO SERVICE.	TERM—YEARS.	REMARKS.
Kimby, John	Private	Feb. 22, 1864	3	Discharged by General Order, June 5, '65.
Rowland, Peter H	do	July 22, 1862	3	Wounded at Gettysburg, Pa., July 2, '63—not on muster-out roll.
Reilly, Michael	do	Aug. 15, 1862	3	Not on muster-out roll.
Robinson, John	do	Aug. 19, 1862	3	Not on muster-out roll.
Smith, John G	do	Aug. 15, 1862	3	Mustered out with company, June 3, '65.
Smith, Thomas	do	July 21, 1862	3	Prisoner from Oct. 14, '63, to Oct. 17, '64—discharged by General Order, June 9, '65.
Smith, William S	do	July 28, 1862	3	Mustered out with company, June 3, '65.
Spain, Patrick	do	July 31, 1862	3	Absent, sick, at muster out.
Smith, Augustus	do	Aug. 18, 1862	3	Wounded at Fredericksburg, Va., Dec. 13,'62—absent, in hospital, at muster out.
Spencer, Michael	do	Aug. 30, 1862	3	Killed at Gettysburg.
Sutherland, Henry	do	Aug. 23, 1862	3	Not on muster-out roll.
Towers, George	do	Aug. 13, 1862	3	Mustered out with company, June 3, '65.
Tully, Henry J	do	Jan. 29, 1864	3	Missing in action at Spottsylvania C. H. Va., May 12,'64—disch. by G. O., June 17,'65.
Trealfall, George D	do	Apr. 7, 1864	3	Tr. to V.R.C.—disch. by G. O., Aug. 26, '65.
Thompson, John	do	Aug. 26, 1862	3	Not on muster-out roll.
Tierney, Thomas	do	Aug. 11, 1862	3	Wounded at Fredericksburg, Va., Dec. 13,'62—not on muster-out roll.
Ulrick, Daniel	do	July 23, 1862	3	Killed at Gettysburg.
Wilt, Henry	do	Aug. 4, 1862	3	Wounded at Spottsylvania C. H., Va., May 12, '64—absent, in hospital, at muster out.
Wright, John	do	Aug. 7, 1862	3	Discharged by General Order, May 15, '65.
Wheeler, George	do	Aug. 23, 1862	3	Tr. to V. R. C.—disch. by G. O., June 28, '65.
Wilt, George	do	Feb. 4, 1864	3	Transferred to Co. E. June 2, '65.
Weadley, Henry	do	Mar. 28, 1864	3	Wounded at Spottsylvania C. H., Va., May 12, '64—transferred to Co. E, June 2, '65.
Wilson, Samuel	do	Aug. 5, 1862	3	Not on muster-out roll.
Wickham, James	do	Aug. 6, 1862	3	Transferred to Battery A, 4th U. S. Artillery.
Whiting, Stephen D	do	Aug. 8, 1862	3	Missing in action at Fredericksburg.
Whitmeyer, David	do	Aug. 13, 1862	3	Died at City Point, Va., Sept. 27, '64.
Young, William A	do	Aug. 19, 1862	3	Prisoner from May 5, '64 to April 21, '65—wounded at Gettysburg—discharged by General Order, Aug. 11, '65.
Young, William	do	Mar. 17, 1864	3	Transferred to Co. E, June 2, '65.
Yocum, Joseph W	do	Aug. 25, 1862	3	Transferred to Co. I—date unknown.
Zellers, George	do	Aug. 8, 1862	3	Transferred to Battery A, 4th U. S. Artillery.

Company D.

NAME.	RANK.	DATE OF MUSTER INTO SERVICE.	TERM—YEARS.	REMARKS.
William A. Peet	Captain	Aug. 25, 1862	3	Resigned Feb. 28, '63.
Garrett Nowlen	do	Aug. 7, 1862	3	Promoted from Adj., Nov. 21, '63—to Br-Maj., Aug. 25, '64—wd. at Fredericksburg—killed at Reams Station, Va., Aug. 25, '64—bu. in Laurel Hill Cem., Philadelphia, Pa.
Louis J. Sacriste	do	Sept. 1, 1862	3	Promoted from 2d Lieut., Co. F, to 1st Lieut., March 1,'63—to Adjt. Nov. 21,'63—to Capt., Sept. 22, '64—to Bv.-Maj., March 13, '65—wd. at Cold Harbor, Va., June 3, '64—mustered out with company, June 3, '65.
Jacob R. Moore	1st Lieut.	Aug. 5, 1862	3	Detailed on staff of Gen. Birney—wounded at Gettysburg.
Eugene Brady	do	Aug. 15, 1862	3	Wd. at Gettysburg, Pa., July 2, '63—pr. fr. Sgt., Nov. 21, '63—killed at Five Forks, Va., March 31, '65—bur. in Cathedral Cemetery, Philadelphia.
John C. Wright	do	July 26, 1862	3	Wounded at Cold Harbor, Va., June 2, '64—promoted from 1st Sgt., May 17, '65—mustered out with company, June 3, 1865.
George L. Reilly	2d Lieut.	Aug. 25, 1862	3	Wounded at Fredericksburg, Va., Dec. 13, '62—discharged Feb. 27, '63.

THE STORY OF THE 116TH REGIMENT.

NAME.	RANK.	DATE OF MUSTER INTO SERVICE.	TERM—YEARS.	REMARKS.
William H. Bibighaus	2d Lieut.	Aug. 15, 1862	3	Promoted from 1st Sgt., Co. C, March 1, '63—died at Washington, D. C., Aug. 6, '63—bu. in Laurel Hill Cem., Philadelphia, Pa.
Bernard McCahey	1st Sgt.	July 10, 1862	3	Wounded at Spottsylvania C. H., Va., May 18, '64—promoted from Sgt., May 17, '65—mustered out with company, June 3, '65.
Richard E. Ker	do	June 24, 1862	3	Transferred to 3d Reg't., U. S. Cav., June, '63.
Daniel Rodgers	Sergeant.	Aug. 16, 1862	3	Wounded at Chancellorsville, Va., May 3, '63—com. 2d Lieut., June 1, '65—not mus.—mustered out with company, June 3, '65.
James Duffy	do			Wounded at Chancellorsville and discharged in consequence—date unknown.
James Cavanaugh	do	Aug. 20, 1862	3	Captured at Reams Station, Va., Aug. 25, '64—promoted from private, March 1, 1865—mustered out with company.
Joseph Slinker	do	Aug. 1, 1862	3	Wounded at Gettysburg, Pa., July 2, '63—trans. to Vet. Reserve Corps, Jan. 7, '64.
Peter Kelly	do	Feb. 25, 1864	3	Wounded at Petersburg, Va., June 22, '64, and April 2, '65—trans. to Co. I, June 3, '65.
William L. Lott	do	Aug. 2, 1862	3	Killed at Reams Station, Va., Aug. 25, '64.
Robert J. Fitzgerald	do	Aug. 13, 1862	3	Missing in action at Gettysburg, Pa., July 2, 1863.
Josiah C. Randolph	do	July 16, 1862	3	Transferred to Co. A, Jan. 26, '63.
Thomas Connard	do	Aug. 2, 1862	3	Not on muster-out roll.
Morris Stowe	do	July 7, 1862	3	Not on muster-out roll.
Andrew E. Ker	do	June 25, 1862	3	Killed at Fredericksburg, Va., Dec. 13, '62.
Alexander Edgar	Corporal	July 8, 1862	3	Mustered out with company, June 3, '65.
Joseph Murphy	do	July 30, 1862	3	Mustered out with company, June 3, '65.
George Allen	do	Aug. 22, 1862	3	Captured at Gettysburg, Pa., July 2, '63—promoted to Corporal, March 1, '65—mustered out with company, June 3, '65.
Thomas P. Crown	do	Aug. 4, 1862	3	Disch. on Surgeon's certificate, March 17, '63.
Michael J. McKenna	do	Aug. 11, 1862	5	Transferred to Vet. Res. Corps, Dec. 14, '64.
David Steen	do	Mar. 18, 1864	3	Transferred to Co. I, June 3, '65—Vet.
Brian McLaughlin	do	Apr. 4, 1864	3	Wounded at Cold Harbor, Va., June 2, '64—transferred to Co. I, June 3, '65.
John Adams	do	Mar. 8, 1864	3	Transferred to Co. I, June 3, '65.
John H. Curry	do	July 15, 1862	3	Killed at Wilderness, Va., May 5, '64.
John Hughes	do	Apr. 27, 1864	5	Captured at Reams Station, Va., Aug. 25, '64—died October 28, '64, in prison.
John Martin	do	July 28, 1862	3	Not on muster-out roll.
Thomas Scarlett	do	June 18, 1862	3	Transferred to Co. A, Jan. 26, '63.
Thomas A. Dorwart	do	Aug. 21, 1862	3	Transferred to Co. A—date unknown.
R. J. Stephenson	do	Aug. 9, 1862	3	Wounded at Fredericksburg, Va., Dec. 13, '62—transferred to Co. A, Jan. 26, '63.
Joseph Surrick	do	July 12, 1862	3	Not on muster-out roll.
John McKinney	do	July 7, 1862	3	Not on muster-out roll.
Isaac Landis	do	Aug. 6, 1862	3	Not on muster-out roll.
Henry Miller	do	Aug. 5, 1862	3	Not on muster-out roll.
Andrew Hart	do	Aug. 22, 1862	3	Deserted at Harper's Ferry, Oct. 29, '62.
Nicholas Martin	do	July 24, 1862	3	Wounded at Gettysburg, Pa., July 2, '63—not on muster-out roll.
Hugh McVey	do	Aug. 13, 1862	3	Wounded at Gettysburg, Pa., July 2, '63—not on muster-out roll.
Alonzo Mahan	Musician	July 17, 1862	3	Disch. on Surgeon's certificate, March 17, '63.
Robert Henry	do	June 28, 1862	3	Transferred to Co. A, January 26, 1863.
Charles Gysel	do	July 10, 1862	3	Not on muster-out roll.
Alexander, Chas. B.	Private	Feb. 26, 1864	3	Discharged by General Order, May 16, '65.
Alexander, Albert	do	Feb. 11, 1864	3	Wounded at Cold Harbor, Va., June 2, '64—transferred to Co. I, June 3, '65.
Ahern, Daniel	do	Aug. 11, 1862	3	Transferred to Co. A, Jan. 26, '63.
Adams, Nathan	do	July 29, 1862	3	Transferred to Co. A, Jan. 26, '63.
Allingham, Robert	do	June 26, 1862	3	Transferred to Co. A, Jan. 26, '63.
Anderson, Thomas	do	July 8, 1862	3	Not on muster-out roll.
Altimus, John S.	do	Aug. 14, 1862	3	Transferred to Co. A, Jan. 26, '63.
Adema, William	do	July 28, 1862	3	Transferred to 4th Artillery, Oct. 26, '62, by Order 154, U. S. A.
Ballinger, Christian	do	Apr. 12, 1864	3	Transferred to Co. I, June 3, '65.

THREE YEARS' SERVICE.

NAME.	RANK.	DATE OF MUSTER INTO SERVICE.	TERM-YEARS.	REMARKS.
Brown, Isaac	Private	July 9, 1862	3	Absent, sick, at muster out.
Benson, John T	do	Feb. 26, 1864	3	Killed at Wilderness, Va., May 5, '64.
Browan, Benjamin	do	April 8, 1864	3	Wounded at Po River, Va., May 10, '64—not on muster-out roll.
Bradley, Wm. T	do	June 18, 1862	3	Not on muster-out roll.
Binder, John E	do	June 30, 1862	3	Not on muster-out roll.
Bakeoven, George	do	July 29, 1862	3	Not on muster-out roll.
Bailey, Edward	do	Aug. 21, 1862	3	Not on muster-out roll.
Burns, William	do	Aug. 22, 1862	3	Not on muster-out roll.
Boylan, John C	do	Aug. 28, 1862	3	Not on muster-out roll.
Caffrey, Stephen	do	Apr. 24, 1864	3	Discharged on Surgeon's certificate, Jan.,'65.
Carr, John H	do	Apr. 13, 1864	3	Wd. at Petersburg, Va., June 16, '64—tr. to V. R. C., Mar. 11, '65—disch. Sept. 5, '66.
Conway, James	do	Mar. 21, 1864	3	Transferred to Co. I, June 3, '65.
Cassady, George	do	Apr. 23, 1864	3	Wounded at Petersburg, Va., June 16, '64—transferred to Co. I, June 3, '65.
Condon, William	do	Mar. 12, 1864	3	Wounded at Petersburg, Va., June 16, '64—transferred to Co. I, June 3, '65.
Cole, John	do	July 14, 1862	3	Transferred to Co. A, Jan. 26, '63.
Campbell, William	do	Aug. 18, 1862	3	Not on muster-out roll.
Conway, Robert	do	June 24, 1862	3	Killed in Wilderness, May 5, '64.
Casey, James	do	July 30, 1862	3	Wounded at Fredericksburg, Va., Dec. 13,'62 —not on muster-out roll.
Connelly, John	do	Aug. 20, 1862	3	Not on muster-out roll.
Cotterell, John	do		3	Promoted to Hos. Stew. U.S. Army, Aug. 2,'64.
Dougherty, Ew'd	do	Aug. 19, 1862	3	Mustered out with company, June 3, '65.
Duffey, John	do	July 30, 1862	3	Disch. on Surgeon's certificate, date unknown.
Dunning, Hugh	do	Aug. 29, 1862	3	Discharged July 7, for wounds received at Gettysburg, Pa., July 2, '63.
De Luar, Albert	do	Feb. 12, 1864	3	Transferred to U.S. Navy, March 1, '64.
Delaney, Finton	do	Apr. 8, 1864	3	Transferred to Co. I, June 3, '65.
Donovan, John	do	Apr. 22, 1864	3	Wounded at Petersburg, Va., June 16, '64—transferred to Co. I, June 3, '65.
Detweiler, Thomas	do	Aug. 11, 1861	3	Transferred to Co. A, Jan. 26, '63.
Deihl, Jacob H	do	Aug. 21, 1862	3	Transferred to Co. A, Jan. 26, '63.
Devonshire, Jere'h	do	Aug. 4, 1862	3	Transferred to Co. A, Jan. 26, '63.
Dampman, Wm. H	do	June 28, 1862	3	Not on muster-out roll.
Davis, John	do	Aug. 29, 1862	3	Not on muster-out roll.
Ellinger, Emanuel	do	Aug. 4, 1862	3	Disch. on Surgeon's certificate, Mar. 3, '63.
Engle, Peter	do	Aug. 15, 1862	3	Transferred to Co. A, Jan. 26, '63.
Fletcher, James	do	Aug. 29, 1862	3	Mustered out with company, June 3, '65.
Farrell, John A	do	Apr. 4, 1864	3	Wounded at Petersburg, Va., June 16, '64—transferred to Co. I, June 3, '65.
Foster, Samuel	do	June 17, 1862	3	Transferred to Battery A, 4th U.S. Artillery, Oct. 26, '64, Order 154.
Fox, Henry	do	June 17, 1862	3	Not on muster-out roll.
Garman, William	do	Aug. 4, 1862	3	Wounded at Petersburg, Va., June 27, '64—discharged by General Order, June 20, '65.
Guinan, Peter	do	July 9, 1862	3	Mustered out with company, June 3, '65.
Gallagher, Martin	do	Aug. 14, 1862	3	Discharged for wounds rec. at Gettysburg, Pa., July 2, '63.
Glasgow, Matthew	do	July 30, 1862	3	Captured at Reams Station, Va., Aug. 25, '64 —died at Philadelphia, Pa., Mar. 27, '65.
Goldey, John	do	June 13, 1862	3	Transferred to Co. A, Jan. 26, '63.
Green, William R	do	June 23, 1862	3	Not on muster-out roll.
Gray, William	do	Aug. 11, 1862	3	Discharged for disability, Oct. 29, '62, at Harper's Ferry.
Hanlon, William	do	Aug. 19, 1862	3	Wounded at Five Forks, Va., Mar. 31, '65—absent, in hospital, at muster out.
Hayden, Patrick	do	Aug. 23, 1862	3	Mustered out with company, June 3, '65.
Harris, Francis M	do	Aug. 15, 1862	3	Discharged by General Order, May 26, '65.
Holt, George C	do	Mar. 25, 1864	3	Wounded at Totopotomy, Va., May 31, '64—transferred to Co. I, June 3, '65.
Hansell, John R	do	Apr. 4, 1864	3	Wounded at Five Forks, Va., Mar. 31, '65—transferred to Co. I, June 3, '65.
Hughes, James	do	Mar. 6, 1865	3	Transferred to Co. I, June 3, '65.
Harker, Edward	do	Apr. 24, 1864	3	Transferred to Co. I, June 3, '65.

NAME.	RANK.	DATE OF MUSTER INTO SERVICE.	TERM—YEARS.	REMARKS.
Hilear, Frederick	Private	Apr. 13, 1864	3	Died at Wilderness, Va., May 4, '64.
Hughes, John	do	Mar. 23, 1864	3	Died at Annapolis, Md., Oct. 9, '64, of wounds received in action at Petersburg—buried in U. S. General Hospital Cemetery, No. 2.
Huss, John	do		3	Died Nov. 11, '64, at Salisbury, N. C., Prison.
Hanna, James	do	Mar. 29, 1864	3	Captured at Reams Station, Va., Aug. 25, '64—died Nov. 5, '64.
Heyle, Samuel	do	Apr. 12, 1864	3	Not on muster-out roll.
Handline, George	do	Aug. 12, 1862	3	Transferred to Co. A, Jan. 26, '63.
Harlen, William	do	Aug. 13, 1862	3	Not on muster-out roll.
Hite, George	do	Aug. 18, 1862	3	Not on muster-out roll.
Hathaway, Wm. E.	do	July 11, 1862	3	Trans. to V. R. C.—wounded at Gettysburg—disch. on Surgeon's certificate, Mar. 14, '63.
Jones, John	do	July 22, 1862	3	Not on muster-out roll.
Kunkle, George	do	Aug. 4, 1862	3	Wounded and captured at Gettysburg, Pa., July 2, '63—absent, in hospital, at muster-out.
King, James L.	do	July 25, 1862	3	Mustered out with company, June 3, '65.
Kilpatrick, James	do	Mar. 6, 1865	3	Transferred to Co. I, June 3, '65.
Kinchner, John	do	July 29, 1862	3	Transferred to Co. I, June 3, '65.
Keiper, William	do	July 7, 1862	3	Not on muster-out roll.
Klopner, August	do	Aug. 22, 1862	3	Not on muster-out roll.
Logue, Frank	do	July 21, 1862	3	Mustered out with company, June 3, '65.
Logue, James	do	July 19, 1862	3	Wounded at Fredericksburg, Va., Dec. 13,'62—absent at muster out.
Long, James	do	Aug. 23, 1862	3	Disch. on Surgeon's certificate, Feb. 16, '63.
Lloyd, Henry	do	Mar. 12, 1864	3	Disch. by General Order, May 25, '65.
Logue, Daniel	do	Sept. 1, 1862	3	Disch. on Surgeon's certificate, Feb 4, '63.
Lawrence, Henry D.	do	Apr. 18, 1864	3	Wd. at Spottsylvania C. H., Va., May 12, '64—transferred to Co. I, June 3, '65.
Lyons, James	do	Apr. 11, 1864	3	Wounded at Cold Harbor, Va., June 3, '64—transferred to Co. I, June 3, '65.
Lawson, Samuel	do	Aug. 20, 1862	3	Transferred to Co. A, Jan. 26, '63.
Llewellyn, Samuel	do	Aug. 14, 1862	3	Transferred to Co. A, Jan. 26, '63.
Lawson, William S.	do	July 1, 1862	3	Not on muster-out roll.
Lemark, Woodman	do	Aug. 11, 1862	3	Not on muster-out roll.
Lumadue, Lewis	do	Aug. 18, 1862	3	Not on muster-out roll.
Lemark, Samuel	do	Aug. 9, 1862	3	Not on muster-out roll.
Landes, William	do	Aug. 23, 1862	3	Not on muster-out roll.
Long, Charles	do	Aug. 22, 1862	3	Disch. on Surgeon's cert.—date unknown.
Martin, John	do	Aug. 28, 1862	3	Wd. at Reams Station, Va., Aug. 25, '64—mustered out with company, June 3, '65.
Murphy, John	do	Aug. 15, 1862	3	Mustered out with company, June 3, '65.
Merrick, Joseph	do	Aug. 7, 1862	3	Disch. on Surgeon's certificate, Apr. 4, '63.
Myers, John D.	do	July 9, 1862	3	Tr. to V. R. C., Feb. 16, '64—discharged by General Order, June 1, '65.
Myers, John	do		3	Died July 22, '63, at Andersonville, Ga.—grave, 3,765.
Merritt, Murtha	do	Apr. 9, 1864	3	Transferred to Co. I, June 3, '65.
Mulholland, John	do	Apr. 25, 1864	3	Captured at Reams Station, Aug. 25, '64—transferred to Co. I, June 3, '65.
Morrissey, John	do	Apr. 2, 1864	3	Killed at Petersburg, Va., June 29, '64.
Moser, William	do	Aug. 22, 1862	3	Transferred to Co. A, Jan. 26, '63.
Malinger, Simon	do	July 1, 1862	3	Wounded at Chancellorsville, May 3, '63—tr. to Battery A, 4th U. S. Artillery, Oct. 26, '62.
Mallon, Edward	do	July 5, 1862	1	Not on muster-out roll.
Murphy, John	do	July 23, 1862	3	Mustered out with company, June 3, '65.
Mills, Jacob	do	Aug. 18, 1862	3	Died on way to Gettysburg.
McFadden, Thos.	do	Aug. 13, 1862	3	Absent, sick, at muster out.
McGonigle, Henry	do	July 15, 1862	3	Mustered out with company, June 3, '65.
McQuaid, Thomas	do	Aug. 29, 1862	3	Mustered out with company, June 3, '65.
McCullough, David	do	Sept. 1, 1862	3	Mustered out with company, June 3, '65.
McLaughlin, Chas.	do	July 2, 1862	3	Mustered out with company, June 3, '65.
McGovern, Edward	do	Apr. 6, 1864	3	Wd. at Petersburg, Va., June 16, '64—disch. on Surgeon's certificate, Apr. 4, '65.
McDowell, Andrew	do	Aug. 6, 1862	3	Wd. at Petersburg, Va., June 16, '64—disch. on Surgeon's certificate—date unknown.
McMenamin, Mat'w	do	Feb. 3, 1864	3	Wounded at Totopotomy, Va., May 31, '64—transferred to Co. I, June 3, '65.

NAME.	RANK.	DATE OF MUSTER INTO SERVICE.	TERM—YEARS.	REMARKS.
McIlhenny, John	Private	Aug. 12, 1862	3	Not on muster-out roll.
McLaughlin, Mich'l	do	Aug. 9, 1862	3	Not on muster-out roll.
McMahon, Thos. J	do	July 3, 1862	3	Not on muster-out roll.
McGiveney, Wm	do	Aug. 23, 1862	3	Disch. on Surgeon's certificate of disability.
Nichols, William	do	June 30, 1862	3	Transferred to Co. A, Jan. 26, '63.
Norcross, Eugene	do	June 1, 1862	3	Not on muster-out roll.
O'Brian, Thomas	do	Aug. 29, 1862	3	Died at Philadelphia, Pa., Feb. 7, '65.
O'Brian, James	do	June 27, 1862	3	Not on muster-out roll.
Powers, John	do	Aug. 29, 1862	3	Mustered out with company, June 3, '65.
Perry, John	do	May 11, 1862	3	Wounded at Petersburg, Va., June 22, '64—transferred to Co. I, June 3, '65.
Pinton, Alfred	do	June 10, 1862	3	Not on muster-out roll.
Pounds, Wm	do	Aug. 18, 1862	3	Not on muster-out roll.
Parker, Franklin B	do	Aug. 21, 1862	3	Not on muster-out roll.
Quigley, Joseph B	do	May 4, 1864	3	Died at Philadelphia, Pa., Aug. 29, of wounds rec. at Petersburg, Va., June 16, '64—bu. rec., died at Portsmouth Grove, R. I., July 2, '64.
Quicksall, Wm	do	July 28, 1862	3	Not on muster-out roll.
Rushworth, George	do	July 15, 1862	3	Killed at Chancellorsville, Va., May 3, '63.
Rodormell, Chas	do	Aug. 17, 1862	3	Transferred to Co. A, Jan. 26, '63.
Robson, William	do	July 7, 1862	3	Not on muster-out roll.
Sweeney, John	do	Aug. 19, 1862	3	Mustered out with company, June 3, '65.
Sweeney, Michael	do	Aug. 23, 1862	3	Wounded at Petersburg, Va., June 16, '64—absent, sick, at muster out.
Snyder, George F	do	Aug. 6, 1862	3	Disch. on Surgeon's certificate, Mar. 3, '63.
Stone, Robert J	do	Apr. 4, 1864	3	Absent, sick, at muster out.
Smith, William	do	Mar. 18, 1864	3	Transferred to Co. I, June 3, '65.
Smith, John A	do	Apr. 12, 1864	3	Died at Philadelphia, Pa., July 26, '64—burial record, Sept. 4, '64.
Serross, Charles	do	Mar. 9, 1864	3	Wounded and captured at Petersburg, Va., June 22, '64—died at Andersonville, Ga., Sept. 30, '64—grave, 10,091.
Sickles, Charles	do	Aug. 18, 1862	3	Transferred to Co. A, Jan. 26, 1863.
Shultz, William	do	Aug. 9, 1862	3	Missing in action at Gettysburg.
Smith, William A	do	Aug. 21, 1862	3	Not on muster-out roll.
Sherin, Francis	do	Aug. 23, 1862	3	Killed at Gettysburg.
Smedley, William	do	June 16, 1862	3	Not on muster-out roll.
Tully, Patrick	do	Aug. 4, 1862	3	Disch. on Surgeon's certificate, March 17, '63.
Twelves, Stephen	do	Aug. 16, 1862	3	Transferred to Co. A, Jan. 26, 1863.
Thompkins, John	do	June 16, 1862	3	Not on muster-out roll.
Wallace, William A	do	Aug. 3, 1862	3	Mustered out with company, June 3, 1865.
Whelan, James	do	Aug. 29, 1862	3	Wounded at Spottsylvania C. H., Va., May 10, '64—transferred to Vet. Res. Corps—discharged by General Order, July 26, '65.
Wilson, John	do	Sept. 1, 1864	3	Disch. on Surgeon's certificate, Feb. 16, '63.
Wallace, Thomas	do	Aug. 7, 1862	3	Disch. Nov. 25, '63, for wds. rec. in action.
Wilson, David	do	Aug. 7, 1862	3	Disch. on writ of *habeas corpus*, May 25, '63.
Wolf, August	do	Apr. 9, 1864	3	Absent, sick, at muster out.
Walker, Theodore A	do	July 20, 1862	3	Killed at Chancellorsville, Va., May 3, '63.
Woodard, John	do	Aug. 16, 1862	3	Transferred to Co. A, Jan. 26, '63.
Whitus, Charles	do	Aug. 22, 1862	3	Not on muster-out roll.
Walton, F. C. V	do	Aug. 14, 1862	3	Wounded at Fredericksburg, Dec. 13, '62—not on muster-out roll.
White, John	do	Aug. 15, 1862	3	Transferred to Battery A, 4th U. S. Artillery, Oct. 26, '62—Order 154.

COMPANY E.

NAME	RANK	DATE	TERM	REMARKS
John McNamara	Captain	Aug. 23, 1862	3	Transferred to Co. B, Jan. 26, '63.
Michael Schoales	do	Mar. 3, 1864	3	Resigned May 17, '64.
Charles Cosslett	do	Mar. 3, 1864	3	Wounded at Wilderness, Va., May 5, at Cold Harbor, June 3, and wounded and captured at William's Farm, June 22, '64—promoted from 2d Lt., June 13, '64—to Brevet-Major, March 13, '65—discharged on Surgeon's certificate, June 22, '65.

400   THE STORY OF THE 116TH REGIMENT.

NAME.	RANK.	DATE OF MUSTER INTO SERVICE.	TERM—YEARS.	REMARKS.
Joseph H. G. Miles	1st Lieut.	Sept. 5, 1862	3	Discharged by special order, Jan. 27, '63.
Robert J. Grogan	do	Mar. 3, 1864	3	Resigned May 17, '64.
Timothy A. Sloan	do	Feb. 16, 1864	3	Wounded at Cold Harbor, Va., June 2, '64—promoted from Sgt. to 2d Lt., June 13, '64—to 1st Lt., June 9, '65—com. Capt., June 27, '65—not mus.—mustered out with company, July 14, '65.
Robert T. Maguire	2d Lieut.	Aug. 23, 1862	3	Wounded at Fredericksburg, Va., Dec. 13, '62—transferred to Co. B, Jan. 26, '63.
Henry Keil	do		3	Promoted from 1st Sgt.—killed at Spottsylvania, May 12, '64.
Silas Younkin	1st Sgt	Feb. 25, 1864	3	Promoted to Cor., Nov. 1, '64—to Sgt., May 1, '65—to 1st Sgt., June 9, '65—com. 2d Lt., July 1, '65—not mustered—mustered out with company, July 14, '65.
Thomas Bowers	do	Aug. 15, 1862	3	Not on muster-out roll.
Patrick Welsh	Sergeant	Feb. 12, 1864	3	Wounded at Petersburg, Va., June 16, '64—promoted from private, May 1, '65—mustered out with company, July 14, '65.
John Reed	do	Feb. 12, 1864	3	Promoted from private, May 1, '65—mustered out with company, July 14, '65.
Edward W. Desher	do	Feb. 13, 1864	3	Wounded at Wilderness, Va., May 5, '64—promoted from private, July 1, '65—mustered out with company, July 14, '65.
Michael Cavanaugh	do	Feb. 18, 1864	3	Promoted to Cor., May 1, '65—to Sgt., July 1, '65—mus. out with company, July 14, '65.
John Cassidy	do	Feb. 15, 1864	3	Wounded at Wilderness, Va., May 5, '64—absent, in hospital, at muster out.
John Murray	do	Feb. 20, 1864	3	Captured at Spottsylvania C. H., Va., May 12, '64—died at Andersonville, Ga.—date unknown.
Henry Marshall	do	Feb. 12, 1864	3	Absent, wounded, at muster out.
Thomas Lacompte	do	Feb. 12, 1864	3	Captured at Petersburg, Va., June 29, '64—discharged by General Order, June 12, '65.
Henry Kelly	do	Aug 5, 1862	3	Died Sept., '62.
Hugh Croll	do	Feb. 15, 1864	3	Promoted to Sgt., May 1, '64—discharged by General Order, May 31, '65.
James J. Byrne	do	Feb. 15, 1864	3	Promoted to Sgt., May 1, '64—not on muster-out roll.
Martin Weiss	do	Feb. 12, 1864	3	Not on muster-out roll.
John H. Davis	do	Feb. 17, 1864	3	Not on muster-out roll.
George W. Bentley	do	June 27, 1862	3	Transferred to Co. B, Jan. 26, '63.
Andrew Fisher	do	June 14, 1862	3	Transferred to Co. B, Jan. 26, '63.
Patrick Costello	do	June 24, 1862	3	Promoted to Com. Sgt., Jan. 26, '63.
Andrew Murphy	do	Aug. 16, 1862	3	Not on muster-out roll.
Lewis Rhole	Corporal	Feb. 10, 1864	3	Promoted to Corporal, May 1, '65—mustered out with company, July 14, '65.
Henry Weadley	do	Mar. 26, 1864	3	Promoted to Corporal, May 1, '65—mustered out with company, July 14, '65.
Henry Dress	do	Feb. 10, 1864	3	Promoted to Corporal, July 1, '65—mustered out with company, July 14, '65.
John Ellis	do	Feb. 8, 1864	3	Wounded at Cold Harbor, Va., June 2, '64, and in action, Oct. 16, '64—discharged by General Order, June 2, '65.
Lot Turney	do	Feb. 24, 1864	3	Promoted to Corporal, May 15, '64—killed at Cold Harbor, Va., June 3, '64.
Thomas Sharp	do	Feb. 10, 1864	3	Killed at Cold Harbor, Va., June 3, '64.
Aaron Tomlinson	do	Feb. 10, 1864	3	Died at Alexandria, Va., June 18, of wounds received at Cold Harbor, Va., June 3, '64—grave 2,181.
Henry Masters	do	Feb. 13, 1864	3	Promoted to Corporal, May 15, '64—captured at Reams Station, Va., Aug. 25, '64—died at Salisbury, N. C., Nov. 13, '64.
S. G. Stotzenberg	do	Feb. 18, 1864	3	Pr. to Cor., June 1, '64—dis. March 1, '65.
Lewis Brown	do	Feb. 13, 1864	3	Not on muster-out roll.
James Donagan	do	Feb. 15, 1864	3	Not on muster-out roll.
William H. Little	do	July 7, 1862	3	Transferred to Co. B, Jan. 26, '63.

THREE YEARS' SERVICE.

NAME.	RANK.	DATE OF MUSTER INTO SERVICE.	TERM—YEARS.	REMARKS.
Daniel Connelly	Corporal	Aug. 12, 1862	3	Transferred to Co. B, Jan. 26, '63.
William Clark	do	Aug. 7, 1862	3	Wounded at Fredericksburg, Va., Dec. 13, '62—transferred to Co. B, Jan. 26, '63.
Augustus Lindsay	do	Aug. 12, 1862	3	Transferred to Co. B, Jan. 26, '63.
John Parker	do	July 19, 1862	3	Transferred to Co. B, Jan. 26, '63.
Francis E. Crawford	do	July 19, 1862	3	Promoted to Q. M. Sgt., Jan. 26, '63.
Thos. H. F. Brady	do	July 22, 1862	3	Not on muster-out roll.
Edward Buckley	do	Aug. 13, 1862	3	Not on muster-out roll.
John Dagney	Musician	Feb. 20, 1864	3	Absent, sick, at muster out.
Wm. J. Curley	do	Feb. 12, 1864	3	
James Monahan	do	Aug. 20, 1862	3	Transferred to Co. B, Jan. 26, '63.
Elberson E. Little	do	July 7, 1862	3	Not on muster-out roll.
Adams, George	Private	Feb. 10, 1864	3	Missing in action, Wilderness, Va., May 5, '64.
Allen, Thomas W.	do	Feb. 15, 1864	3	Not on muster-out roll.
Anderson, Nicholas	do	Feb. 22, 1864	3	Not on muster-out roll.
Allen, Charles	do	July 21, 1862	3	Not on muster-out roll.
Alcom, George	do	July 29, 1862	3	Not on muster-out roll.
Armstrong, Wm.	do	Aug. 20, 1862	3	Not on muster-out roll.
Baker, John	do	Sept. 21, 1864	3	Drafted—mus. out with company, July 14, '65.
Barth, Charles G.	do	Feb. 11, 1864	3	Mustered out with company, July 14, '65.
Barrett, Richard	do	Feb. 13, 1864	3	Mustered out with company, July 14, '65.
Byarly, James	do	Mar. 17, 1864	3	Mustered out with company, July 14, '65.
Braddish, Stephen	do	Mar. 29, 1864	3	Absent, sick, at muster out.
Bartlett, Thomas A.	do	Feb. 16, 1864	3	Disch. by General Order, May 15, '65.
Barker, Richard	do	Feb. 24, 1864	3	Killed at Spottsylvania C. H., May 18, '64.
Brossen, Clement	do	Feb. 15, 1864	3	Not on muster-out roll.
Brand, George	do	Feb. 17, 1864	3	Not on muster-out roll.
Bagshaw, Walter	do	Aug. 18, 1862	3	Transferred to Co. B, Jan. 26, '63.
Bishop, Charles	do	June 30, 1862	3	Transferred to Co. B, Jan. 26, '63.
Brosnahan, Tim	do	July 28, 1862	3	Not on muster-out roll.
Bowser, Levi	do	Aug. 1, 1862	3	Not on muster-out roll.
Barlow, William	do	Aug. 11, 1862	3	Transferred to Battery A, 4th U. S. Artillery.
Bryan, Albert C.	do	Aug. 18, 1862	3	Not on muster-out roll.
Brown, Joseph F.	do	June 14, 1862	3	Not on muster-out roll.
Caldwell, James W.	do	Feb. 18, 1864	3	Mustered out with company, July 14, '65.
Cosgrove, Edw. P.	do	Sept. 25, 1863	3	Drafted—mus. out with company, July 14, '65.
Curran, Patrick	do	Feb. 16, 1864	3	Absent, wounded, at muster out.
Connelly, Austin	do	Feb. 15, 1864	3	Discharged by General Order, June 9, '65.
Cannon, Bernard	do	Aug. 4, 1862	3	Transferred to Co. B, Jan. 26, '63.
Carlin, James A.	do	Aug. 18, 1862	3	Transferred to Co. B, Jan. 26, '63.
Coates, Lawrence J.	do	Aug. 10, 1862	3	Transferred to Co. B, Jan. 26, '63.
Cummings, James	do	Aug. 24, 1862	3	Transferred to Co. B, Jan. 26, '63.
Chambers, William	do	Aug. 13, 1862	3	Transferred to Co. B, Jan. 26, '63.
Curry, Patrick	do	Aug. 23, 1862	3	Not on muster-out roll.
Collins, Thomas	do	Aug. 5, 1862	3	Not on muster-out roll.
Cloud, Alfred J.	do	Aug. 19, 1862	3	Honorably discharged, disability, Dec., '62.
Daily, Terrence	do	Feb. 15, 1864	3	Mustered out with company, July 14, '65.
Donald, George	do	Apr. 8, 1864	3	Absent, sick, at muster out.
Dodd, George A.	do	Feb. 20, 1864	3	Killed at Cold Harbor, Va., June 3, '64.
Davis, Joseph	do	Feb. 8, 1864	3	Not on muster-out roll.
Dixon, John	do	Feb. 17, 1864	3	Not on muster-out roll.
Dougherty, Samuel	do	Feb. 11, 1864	3	Not on muster-out roll.
Davidson, George	do	July 9, 1862	3	Transferred to Co. B, Jan. 26, '63.
Daisley, Thomas	do	July 14, 1862	3	Transferred to Co. B, Jan. 26, '63.
Dailey, John M.	do	Aug. 13, 1862	3	Not on muster-out roll.
Ellis, Samuel	do	Feb. 23, 1864	3	Discharged by General Order, June 10, '65.
Elfert, Charles	do	Feb. 24, 1864	3	Killed at Wilderness, Va., May 6, '64—buried in Wilderness burial grounds—grave, 536, Sec. C, Div. B.
Elliott, George	do	Aug. 2, 1862	3	Transferred to Co. B, Jan. 26, '63.
Elleman, Philip H.	do	Aug. 11, 1862	3	Transferred to Co. B, Jan. 26, '63.
Essert, Charles	do		3	Died May 6, '64, at Fredericksburg.
Flynn, James	do	Feb. 16, 1864	3	Absent, sick, at muster out.
Glotfelty, James	do	Feb. 24, 1864	3	Mustered out with company, July 14, '65.
Goggins, Peter	do	Feb. 20, 1864	3	Wd. at Wilderness, Va., May 5, '64—missing in action at Deep Bottom, Aug. 14, '64.
Gasper, Henry	do	Aug. 14, 1862	3	Transferred to Co. B, Jan. 26, '63.

NAME.	RANK.	DATE OF MUSTER INTO SERVICE.	TERM—YEARS.	REMARKS.
Gravell, William	Private	July 14, 1862	3	Not on muster-out roll.
Geddis, Alexander	do	Aug. 5, 1862	3	Not on muster-out roll.
Hall, Joseph	do	Feb. 13, 1864	3	Transferred to Vet. Res. Corps, Nov. 20, '64.
Holter, Michael	do	Feb. 8, 1864	3	Tr. to Co. H, 16th reg. V. R. C., Jan. 25, '65 disch. by General Order, July 15, '65.
Hughes, Lewis W	do	June 14, 1862	3	Transferred to Co. B, Jan. 26, '63.
Holden, Thomas N	do	July 17, 1862	3	Not on muster-out roll.
Howell, Edward	do	Aug. 14, 1862	3	Not on muster-out roll.
Hendricks, Abraham	do		3	Died Jan. 15, '63, at Fredericksburg—grave, 16, Sec. A, Div. D.
Johnston, Joseph W	do	June 14, 1862	3	Wounded at Fredericksburg, Va., Dec. 13, '62—transferred to 16th reg. V. R. Corps.
James, Charles	do	July 14, 1862	3	Not on muster-out roll.
Jard, Jacob	do		3	Died Nov. 25, '64.
Kramer, Charles	do	Mar. 16, 1864	3	Absent, wounded, at muster out.
Kelly, John	do	Feb. 20, 1864	3	Not on muster-out roll.
Kennedy, Moses	do	Aug. 5, 1862	3	Not on muster-out roll.
Larner, Thomas	do	Mar. 21, 1865	3	Substitute—mustered out with Co. July 14, '65.
Luder, Charles	do	Feb. 13, 1864	3	Wd. at Spottsylvania C. H., Va., May 12 and 18, '64—absent, in hospital, at muster out
Lachman, Tobias	do	Feb. 11, 1864	3	Wd. at Spottsylvania C. H., Va., May 12, '64 disch. by General Order, May 26, '65.
Lewders, Frederick	do	Feb. 13, 1864	3	Killed at Deep Bottom, Va., Aug. 16, '64—bu. in Nat. Cem., Ft. Harrison, Sec. A, grave 83
Laycock, Hugh	do	Feb. 18, 1864	3	Cap. at Petersburg, Va., June 22, '64—died at Andersonville, Ga., Aug. 11, '64—grave, 5,314
Logue, John	do	Feb. 15, 1864	3	Died at Washington, D. C., Dec. 25, '64—buried in National Cemetery, Arlington, Va.
Law, Samuel	do	Feb. 8, 1864	3	Not on muster-out roll.
Lincke, Henry	do	July 22, 1862	3	Transferred to Co. B, Jan. 26, '63.
Link, Frederick	do	July 28, 1862	3	Not on muster-out roll.
Murphy, Thos., 1st	do	Feb. 22, 1864	3	Wd. at Wilderness, Va., May 5, '64—tr. to V. R. C.—disch. on Surg. cert., May 6, '65.
Murphy, Thos. 2d	do	Feb. 22, 1864	3	Captured at Reams Station, Va., Aug. 25, '64—died at Annapolis, Md., Sept. 22, '64.
Megary, Peter	do	Feb. 24, 1864	3	Not on muster-out roll.
Murray, Owen	do	Feb. 18, 1864	3	Not on muster-out roll.
Manning, James	do	Feb. 23, 1864	3	Not on muster-out roll.
Miller, James	do	Feb. 16, 1864	3	Not on muster-out roll.
Mooney, Owen J	do	Aug. 20, 1862	3	Transferred to Co. B, Jan. 26, '63.
Murray, John	do	Aug. 14, 1862	3	Transferred to Co. B, Jan. 26, '63.
Mohegan, David	do	Aug. 13, 1862	3	Not on muster-out roll.
Miller, Christian	do	June 26, 1862	3	Not on muster-out roll.
Mullin, Patrick	do	Aug. 11, 1862	3	Transferred to Battery A, 4th U. S. Artillery.
Middleton, Robert	do	Aug. 14, 1862	3	Wounded at Fredericksburg, Va., Dec. 13, '62—not on muster-out roll.
Maloney, William	do	Aug. 16, 1864	3	Not on muster-out roll.
McGranahan, James	do	Feb. 14, 1864	3	Absent, wounded, at muster out.
McGinn, John H	do	Feb. 14, 1864	3	Absent, on detached service, at muster out.
McGonegal, Corne's	do	Feb. 5, 1864	3	Disch. on Surgeon's certificate, Oct. 4, '64.
McCuen, John	do	June 21, 1862	3	Transferred to Co. B, Jan. 26, '63.
McHugh, James	do	Aug. 2, 1862	3	Transferred to Co. B, Jan. 26, '63.
McMahon, George	do	Aug. 14, 1862	3	Transferred to Co. B, Jan. 26, '63.
McCullough, Jno. H	do	Aug. 15, 1862	3	Transferred to Co. B, Jan. 26, '63.
Nelson, Albert	do	Feb. 8, 1864	3	Captured at Reams Station, Va., Aug. 25, '64—died at Andersonville, Ga.—date unknown
O'Connor, Joseph D	do	Feb. 15, 1864	3	Discharged by General Order, July 14, '65.
O'Rourke, Francis	do	Feb. 25, 1864	3	Absent, sick, at muster out.
O'Brien, John	do	Aug. 6, 1862	3	Not on muster-out roll.
O'Callaghan, Wm	do	Aug. 15, 1862	3	Wounded at Fredericksburg, Va., Dec. 13, '62—transferred to Co. B, Jan. 26, '63.
Perdy, Edward	do	June 16, 1864	3	Absent, sick, at muster out.
Perdy, Benjamin	do	Feb. 23, 1864	3	Not on muster-out roll.
Pilkington, John	do	Aug. 12, 1862	3	Transferred to Co. B, Jan. 26, '63.
Porter, Aubrey	do	Aug. 15, 1862	3	Transferred to Co. B, Jan. 26, '63.
Parmer, Watson G	do	July 5, 1862	3	Not on muster-out roll.
Patton, Neal	do	Aug. 14, 1862	3	Not on muster-out roll.

NAME.	RANK.	DATE OF MUSTER INTO SERVICE.	TERM—YEARS.	REMARKS.
Quinn, Michael	Private	Aug. 5, 1862	3	Not on muster-out roll.
Reed, Joseph	do	June 1, 1864	3	Wounded at Cold Harbor, Va., June 3, '64—absent, in hospital, at muster out.
Richard, David	do	Feb. 15, 1864	3	Absent, sick, at muster out.
Rey, James	do	Feb. 10, 1864	3	Not on muster-out roll.
Roberts, William	do	Feb. 10, 1864	3	Not on muster-out roll.
Russell, John	do	June 24, 1862	3	Transferred to Co. B, Jan. 26, '63.
Ryan, John	do	Aug. 18, 1862	3	Transferred to Co. B, Jan. 26, '63.
Robson, John P	do	June 27, 1862	3	Not on muster-out roll.
Richmond, Sam'l G	do	Aug. 18, 1862	3	Transferred to Co. B, Jan. 26, '63.
Sherlin, Patrick	do	Feb. 25, 1864	3	Prisoner from Aug. 25 to Sept. 27, '64—absent, sick, at muster out.
Shadle, William	do	Feb. 10, 1864	3	Wounded at William's Farm, Va., June 22, '64—absent, in hospital, at muster out.
Stuck, Peter	do	Feb. 24, 1864	3	Wounded at Wilderness, Va., May 5, '64—absent, in hospital, at muster out.
Sharpe, Charles W	do	Feb. 19, 1864	3	Discharged by General Order, May 26, '65.
Shannon, David	do	Feb. 24, 1864	3	Killed at Petersburg, Va., June 16, '64
Schmid, John L	do	Feb. 24, 1864	3	Not on muster-out roll.
Storm, Jacob	do	Feb. 13, 1864	3	Not on muster-out roll.
Smith, Thomas	do	Feb. 22, 1864	3	Not on muster-out roll.
Sperling, Fred'k	do	Aug. 13, 1862	3	Transferred to Co. B, Jan. 26, '63.
Sally, Patrick	do	July 7, 1862	3	Transferred to Co. B, Jan. 26, '63.
Stokes, Charles	do	July 14, 1862	3	Transferred to Co. B, Jan. 26, '63.
Shields, James	do	Aug. 15, 1862	3	Transferred to Co. B, Jan. 26, '63.
Sharpe, Morris	do	July 18, 1862	3	Transferred to Co. B, Jan. 26, '63.
Scott, Patrick	do	Aug. 13, 1862	3	Transferred to Co. B, Jan. 26, '63.
Smith, Thomas H	do	July 17, 1862	3	Not on muster-out roll.
Shields, James W	do	Aug. 16, 1862	3	Not on muster-out roll.
Tharp, Chas. V	do		3	
Tomlin, George	do	Feb. 29, 1864	3	Wounded at Petersburg, Va., June 16, '64—absent, in hospital, at muster out.
Tully, Henry J	do	Jan. 29, 1864	3	Discharged by General Order, June 17, '65.
Turpin, Wilson	do	Feb. 23, 1864	3	Killed at Cold Harbor, Va., June 3, '64.
Turner, William	do	July 19, 1862	3	Not on muster-out roll.
Wildoner, George	do	Feb. 23, 1864	3	Wounded at Cold Harbor, Va., June 2, '64—mustered out with company, July 14, '65.
Wilt, George	do	Feb. 4, 1864	3	Mustered out with company, July 14, '65.
Williams, William	do	Feb. 15, 1864	3	Absent, sick, at muster out.
Wilmer, George	do	Feb. 24, 1864	3	Discharged by General Order, May 26, '65.
Wright, Joseph	do	Feb. 16, 1864	3	Wounded at Cold Harbor, Va., June 2, '64—discharged by General Order, June 2, '65.
Wiley, John M	do	Feb. 24, 1864	3	Capt'd at William's Farm, Va., June 22, '64—died at Andersonville, Ga., Oct. 10, '64—grave, 10,632.
Wardlow, Richard	do	Feb. 13, 1864	3	Not on muster-out roll.
Wallace, George W	do	Feb. 17, 1864	3	Not on muster-out roll.
Watling, Charles	do	Aug. 6, 1862	3	Transferred to Co. B, Jan. 26, '63.
Warner, Henry	do	June 26, 1862	3	Not on muster-out roll.
Young, William	do	Mar. 17, 1864	3	Absent, sick, at muster out.
Yard, Jacob	do	Feb. 13, 1864	3	Died at Washington, D. C., Nov. 25, '64.
Young, Silus	do		3	Wounded at Wilderness, May 5, '64—capt'd and died in prison at Salisbury, N. C.
Zang, Malchior	do	Feb. 11, 1864	3	Killed at Po River, Va., May 10, '64.

Company F.

NAME.	RANK.	DATE OF MUSTER INTO SERVICE.	TERM—YEARS.	REMARKS.
Wellington Jones	Captain	Feb. 23, 1864	3	Disch. on Surgeon's certificate, June 27, '64.
Wm. A. Shoener	do	Feb. 23, 1864	3	Promoted from 2d Lieut., Jan. 17, '65—disch. by special order, June 14, '65.
Joseph B. Kite	1st Lieut.	July 17, 1862	3	Resigned Dec. 4, '62.
Peter H. Frailey	do	Feb. 23, 1864	3	Disch. on Surgeon's certificate, June 2, '64.
George Reber	do	Feb. 19, 1864	3	W'd. at Wilderness, Va., May 8, '64—pr.fr.Sgt., Feb. 14, '65—com. Capt., June 15, '65—not mus.—mus. out with company, July 14, '65.

NAME.	RANK.	DATE OF MUSTER INTO SERVICE.	TERM—YEARS.	REMARKS.
Louis J. Sacriste	2d Lieut.	Sept. 1, 1862	3	Promoted to 1st Lieut. Co. D, Mar. 1, '63.
Edward S. Kline	1st Sgt.	Feb. 19, 1864	3	Wd. at Reams Station, Va., Aug. 25, '64—mus. out with company, July 14, '65—Vet.
Robert Scarlett	do	Aug. 7, 1862	3	Discharged for disability, Feb. 11, '63.
Wm. M. Wagner	Sergeant	Feb. 19, 1864	3	Wd. at Cold Harbor, Va., June 2, '64—com. 2d Lieut., July 1, '65—not mustered—mustered out with company, July 14, '65—Vet.
Horace B. Klock	do	Feb. 19, 1864	3	Mus. out with company, July 14, '65—Vet.
Charles Maurer	do	Feb. 19, 1864	3	Pr. to Sergeant. Feb. 1, '65—mustered out with company, July 14, '65—Vet.
Daniel Moyer	do	Feb. 19, 1864	3	Missing in action, at Spottsylvania C. H., Va., May 12, '64.
James Dempsey	do		3	Died, 1863, at Fredericksburg, Va.—grave, 37, Sec. A, Div. D, Nat. Cem., Fredericksburg.
Levi P. Miller	Corporal	Feb. 19, 1864	3	Promoted to Corp., July 1, '64—mustered out with company, July 14, '65—Vet.
William L. Hutton	do	Feb. 19, 1864	3	Wounded at Fredericksburg, Dec. 13, '62, while member of Co. K, 127th Pa Vols.—wd. at Deep Bottom, Aug. 18, '64—wd at Five Forks, March 31, '65—mustered out with company.
Solomon Kamp	do	Feb. 19, 1864	3	Promoted to Corp., Feb. 1, '65—mustered out with company, July 14, '65—Vet.
Wm. H. Webber	do	Feb. 19, 1864	3	Promoted to Corp., May 1, '65—mustered out with company, July 14, '65.
Franklin Wagner	do	Feb. 19, 1864	3	Promoted to Corp., June 1, '65—mustered out with company, July 24, '65.
Solomon Everly	do	Feb. 19, 1864	3	Wounded at Totopotomy River, Va., May 31, '64—absent, sick, at muster out—Vet.
Chris. Dieffenderfer	do	Feb. 19, 1864	3	Captured at Reams Station, Va., Aug. 25, '64—died at Salisbury, N. C., Nov. 4, '64.
Adam Wagner	do	Feb. 19, 1864	3	Killed at Petersburg, Va., June 14, '64—Vet.
William Moser	do	Feb. 19, 1864	3	Died at Alexandria, Va., June 14, of wounds received at Cold Harbor, June 3, '64—buried in National Cemetery, Arlington.
William Emrich	do	Feb. 19, 1864	3	Missing in action at Spottsylvania C. H., Va., May 12, '64—Vet.
Dan. B. Berkheiser	do	Feb. 19, 1864	3	Killed at Reams Stat'n, Va., Aug. 26, '64—Vet.
Jacob Shrader	Musician	Feb. 19, 1864	3	Prisoner from August 25, '64, to March, '65—mus. out with company, July 14, '65—Vet.
Daniel Kramer	do	Feb. 19, 1864	3	Wounded at Wilderness, Va., May 5, '64—mustered out with company, July 14, '65.
Aikman, William	Private	Feb. 19, 1864	3	Discharged by General Order, June 16, '65.
Adams, David M.	do	Apr. 12, 1864	3	Missing in action at Spottsylvania C. H., Va., May 12, '64.
Berger, John A.	do	Feb. 19, 1864	3	Killed at Cold Harbor, Va., June 3, '64.
Berkheiser, Benj.	do	Feb. 19, 1864	3	Missing in action at Spottsylvania C. H., Va., May 12, '64.
Berger, Henry A.	do	Feb. 19, 1864	3	Killed at Po River, Va., May 10, '64.
Brigel, Franklin	do	Feb. 19, 1864	3	Missing in action at Reams Station, Va., Aug. 25, '64—Vet.
Brummer, D. H.	do	Feb. 19, 1864	3	Missing in action at Po River, Va., May 10, 1864.
Baxter, John	do	Aug. 12, 1862	3	Killed at Fredericksburg, Va., Dec. 13, '62.
Bright, Philip F.	do	July 30, 1862	3	Not on muster-out roll.
Corloy, John	do	Aug. 16, 1862	3	Transferred to Co. A, Jan. 26, '63.
Cummings, John	do	Aug. 19, 1862	3	Transferred to Co. A, Jan. 26, '63.
Collins, William	do	July 12, 1862	3	Not on muster out roll.
Charters, Thomas	do	July 12, 1862	3	Not on muster-out roll.
Camden, John	do	Apr. 18, 1864	3	Not on muster-out roll.
Ditzler, Thomas	do	Feb. 19, 1864	3	Mustered out with company, July 14, '65.
Dry, William	do	Mar. 13, 1865	1	Mustered out with company, July 14, '65.
Ditzler, Elias	do	Feb. 19, 1864	3	Absent, sick, at muster out.
Day, James	do	Feb. 19, 1864	3	Captured at Reams Station, Va., Aug. 25, '64—died at Salisbury, N. C., Nov. 4, '64—burial record, Dec. 20, '64.
Derulf, Elam	do	Feb. 19, 1864	3	Missing in action at Reams Station, Va., Aug. 25, '64.

NAME.	RANK.	DATE OF MUSTER INTO SERVICE.	TERM-YEARS.	REMARKS.
Dohrman, John F.	Private	Feb. 19, 1864	3	Mis. in action at Petersburg, Va., June 22,'64.
Dolan, Michael	do	Aug. 5, 1864	3	Absent, in arrest, at muster out.
Dyson, Freeman	do	Aug. 6, 1862	3	Transferred to Co. A, Jan. 26, '63.
Duffy, James F.	do	Aug. 16, 1862	3	Transferred to Co. A, Jan. 26, '63.
Dougherty, Thomas	do	Aug. 28, 1862	3	Transferred to Co. A, Jan. 26, '63.
Dougherty, Patrick	do	Aug. 30, 1862	3	Not on muster-out roll.
Dempsey, James K.	do	Sept. 2, 1862	3	Not on muster-out roll.
Everly, Moses	do	Feb. 19, 1864	3	Wounded at Cold Harbor, Va., June 2, '64—mustered out with company, July 14, '65.
Eckman, Owen	do	Apr. 12, 1864	3	Wounded at Spottsylvania C. H., Va., May 12, '64—tr. to Vet. Res. Corps, Jan. 27, '65.
Evely, Joshua	do	Feb. 19, 1864	3	Killed at Totopotomy River, Va., May 31, '64—Vet.
Emsley, William	do	Aug. 13, 1862	3	Transferred to Co. A, Jan. 26, '63.
Ellis, Samuel	do	Aug. 18, 1862	3	Not on muster-out roll.
Faust, Semaria	do	Feb. 19, 1864	3	Mustered out with company, July 14, '65.
Freeze, Gideon	do	Feb. 19, 1864	3	Mustered out with company, July 14, '65.
Freeze, John	do	Feb. 19, 1864	3	Died at City Point, Va., June 27, '64.
Fahl, Daniel	do	Feb. 19, 1864	3	Missing in action at Petersburg, Va., June 16, '64.
Garth, John S.	do	July 30, 1862	3	Not on muster-out roll.
Green, John	do	Aug. 9, 1862	3	Not on muster-out roll.
Gorman, Samuel	do	Sept. 1, 1862	3	Not on muster-out roll.
Hahn, John G	do	Mar. 24, 1864	3	Wounded at Five Forks, Va., March 31, '65—wounded at Reams Station, Aug. 25, '64—disch. Aug. 7, to date July 14, '65—Vet.
Hendricks, A. W.	do	Feb. 28, 1864	3	Brigade Hospital Steward—mustered out with regiment.
Henny, Daniel	do	Feb. 19, 1864	3	Captured at Reams Station, Va., Aug. 25, '64 wounded at Wilderness—discharged by General Order, June 27, '65.
Hunker, John J.	do	Feb. 19, 1864	3	Died at Brandy Station, Va., April 20, '64—buried in Military Asylum Cemetery, D. C.
Hoffman, Peramus	do	Feb. 19, 1864	3	Died at Annapolis, Md., Oct. 14, '64.
Herring, Levi	do	Feb. 19, 1864	3	Died at Washington, D. C., Sept. 13, '64—burec., buried in Cypress Hill Cem., L. I.
Heinback, Lewis	do	Feb. 19, 1864	3	Killed at Petersburg, Va., June 16, '64.
Houck, Charles T.	do	Feb. 19, 1864	3	Killed at Cold Harbor, Va., June 3, '64.
Johnson, Joseph M	do	Feb. 19, 1864	3	Killed at Po River, Va., May 10, '64.
Kramer, Francis S.	do	Feb. 19, 1864	3	Mustered out with company, July 14, '65.
Kamp, Reuben	do	Feb. 19, 1864	3	Absent, sick, at muster out.—Vet.—prisoner.
Kramer, Samuel	do	Feb. 19, 1864	3	Absent, sick, at muster out.
Knapp, Cyrus	do	Feb. 19, 1864	3	Wounded at Wilderness, Va., May 5, '64—discharged by General Order, June 27, '65.
Kramer, Thomas S.	do	Feb. 19, 1864	3	Died at Annapolis, Md., March 13, '65—Vet.
Koch, Isaiah	do	Feb. 19, 1864	3	Missing in action at Reams Station, Va., Aug. 25, '64.
Kramer, Francis	do	Feb. 19, 1864	3	Mustered out with company.
Kramer, George	do	Feb. 19, 1864	3	Wounded at Cold Harbor.
Kramer, Daniel	do			Wounded at Wilderness—mustered out with company.
Knight, Thomas	do	Aug. 6, 1862	3	Not on muster-out roll.
Kelley, Henry C.	do	Aug. 14, 1862	3	Not on muster-out roll.
Kite, William S.	do	Aug. 19, 1862	3	Wounded at Fredericksburg, Va., Dec. 13, '62—transferred to Co. A, Jan. 26, '63.
Kanady, Thomas	do	Aug. 23, 1862	3	Not on muster-out roll.
Kalsher, Charles	do	Apr. 18, 1864	3	Not on muster-out roll.
Lawrence, Jeremiah	do	Feb. 19, 1864	3	Mustered out with company, July 14, '65—Vet.
Lahone, Jonathan	do	Feb. 19, 1864	3	Wounded at Po River, Va., May 10, '64—mustered out with company, July 14, '65.—Vet.
Lynn, Daniel	do	Apr. 12, 1864	3	Mustered out with company, July 14, '65—wounded June 16, '64.
Lister, Thomas J.	do	Aug. 6, 1862	3	Not on muster-out roll.
Lister, William	do	Aug. 23, 1862	3	Not on muster-out roll.
Lynch, James	do	Apr. 18, 1864	3	Not on muster-out roll.
Moyer, June	do	Feb. 19, 1864	3	Mus. out with company, July 14, '65—Vet.

NAME.	RANK.	DATE OF MUSTER INTO SERVICE.	TERM—YEARS.	REMARKS.
Moyer, Lewis E.	Private	Feb. 19, 1864	3	Mustered out with company, July 14, '65.
Morgan, Joseph P.	do	Feb. 19, 1864	3	Wounded at Cold Harbor, Va., June 2, '64—mustered out with company, July 14, '65.
Murphy, Daniel	do	Feb. 19, 1864	3	Mus. out with company, July 14, '65—Vet.
Miller, Tobias W.	do	Feb. 19, 1864	3	Discharged Jan. 19, '65, for wounds received at Cold Harbor, Va., June 2, '64.
Miller, Lewis M.	do	Feb. 19, 1864	3	Discharged by General Order, May 31, '65.
Moyer, Albert I.	do	Feb. 19, 1864	3	Discharged by General Order, May 15, '65.
Mengle, Reuben	do	Feb. 19, 1864	3	Discharged by General Order, July 6, '65.
Moyer, Charles H.	do	Feb. 19, 1864	3	Missing in action at Spottsylvania C. H., Va., May 12, '64.
Moyer, Charles	do	Feb. 19, 1864	3	Missing in action, Po River, Va.. May 10,'64.
Murray, Matthew	do	July 26, 1862	3	Transferred to Co. A, Jan. 26, '63.
Mills, Charles	do	Aug. 22, 1862	3	Wounded at Fredericksburg, Va., Dec. 13,'62—transferred to Co. A, Jan. 26, '63.
Miller, Thomas	do	July 12, 1862	3	Wounded at Gettysburg—transferred to Battery A, 4th U. S. Artillery.
Moore, Jesse	do	Aug. 30, 1862	3	Not on muster-out roll.
McNamara, Matthew	do	July 29, 1862	3	Transferred to Co. A, Jan. 26, '63.
McCready, James	do	Aug. 11, 1862	3	Transferred to Co. A, Jan. 26, '63.
McGlensey, Charles	do	Aug. 18, 1862	3	Not on muster-out roll.
McCutcheon, John	do	Aug. 23, 1862	3	Not on muster-out roll.
McGinty, Hugh	do	Aug, 23, 1862	3	Not on muster-out roll.
McDonnell, James	do	Aug. 23, 1862	3	Not on muster-out roll.
Neyer, Isaac	do	Feb. 19, 1864	3	Discharged by General Order, June 6, '65.
Peteas, Robert	do	July 12, 1862	3	Not on muster-out roll.
Rahn, Jacob	do	Feb. 19, 1864	3	Mustered out with company, July 14, '65.
Reppert, Henry	do	Feb. 19, 1864	3	Wounded at Spottsylvania C. H., Va., May 18,'64—mus. out with company, July 14,'65.
Reber, Franklin	do	Feb. 19, 1864	3	Prisoner from May 14,'64, to April 12,'65—discharged by General Order, June 22, '65.
Reinheimer, A L.	do	Feb. 19, 1864	3	Wounded at Cold Harbor, Va., June 2,'64—transferred to Vet. Res. Corps, April 28, '65 discharged by General Order, July 24, '65.
Reber, Joseph B.	do	Feb. 19, 1864	3	Captured at Reams Station, Va., Aug. 25'64—died at Salisbury, N. C., Jan. 26, '65—Vet.
Reppert, Amos	do	Feb. 19, 1864	3	Died at New York, Oct. 27, '64.
Raush, Nathan	do	Feb. 19, 1864	3	Died July 22, of wounds received at Petersburg, Va., June 16,'64—buried in Cyp. Hill Cemetery, L. I.
Reichert, Charles K	do	Feb. 19, 1864	3	Died June 20, of wounds received at Cold Harbor, Va., June 3, '64.
Reichert, Christian	do	Feb. 19, 1864	3	Missing in action at Reams Station, Va., Aug. 25, '64.
Robinson, Joseph H.	do	Mar. 24, 1864	3	Not on muster-out roll.
Shoener, Morgan	do	Feb. 19, 1864	3	Prisoner from May 5 to Dec.,'64—mustered out with company, July 14, '65—Vet.
Smith, Clayton	do	Apr. 12, 1864	3	Transferred to Vet. Res Corps—discharged on Surgeon's certificate, June 7, '65.
Shoener, Richard	do	Feb. 19, 1864	3	Killed at Cold Harbor, Va., June 3, '64—Vet.
Sacriste, Sebastian	do	July 30, 1862	3	Transferred to Co. A, Jan. 26, '63.
Stewart, William	do	July 26, 1862	3	Transferred to Battery A, 4th U. S. Artillery.
Smith, John	do	Aug. 8, 1862	3	Not on muster-out roll.
Stevens, Charles	do	Aug. 14, 1862	3	Not on muster-out roll.
Stait, Daniel	do	Aug. 22, 1862	3	Wounded at Fredericksburg, Va., Dec. 13,'62—not on muster-out roll.
Titlow, Abr'm S.	do	Aug. 30, 1862	3	Not on muster-out roll.
Thompson, John	do	Mar. 24, 1864	3	Not on muster-out roll.
Updyke, Amos	do	July 12, 1862	3	Not on muster-out roll.
Ubele, Joshua	do		3	Killed May 30,'64, at Totopotomy Creek,Va.
Ubele, Moses	do		3	Wounded at Cold Harbor, June 3, '64.
Woollis, Willoug'y	do	Feb. 19, 1864	3	Wounded at Spottsylvania C. H., Va., May 12, '64—mustered out with Co., July 14, '64.
Webber, Franklin	do	Feb. 19, 1864	3	Wounded at Cold Harbor, Va., June 2, '64—tr. to Vet. Res. Corps, June 6, '65.
Wanner, William	do	Feb. 19, 1864	3	Died at Washington, D. C., Jan. 5 '65—bu. record, Feb. 6,'65—buried in Nat. Cem., Arlington, Va.—Vet.

NAME.	RANK.	DATE OF MUSTER INTO SERVICE.	TERM—YEARS.	REMARKS.
Webber, John	do	Feb. 19, 1864	3	Captured at Spottsylvania C. H., Va., May 12, '64—died at Andersonville, Ga., Sept. 7, '64—grave, 8,081.
White, James	do	Feb. 19, 1864	3	Killed at Wilderness, Va., May 5, '64.
Wagner, Joseph	do	Feb. 19, 1864	3	Died July 17, of wounds received at Petersburg, Va., June 22, '64—bu. in Nat. Cem., Arlington—Vet.
Wagner, John	do	Feb. 19, 1864	3	Died Jan. 7, '65
Wagner, Martin M	do	Feb. 19, 1864	3	Missing in action at Po River, Va., May 10, '64—Vet
Wadsworth, Job	do	July 26, 1862	3	Transferred to Co. A, Jan. 26, '63.
Wright, John C	do	July 26, 1862	3	Transferred to Co D—date unknown.
Williams, James	do	Mar. 28, 1864	3	Not on muster-out roll.
Webber, Wm. H	do		3	Mustered out with company.

Company G.

NAME.	RANK.	DATE OF MUSTER INTO SERVICE.	TERM—YEARS.	REMARKS.
Lawrence Kelley	Captain	Aug. 2, 1862	3	Discharged by special order, Jan. 27, '63.
Frank R. Leib	do	Mar. 9, 1864	3	Wd. at Cold Harbor, Va., June 3, '64—Bv. Major, Mar. 13, '65—discharged by G. O., Oct. 3, '64.
Francis McGuigan	do	Aug. 12, 1862	3	Pr. fr. priv. Co. B to 1st Lt., Apr. 4, '64—to Capt., Jan. 9, '65—disch. by G.O., June 3, '65.
S. G. Vanderheyden	do	Mar. 9, 1864	3	Wd. at Spottsylvania C. H., Va., May 18, '64—pr. fr. 2d to 1st Lt., Jan. 9, '65—to Capt., June 12, '65—mus. out with Co., July 14, '65.
Edmund Randall	1st Lieut.	July 8, 1862	3	Discharged by special order, Jan. 27, '63.
Garrett Nowlen	do	Aug. 2, 1862	3	Wd. at Fredericksburg, Va., Dec. 13, '62—disch. as 2d Lt., Jan. 27, '63—com. 1st Lt., Feb. 27, '63—promoted to Adj., Mar. 1, '63.
William A. Klock	1st Sgt.	Feb. 29, 1864	3	Wd. at Petersburg, Va., June 16, '64—pr. to 1st Sgt., Jan. 1, '65—com. 1st Lt., June 6, '65—not mus.—mus. out with Co., July 14, '65—Vet.
Edward J. Rogers	do	June 17, 1864	3	Wounded at Fredericksburg, Va., Dec. 13, '62—not on muster-out roll.
Israel Seitzinger	Sergeant.	Apr. 5, 1864	3	Mustered out with company, July 14, '65.
George A. Cook	do	Feb. 10, 1864	3	Wounded at Petersburg, June 16, '64—mustered out with company, July 14, '65.
James F. Kressley	do	Mar 3, 1864	3	Promoted to Sgt., June 1st, '65—mustered out with company, July 14, '65.
Charles M. Garber	do	Mar. 9, 1864	3	Promoted to Sgt., June 1st, '65—mustered out with company, July 14, '65.
Jas. M. Seitzinger	do	Apr. 5, 1864	3	Promoted to Sgt., June 3, '64—wounded at Reams Station, Va., Aug. 25, '64—disch. by General Order, May 31, '65.
Charles Shelley	do	Feb. 29, 1864	3	Promoted to Com. Sgt., June 11, '65—Vet.
Wm. H. Harman	do	June 15, 1862	3	Transferred to Co. A, Jan. 26, '63.
George H. Bunting	do	June 20, 1862	3	Not on muster-out roll.
Thomas McKelvey	do	June 24, 1862	3	Not on muster-out roll.
John C. Marley	do	July 8, 1862	3	Killed at Fredericksburg, Va., Dec. 13, '62.
Amos F. Butler	Corporal	Mar. 3, 1864	3	Promoted to Corporal, July 26, '64—mustered out with company, July 14, '65—Vet.
H. M. Seitzinger	do	Mar. 10, 1864	3	Promoted to Corporal, July 26, '64—mustered out with company, July 14, '65.
John McKinsey	do	Mar. 7, 1864	3	Promoted to Corporal, Oct. 25, '64—mustered out with company, July 14, '65.
N. M. Bretzieus	do	Mar. 24, 1864	3	Promoted to Corporal, Apr. 15, '65—mustered out with company, July 14, '65.
Halley Barr	do	Mar. 10, 1864	3	Promoted to Corporal, June 1, '65—mustered out with company, July 14, '65.
Benjamin Dewalt	do	Mar. 12, 1864	3	Wounded at Reams Station, Va., Aug. 25, '64—promoted to Corporal, June 1, '65—mustered out with company, July 14, '65.
Ephraim W. Ney	do	Mar. 31, 1864	3	Promoted to Corporal, June 1, '65—mustered out with company, July 14, '65—Vet.

NAME.	RANK.	DATE OF MUSTER INTO SERVICE.	TERM—YEARS.	REMARKS.
Henry R. Quinter	Corporal	Mar. 10, 1864	3	Wounded at Petersburg, Va., June 22, '64—disch. by General Order—date unknown.
Abraham Foust	do	Mar. 5, 1864	3	Wd. and cap. at Spottsylvania C. H., Va., May 12, '64—died at Richmond—date unknown.
Samuel S. Kramer	do	Feb. 29, 1864	3	Missing at Petersburg, Va., June 22,'64—Vet.
Charles Gallagher	do	July 29, 1862	3	Transferred to Co. A, Jan. 26, '63.
Frederick Wagner	do	June 16, 1862	3	Pr. to Hospital Steward—date unknown.
William H. Milner	do	June 16, 1862	3	Wounded at Fredericksburg, Va., Dec. 13,'62—not on muster-out roll.
Francis Adams	do	June 24, 1862	3	Not on muster-out roll.
Samuel White	do	June 24, 1862	3	Not on muster-out roll.
James Byrnes	do	July 29, 1862	3	Wounded at Fredericksburg, Va., Dec. 13,'62—not on muster-out roll.
Charles Kleeplatt	do	Aug. 1, 1862	3	Not on muster-out roll.
John McCormick	do	July 8, 1862	3	Tr. to Battery A, 4th U. S. Artillery—killed.
Edward Harris	Musician	Mar. 15, 1864	3	Not on muster-out roll.
James Kelley	do	June 26, 1862	3	Not on muster-out roll.
Henry Adams	do	June 26, 1862	3	Transferred to Co B—date unknown.
Adams, Cassius	Private	Mar 19, 1864	3	Wounded at Petersburg, Va., June 22, '64—discharged by General Order, June 15, '65.
Allen, John	do	July 25, 1862	3	Not on muster-out roll.
Berger, George	do	Feb. 29, 1864	3	Absent, sick, at muster out.
Boyer, Elias	do	Feb. 29, 1864	3	Wounded at Wilderness, Va., May 5, '64—tr. to Vet. Reserve Corps—date unknown.
Barr, John	do	Feb. 20, 1864	3	Died May 25, '64.
Buchner, Adam	do	Mar. 24, 1864	3	Captured at Po River, May 10, '64—died at Andersonville, Ga., July 27,'64—grave, 4,084.
Becker, William H	do	Mar. 10, 1864	3	Missing in action, July 26, '64.
Brocklehurst, Rob't	do	July 8, 1862	3	Transferred to Co. A, Jan. 26, '63.
Barr, Dennis	do	June 28, 1862	3	Not on muster-out roll.
Brown, James	do	June 30, 1862	3	Not on muster-out roll.
Busby Samuel	do	June 27, 1862	3	Not on muster-out roll.
Chambers, Morgan	do	Feb. 29, 1864	3	Wounded in action, Sept. 25, '64—absent, in hospital, at muster out.
Christ, Charles	do	Mar. 10, 1864	3	Disch. by General Order, date unknown.
Cooper, Thomas	do	Mar. 5, 1864	3	Killed at Petersburg, Va., June 22, '64.
Cook, John G	do	Aug. 18, 1862	3	Died Nov. 7,'62—bu. in Mil. Asy. Cem., D.C.
Cole, Neil	do	July 12, 1862	3	Not on muster-out roll.
Deitzler, Henry	do	Feb. 29, 1864	3	Captured at Reams Station, Va., Aug. 25, '64—died Mar. 28, '65—buried in Nat. Cem., London Park, Baltimore, Md.
De Bowman, Chas	do	Aug. 1, 1862	3	Not on muster-out roll.
Dennis, John	do	July 10, 1862	3	Not on muster-out roll.
Dorsey, Dennis	do	July 23, 1862	3	Not on muster-out roll.
Doyle, William	do	July 11, 1862	3	Not on muster-out roll.
Dunn, John, 1st	do	June 16, 1862	5	Not on muster-out roll.
Dunn, John, 2d	do	Aug. 28, 1862	3	Transferred to Co. A, Jan. 26, '63.
Edmonston, Rob't	do		3	Discharged by special order, Mar. 18, '64.
Fennel, William	do	Mar. 10, 1864	3	Mustered out with company, July 14, '65.
Freeby, George	do	Mar. 10, 1864	3	Disch. on Surgeon's certificate, Dec. 18, '64.
Fields, John	do	June 13, 1862	3	Not on muster-out roll.
Franks, Frank B	do	June 30, 1862	3	Not on muster-out roll.
Gearing, John	do	Mar. 24, 1864	3	Mustered out with company, July 14, '65.
Goodman, George	do	Apr. 18, 1864	3	Mustered out with company, July 14, '65.
Green, Jesse	do	Apr. 5, 1864	3	Wounded at Cold Harbor, Va., June 2, '64—discharged by General Order, July 7, '65.
Gebhert, Edm'd L	do	Feb. 29, 1864	3	Died at Washington, D. C., Oct. 16,'64—bur. in National Cemetery, Arlington, Va.
Giltman, John	do	July 12, 1862	3	Transferred to Co. A, Jan. 26, '63.
Green, Wm	do	July 8, 1862	3	Not on muster-out roll.
German, Wm	do	July 21, 1862	3	Not on muster-out roll.
Gorman, Bernard	do	July 25, 1862	3	Not on muster-out roll.
Gibbs, James	do	July 29, 1862	3	Not on muster-out roll.
Gravell, George	do	Aug. 1, 1862	3	Transferred to company A, Jan. 26, 1863.
Giger, John	do	Aug. 13, 1862	3	Transferred to company A, Jan. 26, 1863.
Gedds, Alexander	do	Aug. 14, 1862	3	Not on muster-out roll.
Heater, Franklin	do	Mar. 17, 1864	3	Mustered out with company, July 14, 1865.

THREE YEARS' SERVICE.

NAME.	RANK.	DATE OF MUSTER INTO SERVICE.	TERM—YEARS.	REMARKS.
Hasler, Frederick	Private	Mar. 3, 1864	3	Wd. at Reams Station, Va., Aug. 25, '64—m. s. out with company, July 14, 1865—Vet.
Hoffman, John H	do	Mar. 5, 1864	3	Mustered out with company, July 14, 1865.
Heinback, Wm. B	do	Feb. 29, 1864	3	Wd. at Spottsylvania C. H., Va., May 12, '64—absent, in hospital, at muster out.
Hartz, Francis	do	Mar. 17, 1864	3	Wd. at Cold Harbor, Va., June 2, 1864—absent, in hospital, at muster out.
Harren, Edward	do	Mar. 25, 1864	3	Wd. at Spottsylvania C. H., Va., May 18, '64—discharged by Gen. Order, July 6, 1865.
Herring, Isaac	do	Feb. 29, 1864	3	Pris. from Aug. 25, 1864, to Feb. 28, 1865—disch. by General Order, June 21, 1865.
Harker, John W	do	Feb. 29, 1864	3	Wd. at Cold Harbor, Va., June 2, 1864—tr. to Vet. Res. Corps—date unknown.
Heinback, Wm	do	Feb. 29, 1864	3	Capt'd at Spottsylvania C. H., Va., May 12, '64—died at Andersonville, Ga.—date unk.
Heinback, John	do	Feb. 29, 1864	3	Capt'd at Petersburg, Va., June 22, '64—died at Andersonville, Ga., Oct. 12, '64—grave 10,814.
Hummel, Jacob	do	Mar. 5, 1864	3	Capt'd at Reams Station, Va., Aug. 25, '64—died at Andersonville, Ga.—date unknown—Vet.
Herring, Paul	do	Feb. 29, 1864	3	Mis. in action at Reams Station.
Hummel, Jonathan	do	Feb. 29, 1864	3	Pris. from July 27, '64, to Mar. 1, '65—disch. by General Order, June 29, '65.
Hoffman, Henry	do	Mar. 10, 1864	3	Missing in action at Reams Station, Va., Aug 25, '64.
Hibbs, Joseph H	do	Aug. 12, 1862		Transferred to Co. A, Jan. 26, '63.
Heinback, S	do			Died Aug. 14, '64, at Andersonville, Ga.—grave 5,688.
Hutchinson, Wm	do	June 24, 1862	3	Transferred to Co. A, Jan. 26, '63.
Hare, William	do	June 24, 1862	3	Killed at Fredericksburg, Dec. 13, '62.
Johnston, Wm. H	do	June 24, 1862	3	Not on muster-out roll.
Jones, William	do	June 24, 1862	3	Not on muster-out roll.
Jones, Frank	do	July 15, 1862	3	Not on muster-out roll.
Kramer, Isaac	do	Mar. 10, 1864	3	Mustered out with company, July 14, '65.
Kissmer, Wm. H	do	Mar. 31, 1864	3	Mustered out with company, July 14, '65.
Koch, George W	do	Jan. 3, 1865	3	Absent, sick, at muster out.
Kramer, George	do	Feb. 19, 1864	3	Capt'd at Petersburg, Va., June 22, '64—died at Andersonville, Ga., Oct. 30, '64—grave, 11,645.
Krouse, Gottlieb	do	Mar. 31, 1864	3	Mis. in act'n at Petersburg, Va., June 22, '64.
Krewson, Alban's L	do	June 13, 1852	3	Not on muster-out roll.
Kavanaugh, Peter	do	July 20, 1862	3	Not on muster out roll.
Kelly, James	do	Aug. 20, 1862	3	Killed at Fredericksburg, Va., Dec. 13, '62.
Long, Lewis D	do	Mar. 12, 1864	3	Wd. at Spottsylvania C H., Va., May 12, '64—disch. by Gen. Order, Aug. 7, '65.
Lutz, Mahlon	do	Mar. 10, 1864	3	Wd. at Cold Harbor, Va., June 2, '64—tr. to Vet. Res. Corps—date unknown.
Lawler, John	do	July 30, 1862	3	Not on muster-out roll.
Matz, Leon D	do	Feb. 29, 1864	3	Wd. at Petersburg, Va., June 16, '64—must. out with company, July 14, 1865.
Moyer, William	do	Mar. 12, 1864	3	Mustered out with company July 14, '65.
Miller, John	do	Apr. 3, 1865	3	Mustered out with company, July 14, '65.
Miller, Thomas	do	Mar. 3, 1864	3	Wd. at Wilderness, Va., May 5, '64—absent in hospital, at muster out.
Moyer, Michael	do	Apr. 5, 1864	3	Tr. to Vet. Res. Corps—date unknown—disch. by General Order, Aug. 23, '65.
Moyer, Jonathan Y	do	Feb. 20, 1864	3	Died at White House, Va., Aug. 12, of wounds received at Cold Harbor, June 3, '64—buried in Nat'l Cemetery, Arlington.
Marberger, John C	do	Mar. 5, 1864	3	Died at Washington, D. C., Sept. 8, of wds. rec. at Reams Station, Va., Aug. 25, '64—buried in National Cemetery, Arlington.
Moyer, James F	do	Mar. 5, 1864	3	Died at Washington, D. C., June 26, '64.
Markland, James	do	June 13, 1862	3	Not on muster-out roll.
Monaghan, Felix	do	June 13, 1862	3	Not on muster-out roll.
Miles, Edward E	do	June 30, 1862	3	Not on muster-out roll.

NAME	RANK	DATE OF MUSTER INTO SERVICE.	TERM—YEARS.	REMARKS.
Martin, Hugh	Private	July 12, 1862	3	Not on muster-out roll.
Moxley, William	do	July 31, 1862	3	Transferred to Co. A, Jan. 26, '63.
Manning, Mark	do	Aug. 1, 1862	3	Not on muster-out roll.
McCafferty, John	do	Feb. 25, 1864	3	Wd. at Cold Harbor, Va., June 2, '64—mus. out with company, July 14, '65.
McVey, William	do	Sept. 28, 1864	3	Trans. to Vet. Res. Corps—date unknown—discharged by General Order, June 28, '65.
McSorley, Patrick	do	July 9, 1862	3	Transferred to Co. A, Jan. 26, '63.
McLane, John	do	July 28, 1862	3	Not on muster-out roll.
McCullow, John	do	July 29, 1862	3	Not on muster-out roll.
McGrickin, Michael	do	June 13, 1862	3	Not on muster-out roll.
McCarty, James	do	July 14, 1862	3	Not on muster-out roll.
McGinley, Charles	do	July 19, 1862	3	Not on muster-out roll.
McLaughlin, Daniel	do	July 7, 1862	3	Not on muster-out roll.
McNulty, Henry	do	July 22, 1862	3	Not on muster-out roll.
McInire, Thomas	do	June 30, 1862	3	Not on muster-out roll.
Norton, Thomas	do	Mar. 31, 1864	3	Not on muster-out roll.
O'Harra, Henry	do	July 7, 1862	3	Wd. at Fredericksburg, Va., Dec. 13, '62—transferred to Co. A, Jan. 26, '63.
O'Conner, John	do	July 7, 1862	3	Not on muster-out roll.
O'Reeson, William	do	Aug. 1, 1862	3	Not on muster-out roll.
Poffenberger, Fran.	do	Mar. 5, 1864	3	Kill'd at Spottsylvania C. H., Va. May 18, '64.
Purdy, Thomas	do	July 29, 1862	3	Not on muster-out roll.
Price, Henry D.	do	July 5, 1862	3	Transferred to Co. B—date unknown.
Porter, Michael	do	July 22, 1862	3	Not on muster-out roll.
Quinn, Terrence	do	Aug. 28, 1862	3	Not on muster-out roll.
Reber, Franklin	do	Mar. 10, 1864	3	Wd. at Wilderness, Va., May 5, '64—discharged by General Order, May 3, '65.
Rehring, Moses	do	Mar. 25, 1864	3	Prisoner from June 23, '64, to April 29, '65—discharged by General Order, June 27, '65.
Roth, Jacob	do	Mar. 3, 1864	3	Trans. to Vet. Res. Corps—date unknown.
Ruck, Cyrus	do	Mar. 25, 1864	3	Capt'd at Petersburg, Va., June 22, '64—died at Lynchburg, Aug. 17, '64—buried in Poplar Grove National Cem., division E, section E, grave, 331.
Ross, John	do	July 12, 1862	3	Not on muster-out roll.
Ryan, Martin V.	do			Died July 24, '64, at Louisville, Ky., grave 63, sec. B, div. 4.
Reager, Timothy	do	July 31, 1862	3	Not on muster-out roll.
Seifried, John	do	Mar. 10, 1864	3	Mustered out with company, July 14, '65.
Sherff, Henry	do	Feb. 29, 1864	3	Mustered out with company, July 14, '65.
Schelthorn, Jacob	do	Mar. 17, 1864	3	Wd. at Spottsylvania C. H., Va., May 12, '64, and at Five Forks, March 31, '65—mus. out with company, July 14, '65.
Smith, Adam S.	do	Mar. 17, 1864	3	Mus. out with company, July 14, '65—Vet.
Sellers, Jacob	do	Apr. 5, 1864	3	Mustered out with company, July 14, '65.
Stout, Daniel	do	Mar. 10, 1864	3	Wd. at Cold Harbor, Va., June 2, '64—discharged by General Order, June 26, '65.
Smith, George S.	do	Feb. 24, 1864	3	Prisoner from Aug. 25, '64, to March 12, '65—discharged by General Order, June 22, '65.
Snyder, Peter	do	Mar. 5, 1864	3	Disch. on Surgeon's certificate, July 28, '64.
Sherman, Adam	do	Feb. 20, 1864	3	Killed at Cold Harbor, Va., June 3, '64—burial record, June 12, '64—buried in National Cemetery, Arlington.
Sherman, John	do	Mar. 10, 1864	3	Died at Washington, D. C., June 30, '64—buried in National Cem., Arlington, Va.
Smith, Samuel	do	Mar. 10, 1864	3	Missing in action July 26, '64.
Schor, Paul	do	July 31, 1862	3	Not on muster-out roll.
Seed, Joseph	do	July 23, 1862	3	Not on muster-out roll.
Smith, Josiah	do	June 16, 1862	3	Transferred to Co. A, Jan. 26, '63.
Scott, Joseph B.	do	July 5, 1862	3	Not on muster-out roll.
Sayer, John	do	July 22, 1862	3	Not on muster-out roll.
Steigwalt, Lewis	do	Mar. 3, 1864	3	Not on muster-out roll.
Trumbo, Henry H.	do	Feb. 20, 1864	3	Kill'd at Spottsylvania C.H.,Va., May 12,'64.
Tucker, William	do	Mar. 3, 1864	3	Died at Washington, D. C., Aug. 5, '64—buried in National Cem., Arlington, Va.
Taylor, Francis	do	June 13, 1863	3	Transferred to Co. A, Jan. 26, '63.

THREE YEARS' SERVICE. 411

NAME.	RANK.	DATE OF MUSTER INTO SERVICE.	TERM-YEARS	REMARKS.
Turner, George	Private	Aug. 22, 1862	3	Transferred to Co. A, Jan. 26, '63.
Tonner, William	do	Aug. 1, 1862	3	Not on muster-out roll.
Torrins, Wm. 1st	do	June 25, 1862	3	Not on muster-out roll.
Torrins, Wm. 2d	do	June 30, 1862	3	Not on muster-out roll.
Thornton, William	do	June 28, 1862	3	Not on muster-out roll.
Vannata, Squire H.	do			Died Dec. 25, '64—buried U. S. General Hosp. Cem., Annapolis, Md.
Wolf, William	do	Mar. 3, 1864	3	Mustered out with company, July 14, '65.
Wanner, Franklin	do	Feb. 29, 1864	3	Died at Annapolis, Md., Dec. 25, '64, grave 756.
Wilson, Andrew	do	Feb. 29, 1864	3	Capt'd at Reams Station, Va., Aug. 25, '64—died at Salisbury, N. C., Feb. 10, '65.
Wintermouth, Geo.	do	Mar. 10, 1864	3	Missing in action at Spottsylvania C. H., Va., May 12, '64.
Wilson, Ambrose O.	do	June 24, 1862	3	Transferred to Co. A, Jan. 26, '63.
Williams, John	do	July 10, 1862	3	Not on muster-out roll
White, Thomas J.	do	July 14, 1862	3	Killed at Wilderness, May 5, '64.
Walls, John	do	July 1, 1862	3	Died of Wounds at Fredericksburg, Va. Dec. 13, '62.
Zanes, William	do	Mar. 7, 1864	3	Wounded at Five Forks, Va., March 31,'65—mustered out with company, July 14,'65.

COMPANY H.

NAME	RANK	DATE OF MUSTER INTO SERVICE	TERM-YEARS	REMARKS
John Smith	Captain	Sept. 1, 1862	3	Wounded at Fredericksburg, Va., Dec. 13, '62—discharged by special order, Jan. 27,'63.
David W. Megraw	do	Mar. 2, 1864	3	Promoted to Major, Jan. 28, '65.
Robert J. Alston	do	Feb. 23, 1864	3	Wounded at Spottsylvania C. H., Va., May 12, '64—pr. from 1st Lt., Feb. 13, '65—com. Major, June 3, and Lt. Col., June 4, '65—not mustered—mustered out with company, July 14, '65.
George A. Henry	1st Lieut.	June 11, 1862	3	Pr. from 2d Lt., Sept 2, '62—dis. Nov. 22,'62.
Francis T. Quinlan	do	Sept. 1, 1862	3	Pr. from 1st Sergeant, Sept. 16, '62—to Captain Co. B, March 7, '63.
Jacob Foerst	do	Feb. 22, 1864	3	Wounded at Cold Harbor, Va., June 5, '64—pr. from Sergt. to 1st Sergt., July 1, '64—to 1st Lt., Feb. 14, '65—mustered out with company, July 14, '65.
Richard H. Wade	2d Lieut.	Aug. 8, 1862	3	Promoted from Q. M. Sergeant, Nov. 1,'62—to Q. M., January 26, '63.
Thompson W. Smith	do	Mar. 2, 1864	3	Disch. on Surgeon's certificate, Oct. 8, '64.
Robert P. Brown	1st Sergt.	Feb. 11, 1864	3	Pr. from Sergeant, Feb. 14, '65—mustered out with company, July 14, '65—Vet.
John A. Graham	do	Feb. 15, 1864	3	Died at Alexandria, June 18, of wounds received at Cold Harbor, Va., June 3, '64 grave 2,135.
John Farley	do	July 15, 1862	3	Killed at Fredericksburg, Va., Dec. 13, '62.
Henry Mertz	Sergeant	Feb. 25, 1864	3	Wounded at Spottsylvania C. H., May 18, '64—pr. from Corporal, July 1, '64—mustered out with company, July 14, '65—Vet.
David C. Jackson	do	Feb. 6, 1864	3	Promoted from Corporal, Dec. 1, '64—mustered out with company, July 14, '65.
David Powell	do	Feb. 25, 1864	3	Promoted to Corporal, Sept. 1, '64—to Sergt., Dec. 1, '64—mustered out with company, July 14, '65—Vet.
John A. Gray	do	Feb. 8, 1864	3	Wounded at Spottsylvania C. H., May 12, '64—promoted from Corporal, Aug. 1, '64—mustered out with company. July 14, '65.
Frederick Shawn	do	Feb. 8, 1864	3	Died July 31, of wounds received at Petersburg, Va., June 24, '64—buried in National Cemetery, Arlington.

NAME.	RANK.	DATE OF MUSTER INTO SERVICE.	TERM—YEARS.	REMARKS.
Henry W. Case	Sergeant	Feb. 27, 1864	3	Died Aug. 13, of wounds received at Spottsylvania C. H., Va., May 12, '64—buried in National Cemetery, Arlington.
Bernard McCahey	......do	July 10, 1862	3	Transferred to Co. D, Jan. 26, '63.
William Keiper	......do	July 7, 1862	3	Transferred to Co. D, Jan. 26, '63.
John Welsh	......do	Aug. 19, 1862	3	Not on muster-out roll.
William Kelly	......do	Aug. 19, 1862	3	Not on muster-out roll.
William Springer	Corporal	Feb. 8, 1864	3	Promoted to Corporal, Oct. 1, '64—mustered out with company, July 14, '65.
John Ward	......do	Oct. 14, 1864	3	Promoted to Corporal, Dec. 1, '64—mustered out with company, July 14, '65.
Frederick D. Rasp	......do	Feb. 6, 1864	3	Promoted to Corporal, Jan. 1, '65—mustered out with company, July 14, '65.
Joseph Gaber	......do	Feb. 16, 1864	3	Promoted to Corporal, May 1, '65—mustered out with company, July 14, '65.
John Robbins	......do	Feb. 22, 1864	3	Promoted to Corporal, June 6, '65—mustered out with company, July 14, '65.
James T. Tompkins	.... do	Feb. 23, 1864	3	Wounded at Petersburg, Va., June 16, '64—absent, in hospital, at muster out—Vet.
William H. Barker	......do	Feb. 8, 1864	3	Mustered out with company, July 14, '65—Vet.
William Wallace	......do	Feb. 26, 1864	3	Promoted to Corporal, Dec. 1, 1864—disch. by General Order, June 3, '65.
John Lutton	......do	Feb. 13, 1864	3	Promoted to Sergeant-Major, June 6, '65.
William Wertz	......do	Feb. 13, 1864	3	Killed at Spottsylvania C. H., Va., May 18, '64.
George Seip	......do	Feb. 24, 1864	3	Captured at Reams Station, Va., Aug. 25, '64—died a Salisbury, N. C., Nov. 8, '64.
John Duffey	......do	July 30, 1862	3	Transferred to Co. D, Jan. 26, '63.
Alexander Edgar	......do	July 8, 1862	3	Transferred to Co. D, Jan. 26, '63.
Robt. J. Fitzgerald	......do	July 13, 1862	3	Transfe red to Co. D, Jan. 26. '63.
John D. Myers	......do	July 9, 1862	3	Transferred to Co. D, Jan. 26, '63.
Horace Greenleaf	......do	July 8, 1862	3	Killed at Fredericksburg, Dec. 13, 1862.
Nicholas Martin	......do	July 24, 1862	3	Transferred to Co. D, Jan. 26, '63.
Chas. J. Dougherty	......do	July 25, 1862	3	Not on muster-out r ll.
Thomas McNeice	......do	Aug. 21, 1862	3	Not on muster-out roll.
James Slavin	......do	Aug. 29, 1862	3	Killed at Fredericksburg, Va., Dec. 13, '62.
Alexander Mahan	Musician	July 17, 1862	3	Transferred to Co. D, Jan. 26, ' 3.
Anderson, Robert	Private	Feb. 4, 1864	3	Prisoner from Aug. 25, '64, to March 4, '65—discharged by General Order, Aug. 7, '65.
Anderson, Joseph	......do	July 11, 1862	3	Not on muster-out roll.
Anderson, Geo. P	......do	July 26, 1862	3	Not on muster-out roll.
Atkinson, Franc. C	......do	Aug. 19, 1862	3	Not on muster-out roll.
Awes, Lewis	......do	Feb. 18, 1864	3	Not on muster-out roll.
Berwick, Alex	......do	Feb. 26, 1864	3	Mus. out with company, July 14, '65—Vet.
Brown, John	......do	Feb. 11, 1864	3	Mustered out with company, July 14, '65.
Black, Josiah B	......do	Feb. 25, 1864	3	Mustered out with company, July 14, '65.
Bennett, James	......do	Aug. 2, 1864	3	Mustered out with company, July 14, '65
Beaty, Samuel	......do	Mar. 31, 1864	3	Wounded at Cold Harbor, Va., June 3, '64—died of wounds, June 23, '64.
Belter, Rudolph	......do	Feb. 11, 1864	3	Died June 23, of wounds received at Cold Harbor, Va., June 3, '64—buried in Nat. Cem., Arlington.
Beilhartz, John	......do	Feb. 27, 1864	3	Captured at William's Farm, Va., June 22, '64—died at Andersonville, Oct. 14, '64—grave 10,943.
Bowser, James W	.... do	Feb. 15, 1864	3	Missing in action at Spottsylvania Court House, Va., May 12, '64.
Buckley, Michael J	......do	Feb. 25, 1864	3	Not on muster-out roll.
Brown, Isaac	......do	July 9, 1862	3	Transferred to Co. D, Jan. 26, '63.
Brewer, George C	......do	July 11, 1862	3	Not on muster-out roll
Harris, William	......do	July 22, 1862	3	Not on muster-out roll.
Boyle, Michael	......do	Mar. 7, 1864	3	Not on muster-out roll.
Caine, George W	......do	Feb. 9, 1864	3	Wounded at Cold Harbor, Va., June 3, '64—absent, in hospital, at muster out.
Clifford, Charles	......do	Feb. 27, 1864	3	Promoted to Sergeant-Major, June 4, '65.
Carroll, James	......do	Feb. 18, 1864	3	Miss. in action at Petersburg, Va., June 16, '64.
Curry, John H	......do	July 15, 1862	3	Transferred to Co. D, Jan. 26, '63.

THREE YEARS' SERVICE. 413

NAME.	RANK.	DATE OF MUSTER INTO SERVICE.	TERM—YEARS.	REMARKS.
Cummings, John	Private	Aug. 19, 1862	3	Transferred to Co. F—date unknown.
Casey, John M	do	Feb. 15, 1864	3	Not on muster-out roll.
Cutinar, Charles	do	July 16, 1862	3	Not on muster-out roll.
Clementine, John	do	Feb. 20, 1864	3	Not on muster-out roll.
Cook, Lewis C	do	Feb. 24, 1864	3	Not on muster-out roll.
Cox, Richard	do	Feb. 11, 1864	3	Not on muster-out roll.
Devine, Dennis	do	Feb. 4, 1864	3	Mustered out with company, July 14, '65.
Door, John	do	Feb. 15, 1864	3	Died at City Point, Va., Feb. 15, '65.
Delaney, Patrick	do	July 9, 1862	3	Not on muster-out roll.
Dubois, George	do	July 12, 1862	3	Not on muster-out roll.
Daly, Roderick	do	July 8, 1862	3	Not on muster-out roll.
Davis, James	do	July 21, 1862	3	Not on muster-out roll.
Develin, Michael	do	July 25, 1862	3	Not on muster-out roll.
Develin, Thomas	do	Aug. 13, 1862	3	Not on muster-out roll.
Dawson, John	do	Feb. 23, 1864	3	Not on muster-out roll.
Diebold, Peter	do	Feb. 3, 1864	3	Wounded at Petersburg, Va., June 16, '64.
Emanuel, John	do	Feb. 3, 1864	3	Wounded at Petersburg, Va., June 16, '64—discharged by General Order, June 16, '65.
Fagan, James	do	Feb. 22, 1864	3	Not on muster-out roll.
Fence, William	do	Feb. 23, 1864	3	Mustered out with company, July 14, '65.
Fence, Suffley	do	Feb. 22, 1864	3	Discharged on Surgeon's certificate, Jan. 7, '65.
Freidle, John S	do	Feb. 27, 1864	3	Captured at Reams Station, Va., Aug. 25, '64—died at Salisbury, N. C., Dec. 25, '64.
Fletcher, James	do	Aug. 29, 1862	3	Transferred to Co. D, Jan. 26, '63.
Foster, John W	do	July 10, 1862	3	Not on muster-out roll.
Fisher, Joseph	do	Aug. 5, 1862	3	Not on muster-out roll.
Frazier, George F	do	Feb. 22, 1864	3	Not on muster-out roll.
Ford, Jeremiah	do	Feb. 15, 1864	3	Not on muster-out roll.
Gibbons, Richard	do	Feb. 4, 1864	3	Mustered out with company, July 14, '65.
Gillespie, Samuel S	do	Sept. 21, 1864	3	Killed at Five Forks, Va., March 31, '65.
Guinan, Peter	do	July 9, 1862	3	Wd. at Fredericksburg, Va., Dec. 13, '62—transferred to Co. D, Jan. 26, '63.
Glasgow, Matthew	do	July 30, 1862	3	Transferred to Co. D, Jan. 26, '63.
Gorman, William	do	Aug. 4, 1862	3	Transferred to Co. D, Jan. 26, '63.
Geary, William	do	July 21, 1862	3	Not on muster-out roll.
Gates, John	do	July 21, 1862	3	Not on muster-out roll.
Golder, John	do	Aug. 19, 1862	3	Not on muster-out roll.
Gunk, Conrad	do	Feb. 15, 1865	3	Not on muster-out roll.
Hamilton, Thos. A	do	Feb. 10, 1864	3	Wd. at Cold Harbor, Va., June 2, '64—mustered out with company, July 14, '65.
Hausburg, Jos. S	do	Feb. 5, 1864	3	Mustered out with company, July 14, '65.
Harlan, John	do	Feb. 6, 1864	3	Discharged by G. O., May 15, '65.
Haughy, John	do	Feb. 11, 1864	3	Died July 25, of wounds received at Cold Harbor, June 3, '64.
Hathaway, Wm E	do	July 11, 1862	3	Transferred to Co. D, Jan. 26, '63.
Himes, James	do	Aug. 16, 1862	3	Not on muster-out roll.
Hewitt, Charles	do	July 21, 1862	3	Not on muster-out roll.
Harron, William	do	Aug. 23, 1862	3	Not on muster-out roll.
Hayden, Patrick	do	Aug. 23, 1862	3	Transferred to Co. D, Jan. 26, '63.
Holmes, James	do	Feb. 20, 1864	3	Not on muster-out roll.
Johnston, Alex	do	Feb. 17, 1864	3	Wounded at Petersburg, Va., April 2, '65—discharged by General Order, June 3, '65.
Keeney, Patrick	do	Feb. 18, 1864	3	Mustered out with company, July 14, '65.
Kelley, Michael	do	Feb. 11, 1864	3	Wounded at Spottsylvania C. H., Va., May 12, '64—discharged by G. O., June 7, '65.
Kinchner, John	do	July 29, 1862	3	Transferred to Co. D, Jan. 26, '63.
Kendel, Jacob	do	Aug. 19, 1862	3	Not on muster-out roll.
Kelley, Charles	do	Feb. 24, 1864	3	Not on muster-out roll.
Lefevre, Calvin J	do	Feb. 10, 1864	3	Wounded at Spottsylvania C. H., May 12, '64—transferred to Co. C, 14th reg. V. R. C.—died at Washington, D. C., July 4, '65.
Leonard, Frank	do	Feb. 16, 1864	3	Captured at Petersburg, Va., June 22, '64—died at Lynchburg, Sept. 10, '64.
Logue, Frank	do	July 21, 1862	3	Transferred to Co. D, Jan. 26, '63.
Lott, William L	do	Aug. 2, 1862	3	Transferred to Co. D, Jan. 26, '63.
Lutz, John L	do	July 14, 1862	3	Not on muster-out roll.

NAME.	RANK.	DATE OF MUSTER INTO SERVICE.	TERM—YEARS.	REMARKS.
Liver, John P.	Private.	Aug. 14, 1862	3	Not on muster-out roll.
Mink, Andrew J.	do	Jan. 13, 1864	3	Absent, sick, at muster out.
Mercer, William	do	Feb. 6, 1864	3	Absent, sick, at muster out—wounded at 2d battle of Spottsylvania.
Miller, Winfield S.	do	Feb. 15, 1864	3	Wounded at Spottsylvania C. H., Va., May 18, '64—absent, in hospital, at muster out.
Maul, Alexander	do	Feb. 15, 1864	3	Wounded at Spottsylvania C. H., Va., May 18, '64—absent, in hospital, at muster out.
Medsker, George	do	Feb. 29, 1864	3	Prisoner from June 22, '64, to March 30, '65—discharged by G. O., July 24, '65.
Marshall, Alex.	do	Feb. 9, 1864	3	Missing in action at Spottsylvania C. H., May 12, '64.
Murphy, John	do	Aug. 15, 1862	3	Wounded at Fredericksburg, Va., Dec. 13, '62—transferred to Co. D, Jan. 26, '63.
Murphy, Joseph	do	July 30, 1862	3	Transferred to Co. D, Jan. 26, '63.
Morris, Owen	do	July 29, 1862	3	Not on muster-out roll.
Mills, Charles	do	Aug. 22, 1862	3	Not on muster-out roll.
McIntyre, Stephen	do	Feb. 18, 1864	3	Wounded at Totopotomy, Va., May 31, '64, and at Five Forks, March 31, '65—ab., in hospital at muster out.
McLaughlin, J. B.	do	Feb. 17, 1864	3	Wounded at Cold Harbor, Va., June 3, '64—discharged by General Order, May 26, '65.
McCarty, Charles	do	Feb. 8, 1864	3	Captured at Reams Station, Va., Aug. 25, '64—died at Salisbury, N. C., Jan. 10, '65
McCullough, David	do	Sept. 1, 1862	3	Wounded at Fredericksburg Va., Dec. 13, '62—transferred to Co. D, Jan. 26, '63.
McQuaid, Thomas	do	Aug. 29, 1862	3	Transferred to Co. D, Jan. 26, '63.
McGonigal, Henry	do	July 15, 1862	3	Transferred to Co. D, Jan. 26, '63.
McNight, Henry	do	Aug. 16, 1862	3	Not on muster-out roll.
McMullin, James	do	Aug. 19, 1862	3	Not on muster-out roll.
McGinty, Hugh	do	Aug. 22, 1862	3	Not on muster-out roll.
McCarty, Daniel	do	Aug. 30, 1862	3	Killed at Fredericksburg, Dec. 13, 1862.
McGurick, Laurence	do	Aug. 29, 1862	3	Not on muster-out roll.
McFarland, Peter	do	Feb. 5, 1864	3	Not on muster-out roll.
McGuire, Thomas	do	Feb. 6, 1864	3	Not on muster-out roll.
Niblo, George	do	Aug. 19, 1862	3	Not on muster-out roll.
Polly, John	do	Feb. 14, 1864	3	Mustered out with company, July 14, '65.
Puhl, John	do	Feb. 8, 1864	3	Wounded at Five Forks, Va., March 31, '65—discharged by General Order, June 5, '65.
Puhl, Nicholas	do	Feb. 25, 1864	3	Prisoner from Aug. 18, 1864, to Feb. 28, 1865—discharged by G. O., June 16, 1865.
Pack, Jacob	do	Feb. 12, 1864	3	Miss. in action at Petersburg, Va., June 15, '64
Parker, Robert	do	Aug. 9, 1862	3	Not on muster-out roll.
Quinn, Charles A.	do	Aug. 10, 1862	3	Not on muster-out roll.
Ruley, Philip	do	Feb. 25, 1864	3	Wounded at Cold Harbor, Va., June 3, 1864—mustered out with company, July 14, 1865.
Ritchie, Edward	do	Feb. 29, 1864	3	Absent, sick, at muster out.
Rosier, Edward H.	do	Mar. 7, 1864	3	Absent, sick, at muster out.
Ralston, William G.	do	Sept. 21, 1864	3	Discharged by General Order, June 3, 1865
Ross, William A.	do	Feb. 16, 1864	3	Transferred to Vet. Res. Corps, Sept. 2, 1864—discharged by General Order, July 31, '65.
Rushworth, George	do	July 15, 1862	3	Transferred to Co. D, Jan. 26, 1863.
Rodgers, Willets	do	Aug. 19, 1862	3	Not on muster-out roll.
Russell, Lewis	do	Aug. 5, 1862	3	Not on muster-out roll.
Stark, Robert C.	do	Feb. 16, 1864	3	Mustered out with company, July 14, 1865.
Shields, John	do	Mar. 26, 1864	3	Absent, sick, at muster out.
Steenburg, Charles	do	Feb. 1, 1865	3	Discharged by General Order, Aug. 9, 1865.
Stewart, Robert	do	April 15, 1864	3	Absent, wounded, at muster out.
Shultz, Isaac	do	Feb. 10, 1864	3	Killed near Darbytown Road, Va, Oct. 8, '64—burial record, Oct. 18, '64—buried in Nat. Cem., City Point, sec. E, div. 2, grave, 151.
Swisher, John	do	Mar. 1, 1864	3	Died at Philadelphia, Pa., July 31, of wounds received at Cold Harbor, Va., June 3, 1864.
Seifritz, Matthias	do	Feb. 11, 1864	3	Died at Alexandria, Va., Sept. 8, of wounds received at Cold Harbor, Va., June 3, 1864.
Shaeffer, Joseph	do	July 15, 1862	3	Not on muster-out roll.
Stevens, John I.	do	July 10, 1862	3	Not on muster-out roll.

THREE YEARS' SERVICE. 415

NAME.	RANK.	DATE OF MUSTER INTO SERVICE.	TERM—YEARS.	REMARKS.
Shannon, Thomas	Private.	July 10, 1862	3	Not on muster-out roll.
Simpson, Stephen E	do	July 15, 1862	3	Not on muster-out roll.
Small, John E	do	July 31, 1862	3	Not on muster-out roll.
Shinn, Thomas A	do	Aug. 13, 1862	3	Not on muster-out roll.
Smith, Charles	do	July 14, 1862	3	Not on muster-out roll.
Stephenson, Wm	do	Feb. 13, 1864	3	Not on muster-out roll.
Shaffer, Thomas	do	Feb. 25, 1864	3	Not on muster-out roll.
Stewart, Wm. H	do	Feb. 9, 1864	3	Not on muster-out roll.
Sikes, Samuel	do	Feb. 9, 1864	3	Not on muster-out roll.
Stetzler, C				Died Nov. 6, 1864, at Beverly, N. J.
Thomas, Alonzo C	do	April 14, 1864	3	Absent, sick, at muster out.
Tompkins, John W	do	Feb. 27, 1864	3	Discharged by General Order, May 24, 1865.
Torpie, John	do	Feb. 6, 1864	3	Missing in action at Cold Harbor, Va., June 3, 1864.
Worsenborger, I	do	Feb. 6, 1864	3	Mustered out with company, July 14, 1865.
Walker, Theodore A	do	July 20, 1862	3	Transferred to Co. D, Jan. 26, 1863.
Whelan, James	do	Aug. 29, 1862	3	Transferred to Co. D. Jan. 26, 1863.
Willoughby, E. B	do	July 3, 1862	3	Not on muster-out roll.
Wood, George H	do	July 21, 1862	3	Not on muster-out roll.
Wilson, David	do	Aug. 7, 1862	3	Not on muster-out roll.
Wood, Charles	do	Aug. 19, 1862	3	Not on muster-out roll.
Wall, James	do	Aug. 23, 1862	3	Not on muster-out roll.
Webb, William H	do	Aug. 29, 1862	3	Not on muster-out roll.

Company I.

Samuel Taggart	Captain	Apr. 14, 1864	3	Killed at Reams Station, Va., Aug. 25, '64—buried in Allegheny Cem., Pittsburg, Pa.
Wm O'Callaghan	do	Aug. 15, 1862	3	Promoted from 2d Lt. Co. B to 1st Lt. May 2, '64—to Capt., Sept. 22, '64—discharged by special order, Feb. 16, '65.
Joseph W. Yocum	do	Aug. 25, 1862	3	Promoted to 2d Lt., May 3, '64—to 1st Lt., Oct. 14, '64—to Capt., March 4 '65—to Bv. Maj., March 13,'65—wd. at Petersburg,Va., June 16 and at William's Farm, June 22,'64—d sch. by special order, May 19, '65.
Robert J. Taggart	do	May 25, 1864	3	Promoted to Sgt., April 25, '64—to 1st Sgt., Sept. 1, '64—to 1st Lt., March 4, '65—to Capt. June 9, '65—com. Major, June 4, '65—not mustered—mustered out with company, July 14, '65.
John Stephens	1st Lieut.	Sept. 18, 1862	3	Discharged May 12, to date Jan. 27, '63.
R. B. Montgomery	2d Lieut.	Sept. 19, 1862	3	Killed at Fredericksburg, Va., Dec 13, '62.
John A. Dickson	1st Sgt.	Feb. 29, 1864	3	Promoted to Sgt., April 25, '64—to 1st Sgt., March 4, '65—wd. at Five Forks, Va., Mar. 31, '65—absent, in hospital, at muster out—Vet.
Thomas J. Murtha	do	July 24, 1862	3	Transferred to Co. B, Jan. 26, '63.
Peter Kelly	Sergeant.	Feb. 25, 1864	3	Mustered out with company, July 14, '65.
George L. Northrop	do	Jan. 9, 1865	3	Pr to Corp., Mar. 1, '65—to Sgt., July 1, '65—mustered out with company, July 14, '65.
Henry Mullen	do	Mar. 23, 1864	3	Absent, sick, at muster out—Vet.
Joseph Guller	do	Mar. 9, 1864	3	Discharged by General Order, June 17, '65.
Thomas McKnight	do	July 12, 1862	3	Transferred to Co. B, Jan. 26, '63.
James E. Craig	do	July 22, 1862	3	Transferred to Co. B, Jan. 26, '63.
Daniel Reen	do	July 16, 1862	3	Transferred to Co. B, Jan. 26, '63.
George Cole	do	July 10, 1862	3	Killed at Fredericksburg, Va., Dec 13, '62.
David Steen	Corporal.	Mar. 18, 1864	3	Mus. out with company, July 14, '65—Vet.
John Adams	do	Mar. 8, 1864	3	Mustered out with company, July 14, '65.
Brian McLaughlin	do	Apr. 4, 1864	3	Mustered out with company, July 14, '65.
William Devereau	do	Feb. 7, 1865	3	Promoted to Corp., July 1, '65—mustered out with company, July 14, '65.
William R. Cowl	do	Apr. 13, 1864	3	Promoted to Corp., April 25, '64—wounded at Spottsylvania C. H., May 12, '64—trans

NAME.	RANK.	DATE OF MUSTER INTO SERVICE.	TERM-YEARS.	REMARKS.
Patrick J. Carrigan	Corporal	Mar. 26, 1864	3	to Co. B, 18th Reg. Vet. Res. Corps—discharged by General Order, July 19, '65. Promoted to Corp., April 25, '65—prisoner from June 22, '64, to April, '65—discharged by General Order, June 3, '65.
John Whigham	do	Mar. 23, 1864	3	Wounded at Petersburg, Va., June 17, '64, and at William's Farm, June 22, '64—disch. on Surgeon's certificate, Jan. 24, '65.
John Jardine	do	Feb. 24, 1864	3	Wounded at Wilderness, Va., May 5, '64—disch. on Surgeon's certificate, May 18, '65.
John A. Fox	do	Aug. 8, 1864	3	Promoted to Corp., March 1, '65—discharged by General Order, June 3, '65.
Benjamin F. Groves	do	Aug. 4, 1862	3	Transferred to Co. B, Jan. 26, '63.
John H. Rowen	do	Aug. 6, 1862	3	Transferred to Co. B, Jan. 26, '63.
William H. Brown	do	Aug. 7, 1862	3	Transferred to Co. B, Jan. 26, '63.
Alexander Downey	do	July 17, 1862	3	Wounded at Fredericksburg, Va., Dec. 13, '62—burial record, Albert Downey, died Jan. 6, '63—buried in Mil. Asy. Cem., D. C.
Thomas Disney	Musician	July 14, 1862	3	Discharged, 1854.
Christopher H. Moore		Mar. 1, 1863	3	Discharged at close of war.
Alexander, Albert	Private	Feb. 11, 1864	3	Mustered out with company, July 14, '65—wounded at Cold Harbor.
Allen, Andrew J.	do	Apr. 9, 1864	3	Wounded at Cold Harbor, Va., June 3, '64—disch. on Surgeon's certificate, Dec. 26, '64.
Allen, John	do	Feb. 25, 1864	3	Wounded at Cold Harbor, Va., June 3, '64—died at City Point, Va., Oct. 22, '64.
Adams, Jacob W.	do	Aug. 18, 1862	3	Transferred to Co. B, Jan. 26, '63.
Ash, William J.	do	July 23, 1862	3	Not on muster-out roll.
Austin, John	do	Aug. 13, 1862	3	Not on muster-out roll.
Broadwater, Henry	do	Jan. 25, 1865	3	Deserted June 20, returned July 5, '65—mustered out with company, July 14, '65.
Beatty, James	do	Feb. 24, 1864	3	Absent, sick, at muster out.—Vet.
Bullinger, Chris.	do	Apr. 12, 1864	3	Absent, sick, at muster out.
Birely, Isaac	do	Aug. 28, 1862	3	Discharged June 1 '63.
Carter, J.	do		3	Died March 16, '64.
Conway, James	do	Mar. 21, 1864	3	Mustered out with company, July 14, '65.
Condon, William	do	Mar. 12, 1864	3	Mustered out with company, July 14, '65.
Close, Joseph J.	do	Mar. 10, 1864	3	Wounded at Wilderness, Va., May 5, '64—mustered out with company, July 14, '65.
Cassady, George	do	Apr. 23, 1864	3	Discharged by General Order, Aug. 4, '65.
Capehart, Daniel	do	Jan. 25, 1865		Not on muster-out roll.
Collins, Henry M.	do	Aug. 13, 1862	3	Transferred to Co. B, Jan. 26, '63.
Collar, Jacob	do	Aug. 18, 1862	3	Transferred to Co. B, Jan. 26, '63.
Clements, Wm. K.	do	Aug. 23, 1862	3	Transferred to Co. B, Jan. 26, '63.
Carr, Samuel	do	Aug. 4, 1862	3	Discharged Jan., '62.
Connelly, William	do	Feb. 26, 1864	3	Not on muster-out roll.
Dwier, Daniel	do	Jan. 20, 1865	3	Discharged by General Order, June 2. '65.
Donovan, John	do	Apr. 22, 1864	3	Absent, sick, at muster out.
Dugan, Daniel	do	Feb. 4, 1864	3	Discharged by General Order, June 14, '65.
Dee, William	do	Feb. 19, 1864	3	Wounded at Spottsylvania C. H., May 18, '64—trans. to Vet. Res. Corps, Dec. 14, '64.
Delaney, Finton	do	Apr. 8, 1864	3	Wounded at Reams Station, Aug 25, 1864—mustered out May 24, 1815.
Drey, Daniel	do	May 2, 1864	3	Wounded at Reams Station, Va., Aug. 25, '64—tr. to 39th Co., 2d Bat. V. R. C, April 11, '65—dis. on Surgeon's certific., July 27, '65.
Delaney, Matthew	do	Aug. 13, 1862	3	Transferred to Co. B, Jan. 26, '63.
Dubree, Lewis	do	July 29, 1862	3	Not on muster-out roll.
Dow, Andrew	do	July 16, 1862	3	Not on muster-out roll.
Daghan, Charles	do	April 4, 1864	3	Not on muster-out roll.
Devlin, Patrick	do	Mar. 1, 1864	3	Not on muster-out roll.
Engles, George H.	do	Aug. 7, 1862	3	Not on muster-out roll.
Flanigan, William	do	Dec. 15, 1864	3	Prisoner from March 2 to April 6, '65—disch. by General Order, June 29, '65.
Farrell, John A.	do	April 4, 1864	3	Absent, sick, at muster out.
Fleming, Patrick	do	Mar. 25, 1864	3	Killed at Wilderness, Va., May 5, '64.

NAME.	RANK.	DATE OF MUSTER INTO SERVICE.	TERM—YEARS	REMARKS.
Farley, John	Private	Aug. 14, 1862	3	Transferred to Co. B, Jan. 26, '63.
Fagan, Edward	do	Aug. 23, 1862	3	Transferred to Co. B, Jan. 26, '63.
Forsythe, George	do	Feb. 24, 1864	3	Not on muster-out roll.
Gallagher, Owen	do	Feb. 29, 1864	3	Wd. at Spottsylvania C. H., Va., May 18, '64—mus. out with company, July 14, '65.
Grant, Thomas	do	Feb. 19, 1864	3	Wounded at Five Forks, Va., March 31, '65—discharged by General Order, June 3, '65.
Gaw, William	do	Aug. 6, 1862	3	Killed at Fredericksburg, Va., Dec. 13, '62.
Holt, George C	do	Mar. 25, 1864	3	Mustered out with company, July 14, '65.
Hughes, James	do	Mar. 6, 1865	3	Mustered out with company, July 14, '65.
Harker, Edward	do	Apr. 24, 1864	3	Mustered out with company, July 14, '65.
Hansell, John R	do	Apr. 4, 1864	3	Absent, wounded, at muster out.
Heebner, Lawrence	do	Apr. 18, 1864	3	Discharged by General Order, May 27, '65.
Hatch, Hannibal	do	Mar. 2, 1864	3	Killed at Wilderness, Va., May 5, '64.
Harvey, Wm. C	do	Mar. 28, 1864	3	Died near Washington, D. C., Oct. 14, '64.
Hoofnagle, Melch'r	do	July 10, 1862	3	Not on muster-out roll.
Hodder, John	do	July 22, 1862	3	Not on muster-out roll.
Hayden, Patrick	do	July 30, 1862	3	Transferred to Co. D.
Haley, James	do	July 11, 1862	3	Transferred to Co. B, Jan. 26, '63.
Haas, Henry	do	July 23, 1862	3	Transferred to Co. B, Jan. 26, '63.
Hill, John	do	Aug. 13, 1862	3	Transferred to Co. B, Jan. 26, '63.
Hamilton, Frank'n	do	Feb. 17, 1864	3	Not on muster-out roll.
Hutchinson, John	do	Feb. 17, 1864	3	Not on muster-out roll.
Jones, Charles	do	Jan. 26, 1865	3	Wounded at Five Forks, Va., March 31, '65—discharged by General Order, July 15, '65.
Johnson, Bartholomew	do	July 23, 1862	3	Killed at Fredericksburg, Va., Dec. 13, '62.
James, Enoch G	do	Feb. 26, 1864	3	Not on muster-out roll.
Kohlenberg, Joseph	do	June 20, 1864	3	Absent, sick, at muster out.
Kilpatrick, James	do	Mar. 6, 1865	3	Absent, on furlough, at muster out.
Kinchner, John	do	July 29, 1862	3	Not on muster-out roll.
Lawson, Andrew	do	Mar. 6, 1865	3	Mustered out with company, July 14, '65.
Lawrence, Henry D	do	Apr. 18, 1864	3	Mustered out with company, July 14, '65.
Lyons, James	do	Apr. 11, 1864	3	Absent, sick, at muster out.
Leech, Frank	do	Mar. 7, 1864	3	Wounded at Reams Station, Va., Aug. 25, '64—disch. on Surgeon's certificate, Feb. 6, '65.
Leech, John	do	Mar. 7, 1864	3	Killed at William's Farm, Va., June 22, '64.
Lutz, Jacob	do	Aug. 15, 1862	3	Transferred to Co. B, Jan. 26, '63.
Lequen, John	do	Aug. 19, 1862	3	Transferred to Co. B, Jan. 26, '63.
Lynch, John	do	Apr. 4, 1864	3	Not on muster-out roll.
Moore, Christ'r H	do	Mar. 31, 1864	3	Mustered out with company, July 14, '65.
Moore, George	do	Jan. 18, 1865	3	Mustered out with company, July 14, '65.
Merritt, Murtha	do	Apr. 9, 1864	3	Mustered out with company, July 14, '65.
Mulholland, John	do	Apr. 25, 1864	3	Mustered out with company, July 14, '65.
Minnich, Joseph	do	Mar. 31, 1864	3	Missing in action at Spottsylvania C. H., Va., May 12, '64—Vet.
Martin, Joseph	do	Feb. 21, 1865	3	Not on muster-out roll.
Mannesley, Wm	do	Aug. 9, 1862	3	Transferred to Co. B, Jan. 26, '63.
Moore, James M	do	Aug. 16, 1862	3	Transferred to Co. B, Jan. 26, '63.
Mabuerry, Isaac M	do	Aug. 18, 1862	3	Transferred to Co. B, Jan. 26, '63.
Manderfield, George C	do	July 7, 1862	3	Not on muster-out roll.
Moore, John	do	Aug. 7, 1862	3	Not on muster-out roll.
McManamin, Mat	do	Feb. 3, 1864	3	Mustered out with company, July 14, '65.
McManus, John	do	Feb. 19, 1864	3	Wounded at Wilderness, Va., May 5, '64—absent, sick, at muster out.
McMullin, John R	do	Aug. 29, 1862	3	Transferred to Co. B, Jan. 26, '63.
McClune, Samuel	do	July 25, 1862	3	Killed at Fredericksburg, Va., Dec. 13, '62.
McDonald, James	do	Aug. 7, 1862	3	Not on muster-out roll.
Neveling, John	do	Jan. 20, 1865	3	Not on muster-out roll.
Oliver, Abraham	do	Aug. 11, 1862	3	Transferred to Co. B, Jan. 26, '63.
Perry, John	do	May 31, 1864	3	Mustered out with company, July 14, '65.
Potts, David	do	Feb. 22, 1864	3	Wounded at Petersburg, Va., June 16, '64—absent, sick, at muster out.
Price, Samuel	do	Mar. 25, 1864	3	Died at Alexandria, Va., July 11, of wds. rec. at Cold Harbor, June 3, '64—grave 2,384.
Rafferty, Charles	do	Mar. 27, 1865	3	Mustered out with company, July 14, '65.
Richardson, Isaac	do	Jan. 20, 1865	3	Mustered out with company, July 14, '65.
Rutherford, Thos	do	Aug. 14, 1862	3	Transferred to Co. B, Jan. 26, '63.

NAME.	RANK.	DATE OF MUSTER INTO SERVICE.	TERM—YEARS.	REMARKS.
Smith, William	Private	Mar. 18, 1864	3	Mustered out with company, July 14, '65.
Smith, George S.	...do...	Apr. 11, 1864	3	Missing in action, June 13, '64.
Searight, William A.	...do...	Feb. 17, 1864	3	Wd. at Spottsylvania C. H., Va., May 12, '64—died at Washington, D. C., July 20, '64.
Shea, Edward	...do...	Apr. 6, 1864	3	Wounded at Wilderness, Va., May 5, '64—died at Washington, D. C., June 3, '64—buried in National Cemetery, Arlington, Va.
Steel, Robert	...do...	Jan. 26, 1865	3	Not on muster-out roll.
Search, Francis	...do...	July 24, 1862	3	Transferred to Co. B, Jan. 26, '63.
Smith, George	...do...	July 29, 1862	3	Not on muster-out roll.
Smick, George N.	...do...	Aug. 29, 1862	3	Not on muster-out roll.
Short, Alfred	...do...	Feb. 19, 1864	3	Not on muster-out roll.
Thompson, Isaac	...do...	Apr. 28, 1864	3	Discharged by General Order, May 10, '65.
Tully, Thomas	...do...	Mar. 11, 1864	3	Transferred to 105th Co., 2d Batt. V. R. C., Jan. 22, '65—discharged on Surgeon's certificate, Aug. 29, '65.
Van Valtenberg, C.	...do...	July 21, 1862	3	Not on muster-out roll.
Van Dien, Albert J.	...do...	July 29, 1862	3	Killed at Fredericksburg, Va., Dec. 13, '62.
Vaughan, Joseph	...do...	Aug. 6, 1862	3	Transferred to Co. B, Jan. 26, '63.
Vanderslice, And.	...do...	Aug. 18, 1862	3	Transferred to Co. B, Jan. 26, '63.
Wallace, Andrew	...do...	Apr. 6, 1864	3	Captured June 11, '64—died at Andersonville, Ga., July 10, '64—grave 3,135.
Winchester, John	...do...	Aug. 28, 1862	3	Killed at Fredericksburg, Va., Dec. 13, '62.
White, George	...do...	Apr. 4, 1864	3	Not on muster-out roll.
Yauger, Uriah	...do...	Mar. 29, 1864	3	Not on muster-out roll.

COMPANY K.

NAME.	RANK.	DATE OF MUSTER INTO SERVICE.	TERM—YEARS.	REMARKS.
John Q. O'Neill	Captain	Sept. 1, 1862	3	Wounded at Fredericksburg, Va., Dec. 13, '62—transferred to 22d reg. V. R. C., April 4, 1863.
John R. Weltner	...do...	Apr. 7, 1864	3	Discharged by special order, June 22, '65.
Patrick Casey	1st Lieut.	Sept. 1, 1862	3	Died at Philadelphia, Pa., Nov. 9, of wounds received October 7, '62.
James D. Cope	...do...	Mar. 17, 1864	3	Captured at William's Farm, Va., June 22, '64—com. Capt., June 22, '65—not mustered out with company, July 14, '65.
Bernard Loughery	2d Lieut.	Sept. 3, 1862	3	Discharged May 12, to date Jan. 27, '63.
Zadock B. Springer	...do...	Apr. 7, 1864	3	Captured at Reams Station, Va., Aug. 25, '64—com. Q. M., June 3, '65—not mustered out with company, July 14, '65.
James E. Joliff	1st Sgt.	Mar. 31, 1864	3	Wounded at Five Forks, Va., March 31, '65—absent, in hospital, at muster out.
E. K. Crathamel	...do...	July 31, 1862	3	Wounded at Fredericksburg, Va., Dec. 13, '62—mustered out with company.
Samuel A. Clear	Sergeant	Feb. 29, 1864	3	Promoted from Corporal, May 29, '64—mustered out with company, July 14, '65.
Wm. H. Sembower	...do...	Feb. 29, 1864	3	Promoted to Sergeant, April 16, '64—mustered out with company, July 14, '65.
James Collins	...do...	Feb. 29, 1864	3	Promoted from Corporal, Dec. 26, '64—mustered out with company, July 14, '65.
Alex. Chisholm	...do...	Feb. 29, 1864	3	Promoted from Corporal, June 1, '64—mustered out with company, July 14, '65.
Edward Spence	...do...	Feb. 29, 1864	3	Died at Annapolis, Md., June 24, of wounds received at Petersburg, Va., June 16, '64.
Thomas P. Crown	...do...	Aug. 4, 1862	3	Transferred to Co. A, Jan. 26, '63.
Joseph Slinker	...do...	Aug. 1, 1862	3	Transferred to Co. A, Jan. 26, '63.
Daniel Root	...do...	Aug. 1, 1862	3	Killed at Fredericksburg, Va., Dec. 13, '62.
Wm. H. Tyrrell	...do...	Aug. 12, 1862	3	Wounded at Fredericksburg, Va., Dec. 13, '62—promoted to 2d Lt. Co. C, May 1, '63.
Hezekiah Dean	...do...	Feb. 29, 1864		Wounded at Petersburg, Va., June 16, '64—mustered out with company.
Warren S. Kilgore	...do...	Mar. 1, 1864		Vet.—served in 85th Pa. V.—Killed at Spottsylvania, Va., May 12, '64.

THREE YEARS' SERVICE.   419

NAME.	RANK.	DATE OF MUSTER INTO SERVICE.	TERM—YEARS.	REMARKS.
Stephen S. Beckett	Corporal	Mar. 7, 1864	3	Promoted to Corp., April 16, '64—wounded at Petersburg, Va., June 16, '64—mustered out with company, July 14, '65.
Lloyd Patterson	do	Mar. 30, 1864	3	Promoted to Corporal, June 4, '64—mustered out with company, July 14, '65.
Andrew J. Seese	do	Mar. 3, 1864	3	Promoted to Corporal, March 16, '65—mustered out with company, July 14, '65.
George W. Ganoe	do	Apr. 1, 1864	3	Promoted to Corporal, June 2, '65—mustered out with company, July 14, '65.
William H. Nycum	do	Feb. 29, 1864	3	Captured—promoted to Corporal, June 2, '65 wounded at Wilderness—mustered out with company, July 14, '65.
Ephraim Keim	do	Feb. 24, 1864	3	Promoted to Corporal, June 2, '65—mustered out with company, July 14, '65.
George J. Cruse	do	Mar. 30, 1864	3	Wounded at Totopotomy, Va., May 31, '64. and at Five Forks, March 31, '65—transferred to Co. G, 18th Regiment Vet. Res. Corps—disch. by General Order, Aug. 14, '65.
Timothy McInerney	do	Mar. 13, 1864	3	Wounded at Five Forks, Va., March 31, '65—absent, in hospital, at muster out.
Rob't J. Brownfield	do	Feb. 29, 1864	3	Died June 12, of wounds received at Spottsylvania C. H., Va., May 12, '64—buried in National Cemetery, Arlington.
Thomas Wallace	do	Aug. 7, 1862	3	Transferred to Co. D, Jan. 26, '63.
Eugene Brady	do	Aug. 15, 1862	3	Transferred to Co. D, Jan. 26, '63.
Michael J. McKenna	do	Aug. 11, 1862	3	Transferred to Co. D, Jan. 26, '63.
George P. Snyder	do	Aug. 6, 1862	3	Transferred to Co. D, Jan. 26, '63.
Charles McLaughlin	do	July 29, 1862	3	Transferred to Co. D, Jan. 26, '63.
George Mahaffey	do	Aug. 5, 1862	3	Disch. on Surgeon's certificate—date unk'n.
John Remanter	do	Aug. 6, 1862	3	Not on muster-out roll.
Joseph Hudson	do	Aug. 8, 1862	3	Killed at Fredericksburg, Va., Dec. 13, '62.
Richard A. McLean	do			Wounded, May 18, '64 at Spottsylvania, Va. —mustered out with company.
Daniel Crawford	do			Killed at Spottsylvania, Va., May 18, '64.
Daniel Rodgers	Musician	Aug. 16, 1862	3	Transferred to Co. D, Jan. 26, '63.
George Allen	do	Aug. 22, 1862	3	Transferred to Co. D, Jan. 26, '63.
Allaman, Jacob	Private	Feb. 29, 1864	3	Wounded at Wilderness, Va., May 5, '64—mustered out with company, July 14, 1865.
Allingham, Robert	do	June 28, 1862	3	Mustered out with company, July 14, 1865.
Bolen, Albert W	do	Mar. 23, 1864	3	Wounded at Spottsylvania C. H., Va., May 12, 1864—mustered out with company, July 14, 1865—Vet in 16th Pa. Cav.
Bagshaw, John H	do	Feb. 15, 1864	3	Wounded at Wilderness, Va., May 5, at Reams Station, Va., August 25, 1864, and at Five Forks, March 31, 1865—absent, in hospital, at muster out.
Bailes, Andrew J	do	Feb. 29, 1864	3	Wounded at Petersburg, Va., June 16, '64—tr. to Veteran Reserve Corps, June 7, '65.
Bricker, William P	do	Mar. 31, 1864	3	Wounded at Wilderness, Va., May 5, '64—tr. to Veteran Reserve Corps, 1864.
Boyd, Parks A	do	Mar. 31, 1864	3	Killed at Wilderness, Va., May 5, 1864.
Burkholder, C	do	Mar. 31, 1864	3	Died of wounds received at Cold Harbor, Va., June 3, 1864.
Bell, Henry J	do	Mar. 23, 1864	3	Killed at Spottsylvania C. H., Va., May 12, '64—Vet
Boylan, John C	do	Aug. 28, 1862	3	Transferred to Co. D, Jan. 26, 1863.
Barker, Thomas	do	Aug. 28, 1862	3	Not on muster-out roll.
Bishop, Albert S	do	Aug. 19, 1862	3	Not on muster-out roll.
Burns, John	do	Aug. 13, 1862	3	Killed at Fredericksburg, Va., Dec. 13 '62.
Berrell, Charles	do	Aug. 11, 1862	3	Not on muster-out roll.
Bibbs, Morris	do	Mar. 7, 1864	3	Not on muster-out roll.
Brooks, Oliver	do	Feb. 29, 1864	3	Not on muster-out roll.
Blair, Alfred, Jr	do	Feb. 29, 1864	3	Not on muster-out roll.
Campbell, John	do	Mar. 31, 1864	3	Wounded at Cold Harbor, Va., June 3, '64—mustered out with company, July 14, '65.
Chisholm, Daniel	do	Feb. 29, 1864	3	Wounded at Petersburg, Va., June 16, '64—pro. to Corporal, March 16, '64—disch. by General Order, June 9, '65.

NAME.	RANK.	DATE OF MUSTER INTO SERVICE.	TERM-YEARS.	REMARKS.
Chalfant, John W	Private	Mar. 22, 1864	3	Discharged by General Order, June 5, '65.
Crawford, Daniel C	do	Feb. 29, 1863	3	Killed at Spottsylvania C. H., Va., May 18, 1864.
Conn, William A	do	Mar. 31, 1864	3	Killed at Spottsylvania C. H., Va., May 18, 1864.
Clemmer, Michael	do	Mar. 31, 1864	3	Killed at Cold Harbor, Va., June 3, 1864.
Cavanaugh, James	do	Aug. 20, 1862	3	Transferred to Co. D, Jan. 26, 1863.
Coffey, Bernard	do	Aug. 2, 1862	3	Not on muster-out roll.
Ditmore, Wm. H	do	Mar. 3, 1864	3	Discharged by General Order, June 28, 1865.
Dean, Stephen H	do	Mar. 30, 1864	3	Wounded and captured at Reams Station, Va., Aug. 25, '64—died at Salisbury, N. C., Dec. 3, '64—burial record, Dec. 13, '64.
Dougherty, Edward	do	Aug. 19, 1862	3	Transferred to Co. D, Jan. 26, 1863.
Durning, Hugh	do	Aug. 19, 1862	3	Wounded at Fredericksburg, Va., Dec 13, '62 —transferred to Co. D, Jan. 26, 1863.
Davis, John	do	Aug. 29, 1862	3	Transferred to Co. D, Jan. 26, '63.
Edwards, Thomas	do	Feb. 20, 1864	3	Discharged by General Order, June 19, 1865.
Ellinger, Emanuel	do	Aug. 4, 1862	3	Transferred to Co. D, January 26, 1863.
Fisher, Michael	do	Mar. 30, 1864	3	Wd. at Cold Harbor, Va., June 3, '64—Discharged on Surgeon's cert., May 18, '65.
Frazier, Albert	do	Mar. 23, 1864	3	Discharged by General Order, June 10, '65.
Finegan, Peter	do	Aug. 29, 1862	3	Killed at Fredericksburg, Va., Dec. 13, '62.
Farrell, John	do	Sept. 2, 1862	3	Not on muster-out roll.
Gilmore, Levi	do	Mar. 30, 1864	3	Died at Alexandria, Va., July 17, of wds. received at Cold Harbor, June 3, '64—Grave 2,413—Vet.
Glendenning, Robert	do	Mar. 31, 1864	3	Wounded and captured at William's Farm, Va., June 22, '64—died July, '64, at Salisbury, N. C. Prison.
Gallagher, Martin	do	Aug. 14, 1862	3	Transferred to Co. D, Jan. 26, '63.
Garoh, Thomas	do	Aug. 16, 1862	3	Not on muster-out roll.
Green, Charles	do	Feb. 29, 1864	3	Not on muster-out roll.
Hart, John	do	Feb. 28, 1864	3	Mustered out with company, July 14, '65.
Hall, Henry	do	Mar. 23, 1864	3	Mustered out with company, July 14, '65.
Hagar, William	do	Mar. 30, 1864	3	Mustered out with company, July 14, '65.
Hayden, John K	do	Mar. 23, 1864	3	Wd. at Po River, Va., May 10, '64—mustered out with company, July 14, '65.
Hayan, George W	do	Feb. 29, 1864	3	Killed at Wilderness, Va., May 6, '64.
Hail, William	do	Mar. 23, 1864	3	Died at Field Hospital, near Brandy Sta., Va.—date unknown.
Haynan, Joseph J	do	Feb. 29, 1864	3	Died March 27, '64—burial record, Thos. Hayman, died at Alexandria, Va., March 29, '64, grave 1,692.
Haus, John	do	Mar. 30, 1864	3	Captured at William's Farm, June 22, '64—died at Andersonville, Ga., Aug. 1, '64, grave 4,474.
Hutchinson, Scott	do	Feb. 29, 1864	3	Died July, '64, at U. S. General Hospital, Alexandria, Va
Hull, Abraham	do	Mar. 23, 1864	3	Died June 23, '64, at Second Corps Field Hospital.
Hull, John J	do	Mar. 23, 1864	3	Died 1865, at U. S General Hospital, Alexandria, Va.
Hanlon, William	do	Aug. 19, 1862	3	Wd. at Fredericksburg, Va., Dec. 13, '62—transferred to Co. D, Jan. 26, '63.
Hudson, Joseph	do	Aug. 19, 1862	3	Killed at Fredericksburg, Dec, 13, '62.
Hickey, Michael	do	Aug. 2, 1862	3	Transferred to U. S. Artillery, Sept., 1862.
Horner, William	do	Aug. 11, 1862	3	Not on muster-out roll.
Harr, James	do	Aug. 29, 1862	3	Not on muster-out roll.
Hughes, James	do	Sept. 1, 1862	3	Not on muster-out roll.
Inks, John H	do	Feb. 24, 1864	3	Died June 15 of wds. rec. at Totopotomy, Va., May 31, '64—bur. in Nat. Cem., Arlington.
Jordon, Joseph A	do	Feb. 29, 1864	3	Trans. to Co. A, 10th reg. Vet. Res. Corps—discharged by General Order, July 29, '65.
James, Francis	do	Aug. 13, 1862	3	Not on muster out roll.
Kearns, John	do	Feb. 24, 1864	3	Mustered out with company, July 14, '65.
Kunkle, George	do	Aug. 4, 1862	3	Transferred to company D, Jan. 26, 1863.
King, James L	do	July 25, 1862	3	Transferred to company D, Jan. 26, 1863.

NAME.	RANK.	DATE OF MUSTER INTO SERVICE.	TERM—YEARS.	REMARKS.
King, Daniel	Private	Aug. 23, 1862	3	Not on muster-out roll.
Lehman, Elias	do	Mar. 31, 1864	3	Absent, sick, at muster-out.
Luckey, John W	do	Mar. 29, 1864	3	Prisoner from Aug. 1, 1864, to Mar. 13, 1865—discharged by General Order, June 20, 1865.
Luckey, Joshua	do	Feb. 29, 1864	3	Died April 8, 1864, at Alexandria, Va.
Long, Charles	do	Aug. 22, 1862	3	Transferred to company D, Jan. 26, '63.
Long, James	do	Aug. 23, 1862	3	Transferred to company D, Jan. 26, '63.
Logue, James	do	Aug. 19, 1862	3	Wounded at Fredericksburg, Va., Dec. 13, '62—transferred to Company D, Jan. 26, '63.
Logue, Daniel	do	Sept. 1, 1862	3	Transferred to company D, Jan. 26, '63.
Leister, William	do	Aug. 28, 1862	3	Not on muster-out roll.
Murray, James	do	Mar. 1, 1864	3	Mustered out with company, July 14, '65.
Mallory, John D	do	Mar. 31, 1864	3	Mustered out with company, July 14, '65—captured while on picket, Oct. 1, '64.
Moore, John	do	Mar. 29, 1864	3	Mustered out with company, July 14, '65.
Morrison, Ross	do	Mar. 30, 1864	3	Wounded at Po River, Va., May 10, 1864—discharged by General Order, June 7, '65.
Maust, Jacob	do	Mar. 3, 1864	3	Died at Alexandria, Va., Mar. 8, '64—int. rec. Mar. 29, '64—grave 1,689.
Martin, John	do	Aug. 28, 1862	3	Transferred to Co. D, Jan. 26, '63.
Merrick, Joseph	do	Aug. 7, 1862	3	Transferred to Co. D, Jan. 26, '63.
Munson, John H	do	July 28, 1862	3	Not on muster-out roll.
Mahaffey, Henry	do	Aug. 8, 1862	3	Not on muster-out roll.
Miles, George H	do	Aug. 12, 1862	3	Not on muster-out roll.
McDonald, John	do	Mar. 1, 1864	3	Discharged by General Order, June 26, '65.
McCuen, John	do	Feb. 29, 1864	3	Discharged by General Order, May 2, '65.
McClean, Rich. S	do	Feb. 29, 1864	3	Wounded at Spottsylvania C. H., Va., May 18, '64—disch. by General Order, June 13, '65.
McDowell, Andrew	do	Aug. 6, 1862	3	Wounded at Fredericksburg, Va., Dec. 13, '62—transferred to Co. D, Jan. 26, '63.
McIlhenney, John	do	Aug. 12, 1862	3	Transferred to Co. D, Jan. 26, '63.
McFadden, Thomas	do	Aug. 13, 1862	3	Transferred to Co. D, Jan. 26, '63.
McGiveney, Wm	do	Aug. 23, 1862	3	Transferred to Co. D, Jan. 26, '63.
McVey, Hugh	do	Aug. 13, 1862	3	Wounded at Fredericksburg, Va., Dec. 13, '62—transferred to Co. D, Jan. 26, '63.
McGinty, Hugh	do	Aug. 19, 1862	3	Not on muster-out roll.
Neal, Henry O	do	Mar. 31, 1864	3	Wd. at Spottsylvania C. H., Va., May 12, '64—Mus. out with company, July 14, '65—Vet.
O'Brian, Thomas	do	Aug. 29, 1862	3	Transferred to Co. D, Jan. 26, '63.
O'Brian, William	do	Sept. 2, 1862	3	Not on muster-out roll.
O'Brian, John	do	Aug. 13, 1862	3	Not on muster-out roll.
O'Hara, John T	do	Aug. 28, 1862	3	Not on muster-out roll.
Oliver, James	do	Mar. 9, 1864	3	Not on muster-out roll.
Prettyman, Jacob	do	Feb. 29, 1864	3	Wounded at Wilderness—absent, sick, at muster out—Vet.
Powers, John	do	Aug. 29, 1862	3	Transferred to Co. D, Jan. 26, '63.
Price, Edward	do	Feb. 29, 1864	3	Not on muster-out roll.
Quinn, James	do	Aug. 12, 1862	3	Not on muster-out roll.
Ryan, Isaac L	do	Feb. 12, 1864	3	Absent, sick, at muster out.
Ryan, John	do	Mar. 8, 1864	3	Absent, sick, at muster out.
Rifle, David J	do	Feb. 29, 1864	3	Killed at William's Farm, Va., June 22, '64.
Rathburn, Milton	do	Feb. 29, 1864	3	Killed at Spottsylvania C. H., Va., May 12, '64.
Roe, Robert	do	Sept. 2, 1862	3	Not on muster-out roll.
Sampsell, Simeon	do	Mar. 28, 1864	3	Absent, sick, at muster out.
Savage, Edmund	do	Mar. 23, 1864	3	Killed at Spottsylvania C. H., Va., May 18, '64.
Shipley, William D	do	Mar. 31, 1864	3	Disch. by General Order, June 2, '65.
Smith, James	do	Mar. 31, 1864	3	Died of wounds received at Wilderness—bu. rec., died at Annapolis, Md., Aug. 24, '64.
Smith, Joseph J	do	Feb. 29, 1864	3	Killed at Spottsylvania C. H., Va., May 12, '64.
Smith, John W	do	Feb. 29, 1864	3	Died June 14, of wounds received at Cold Harbor, Va., June 3, '64—buried in Nat. Cemetery, Arlington.
Sickels, Daniel	do	Feb. 29, 1864	3	Wounded and captured at Spottsylvania C. H., Va., May 12, 1864—died at Andersonville, Ga., July 9, 1864—burial record, July 19, 1864—grave, 3,586.

NAME.	RANK.	DATE OF MUSTER INTO SERVICE.	TERM—YEARS.	REMARKS.
Sweeney, John	Private	Aug. 19, 1862	3	Transferred to Co. D, Jan. 26, 1863.
Sweeney, Michael	do	Aug. 23, 1862	3	Transferred to Co. D, Jan. 26, 1863.
Sheean, John	do	Aug. 15, 1862	3	Not on muster-out roll.
Sheets, Jonathan	do	Feb. 29, 1864	3	Transferred to V. R. corps.
Toner, John	do	Feb. 17, 1864	3	Mustered out with company, July 14, '65.
Taylor, Benjamin	do	Mar. 23, 1864	3	Died May 5, '64—bu. in Mil. Asy. Cem., D. C.
Tierman, John, Jr.	do	Feb. 29, 1864	3	Killed at Wilderness, Va., May 6, 1864.
Thorndell, Thos. T.	do	Mar. 7, 1864	3	Killed in action at Five Forks, Va., March 31, 1865
Tully, Patrick	do	Aug. 14, 1862	3	Transferred to Co. D, Jan. 26, '63.
Townsend, Egbert	do	Aug. 16, 1862	3	Not on muster-out roll.
Tracy, Edward	do	Sept. 1, 1862	3	Not on muster-out roll.
Torbert, Ed. W.	do	Sept. 2, 1862	3	Not on muster-out roll.
Umble, Newton	do	Apr. 1, 1864	3	Captured at Reams Station, Va., Aug. 25, '64 —died at Salisbury, N. C., Oct. 19, '64.
Whitaker, Warren	do	Feb. 8, 1864	3	Mustered out with company, July 14, '65.
Whoolery, Wm.	do	Feb. 29, 1864	3	Mustered out with company, July 14, '65.
Williams, Thos. B.	do	Feb. 29, 1864	3	Wounded at Po River, Va., May 10, '64—discharged by General Order, June, 13, '65.
Watson, Aaron S.	do	Feb. 29, 1864	3	Transferred to Vet. Res. Corps, Jan. 24, '65.
Wilson, John	do	Sept. 1, 1862	3	Transferred to Co. D, Jan. 26, '63.
Wallace, Wm. A.	do	Aug. 5, 1862	3	Wounded at Fredericksburg, Va., Dec. 13, '62—transferred to Co. D, Jan. 26, '63.
Wilson, Thomas	do	Sept. 1, 1862	3	Killed at Fredericksburg.
Williams, John	do	July 25, 1862	3	Died February 9, '63.
Wilkinson, Thomas	do	Sept. 2, 1862	3	Not on muster-out roll.
Wood, John W.	do	Feb. 29, 1864	3	Honorably discharged—date unknown.
Yauger, Charles	do	Mar. 23, 1864	3	Wounded at Cold Harbor, Va., June 3, '64 —mus. out with company, July 14, '65—Vet.

UNASSIGNED MEN.

NAME.	RANK.	DATE OF MUSTER INTO SERVICE.	TERM—YEARS.	REMARKS.
Agan, Thomas	Private.	Mar. 30, 1864	3	Not accounted for.
Ankins, John W.	do	Mar. 10, 1864	3	Not accounted for.
Bronson, John	do	Mar. 30, 1864	3	Not accounted for.
Brown, John	do	Feb. 29, 1864	3	Not accounted for.
Dugman, Michael	do	Jan. 19, 1865	3	Substitute—not accounted for.
Geggus, Lewis	do	Mar. 21, 1864	3	Not accounted for.
Gallagher, Simon	do	Feb. 8, 1864	3	Not accounted for.
Hammer, Henry	do	Mar. 11, 1864	3	Discharged by General Order, June 5, 1865.
McCormick, Zach	do	Feb. 24, 1864	3	Not accounted for.
Wandel, Benjamin	do	Feb. 10, 1864	3	Not accounted for.

www.ingramcontent.com/pod-product-compliance
Lightning Source LLC
Chambersburg PA
CBHW021416300426
44114CB00010B/512